Essential
SQL Server™ 2000

An Administration Handbook

Buck Woody

Addison-Wesley

Boston • San Francisco • New York • Toronto • Montreal
London • Munich • Paris • Madrid
Capetown • Sydney • Tokyo • Singapore • Mexico City

005.7585 WOO

Many of the designations used by manufacturers and sellers to distinguish their products are claimed as trademarks. Where those designations appear in this book, and Addison-Wesley was aware of a trademark claim, the designations have been printed with initial capital letters or in all capitals.

The author and publisher have taken care in the preparation of this book, but make no expressed or implied warranty of any kind and assume no responsibility for errors or omissions. No liability is assumed for incidental or consequential damages in connection with or arising out of the use of the information or programs contained herein.

The publisher offers discounts on this book when ordered in quantity for special sales. For more information, please contact:

Pearson Education Corporate Sales Division
201 W. 103rd Street
Indianapolis, IN 46290
(800) 428-5331
corpsales@pearsoned.com

Visit AW on the Web: www.aw.com/cseng/

Library of Congress Cataloging-in-Publication Data

Woody, Buck.
    Essential SQL Server 2000 : an administration handbook / Buck Woody.
        p. cm.
      ISBN 0-201-74203-9 (alk. paper)
    1. Client/server computing. 2. Relational databases. 3. SQL server.
I. Title.
      QA76.9.C55 W665 2002
      005.75'85--dc21

                                                                  2001053740

ISBN 0-201-74203-9
Text printed on recycled paper
1 2 3 4 5 6 7 8 9 10—CRS—0504030201
First printing, December 2001

I'd like to dedicate this book to my daughter, Christina.
You have been an inspiration to me, the driving force
behind my dreams. It has been my greatest privilege
in life to watch you grow and learn. My only hope
is that no matter what, you'll always want
to have an ice cream with your dad.

Contents

Preface

This book is written for the technical professional. It's a mix of a little theory and a lot of practical hands-on examples and real-world explanations.

The book is divided into two parts. The first part (Chapters 1–10) deals with the day-to-day things you need to know as a database administrator (DBA).

- Chapter 1 explains how to use the book. It introduces databases in general and SQL Server in particular. This chapter also explains what a DBA does, and details the various versions of SQL Server 2000.

- Chapter 2 displays an install of SQL Server 2000 as well as an overview of upgrading a SQL Server 7 or 6.5 database server to SQL Server 2000.

- Chapter 3 familiarizes you with the tools available for SQL Server 2000. This chapter also shows the tools' changes from earlier versions.

- Chapter 4 introduces you to methods of accessing data, both from internal SQL Server 2000 tools and by using other programs. This chapter also covers the connection methods for SQL Server 2000.

- Chapter 5 explains the methods used to import and export data for SQL Server 2000, and how to automate data transfer from existing sources, such as text files or other databases, to another destination.

- Chapter 6 introduces you to automating SQL and other tasks such as operating system commands to full-scale programming with conditional branching.

- Chapter 7 focuses on the maintenance of your databases. This is the most important chapter in the book.

- Chapter 8 explains backing up and restoring SQL Server 2000 databases to disk or tape as well as the recovery models SQL Server uses for its databases and how they affect backups and restoration.

- Chapter 9 shows how to tune SQL 2000 Server, both with hardware and the nondesign options.
- Chapter 10 details SQL Server 2000 security.

The second part (Chapters 11–15) contains introductions and overviews to the more advanced features in SQL Server™ 2000. I've also included a sizing exercise for your servers as well as a discussion about hardware.

- Chapter 11 describes replication and shows a simple replication schema.
- Chapter 12 gives a basic understanding of Microsoft's Analysis Services. Here you'll see a start-to-finish example of how OLAP cubes work, as well as the process to use Microsoft Excel as an OLAP client.
- Chapter 13 provides an overview of the XML technology in SQL Server 2000.
- Chapter 14 shows how to ask plain-English questions from SQL Server 2000 databases.
- Chapter 15 explains named instances and how to set them up and connect to them.

The book concludes with two appendixes.

- Appendix A gives a sample server sizing exercise.
- Appendix B details hardware for SQL Server 2000.

Acknowledgments

No book is written by one person's efforts alone. I'd like to thank all the wonderful staff at Addison Wesley for their help in getting this book to press. I'd especially like to thank Stacie Parillo, who helped me get started with the book, and Mary O'Brien and Alicia Carey, who helped me finish it.

I'd also like to acknowledge the professionals at the Tampa SQL User Group who have taught me in more ways than they know over the years. I would especially like to mention Jose Amado-Blanco, who mentors me in SQL Server constantly, along with Marty Hensler.

Thanks to Marjorie, my wife, who is the nicest person I know.

Chapter **1**

Introduction

Chapter at a Glance

Read this chapter to find out how to use this book. Read this chapter if you are new to databases or SQL Server, need an overview of what a database administrator (DBA) does, or need to know about the versions of SQL Server 2000 and where to install them.

The Resources section contains references for:

- Versions of SQL Server 2000
- An overview of using SQL Server 2000 on CE devices
- The Microsoft Developer Network
- The Microsoft Data Access site

There are no prerequisites for this chapter.

Overview

So your boss just popped into your cubicle and said "Hey! We've got another project coming. I've just bought Brand X enterprise software, and it uses Microsoft SQL Server 2000 as the back end. You'll need to learn how to use it."

Maybe you're a developer and you don't have a full-time DBA available to manage the system you're designing. Or perhaps you're already a database professional, but you use another database package; or you're taking that next step up from Microsoft Access or some other small database system, and you need to learn the ropes.

This book is designed to help the technical professional install and manage SQL Server 2000.

How You Can Use This Book (You Really Should Read This Part)

This book is arranged to help you quickly locate real-world topics, and it provides practical information about them. It's arranged in two parts—the first covers common topics you'll deal with constantly, and the second section deals with a few of the more elaborate features of SQL Server 2000.

You could sit and read the whole book cover to cover, but it's designed so that you can "pick and choose" what you want or need to know. Read each chapter's Chapter at a Glance section to find out if the subject you're interested in is in the chapter, and look at the prerequisites as well.

This book is designed for the technical professional. I do not spend a lot of time on why something works; I spend more time on how it works. Because you already have a technical background, I won't be covering what a hard drive is or what "backup" means. I will cover what impact the choice of a hard drive has and how to do backups. That being said, I'm not going to skimp on the technical content either. I want to make sure that you have enough theory to know what's going on.

The book is structured so that you can skip around a bit if need be. Here's how it's laid out:

- *Chapter at a Glance*—Read this to see what's in the chapter. You'll also find out if there are any prerequisites before reading the chapter. The prerequisites explain a concept I'll leverage in that chapter.

- *Overview*—This section provides a broad overview of the chapter. If you understand all the concepts discussed here, you may not need to read the entire chapter—but skip right to the Examples and Resources sections.

- *Detail*—This section further explains each topic, including process and theory.

- *Graphical*—In this section, I show, step by step, the graphical tools to perform the tasks involved with this topic.

- *Command Line*—One of the great features I've always admired about Microsoft SQL Server in all its versions is that you can do virtually everything with either a command or a graphical tool. This section often mirrors the Graphical section, explaining the commands used to perform tasks.

- *Examples*—The Examples section shows real-world implementations of the topic. It's intended to be a training tool, but I try to make the examples useful.

- *Rosetta Stone*—This section answers the question, *"If I know where it is in Oracle or Microsoft Access, where is it in SQL Server 2000?"* With such a large product as Oracle and as small a product as Microsoft Access, there's often no one-to-one mapping of tools and concepts. I try to point out the similarities in one tool or command in both these products' counterparts wherever I can.

- *Resources*—Here I list other Web references so that you can get more information about the topic.

The DBA Role

There are basically three types of database administrators:

- *The maintenance DBA.* This technical professional manages, supports, and can recover one or more SQL Servers. This book is aimed squarely at helping you become a maintenance DBA.

- *The database developer.* This professional has a programming background and does a lot of Structured Query Language (SQL) development.

- *The data architect.* This professional has the job of looking at a company's processes, defining what data is to be stored and how it will be accessed. They also are often called on to implement the advanced SQL Server 2000 features that I describe in the last part of the book.

If you're in the first group (or want to be), this book will tell you what you need to know to do your job. If you're in the second or third group, this book can help you use SQL Server 2000 to fulfill your responsibilities, and it provides a good starting point for learning about the product.

Duties of a DBA

What is required of a DBA? Although this is by no means an exhaustive list, here are some common tasks:

- Understand how SQL Server 2000 can be used
- Select the right hardware to run SQL Server 2000
- Select and install the proper version

- Create a new database
- Create and manage users
- Create a maintenance plan
- Troubleshoot
- Back up databases
- Recover databases
- Transfer databases
- Export and import data
- Secure the system
- Monitor the system

There are many other tasks, of course, but these are the ones you'll work with daily or weekly.

SQL Server 2000—Overview

It's important to know the background of database servers; or to you, maybe, it isn't. If you're not exactly sure what separates SQL Server 2000 from Microsoft Access or just a bunch of spreadsheets, read on. Otherwise, you can skip to the topic of versions.

Relational Database Management Systems and Their Uses

So just what is a Relational Database Management System (RDBMS)? Put simply, an RDBMS is a collection of software that stores, modifies and retrieves data, and accesses it through relationships between sets of data. Many vendors offer products that do this, but I'm talking about the "big leagues"—databases that are accessed in really fast, optimized ways.

The data at this level is usually mission-critical, and it is used by a lot of people at once—think Amazon.com or the stock market. The data is also usually accessed through many methods, such as over the Internet or through distributed applications. The idea is that the access method is abstracted from the data storage and retrieval; in other words, the programs don't have to worry about managing data, just about getting to it.

The leading enterprise-level database system vendors are pretty varied in how they implement data access, but they all have a few things in common.

- They support multiple users (called concurrency).
- They are very fast.

- They are very robust (have a feature-rich offering).
- They are highly available.
- They are recoverable, usually to a specific point in time.
- They have user security that is separate from or in combination with the operating system.

Microsoft's SQL Server 2000 is the easiest RDBMS to administer and maintain that I've ever used. Some have argued that this ease of use sacrifices the level at which a system can operate. I haven't observed this.

Some companies tout their database software as being more powerful than SQL Server, but many multiterabyte SQL Server 2000 databases are turning in some of the best response numbers in the industry. The rich tool set included makes it easy to manage and support. For ease of use and great power and scalability, SQL Server 2000 is hard to beat.

Versions

Microsoft's SQL Server 2000 comes in five versions: Enterprise, Standard, Personal, CE, and Microsoft Desktop Engine (MSDE). There are a couple of developer editions as well, mirroring the Enterprise and Standard editions, with a connections limitation. I won't cover those separately because they have the same benefits and requirements as the production versions.

Let's take a quick look at each of these versions, along with when and where you would use them. I'll start with the smaller versions and work up to the larger offerings. Keep in mind that the figures in the charts are minimums, and you'll most certainly need more RAM to use the software. The same holds true for the central processing unit (CPU) speeds listed, and to further exploit the multiple CPU capabilities of some of these versions, you'll need to install a higher operating system such as Windows 2000 Advanced Server.

One fact is worth mentioning before I start describing the versions. You'll notice that many of them require Internet Explorer (IE) to be installed. There are two reasons for this: (1) the Books Online program that serves as the documentation for SQL Server 2000 uses HTML help technology; (2) the Extensible Markup Language (XML) features in SQL Server 2000 require the IE browser to work.

CE

You might not ever work with the CE version of SQL Server 2000; but as the workforce grows increasingly mobile, you'll have an advantage if you read up on this latest offering of the SQL Server 2000 family. Although it isn't for use on a server, it allows SQL Server to scale to even the smallest of devices. I've included a Web reference for CE at the end of the chapter. Table 1.1 shows the requirements for SQL Server 2000 CE.

Why Use the CE Version Even though this version is surprisingly feature-rich, it is best suited for distributed applications. You'll find the CE is useful when you've developed an application that uses SQL Server 2000 as the back end and you want to develop a CE application to be able to use it while disconnected from your main server.

CE supports remote data access and merge replication with SQL Server 2000. You can also use Microsoft's Internet Information Services to facilitate the transfer of data. A good example of this type of application would be the ability to track projects in the field and sync up with the primary server, even over the Internet.

MSDE

The Microsoft Desktop Engine is an RDBMS engine that is almost identical to the one found in SQL Server 2000, but it is not quite as robust as its bigger brothers. It is positioned as a back-end replacement for the Microsoft Jet Engine that is used in technology such as MS Access and WINS on a Microsoft network. This product ships as part of Microsoft Access 2000 and is also available separately.

MSDE lacks the management tools you'll need, as well as some of the extended functions that allow you to perform automated checks, but if you have SQL Server 2000 software installed in another version on the same network, you can manage it remotely. Table 1.2 shows what you'll need to run MSDE.

Why Use MSDE This version is best for small Web or workflow applications. The objects you create are directly transportable to a SQL Server 2000

Table 1.1 SQL Server CE

Computer	Handheld PC Pro (H/PC Pro) or Palm-size PC (P/PC)
Operating system	Microsoft Windows CE operating system version 2.11 or later, Windows CE 3 or later for a Pocket PC
Memory	1MB–3MB
Drive space	N/A
Other requirements	N/A

Table 1.2 SQL Server MSDE

Computer	Intel (or compatible) 166MHz
Operating system	NT Server 4 (SP5+) NT Server 4 Enterprise Edition (SP5+) Windows 2000 Server, Advanced Server, and Datacenter Microsoft Windows 98 Microsoft Windows Millennium Edition (Me) Windows NT Workstation 4 with SP5 or later Microsoft Windows 2000 Professional
Memory	32MB
Drive space	44MB
Other requirements	VGA monitor, CD, keyboard—the usual stuff—as well as (surprise) MS Internet Explorer 5 or later installed on the server

server by just backing the database up or using the attachment features in SQL Server 2000. MSDE will scale to two processors.

This product can also be bundled with an application that allows the database to be seamlessly upgraded to SQL Server 2000 later, if desired.

Small Size   Because it contains no tools, MSDE is a much smaller installation than other versions of SQL Server 2000.

Price   It's a lot less expensive to use MSDE than to purchase the full version of Microsoft SQL Server. If you're a developer, MSDE can be distributed royalty-free with your applications.

Robustness   MSDE isn't limited in the number of connections it will accept, but you shouldn't be fooled into thinking that this is the product to use for full-size applications. Its query engine is tuned to work with five or so users concurrently, and you'll notice a huge drop-off in performance if you have 20 or more users access the engine.

MSDE uses a "write-ahead" log, just like SQL Server 2000 (more on this in Chapter 4). This means that every transaction (group of data) is written first to a log file and then to the database. This logging process allows each transaction, if necessary, to be "unwritten"—a process called "rolling back." It also allows the server to move back to a consistent state if a power outage, network error, or the like occurs.

Personal

The Microsoft SQL Server 2000 Personal Edition is almost identical to its big brother, the Standard Edition. It is primarily intended for a single-use application or development. It includes most of the same features as the Standard Edition but has limits on some of the depth of those functions. There are also limits on things like clustering, network libraries, full-text indexing, and encryption, in some cases, depending more on the operating system than the database engine. Table 1.3 shows the minimum requirements to run MS Personal.

Why Use the Personal Version   The primary reason to use this version is that it can be installed on several operating systems, from Windows 98 and up. MSDE and Personal are the only SQL Server 2000 versions that will install on Windows NT Workstation or Windows 2000 Professional.

You can also run just about any application that is designed to use SQL Server 2000 as a back end, with a few caveats, including the fact that the Personal Edition does not scale past two processors, and the Analysis Services do not run if you're using a Win9*x* or a Windows Me operating system. You also don't have access to indexed views when using Personal.

Table 1.3 SQL Server Personal

Computer	Intel (or compatible) 166MHz
Operating system	NT Server 4 (SP5+)
	NT Server 4 Enterprise Edition (SP5+)
	Windows 2000 Server, Advanced Server, and Datacenter
	Microsoft Windows 98
	Microsoft Windows Millennium Edition (Me)
	Windows NT Workstation 4 with SP5 or later
	Microsoft Windows 2000 Professional
Memory	32MB
Drive space	270MB for full installation of server
	250MB for typical installation of server
	95MB for minimum installation of server
	50MB for minimum installation of Analysis Services (130MB for typical installation)
	80MB for Microsoft English Query
Other requirements	VGA monitor, CD drive, keyboard—the usual stuff—as well as (surprise) MS Internet Explorer 5 or later installed on the server

Light Footprint   Keep in mind you're running a full server package on a non-server operating system, in most cases. For this level of sophistication, it's still not a resource hog.

(Mostly) Everything You Need as a Developer   If you're a developer, the Personal Edition can be useful to have on your local system to program and test your applications if you don't have the Developer Edition of SQL Server 2000. There is, however, a complete set of all versions in the Developer Edition. The Microsoft Developer Network is the place to find information on these editions of the software.

All database objects created here will transport directly to the other versions, other than the limitations described earlier.

Standard

This version is the one that sells best for Microsoft, sometimes because of pricing alone. Don't let the price mislead you, however; this version can handle small- to midrange servers and is what many software vendors choose as their back end. Table 1.4 shows what you'll need, at a minimum, to run the Standard Edition.

Why Use the Standard Edition   Microsoft SQL Server 2000 Standard Edition has all the features in the versions described earlier as well as the additions discussed on the next page.

Table 1.4   SQL Server Standard

Computer	Intel (or compatible) 166MHz
Operating system	NT Server 4 (SP5+)
	NT Server 4 Enterprise Edition (SP5+)
	Windows 2000 Server, Advanced Server, and Datacenter
Memory	64MB (!)
Drive Space	270MB for full installation of server
	250MB for typical installation of server
	95MB for minimum installation of server
	50MB for minimum installation of Analysis Services (130MB for typical installation)
	80MB for MS English Query
Other requirements	VGA monitor, CD, keyboard, as well as MS Internet Explorer 5 or later installed on the server

Good Scalability The Standard Edition scales to four processors and can be configured to use all or any number of them. This version also takes advantage of the speed of your drives as well as the RAM installed in your server, making it a solid choice for mid- to high-range applications.

Feature Set The Standard Edition ships with most everything you'll need out of the box: Database engine, management tools, Web wizards and interfaces, XML support, replication, import and export facilities in multiple ways (with data transforms), English Query (sometimes called Natural Language Processing), and Analytical Services (OLAP). It's worth noting that the Analytical Services can be installed as a separate product, without using SQL Server 2000 at all.

Without sounding like a Microsoft marketing pitch, with all these features, there really won't be much to buy from third-party vendors. However, if you're looking for indexed views or Web-enabled analysis, you'll need the Enterprise version.

Enterprise

This version is the big "workhorse" SQL Server of the bunch. It requires the most hardware and attention and does the most the fastest. If you are a new DBA, it is unlikely that you'll be asked to manage an Enterprise installation, but you might be asked to manage a database on one. Table 1.5 shows what you'll need, at a minimum, to run the Enterprise version. Specific requirements will change, of course, based on the use and size of your database(s).

Table 1.5 *SQL Server Enterprise*

Computer	Intel (or compatible) 166MHz
Operating system	NT Server 4 Enterprise Edition (SP5+) Windows 2000 Advanced Server and Datacenter
Memory	64MB (!)
Drive space	270MB for full installation of server 250MB for typical installation of server 95MB for minimum installation of server 50MB for minimum installation of Analysis Services (130MB for typical installation) 80MB for Microsoft English Query
Other requirements	VGA monitor, CD drive, keyboard—the usual stuff—as well as (surprise) MS Internet Explorer 5+ installed on the server

Why Use the Enterprise Version   This version is touted as Microsoft's flagship for large enterprises and hosted environments. In addition to all the features available in the versions described previously, Enterprise has the following features.

Speed and Capacity   If you use Windows 2000 Datacenter Server as the operating system, the Enterprise Edition can scale to 64GB of RAM and up to 32 processors.

Enterprise clusters and scales best, and also takes advantage of vendor devices that allow "snapshot" backups, which have no database impact during the backup operation. The version also allows four-node fail-over clusters so that any node can recover the processing of any other node. Whenever Microsoft posts statistics about SQL Server, you can bet they're running the Enterprise version.

Better Analysis Services   This feature provides you with slice-and-dice data, showing it in various dimensions. This was once called Online Analytical Processing (OLAP). SQL Server 2000 Enterprise has the optimizations and memory configurations to run these intensive queries faster than the other versions. This information, sometimes called a "cube," can be viewed over the Web with this version.

Indexed Views   Indexed views are used to allow a view (more about views when I cover the SQL Server objects later) to have the same speed benefits as other SQL objects. For an RDBMS to truly be considered ready for large-scale applications, this feature is a must.

Microsoft implements this feature a little differently from other vendors, who sometimes call this feature a "materialized view"—you don't have to write code to use the feature; it's handled automatically.

Distributed Partitioned Views   This feature allows data to reside on various servers in a highly tuned manner but to still be treated as a single set of data when you access them. This feature is implemented different from other vendors' products in that the group of servers does not have to be connected to the same physical drive set. MS calls this "shared nothing."

SAN/NAS Integration   SQL Server 2000 Enterprise Edition has been engineered to provide direct hooks for System Area Network (SAN) and Network

Attached Storage (NAS) support. A SAN is a self-contained storage infrastructure attached to the server, and NAS allows data to be transferred quickly to various network-attached devices.

For further comparisons between the various versions of SQL Server 2000, see the Resources section at the end of this chapter.

SQL Server Licensing

There are two primary types of licensing that Microsoft invokes for SQL Server 2000. As always, this is subject to change, so make sure you check with Microsoft before purchasing your software. There are many caveats and modifiers to the following license types, so be sure to check Microsoft's SQL Server product Web page for more information.

Per Processor

Using per processor, you pay for a processor license for each processor on the server running the SQL Server software. A per processor license allows an unlimited number of users to connect from either inside or outside your corporate network. Using this model, you don't need to purchase additional server licenses, client access licenses (CALs), or Internet connector licenses.

Server/Per Seat (CAL)

Server/per seat (CAL) licensing requires a separate server license for each server on which the software is installed and a CAL for each client device. You can use this model for either the SQL Server 2000 Standard or Enterprise editions.

Clients

So how do you connect a client system to SQL Server 2000? I'll divide this explanation into two types—from a program and programmatically.

From a Program

As a maintenance DBA, you may be asked to connect client programs to your server. There are basically two ways this happens: (1) through Open Database Connectivity (ODBC), or (2) Object Linking and Embedding Database (OLE-DB).

ODBC   ODBC is an older technology that involves loading a software driver and filling in some values in a graphical screen. If the client machine has a Windows operating system, this software driver system is already installed in some version or other in the Control Panel, but you'll need to upgrade it to the latest version to work with SQL Server 2000. This software driver and the corresponding settings provide the connection layer between the software program and the database. Programs and Web pages can use the driver and settings.

Although an older technology, you'll still run into ODBC now and again. I'll discuss it again in Chapter 4.

OLE-DB   A newer method of client access is through a technology called OLE-DB. It process involves connecting to the server through a program string. It is used quite often in Visual Basic or by using Active Server Pages on an Internet server. If your client program or web page is using OLE-DB, the only setup usually involves a client-side configuration that is defined by the vendor.

Programmatically

There are three basic types of connections you can make to a SQL Server 2000 database using programming—ODBC, DB-Library, or OLE-DB. You can read more about using all these technologies in the MSDN library, which I've referenced for you at the end of this chapter.

ODBC   Although ODBC is an older technology, it's still supported in the current versions of Visual Basic as well as languages like Perl and Visual C++. Within ODBC, the connection method used in Visual Basic is Remote Data Objects (RDO) or Data Access Objects (DAO), both of which aren't suited to a large-scale application.

DB-Library   DB-Library is a technology used by the C programming language and is an Application Programming Interface (API). It has lots of C functions and macros that allow an application to interact with SQL Server.

OLE-DB   OLE-DB is Microsoft's robust low-level API that is used for accessing SQL Server 2000 data. It is used by all the latest programming languages Microsoft makes and is supported in the .NET infrastructure. The subsets of this newer technology are ActiveX Data Objects (ADO) and the new ADO.NET method—the successor to ADO.

If you're writing code today in a Microsoft language, your best bet is an OLE-DB method.

Other Programmatic Methods

There are a few other methods of connecting to SQL Server 2000 programmatically. Within this rare family of connection methods are the ODBC API,

ODBC Direct (for Microsoft Office installs that don't have Visual Basic licenses), and VB-Library. These programming methods are outside the scope of this book; but if you're interested in them, you can check the Microsoft MSDN Web site for more information on using these technologies. For further information on all these methods, see the Microsoft Data Access reference.

Resources

Books Online is the absolute reference for all matters SQL Server. More about Books Online in Chapter 3.

The definitive Web resource from Microsoft on SQL Server 2000 versions:
http://www.microsoft.com/sql/techinfo/planning/ChoosEd.doc

Microsoft Developer Network:
http://msdn.microsoft.com

SQL Server 2000 CE information:
http://www.microsoft.com/sql/productinfo/SQL2000_CE.doc

SQL Server 2000 Windows CE Edition FAQs
http://www.microsoft.com/technet/SQL/sqlcefaq.asp

Microsoft's Data Access page:
http://www.microsoft.com/data/

MSDN online documentation:
http://msdn.microsoft.com/sqlserver/

Chapter 2

Installing/Upgrading SQL Server 2000

Chapter at a Glance

Read this chapter if you've never done an install of SQL Server before or you want to see an install before you do one. Also read this chapter if you want a quick overview of upgrading a SQL Server 7 or 6.5 database server to SQL Server 2000.

The prerequisites for this chapter are to have a basic understanding of computer hardware and to read Chapter 1 to understand the version you wish to install. Chapter 1 also discusses ODBC and OLE-DB, access methods mentioned in this chapter.

The Resources section contains sites that reference:

- Hardware
- Access databases
- English Query and MDAC

Overview

You've probably run into people who installed a product once and put it on their resume. Although you can get away with doing that with a lot of products, I don't recommend it for large-scale database systems.

For the most part, a SQL Server 2000 install involves selecting a server, determining requirements, and making proper choices during the setup program. However, don't just pop that CD in the drive and click on the first Next button you see.

Microsoft is legendary for making things easy to install—but that shouldn't lull you into thinking that one size fits all when it comes to your implementation of SQL Server 2000. This is a powerful package, and the choices you make during the install can have dramatic effects on how, or even if, the system performs later.

In this chapter, I perform another install; and along the way, I explain why you'd choose a certain option over. Many of the software packages that require SQL Server 2000 as a back end don't explain how to install it properly. Here, I spend extra time going over the installation, including screenshots. I also discuss an upgrade of SQL Server 7 to SQL Server 2000.

There are plenty of things you need to plan before you start the install. At the very least, you'll need to specify in detail your use of the software, determine what kind of server you need to buy, and then select the best installation options. I discuss the impact of your decisions and the best settings to pick based on the way you'll use your server.

Detail—Setup

Everything you need to know to install SQL Server 2000 is included in Books Online. Unfortunately, until you perform some sort of an install, you don't *have* Books Online. After you read this chapter, you might want to install the client tools portion on an administrative workstation so that you will have Books Online to read for more information.

I'll begin by describing a new install of SQL Server 2000. By *new* I mean installing SQL Server for the first time on a new, or newly configured, server. If an earlier version of SQL Server is already installed, you can skip ahead to the Detail—Upgrade section.

Requirements

The first thing to do is specify your requirements for the system. What do you want this server to do? Will it act as a Web database platform, or will it be used for data warehousing? You'll use these facts to make your decisions for the install. The software that is using SQL Server as a back end may dictate your choices. If so, read ahead anyway so you'll understand the process for choosing hardware and configuring your server installation.

SQL Server 2000 can be installed on devices ranging from small, handheld computers to clustered superservers. For this example, I cover the installation of a standard SQL Server running on Windows 2000 Server. I have set up my example server as a back end on a Web-based application running an in-house time-card and accounting system. I've included a sample sizing exercise for the server in Appendix A.

Hardware

You may have inherited a server that is already built and running. It's still important to know what factors affect the performance of your server so that you can intelligently answer the question: "Why is this running so slowly?"

The factors in a hardware decision include RAM, CPUs, storage type and capacity, and network I/O. This is a lengthy topic, so to maintain the flow of this explanation, I've included a full hardware discussion in Appendix B.

Environment

Along with hardware and functional requirements, environmental conditions factor into the installation. Keep these in mind:

- Will this server be a domain controller on the network? Does it do more that just serve SQL Server 2000? Here the important factors become Network Interface Card (NIC), memory, and processor.
- Will this server be used for large databases? Hard drive performance takes the forefront in this situation.

These types of questions illustrate that it is vital to think through what you're planning to do with the software. That analysis will help you make intelligent choices during hardware selection and software installation.

I make the example system a *member server* of an NT domain. This security choice gives me the ability to access the security of the network for setting up accounts but doesn't force the server to authenticate users, which would take away valuable CPU and NIC cycles. The other benefit is that a member server has both *domain* and *local* security, very helpful in a Web server like this one.

NOTE: If you're using a Novell network or some other network operating system, my recommendation for SQL Servers is to make the NT server that houses SQL Server 2000 a Stand-Alone-Server in a Workgroup and then use NetWare Directory Services (NDS) or some other security add-in to manage the accounts. Unless you are forced to, don't set up SQL Server as a domain controller.

One final item regarding the environment on your server—don't install other server software on the same system as the SQL Server 2000 RDBMS. Many packages, such as Microsoft Exchange, don't get along well with SQL Server 2000. Take my advice. Make this server a one-package installation. This, of course, doesn't include things like tape backup software, mail clients, or vendor-specific add-ons for SQL Server.

Graphical—Setup

Now that you've decided on the size of the server, the hardware configuration, and the environment, you begin the setup by installing Windows 2000 Server with the appropriate drivers. Since Windows 2000 installs with Internet Explorer 5, you won't need to install that separately. You need to make sure you have IE 5 because *Books Online* and XML require it, as I mentioned in Chapter 1.

NOTE: If you're using NT 4 as the server's OS, you also need to install NT Service Pack 5 or higher. I recommend NT Service Pack 6a with all applicable patches.

You can also set up the tape drive and software and even install a mail client on the server. You'll need the mail client later.

I'll perform a standard SQL Server 2000 installation on the example system. I'll show you the screenshots of the installation, just in case you're not sitting in front of your server at the moment. I also explain most of the choices that you'll see, even if you're not going to select them on your installation.

If the installation is interrupted, just start the install again. The program is smart enough to pick up where it left off.

First, slide the SQL Server 2000 CD into the drive. The system should autoplay the CD because that's the default; but if it doesn't, you can open the CD drive letter and double-click the file autoplay.exe to start the process.

The first screen you're presented with is the beginning installation panel, shown in Figure 2.1.

This screen contains the choice for installing SQL Server 2000 Components, which starts the install. The choice SQL Server 2000 Prerequisites installs things like Internet Explorer 5 and any service packs that need to be on the server before the install. Two other options are Read the Release Notes and Visit Our Web Site. This Web site is the central place for information, white papers, downloads, and the like for SQL Server 2000.

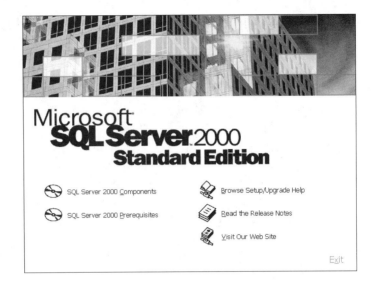

Figure 2.1
Installation
begins

Just select SQL Server 2000 Components. The screen shown in Figure 2.2 appears. This screen gives you three choices: Install Database Server, Install Analysis Services, and Install English Query.

The Install Analysis Services option installs the Online Analytical Processing program of SQL Server 2000. This is essentially a very powerful way to look at data from many dimensions. This feature can be installed separately from SQL

Figure 2.2
Installation
components

Server 2000, using another RDBMS as a back end. I cover this software in greater detail in Chapter 12.

The option to Install English Query allows your users to type questions like "How many authors are there?" from your database. See the English Query Example Web site in the Resources section at the end of the chapter for an example of this technology. I cover this feature in greater detail in Chapter 14.

After you select the Install Database Server option, the Welcome screen appears, as shown in Figure 2.3. This is just an information screen. Pick Next to show the screen in Figure 2.4. Next, you're asked to select the name of the computer where you are installing SQL Server 2000. Leave this set at the default. However, you could install SQL Server 2000 across the network to another machine—if you have the security rights and connectivity to do so.

You also have the choice, if the system is configured properly, to install SQL Server 2000 on a *virtual* computer. A virtual computer is just a single name for a group of computers—sometimes called a cluster.

Microsoft SQL Server 2000 can act as a fail-over type of cluster, where one machine can take over for another automatically, without the users noticing the interruption. Doing this entails several caveats, which are covered in more depth in Books Online.

Select Next, which brings up the Installation Selection screen, as shown in Figure 2.5. Here you select whether this is a new installation or a new instance on this server. Select the first option since this is a new installation.

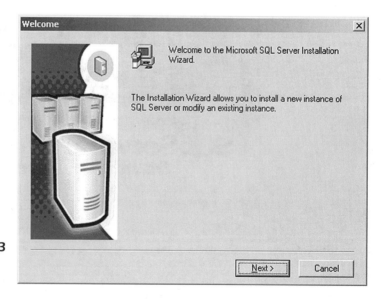

Figure 2.3
Welcome
screen

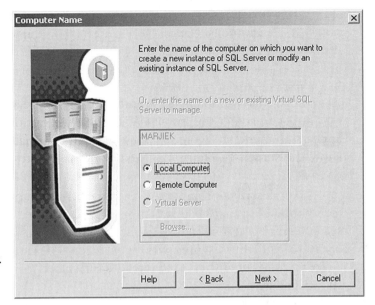

Figure 2.4
Computer
Name

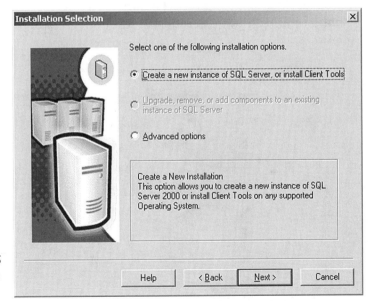

Figure 2.5
Installation
Selection

An *instance* is an entirely new installation of SQL Server 2000 in conjunction with a current installation. This is useful if systemwide settings need to be different on the same server, or if you want to be able to shut down one instance of a server and not affect the other. I discuss instances in more depth in the last chapter of this book.

There's also an *Advanced* options choice, which allows even more customization. You can click *Help* here if you're interested in what these options cover. For most standard installations, it isn't necessary to change them. Leave the first option selected, and click Next to bring up the screen shown in Figure 2.6.

The next screen prompts you to enter the name and company information to be imbedded in your installation of SQL Server 2000. Do that, and then select Next to continue to the screen shown in Figure 2.7.

Here you are presented with what Microsoft calls a EULA—an *End-User License Agreement*. After you've read it all, select Yes to bring up the screen shown in Figure 2.8.

This screen allows you to pick whether you are installing *Client Tools Only*, which is a great selection for an administrative workstation; *Server and Client Tools*, which is a perfect choice for this installation; or *Connectivity Only*, which is used for client machines. The first two options are fairly descriptive—the third option allows you to install just enough of SQL Server to connect to it

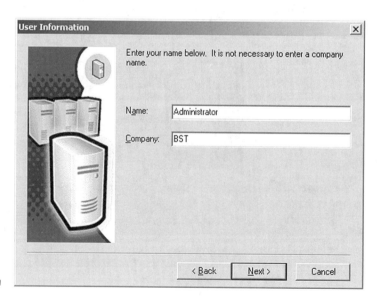

Figure 2.6
User
Information

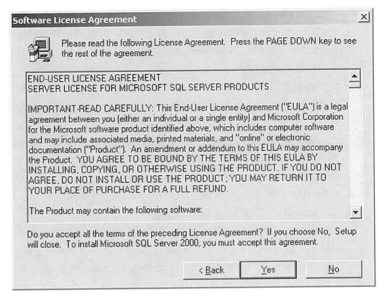

Figure 2.7
License
agreement

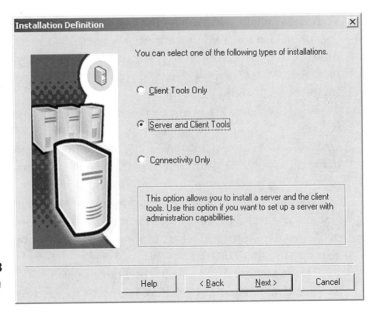

Figure 2.8
Installation
Definition

from a client that uses a two-tier architecture. The third option installs Open Database Connectivity (ODBC) drivers and Microsoft Database Access Components (MDAC) version 2.6. I need to linger on this screen a moment to fully explain this option.

An ODBC driver is simply a set of software drivers that establishes connections to a SQL Server. You won't always need to visit every desk to upgrade those drivers, although this is advisable.

There is a caveat, though. If your program has some commands specific to SQL 6.5 or SQL 2000, your program may break if the wrong ODBC driver is used. See Books Online, Level 1: Handling Discontinued Functionality, for more information. This is due less to ODBC drivers than to SQL Server 2000 behaving in a different way from SQL 6.5.

I mentioned ODBC in Chapter 1 and explained that most new programs use OLE-DB. OLE-DB, you'll recall, doesn't often need a great deal of configuration from the client side, but it may require MDAC 2.6 to operate properly.

If the client program doesn't bundle the installation of MDAC 2.6 with its installation, you'll need to install it manually. You can use this part of the SQL Server 2000 installation program to install it, or MDAC can be installed from a separate package. This package is available at the Universal Data Access (UDA) Web site you can reference at the end of this chapter.

MDAC isn't a single program; it's a set of software. Different versions of MDAC can produce different results for programs. Sometimes those results are incorrect. MDAC is now referred to as UDA, for Universal Data Access. Here's the technical rundown on the versions.

MDAC version 2.1 is installed with SQL Server 7 and can also be installed separately. Various other programs bundled this version. This is called *slip-streaming* because you may not have been made aware that the program made the change to your system. This version is very stable and is probably the most widely used version of MDAC as of this writing.

Version 2.5 of MDAC was shipped with Microsoft Office 2000, SR2. It is also distributed with Microsoft Project 2000, and some add-ins to data-aware programs like AutoCAD have shipped it as well. Windows 2000 in all versions also ships with MDAC 2.5.

There was, however, a major bug in this version—it returned empty results to some date-range queries. There is a patch to this version, which you can find at the end of this chapter in the Resources section.

MDAC version 2.6 is installed with SQL Server 2000 and is also a separate directory on the SQL 2000 CD. This version will be installed regardless of which option you pick on this screen—but read on.

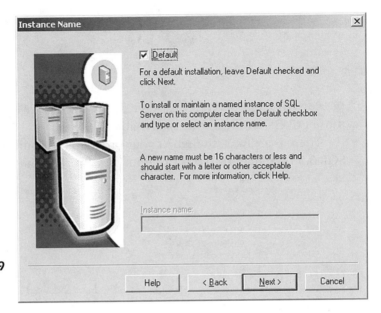

Figure 2.9
Instance
Name

MDAC isn't a set of software that shows up in your Programs area on the Start menu. The only easy way you can tell what version you have or change that version to an earlier one is with a piece of software called the Component Checker. This utility is available from Microsoft.

You can't go backward on the MDAC versions on Windows 2000. You can always use this third option on this screen to install MDAC 2.6 on Windows 2000.

Now that we've completed *that* discussion, you can click Next to show the screen in Figure 2.9. On this screen you indicate that this is the default instance or you name a new instance. I cover instances in greater detail in Chapter 15.

Because this is a new installation, pick Next, and the screen shown in Figure 2.10 appears. Here you select the type of installation you are going to perform. For most installations, including this one, the proper selection is Typical. This option installs the following:

- Database Server
- Upgrade Tools
- Replication Support

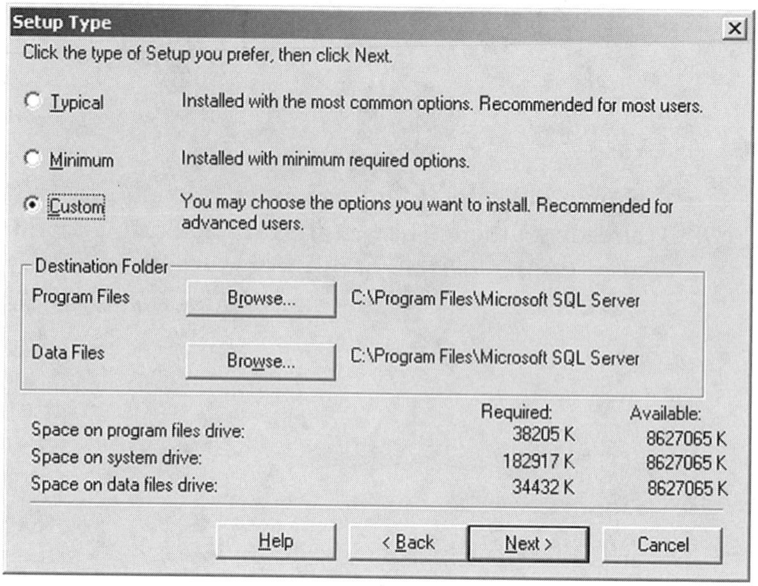

Figure 2.10
Setup Type

- Full-Text Search
- Client Management Tools
- Client Connectivity
- Books Online

The next option is Minimum. This option is normally selected for systems that are going to be managed remotely or on a server with limited space. Here's what's installed with this option:

- Database Server
- Replication Support
- Full-Text Search
- Client Connectivity

You normally pick Typical for this type of server, but the option to select here is Custom. You're not going to change anything, but choosing this option allows you to step through each screen and examine what would be installed.

Also on this screen you can select where various parts of the software will be installed. Select the *binaries*, or program files, to be placed on the system's primary drive. Select the databases to be installed on the larger drive, keeping in mind the hardware discussion in Appendix B.

Select Browse next to the words Data Files—this brings up the next screen, shown in Figure 2.11. Change the selection shown here to drive c: if it isn't already set there. This sets the default location for future databases. This action also sets the location of the system databases, which SQL Server 2000 uses to track itself, as well as the scratch area that SQL Server uses, called *tempdb*. I cover those system databases in the next chapter.

Log files, discussed further in Appendix B, will be stored on the same drive as the database unless specified otherwise in the CREATE statement for a database. Select OK on this screen. Then select Next when you return to the Setup Type screen.

Figure 2.12 shows the selections just as they would be with a *typical* install, as described earlier. You can peruse which selections are made and even change those selections if you like. Select Next to bring up the screen shown in Figure 2.13.

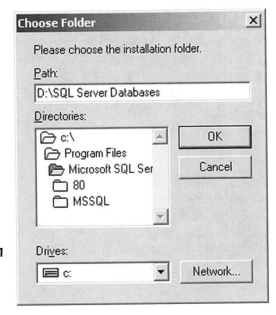

Figure 2.11
Data files
location
selection

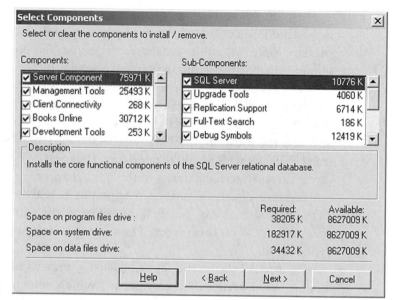

Figure 2.12
Select
Components

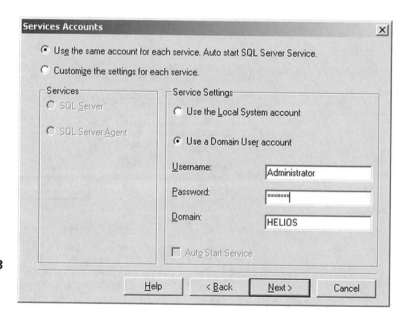

Figure 2.13
Services
Accounts

In this screen you select the accounts used to start two services: SQL Server and SQL Server Agent.

The SQL Server service starts the engine that runs the RDBMS, and its security can be set in one of two ways: Use the Local System account or Use a Domain User account. You'll want to choose the latter most of the time. This allows SQL Server to have access to the same kinds of things a user would, such as network drives, mail accounts, and so forth. The Local System account, which is just a subset of the operating system, can't do those things.

There are security ramifications to these choices, which I discuss further in Chapter 10. SQL Server Agent is covered in more depth in Chapter 6. For this test installation, it's very important that the security for this account be set to Domain User account, for the same reasons cited for the SQL Server account. This becomes critical if you're going to use replication or notifications by e-mail from within SQL Server 2000.

Notice also that you could set the services to use different settings from each other. This isn't normally necessary, but selecting this option does have one advantage—you can set both services to auto-start.

If you leave the selection the way you have it here, SQL Server will start automatically, but SQL Server Agent will not. I'll make that mistake on purpose here and rectify it later. Also set the name, password, and domain of the account used to start SQL Server and SQL Server Agent.

Notice that a domain administrator's account has been used. Although not required, it does allow SQL Server 2000 to do anything the domain administrator can. That gives this server a lot of power and gives me the ability to show more examples of things later. I don't recommend this setting in the field, but I do suggest making a special user in Windows to run SQL Server and granting that account those rights that are necessary to do its job. Use your Active Directory skills if you're installing on Windows 2000 to manage what this account can do. You can always grant it more power later.

Select Next to bring up the screen shown in Figure 2.14. In this screen, select how SQL Server 2000 will validate users. There are two options: Windows Authentication Mode and Mixed Mode.

Windows Authentication Mode allows you to manage SQL Server accounts using only Windows domain accounts that this server can see. This means all trusted domains as well as any local security accounts that you may create on this server. I tend not to choose this option.

Mixed Mode allows *both* Windows NT domain accounts and accounts that you create within SQL Server 2000 to be granted rights within a database. Choose this option to allow the most flexibility. There may be programs or

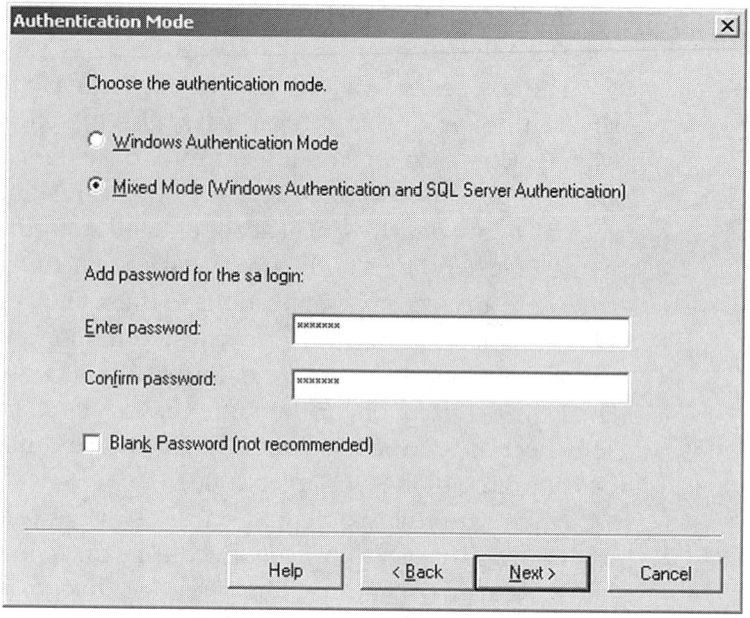

Figure 2.14
Authentication
Mode

users that you want to access SQL Server but that you don't necessarily want on your Windows domain.

Notice on this screen that when you select Mixed Mode, you can set the sa (master account) to either have a password or not. In earlier versions of SQL Server, this password was blank by default. You'll definitely want to set one, as I have here. Mine is letmein. You should *never* leave this password blank.

I cover security in more detail in Chapter 10. Now select Next, to bring up the screen shown in Figure 2.15. This screen allows you to choose another character set and set the sort order for SQL Server 2000. The character set option is useful if you use another language for your databases or to match another SQL Server.

The sort order is called *collation*. Don't worry about the collation option too much because SQL Server 2000 can have databases of various collations in the same instance or server and can even mix collations within a database.

You should leave these settings at their defaults, which is dictionary sort order, case-insensitive, for most servers unless there's a good reason or your front-end program has other requirements. See Books Online, Collation, for more information on what the various settings affect.

Select Next to bring up the screen shown in Figure 2.16. In this screen, you select the method SQL Server 2000 uses to talk with applications and other

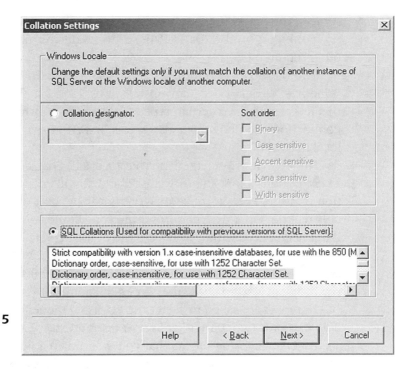

Figure 2.15
Collation
Settings

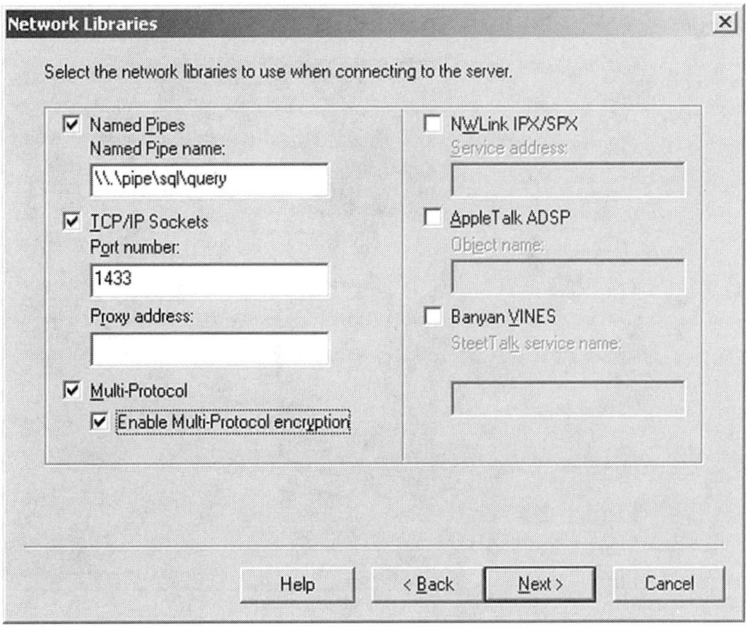

Figure 2.16
Network
Libraries

servers. You'll need to match the network settings your clients use, but you can leave the Port option for TCP/IP set to its default unless the programs have other requirements.

The Named Pipes option selected is simply NetBEUI—the native format for Windows NT networks. Many installations don't use this option, but I've found that it is required for certain types of upgrades, transfers, and even some sticky connection problems. You also select TCP/IP if that's what you use on your local network.

Notice that I've selected Multi-Protocol and Enable Multi-Protocol Encryption. These options allow you to write code that will encrypt the database information transfers even at the SQL Server level, beyond what your network protocols will do. On a production server, you shouldn't select protocols that you don't need because they will slow down the server.

Select Next, and the screen shown in Figure 2.17 appears. This screen allows you to go back and change anything you think you might have set incorrectly. Select Next to show the screen in Figure 2.18.

Here you are asked to select the licensing mode for this server. SQL Server 2000 has only two: either Per Seat or Per Processor.

Per Seat licensing means that you will obtain a license for each client that accesses the server. Microsoft provides several methods for obtaining these

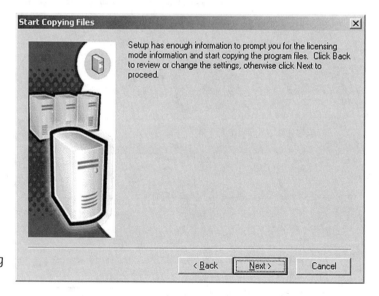

Figure 2.17
Start Copying
Files

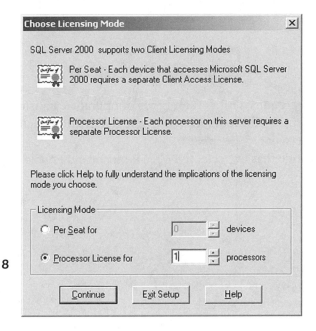

Figure 2.18
Choose
Licensing
Mode

licenses, so check with your Microsoft representative, or call Microsoft directly, to make sure you're covered.

Per Processor licensing means that you are allowed unlimited connections to the server, but you must purchase a license for each processor on the server. This option is often economical; but again, check with your Microsoft representative for more information. I discuss and reference these licensing options further in Chapter 1.

Make your selections here, and then click Continue. You're shown the screen in Figure 2.19. This screen informs you that the MDAC software is being upgraded on this server. The important thing to note is that if for some reason your server acts as a client to some other software, you might already have MDAC installed in another version.

Figure 2.19
MDAC
installation

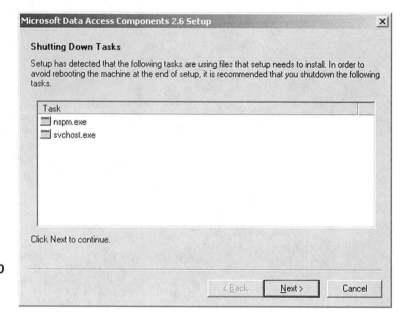

Figure 2.20
Shutdown
services

Once you move on from this panel, the screen shown in Figure 2.20 appears. When you perform an installation on your system, you may receive a screen similar to this one. It's informing you that software is running that will require this system to reboot when you're through with the install. Microsoft has gone a long way toward limiting the number of reboots for Windows 2000, hence the warning. If you shut down these services now, you won't have to reboot; so do that. Select Next, and the screen shown in Figure 2.21 is displayed.

This screen allows you to continue with the installation of MDAC 2.6. Select *Finish*, which brings up the screen shown in Figure 2.22.

This screen shows that you're installing the *Full-Text* engine. Once you leave this panel, the screen shown in Figure 2.23 appears.

SQL Server 2000 uses HTML-based help, and that fact is shown here. Next, the screen in Figure 2.24 appears. Here you see the progress of the install, which continues in Figure 2.25.

Now the SQL Server 2000 engine is started to allow the server to configure itself. The screen shown in Figure 2.26 appears next. This rather ambiguous message informs you that the registry, filesystem, permissions, and lots of other

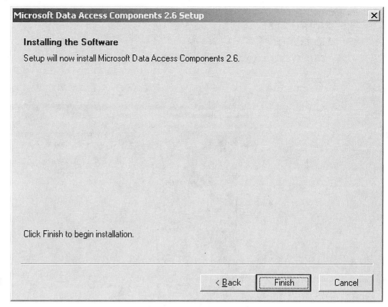

Figure 2.21
Microsoft
Data Access
Components
2.6 Setup

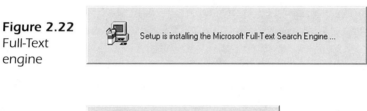

Figure 2.22
Full-Text
engine

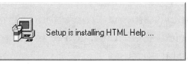

Figure 2.23
HTML help

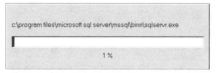

Figure 2.24
File copy
progress

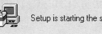

Figure 2.25
Starting SQL
Server

Figure 2.26
Updating
your system

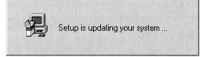

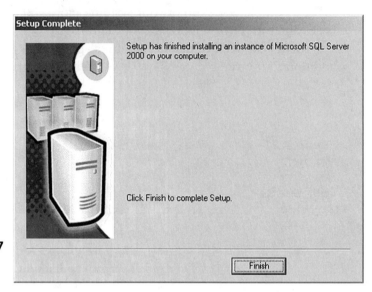

Figure 2.27
Setup
Complete

things on the server are being manipulated to finish the installation, as shown in Figure 2.27.

Because you properly stopped the offending services earlier, you don't have to reboot. Just select *Finish*, and you're ready to begin using the RDBMS. That completes the installation.

If you have an earlier version of SQL Server installed, read the next section to discover how to perform an upgrade.

Detail—Upgrade

You may already have a Microsoft SQL Server version 6.5 or version 7 in place. If so, your decisions on hardware and function are probably already made. You might add memory or hard drive space as part of an upgrade, but that's not always guaranteed. Even so, you still have quite a few details to work out before you perform your upgrade.

I suggest setting up a test system that has your current version of databases installed and upgrading that system first. Test your applications to make sure the data looks and works as it's supposed to. If this process is successful, you can proceed to upgrade the primary server.

If this scenario isn't possible because of budget or time, at least be sure to make a complete backup of your system before you begin, including the databases and the NT or Windows 2000 Server.

You'll also need to decide whether you want SQL Server 2000 to run in addition to the version you have or you wish to replace the version currently installed with SQL Server 2000. The latter choice is the one most often selected, so it's the one I cover here.

Even though you're performing a complete upgrade of your current install, you still have choices. You can upgrade to the same server, called *in-place*, or you can install SQL Server 2000 on another system and have a wizard copy the databases from the current 7 server. Again, *Books Online* is the best reference for the latest information on performing these various types of upgrades.

Most of the upgrade types are wizard-driven. Even without the wizard, an upgrade is pretty easy.

This sample server has Windows NT 4 with Service Pack 6a installed running SQL Server version 7, with no SQL service packs applied.

Requirements

You'll need at least NT 4 with NT Service Pack 5 installed or Windows 2000, regardless of the version you're upgrading. The latest service pack for NT is available at *http://www.microsoft.com/ntserver/nts/downloads/recommended/ SP6/allSP6.asp*

If you're upgrading SQL Server 6.5, remember that this is a complete architectural change. The impacts I discuss are just a few of the large issues you'll face on this upgrade, and I suggest you search the documentation for more information on this version. This is not an upgrade to be taken lightly.

The requirements are as follows:

■ SQL Server 6.5 Service Pack 5 or later. If you're going to upgrade the system to another computer, you'll still need at least SQL Server Service Pack 3 or later. I recommend you get Service Pack 5a regardless before you start the upgrade. These service packs are available at *http://support.microsoft.com/support/kb/articles/Q197/1/77.ASP*

- The Named Pipes protocol must be installed, even if you use the "upgrade to tape" option. If the protocol is not installed on your 6.5 instance, you'll need to run the 6.5 setup program to add it.
- Make sure you have at least one and a half times the current database size free on your server; and if you're doing one in-place, double that.

That's it for SQL Server 6.5—however, there are a few "gotchas":

- SQL Server 6.5 doesn't recognize hyphens as a valid part of a computer's name, so replace them with underlines.
- When the upgrade completes, SQL Server 6.5 is still installed on your server. You'll need to manually remove it if you don't want it anymore.
- After you've performed the upgrade, you'll need to set up a maintenance wizard and run all the steps so that the database is optimized and all the latest indexes and statistics are current. I cover that more in Chapter 7.

The only requirement for an upgrade to SQL Server 7 is that the Named Pipes protocol must be installed, even if you use the "upgrade to tape" option. A 7 upgrade is mostly a "Next... Next... Finish" kind of thing, if you're doing an in-place upgrade. There aren't as many "gotchas" here, but some of them are as follows:

- When you're through, the SQL Server 7 instance is gone. Only Books Online remains from version 7. This assumes, of course, that you picked the options to upgrade your current installation and not just to add SQL Server 2000 to the server.
- SQL Server Profile Traces aren't upgraded.
- SQL Server registrations aren't upgraded.
- Clients on 7 are not able to read Data Transformation Services (DTS) packages created or updated with a SQL Server 2000 client.
- Database Diagrams created with 7 are not visible in SQL Server 2000.
- After you've performed the upgrade, you'll want to set up a maintenance wizard and run all the steps so that the database is optimized and all the latest indexes and statistics are current. More on this in Chapter 7.

Graphical—Upgrade

I'll now demo in detail an upgrade of an existing SQL Server 7 server to SQL Server 2000.

1. Put the SQL Server 2000 CD in the CD-ROM drive on your server. If your server is not set to auto-play CDs, double-click the drive letter of the CD-ROM and then double-click Autorun.exe.

2. Select SQL Server 2000 Components when the first screen appears.

3. Select Install Database Server at the next screen.

4. At the Welcome screen, click Next.

5. Next you'll see a Computer Name dialog box. Local Computer should be checked here, and the name of your server should already be in place. Now click Next.

6. This brings up the Installation Selection dialog box. Select Upgrade, remove, or add components to an existing instance of SQL Server, and click Next.

7. Next you'll see the Instance Name dialog box. The setting here defaults to Default. Now click Next.

8. The Existing Installation dialog box appears next. Select Upgrade your existing installation. Select Next.

9. Now you see the Upgrade dialog box. Here you are asked if you want to proceed with the upgrade.

10. Select Yes, upgrade your (and here it will detail the type of upgrade it will do).

11. Now select Next. The upgrade continues.

12. Eventually you'll see a Connect to Server dialog box. You're asked here to pick the authentication mode.

13. You are asked to set the account that connects to SQL Server. This should be set to The Windows account information you use to log on to your computer with (Windows).

14. Now you'll see the Start Copying Files dialog box. Select Next here.

15. Over the years, I've found that if Microsoft tells you to reboot the system, reboot the system. At the Setup Complete dialog box, select Yes, I want to restart my computer now. Then pick Finish.

16. Next, test your upgrade. Run your applications against a sample of known data, and make sure you check the results carefully.

There are two problems with upgrading that I'm aware of as of this writing. The first is that if you upgrade any version of the Microsoft database engine, you might not get the client tools installed. See Microsoft's Web site for the fix at *http://www.microsoft.com/technet/support/kb.asp?ID=274390*

The other issue I know about is one that you should run into only on rare occasions, but I mention it here for completeness. The problem involves restoring the system databases from a previous version. Attempting to restore one of those databases produces an error. For the workaround, see the article on Microsoft's Web site at *http://www.microsoft.com/technet/support/kb. asp?ID=264474*

As always, try your upgrade on a test system first.

Rosetta Stone

If you're upgrading a database not from Microsoft SQL Server but from Oracle or Microsoft Access, the process gets a bit more complicated. You don't just upgrade the Oracle or Access database in-place. I take a high-level look at some options for each process.

One generic note here: You'll want to take into account the space requirements for upsizing an Access database or transferring an Oracle instance. These activities can take a huge toll on the tempdb database (temporary storage database) that SQL Server 2000 uses. This space should be reclaimed when SQL Server stops and starts, but be aware that you'll need extra room for a transfer or an upgrade.

Oracle

Microsoft SQL Server 2000 has a built-in utility called Data Transformation Services. This product connects to many database types and transfers that data to SQL Server or even between other databases. I cover this product further in Chapter 5. One method of upgrading an Oracle database to SQL Server 2000 is to install SQL Server 2000 on server A, connect to server B running Oracle, and use DTS to transfer the data. This is the most common method I've used. If you follow this method, you'll need the Oracle connection tools installed on the SQL Server 2000 machine.

Another method for upgrading an Oracle instance to SQL Server 2000 is to export the data from Oracle into a text file and import the data into SQL Server using DTS, the bulk copy program (bcp), or a custom-designed interface. I'll also cover those kinds of import methods in Chapter 5. This process is normally used only for subsets of data, not for an entire database.

Microsoft Access

Microsoft Access databases can be upsized to SQL Server 2000 with a set of tools downloaded from the Web, which you can reference in the Resources section. These tools, designed for SQL Server 7, move your Microsoft Access database objects into SQL Server 2000.

Resources

Storage capacity planning:
  http://www.microsoft.com/SQL/techinfo/storageeng.htm
Hardware information:
  http://www6.tomshardware.com/
  http://www.geek.com
Supersize your access databases:
  http://www.microsoft.com/AccessDev/ProdInfo/AUT97dat.htm
English Query Web site:
  http://www.ask.com
Universal Data Access (aka MDAC) download page:
  http://www.microsoft.com/data/download.htm

Chapter 3

Tools

Chapter at a Glance

This chapter familiarizes you with the tools available for SQL Server 2000. Read this chapter if you're new to SQL Server or you want to see the changes from earlier versions. The Resources section contains references for:

- osql
- Query Analyzer
- Hints for connecting an older version of Enterprise Manager to SQL Server 2000
- Setting SQL Server 2000 options

There are no prerequisites for this chapter, although Chapter 2 is recommended, along with Appendixes A and B.

Overview

Often the quickest way to get familiar with a piece of software is to jump right in and start using the tools that come with it. I've used this approach before, but I usually hit a wall quickly. It's great when I run into someone who knows the product and shows me the shortcuts and tricks to using the tools properly.

In this chapter, I explain the tools that create, delete, and manage SQL Server objects. These tools also back up and restore databases, create users, grant rights, and monitor and optimize the system. In a word, they control the complete operation of SQL Server 2000. The primary tools you'll use to manage SQL Server 2000 are *Books Online*, *Enterprise Manager*, and *Query Analyzer*.

Books Online contains the references for SQL Server 2000. They are given special treatment in this chapter because they contain several methods for accessing the same type of data.

Enterprise Manager is the primary management tool for SQL Server 2000. Once a server is registered with Enterprise Manager, you can create and delete databases, back up and restore databases, manage all SQL Server 2000 objects, manage security, and more.

Query Analyzer is the primary command-line interface for SQL Servers. Although it is a graphical tool, its primary use is command-driven. Other command-line tools include osql and bcp. The osql tool is an operating system command-line query tool, and bcp is an import and export utility.

Detail

SQL Server 2000 tools can be installed in two places: on the server or on a workstation that you use to manage a server. See Chapter 2 for a discussion on installation. Once the tools are installed, you can perform the same management tasks from either location. The tools I discuss can be installed on everything from Windows 9x and Me platforms to all flavors of Windows NT and 2000. Personally, I'm in favor of using Windows NT or Windows 2000 Professional on an administrator's workstation, but you do have other options.

You can perform the examples I cover in this chapter using a server or workstation along with me, but I suggest that you do them against a test server.

The SQL Server 2000 tools are in the Start button under Programs, Microsoft SQL Server. I begin the tour of the tools for SQL Server 2000 in the first place that you should become familiar with—the reference tool.

Reference

Even if you've dealt with help references in other packages, you should explore Books Online. It's the primary reference for SQL Server 2000, and it is much more than just the documentation. This tool is arranged in such a way that it is useful to the novice and the professional, to the DBA and the developer.

Books Online

The search features within Books Online are very powerful, but as when you search for information on the Internet, you can sometimes get a lot more results than you are able to use. For a hands-on demonstration of Books Online, see the Graphical section in this chapter.

Administration

Next I discuss the tools used to manage SQL Server 2000. I examine the graphical and command-based methods to control the server and its environment.

Enterprise Manager

Enterprise Manager is the tool you'll use most often for administrative tasks. It's a Microsoft Management Console (MMC) utility that displays SQL Server objects in the left panel and content for those objects in the right panel.

In Figure 3.1, I've selected Start, Programs, Microsoft SQL Server, and then Enterprise Manager. If you're following along, you can either double-click the Microsoft SQL Servers item or click the plus sign next to it to expand the tree. This action holds true for all objects in the tree.

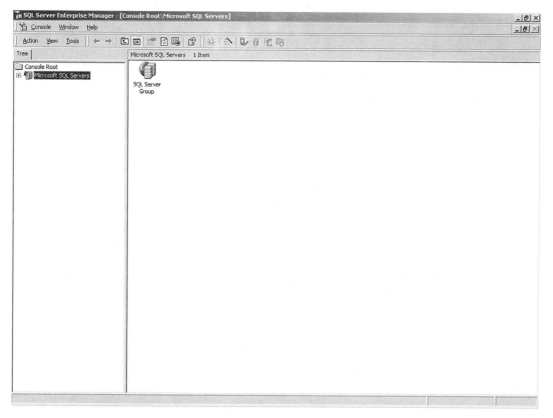

Figure 3.1   *Enterprise Manager*

The first object you're shown is the SQL Server group. A group is just a logical arrangement of servers. All servers registered to this Enterprise Manager belong to the default group unless you create another group and place the server name there.

As you progress down the default group, you see the server names this console is aware of. These servers can be SQL Server 2000, SQL Server 7, or even SQL Server 6.5 versions and, with a few caveats, even earlier.

If you're running Enterprise Manager on your server, that name appears here. If you're on a workstation or want to work with another server, you'll need to register it. This registration sets a connection from Enterprise Manager to as many servers as you like. See the Graphical section later in this chapter, Enterprise Manager, Registering a SQL Server in Enterprise Manager, for the steps to register a server. Double-click the name of your server, and you're shown the screen in Figure 3.2.

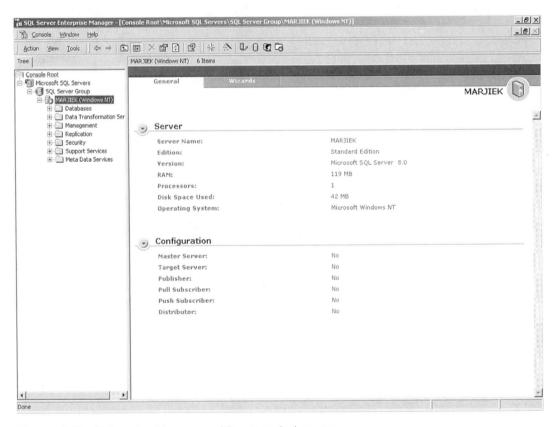

Figure 3.2 Enterprise Manager with expanded server

Notice the content in the right-hand panel—it's actually a Web page view called a taskpad. Parts of it are active, and tabs at the top provide more utilities. The taskpad is quite useful and is context-sensitive to the objects in the left-hand pane. For instance, the Server object's taskpad view shows the edition and disk space used; and the Database object displays the size and space used by the database the last time a backup was made and more database information.

You can also access the database wizards in the taskpad, which can be helpful if you've not worked with SQL Server before. Wizards can do everything from creating a maintenance plan to setting up replication.

There are views available other than the taskpad. Right-click the Server object and select View from the menu that appears. I tend to use the detail view for most of the administration that I do, so I'll switch my view to detail in Figure 3.3.

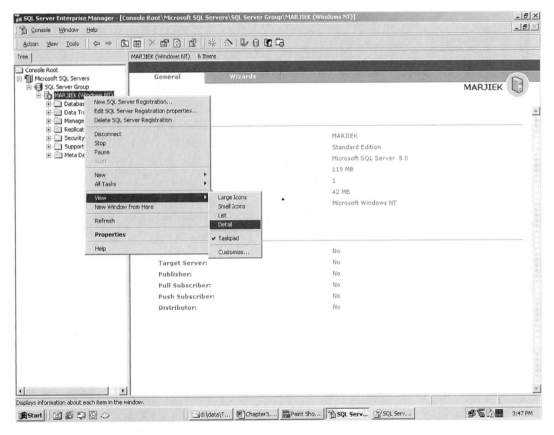

Figure 3.3   Switching views on objects

The right-click menu often changes based on the object you're exploring, but a few menu items are constant. A few of these are self-explanatory, such as Refresh, Delete, and New.

New Window from Here displays a new window at that starting point.

Export List is a useful feature—I'd like to see this on everything Microsoft makes, especially operating systems. Selecting this menu item creates a text file listing of the objects underneath the object you've selected.

Select the name of the server, and then right-click and select Export List . . . from the menu that appears, as shown in Figure 3.4.

You're then asked to select a location for the text file. Set your example to output to C:\TEMP\TEST.TXT, as shown in Figure 3.5. And next you open it, using Notepad, as shown in Figure 3.6

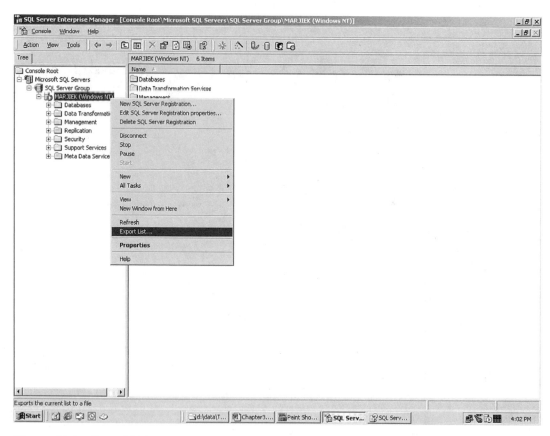

Figure 3.4   Export List

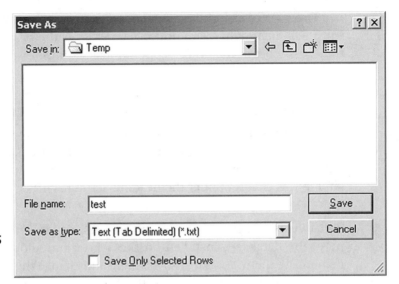

Figure 3.5
Export file
options

Figure 3.6
Export file
contents

This type of exercise is useful if you're creating manuals, batch files, and so forth. The final right-menu option, Properties, is the primary method you'll use to access most of the object's operational settings. I will do this for the Server object.

Server Properties   A common DBA task is to manage the settings for a SQL Server. Although there are settings for most every object in SQL Server 2000, there are options that affect all objects on this installation. We'll make some changes to the configuration for the example server in the Graphical section later in this chapter under the heading Setting SQL Server Configuration.

Databases   The next object on the tree pane is Databases. This object displays the databases installed on the server and allows you to manage and manipulate them. You can also examine and change the data in the database by using this object. Double-click the Databases object to display the screen shown in Figure 3.7.

The databases you're shown here are installed if you pick a standard installation as you did in Chapter 2. Let's take a quick look at each database and its purpose.

The master database is the main database for SQL Server 2000. It contains most everything that the server uses to operate, including many system tables that are accessed in one way or another by all users—even the logins to the server are stored here. You should not change this database in any fashion. You also should back up this database after any major change and after adding any users.

Search Books Online for System Tables, Overview, for a complete description of what the master database stores and how that information is used. Save this as a favorite—the more you use SQL Server 2000, the more knowledge you need about this database.

The model database is used as a template for creating new databases. If you don't specify a particular option when you create a new database, this database will place options found in it on the new database. If you have users, procedures, or any other object that you want to show up in every new database, put them here. Don't delete this database, and keep a backup of it in case you change something drastic.

The msdb database is used by SQL Server Agent for scheduling and saving jobs and for replication of data from one server to another. I detail that further in Chapter 6. It can also store DTS packages, which I cover in Chapter 5. Don't delete this database, either.

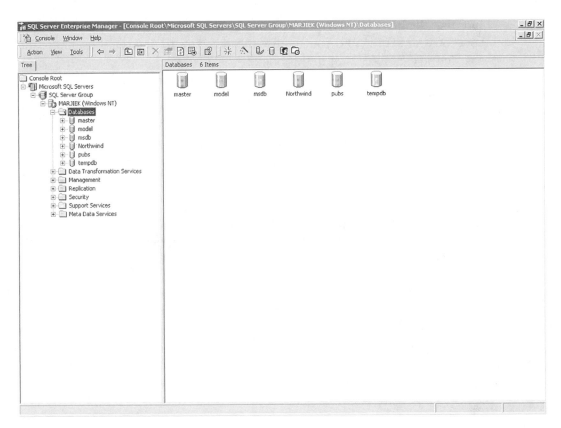

Figure 3.7 Databases

The tempdb database is SQL Server's "scratch" area. This database is used in lots of circumstances, such as in certain types of queries and for SQL Server's internal calculations. These calculations involve sorting, grouping, and distinct operations, which can cause this database to grow quite large. It's destroyed and created automatically each time SQL Server 2000 is started, so don't try to delete it or access it directly. Don't try to back it up, either—there's no point.

The next two databases are sample databases. Some DBAs recommend deleting them; others keep them for testing.

Northwind is a sample database that Microsoft Access users will recognize. It is used for examples and testing.

The pubs database has been with SQL Server since the first versions. Even though it's just an example database, I never recommend deleting it. For one thing, it's very small; and for another, it's handy to have around. You may not be sure that the errors you're getting one day are a result of your database, your code, or your server; and you can use this database to find out. I use this database in the examples later in this book.

Database Objects   Let's open a database to examine the objects in it. Double-click the Northwind database to see the screen shown in Figure 3.8. Let's look at each of these objects.

Diagrams   Database Diagrams are pictorial representations of the tables and relationships in a database. These are sometimes referred to as Entity Relationship Diagrams (ERDs). This tool can be used to view *and* alter the objects in your database, so use it with great care. You can also use this tool to create a set of SQL Server 2000 commands for changes you make in the tool. This tool is the easiest way to establish relationships between tables. See the Graphical

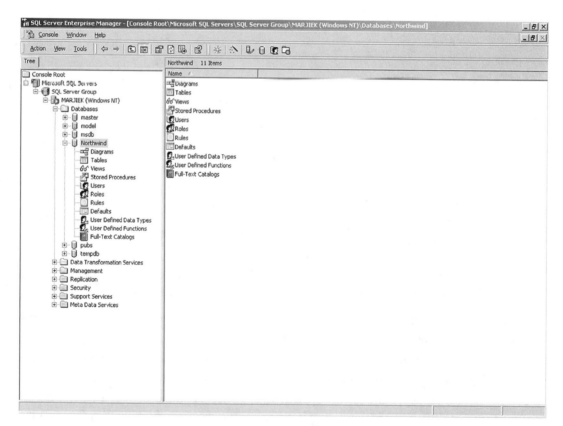

Figure 3.8   Northwind database objects

section, Enterprise Manager, Creating a Database Diagram, for an example of using this tool.

Tables   Tables are rows and columns of information, much like a Microsoft Excel spreadsheet, that are the heart of data storage in a relational database server. Right-click any table to view and alter the structure, delete or copy the table, or even run a query against the data. These tasks are shown in the Graphical section, under the Enterprise Manager, Tables, heading. You can also use Enterprise Manager to set permissions for tables; I cover that further in Chapter 10.

Views   Views are SQL commands that present a set of data as if it were a table. Right-click any view and select Properties to see these commands, or click Open View and then Return all rows to see the data set the view displays. Views are also used to limit the amount of data that is returned to the user or to hide a complex set of table relationships from the user.

Stored Procedures   Stored procedures are SQL Server programs that are stored and run on the SQL Server. They can accept input, create output, and do just about anything you can do on SQL Server. To view the code for the program, right-click a stored procedure and select Properties. Stored procedures have a couple of big advantages. They run on the server, so they can use the power of the server to run quickly. Also, security is simplified because rights need to be granted only on the stored procedure, not on all the different objects in the database. I detail this advantage in Chapter 10.

Users   There are two types of users in SQL Server 2000: server users and database users. This is where the database users are set up. I explain this process in depth in Chapter 10.

Roles   Roles are yet another security aspect. They allow users to be grouped by definition, and then rights can be granted to the role rather than the user. Think of groups on a network operating system, and you've got the idea. Chapter 10 covers this topic in more detail.

Rules   Rules are used to set limits on what type of data can be entered into a database. Right-click a rule and select Properties to see its definition; then click Bind Columns to see which columns of data have this rule applied. Once there, you'd have to pull down the menu for the tables to show which ones are using the rule.

This isn't very intuitive, but there are other ways to see what rules are applied to a table. Rules are largely supported for backward compatibility, since the new way of enforcing data integrity is by the use of constraints entered directly into the table's definition. See Books Online, Rules, if you'd like to learn more about these objects and their replacements.

Defaults   Defaults are a bit like rules and are also here for backward compatibility, except that they don't restrict data. They add data if you don't—as the name implies.

Right-click a default and select Properties to view a default's definition. You'll see they are also bound to a table or tables, just like rules.

User Defined Data Types   If the types of data natively stored by SQL Server 2000 (bigint, int, smallint, tinyint, bit, decimal, numeric, money, smallmoney, float, real, datetime, smalldatetime, char, varchar, text, nchar, nvarchar, ntext, binary, varbinary, image, cursor, sql_variant, table, timestamp, uniqueidentifier) don't fill a particular need, you can create your own. These new data types are dependent on the types already supported by SQL Server 2000. They are normally used to create catalog IDs, store numbers, and so forth. Right-click a User Defined Data Type (UDT) and select Properties to view its definition. Search on Data Types in Books Online to learn what each native data type stores to see if you need to create a UDT.

User Defined Functions   SQL Server 2000 has several built-in functions. A function is a command that works like typing DIR at a command prompt at an operating system prompt. Functions can either return data or perform work, based on what the developer wrote them to do. Besides using the standard SQL Server 2000 functions, you can create your own. Functions can return or manipulate data, and they are powerful because unless they are called on in the SELECT statement, they don't run. This can result in a huge time savings over using views. Right-click a User Defined Function and select Properties to view its definition. Search in Books Online, User Defined Functions for instructions on creating your own functions.

Full-Text Catalogs   Full-Text Catalogs are reference files that are stored on the operating system used to search free-form text in a database field. They work hand in hand with the Microsoft Search service, which you may have seen in Internet Information Server (IIS). These catalogs allow complex searching in large text fields. One important item to note: If your application uses these catalogs, you'll need to follow a specific set of procedures to keep these catalogs up to date. If you're asked to manage a database with this type of index, you should research the topic before you take charge. In many instances, the developers write jobs or scheduled tasks that handle this maintenance for you.

Data Transformation Services   Data Transformation Services is a tool that allows movement of data from several types of sources to either the same or different types of destinations. You can, for example, move data from a text file to a Microsoft Access database, or from several SQL Server 2000 databases to an Oracle database, and many other combinations. The beauty of this tool lies in its ability not only to move the data around but also to transform the data, based on conditions or programming that you create. I examine this tool in depth in Chapter 5.

Management   This object contains the management tools, most of which I cover in more depth in other sections of this book.

SQL Server Agent   SQL Server Agent is the scheduling tool used by SQL Server 2000. It manages jobs, which in turn contain tasks. These tasks can be SQL commands, various scripting language commands, or even operating system commands. You can set up reusable schedules and have the agent send you a report on its success or failure. I cover the SQL Server Agent in Chapter 6.

Backup   This section of Enterprise Manager allows you to define places to send backups and to perform and schedule backups. I discuss this topic further in Chapters 7 and 8.

Current Activity   The Current Activity tree item displays activity in the database as well as the current locks. I use this tool in several examples in Chapter 9.

Database Maintenance Plans   Database maintenance plans are stored settings that schedule maintenance for one or more databases. This is one of the first activities you should perform on your server—setting up maintenance on your databases could be the most important thing you do as a DBA. I detail this tool further in Chapter 7.

SQL Server Logs   Any information that SQL Server stores about itself can be found here. SQL Server 2000 starts and maintains a log of its activities each time it starts. Six of these logs are kept at one time on the server, with the latest one replacing the oldest one. SQL Server 2000 also stores some information in the Windows NT/2000 application log, but more information is stored here than in those logs, as shown in Figure 3.9.

Replication This menu item sets up and monitors the automatic or periodic transfer of data from one server to another. I cover this process in Chapter 11.

Security This management tool sets up the server users. There are also roles here, but these roles are for the entire server, not just a particular database.

Other functions in this section are linked or remote servers, which provide a method of querying remote servers as if they were local to this server. I explore security more in Chapter 10.

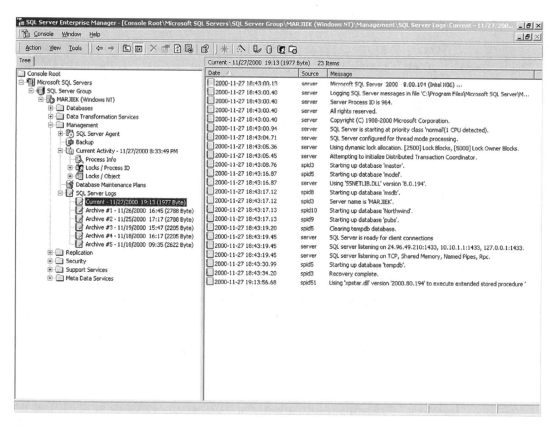

Figure 3.9 SQL Server activity logs

Support Services   The Support Services item includes three objects: Distributed Transaction Coordinator, Full-Text Search, and SQL Mail.

The Distributed Transaction Coordinator is a service that takes data from a client program and groups it in one guaranteed unit, called a *transaction*, with one or more databases or servers. There isn't any configuration to do here, but you can stop or start the service by right-clicking it.

The Full-Text Search object can clean up the Full-Text Catalogs, and you can also display the locations of the files that store the catalog data using this object. Right-click the object to access these functions.

SQL Mail is the object you access to start the SQL Mail configuration. This object allows SQL Server 2000 to access mail.

Meta Data Services   Meta Data is data about data. This object stores more information that SQL Server 2000 uses to run as well as data that is used by the Data Transformation Services. Data for Online Analytical Processing (OLAP) is also stored here. This repository can be used for other purposes by outside programs.

Service Manager

The Service Manager tool controls the state of the SQL services I discussed in Chapter 2. You can access it by selecting the Start button, then Programs, Microsoft SQL Server, Service Manager. You can also access the Service Manager on the server by double-clicking the small SQL Server 2000 icon in the system tray, as shown in Figure 3.10.

Figure 3.10
Service
Manager

With this tool you can start or stop a SQL Server engine and other services associated with it. The pause feature keeps the service working but won't accept any new connections. The server can be local or remote as long as you have the proper rights. The tool also shows the state of a service on that server.

Data Access

The first set of tools I examined primarily dealt with managing the server. Although you can use the tables object to access data, it's better to use another tool: Query Analyzer. This tool is the primary DBA method for typing commands into SQL Server. There are also two other methods for typing commands into SQL Server 2000: osql and isql. I examine those command-line tools in Chapter 4.

Query Analyzer

To use Query Analyzer, click the Start button, then Programs, Microsoft SQL Server, Query Analyzer. You could also start it from inside Enterprise Manager in the Tools menu. You're asked to log in, as shown in Figure 3.11. Type in the name of the server you want to access, which can be local or remote, and the name and password authorized to use that server. Enter the name of your server with the username sa and the password.

Notice that you could use your current NT account, called a trusted connection, if your server is set to allow that type of authentication. After you enter the proper information, you're presented with the screen in Figure 3.12.

Figure 3.11
Query Analyzer
login

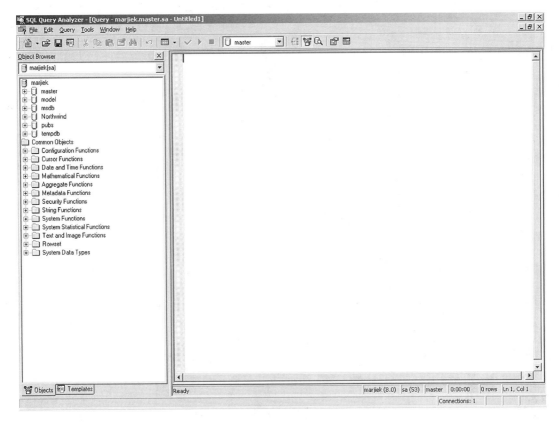

Figure 3.12   Query Analyzer

I'll present a quick tour of this screen before I examine the various menu options. On the title bar, you'll notice the name of the server, the database, and the user who is currently logged on. You can have several queries open at one time, and having this information right at the top of the screen can be helpful.

Just below the title bar is the menu bar. Below the menu bar are groups of icons called a toolbar. All the commands on the toolbar are available on the menu bar, so I won't cover them here. As with most Microsoft products, you can rest the pointer over an icon to discover its meaning.

Note the database selection drop-down menu. Use this icon bar item to set the database that the query you type affects.

To the left of the screen is the Object Browser. This panel gives quick access to database objects such as tables and views that I detailed earlier. To see an example of this feature, expand the pubs database item, then expand User Tables, and right-click dbo.authors. Select Script Object to New Window As, then Select, as shown in Figure 3.13.

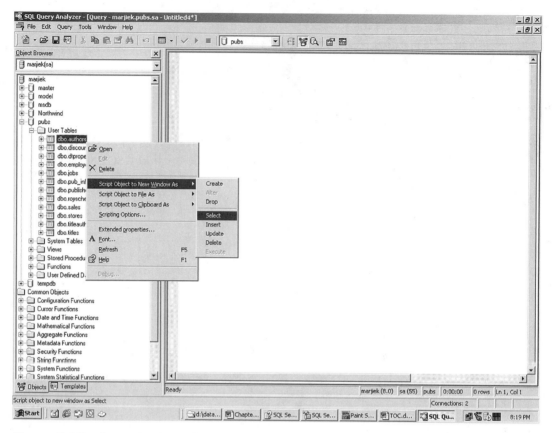

Figure 3.13   Query Analyzer Object Browser

Notice that a set of commands has been placed in the right-hand window, the command area. Next press the F5 key to commit the process, and you've run a simple SQL query on this example server.

Notice the *Templates* tab at the bottom of this panel. The *Templates* panel contains scripts that contain SQL syntax. Once you've selected that tab and expanded the *Create Table* template, double-click the *Create Table Basic Template*. Notice that Query Analyzer inserts the commands to create a table in the command area on the right. You can edit the information in the <> brackets and run the command, or you can simply select *Edit*, then *Replace Template Parameters...* from the *menu bar* for a graphical replacement of the required variables.

One more note on templates: You can create your own for later use. After you type a query, replace any constants you wish with brackets <> and type a variable name in them. Save the query from the menu bar as a template file, and you can use it again.

If you highlight the command CREATE TABLE in the command area, you can press Shift+F1 and jump straight to that topic in Books Online. Templates, combined with this context-sensitive help feature, can quickly bring you up to speed on many SQL statements.

When you run the command by pressing F5 or Ctrl+E, the screen splits to display the results. Commands won't run until you press F5 or select the little green arrow in the icon bar, even if you press the Enter key. SQL Server treats a return character as whitespace.

Another useful trick is highlighting just a portion of the code in the command area and pressing F5—only the highlighted portion will run.

Other hotkeys are available in Query Analyzer. Table 3.1 shows the more common ones.

If you tried the template example earlier, you may have noticed that some words in the command area are displayed in color. These colors have meaning, and the fact that the words have turned a color lets you know that you've typed something correctly. Table 3.2 shows what the colors indicate.

If you receive an error in the Results pane after typing something and running it, check to make sure the colors look right. Chances are you'll catch a typo.

Let's explore the menu bar next. I may appear to jump around a bit as far as topics go, but I'll explain the pertinent menu choices all at once so that you can use them in subsequent chapters. Table 3.3 displays the menu items and what they do.

There are more items in the menu tree than I've covered. Books Online has more information on these items. In the Command Line section later in this chapter and in the following chapters, I use the Query Analyzer frequently.

Monitoring

Monitoring is one of those tasks that you might not be asked to do but you should do anyway. SQL 2000 Profiler is one of the tools you'll use to do that. I cover monitoring more fully in Chapter 9.

Profiler

The SQL 2000 Profiler is the primary tool that you use to monitor the server. You can also use Profiler to track SQL statements for troubleshooting or to monitor the behavior of the server engine that you normally can't see. You can also use Query Analyzer and Windows NT/2000 Performance Monitor to monitor certain aspects of the server.

Table 3.1 Shortcut Keys ("Hotkeys")

Keys	Function Performed
Alt+Break	Cancel a query
Ctrl+O	Connections: Connect
Alt+F1	Database object information
Ctrl+Shift+Delete	Editing: Clear the active Editor pane
Ctrl+C	Editing: Copy. You can also use Ctrl+Insert
Ctrl+X	Editing: Cut. You can also use Shift+Del
Ctrl+F	Editing: Find
Ctrl+V	Editing: Paste. You can also use Shift+Insert
F3	Editing: Repeat last search or find next
Ctrl+H	Editing: Replace
Ctrl+A	Editing: Select all
Ctrl+Z	Editing: Undo
F5	Execute a query. You can also use Ctrl+E
F1	Help for SQL Query Analyzer
Shift+F1	Help for the selected Transact-SQL statement
Ctrl+N	New query window
F8	Object Browser (show/hide)
F4	Object Search
Ctrl+F5	Parse the query and check syntax
Ctrl+P	Print
Ctrl+D	Results: Display results in grid format
Ctrl+T	Results: Display results in text format
Ctrl+Shift+F	Results: Save results to file
Ctrl+R	Results: Show Results pane (toggle)
Ctrl+S	Save
Ctrl+Shift+Insert	Templates: Insert a template
Ctrl+Shift+M	Templates: Replace template parameters
Ctrl+L	Tuning: Display estimated execution plan
Ctrl+K	Tuning: Display execution plan (toggle On/Off)
Ctrl+you	Tuning: Index Tuning Wizard
Ctrl+Shift+S	Tuning: Show client statistics
Ctrl+Shift+T	Tuning: Show server trace
Ctrl+U	Use database

Table 3.2   Query Analyzer Color Codes

Color	Meaning
Blue	Keyword
Dark green	Comment
Dark red	Stored procedure
Gray	Operator
Green	System table
Magenta	System function
Red	Character string

Table 3.3   Query Analyzer Menu Items

Menu	Item	Meaning
File	Connect . . .	Makes a connection to a server. Just like the login when you first started.
	New	Opens a new window, remains connected to the same server and database.
Edit	Bookmark	Sets a placeholder for you in the text. Doesn't affect the query.
Query	Parse	Doesn't run the command but does check it to make sure it would run.
	Display Estimated Execution Plan	Shows a graphical representation of the way SQL Server 2000 will resolve the query. Useful for tracking down poorly performing queries. This is only an estimation; you can also choose another menu item from this tree that shows you the plan that is actually used.
	Show SQL Server Trace	A new tab appears in the Results pane that displays the information moving to and from the SQL Server Engine.
	Show Client Statistics	A new tab appears in the Results pane that displays information about the query—how long it took, which parts took the longest, and so forth.
Tools	Object Browser	Shows or hides the Object Browser panel.
	Object Search	A useful tool. This item works like the advanced search in Microsoft Word—it lets you find any object in the database.
	Manage Indexes	Brings up a dialog box to alter or create indexes.
	Manage Statistics	Statistics help SQL Server 2000 locate information quickly. This item brings up a dialog box to help you manage them. I examine these statistics in Chapter 9.
	Options	This item brings up a tabbed dialog box with numerous settings for the Query Analyzer environment.

I won't spend a great deal of time on Profiler in this chapter, but I will show you an overview of its use. Click on *Start, Programs, Microsoft SQL Server,* then *Profiler,* as shown in Figure 3.14.

You need to connect to a server to monitor it, creating a session called a Trace. To do this, select the menu item *File,* then *New,* then *Trace,* which brings up the login dialog box, as you can see in Figure 3.15.

Figure 3.14
Profiler

Figure 3.15
Profiler login

After you log in, you're shown the General Trace Properties in Figure 3.16. This panel has quite a few things to fill out, but I'll save those for Chapter 9. For now, you'll concentrate on *using* the tool rather than everything that it can do.

You can leave the panels as they are. Before you move on, notice that the trace can be run as is, saved to a table, or saved to a file. Recording these traces can be useful for troubleshooting.

Next select the Run button, and Profiler begins to record activities from the SQL Server. The items that it is recording aren't important right now, but just to see the type of output it produces, open Query Analyzer and perform a very basic query against the pubs database. You can see the results of that activity displayed in the Profiler screen displayed in Figure 3.17.

Here you see the actual SQL statement you typed in Query Analyzer in Profiler's output, line by line. Clicking on a line in the top panel displays what SQL Server "saw" coming in.

You use the green arrow on the icon bar to start or continue a trace, use the double bars next to it to pause one, and use the red square to stop the trace. You can also use the shortcut keys shown in Table 3.4 to manage Profiler.

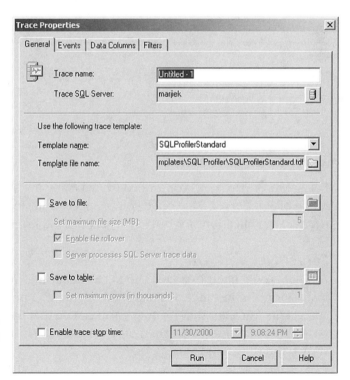

Figure 3.16
Profiler Trace
Properties—
General tab

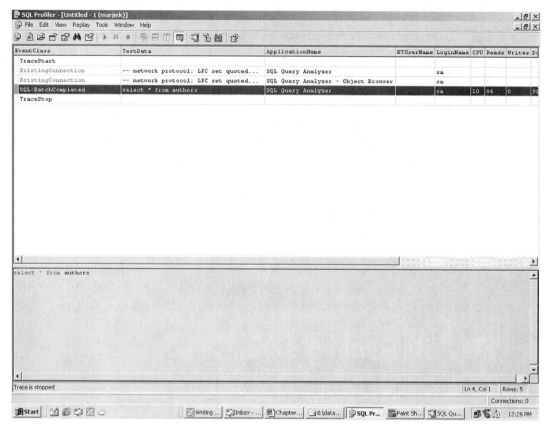

Figure 3.17 Profiler output

Network Configuration

For the most part, you won't need to make any major changes to the configuration of SQL Server 2000 once you've successfully installed it. You might want to make modifications for how SQL Server 2000 listens on the network.

Server Network Utility

At times you'll need to adjust the network settings for your SQL Server 2000 installation. For instance, you may add or change a protocol on the network or add clients using another protocol. You can do that by selecting *Start, Programs, Microsoft SQL Server,* and then *Server Network Utility.* When you do, you're shown the screen in Figure 3.18.

Table 3.4 Profiler Shortcut Keys

Keys	Function Performed
Ctrl+Shift+Delete	Clear a trace window
Ctrl+F4	Close a trace window
–	Collapse a trace grouping
Ctrl+C	Copy
Alt+Delete	Delete a trace
+	Expand a trace grouping
Ctrl+F	Find
F3	Find the next item
Shift+F3	Find the previous item
F1	Display available help
Ctrl+N	Open a new trace
Alt+F7	Replay the settings
Ctrl+F10	Run to cursor
F5	Start a replay
F11	Step
Shift+F5	Stop a replay
F9	Toggle a breakpoint

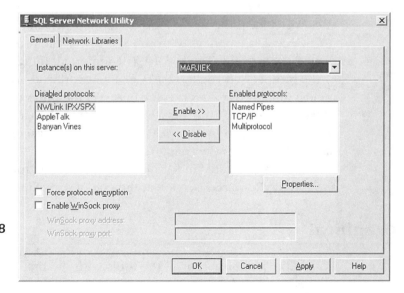

Figure 3.18
SQL Server
Network
Utility

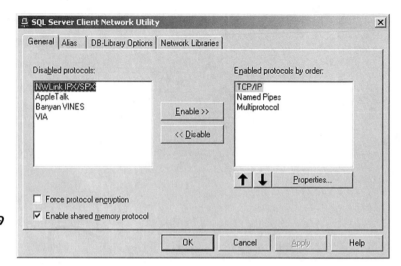

Figure 3.19
Client Net-
work Utility

Here you can select an instance and then add or delete the protocols you want that instance to listen on. Once you've done that, you can select the protocol and press the Properties button. This brings up a dialog box that can further tweak the settings particular to that protocol.

Client Network Utility

The Client Network Utility is the counterpart of the Server Network Utility. It sets up the way an application talks to the server. This utility is also found on a client machine if the Server Tools or Connectivity Only options are installed.

Select Start, Programs, Microsoft SQL Server, and then Client Network Utility to display the screen in Figure 3.19. The important thing to note here is the order of the protocols. If you have a TCP/IP network and users are having problems connecting to your server, check here. Set the order of the protocols to match what you have on your network. Make this change even if you are able to connect—it can help the speed of your client system immensely. I use these tools extensively in the chapters that follow.

If you're interested in learning more about the tools, check out Books Online and the Resources section at the end of the chapter.

Graphical

I begin the graphical tour of the tools with the first place you should start—Books Online.

Books Online

Books Online is the primary resource for SQL Server 2000. It's an electronic help file, a complete set of manuals, and a how-to book all in one.

Using Books Online

From the Start menu, look for Programs, Microsoft SQL Server, and then Books Online, and the screen in Figure 3.20 appears.

Here you see the first section you'll examine in Books Online—the Contents tab. This tab includes a table of contents and a glossary as well as a how-to section. There's also a developer's guide in this tab for SQL Server applications in several languages. This section is topic-oriented, so look up the installation process you followed in Chapter 2.

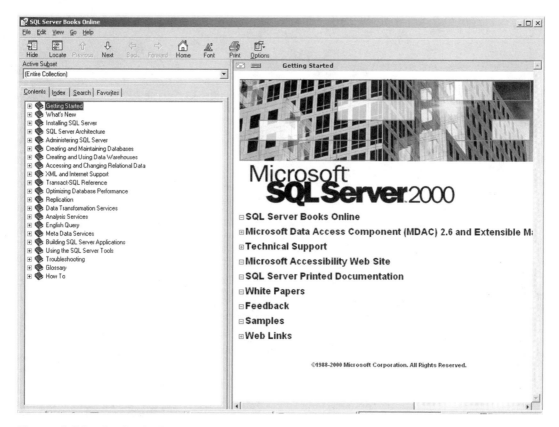

Figure 3.20   Books Online main page

Double-click Installing SQL Server and then Overview of Installing SQL Server 2000. You're shown the display in Figure 3.21. In this screen you see the hyperlinks in the right-hand side of the panel that allow you to jump around through a topic. This tab is where you can quickly locate a topic and logically follow a progressive thread, just like in a book.

The next tab you'll examine is the Index tab, shown in Figure 3.22. This is where you spend most of your time. This tab is more like the index in a book—except you type in the word you want information on, and it jumps to that section of help. One of the best uses of this type of search is when you know the command or concept you need help with but can't remember the exact syntax or process. As an example, enter CREATE DATABASE in the Index tab, and Books Online jumps to the information on that topic. Since you've typed in an exact command, it displays those words. Double-click that section,

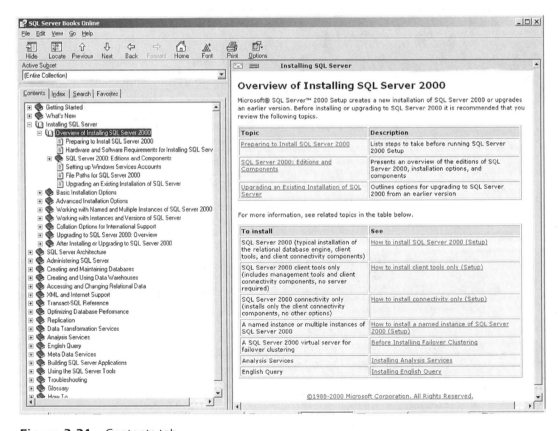

Figure 3.21 Contents tab

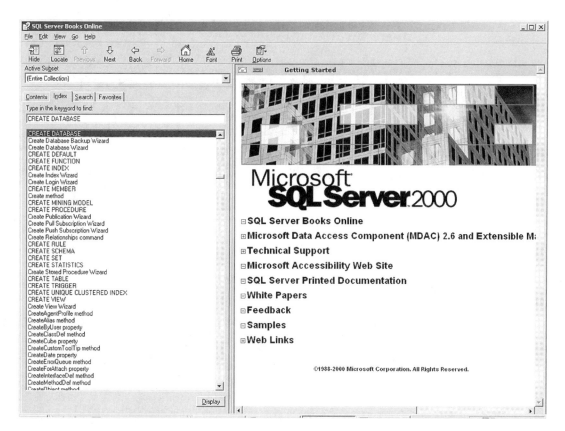

Figure 3.22   Index tab

and two types of information are displayed: Syntax for T-SQL and topics from the section titled Installing SQL Server, as shown in Figure 3.23.

The next section is the Search tab. This tab means exactly what it says—you type in a word or phrase and back comes a huge range of topics to look through. This tab is the one you use when you're not exactly sure of what you're looking for. You can also type in a Boolean search here—use AND, OR, NOT, or NEAR with your words to narrow the search.

An interesting behavior on this tab is the fact that it highlights the word(s) you've searched on. In most cases this is a useful feature, but you can turn it off. Click View in the menu bar, and then click Highlights. Repeat the process to turn it back on. You can see this feature in Figure 3.24.

The last tab isn't used for searching. The Favorites tab is used to store something you've searched on earlier, to make your own list of topics. Once you've located information you want to keep track of, select the Favorites tab. Now

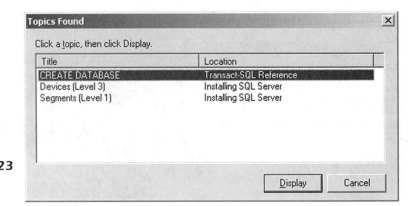

Figure 3.23
Index tab
topics

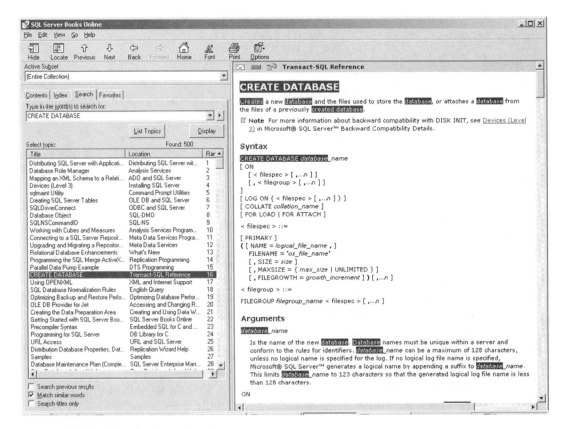

Figure 3.24 Search tab

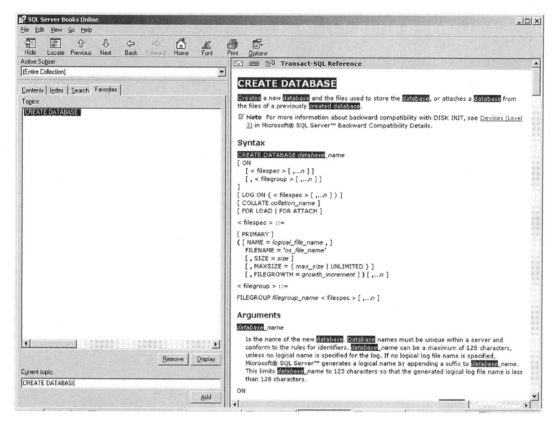

Figure 3.25   Favorites tab

select Add, and that topic's title is saved in the left-hand panel. The Favorites tab is shown in Figure 3.25.

Enterprise Manager

This is the main tool used to manage the objects in SQL Server 2000. To start it, select Start, Programs, Microsoft SQL Server, and then Enterprise Manager.

Registering a SQL Server in Enterprise Manager

In this example, you'll unregister your own server and then you'll reregister it. Start by right-clicking your server's name and selecting Delete SQL Server Registration from the menu that appears, as shown in Figure 3.26.

Now that the server is gone, you will need to register it. Begin by right-clicking the SQL Server Group item, and select New SQL Server Registration from the menu that appears. You'll see the screen shown in Figure 3.27.

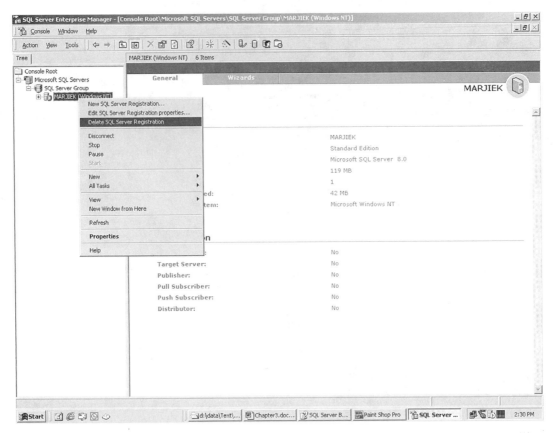

Figure 3.26 Delete registration

Next a wizard starts. Wizards are sprinkled throughout Enterprise Manager, and they make it easy to perform most tasks. You can also access the wizards by selecting Tools and then Wizards from the menu in Enterprise Manager.

Cancel the wizard by selecting From now on you want to perform this task without using a wizard. Do that for two reasons: You want to see what happens if the wizard doesn't start, and the wizard doesn't need much explanation.

Select Next, and you're presented with the screen shown in Figure 3.28 on page 76. This is also the screen you'd see if you right-clicked a server name and selected Properties.

Begin by typing in the name of the server you want to register—or its IP number if you're using TCP/IP on your network. Something to keep in mind is that you need to have some sort of name resolution like DNS, WINS, or even a HOSTS file entry to that server to be able to use the name. You can register

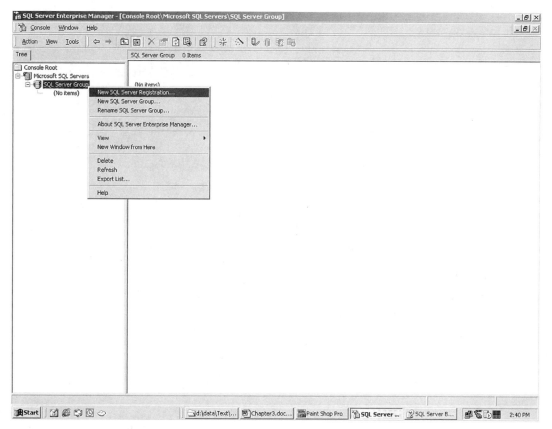

Figure 3.27   *New SQL Server registration*

servers across the Internet or any other network. If you run into trouble here, see the earlier section Client Network Utility.

Next select the type of security you'll use to connect to the server. If you set up your server the way I did in Chapter 2, you can select either mode. If you select *Use Windows authentication,* you'll need to be either a domain administrator (by default) or at least an administrator on the SQL Server.

You can also set the registration to *Use SQL Server authentication* and enter the name and password you used when you installed SQL Server. Notice you can also select the option to have the system prompt for this name and password each time this tool is used. This is handy if more than one person uses the same login on a Windows NT/2000 system or you're setting these tools to be used from Windows 9*x* or Me. Those systems, without this setting, could allow any user to use your credentials to access the registered SQL Server. The

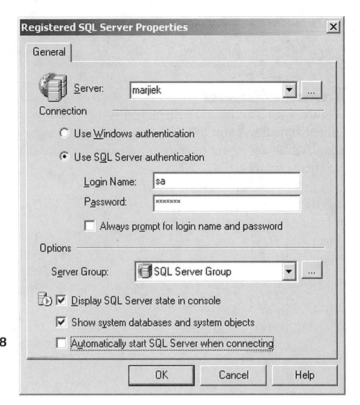

Figure 3.28
Registered
SQL Server
Properties

Display SQL Server state in console option shows the current state in Enterprise Manager.

The next item, Show system databases and system objects, displays just what it says. To be safe, turn this option off; to see them, turn it on. If you're using certain versions of SQL Server, this setting is off by default, so if you don't see the system databases I discussed on your system, change this setting.

The setting Automatically start SQL Server when connecting means that whenever you connect, the server tries to start if it is stopped. This setting is fine if you're using SQL Server 2000 on your own system, but you might want to remove the option for all the production servers you connect to in your enterprise. You may not want to start a server that another administrator has stopped for a reason.

Select OK and you see the server registered in Enterprise Manager once again. You can repeat this process for as many servers as you're allowed to administer. With the servers registered, you can change the systemwide settings using Enterprise Manager.

Setting SQL Server Configuration

To change your example serverwide settings, you first right-click your server's name in Enterprise Manager and then select Properties.

General Properties   Once you do that, you're presented with the screen in Figure 3.29. The first tab displayed is the General panel. This tab is informational and allows you to correct the default behavior of the installation for setting SQL Server Agent to start automatically. Make that change and then move to the next tab.

Memory Properties   Select the next tab and you're shown the screen in Figure 3.30. SQL Server 2000 can dynamically obtain and release memory from the operating system. This is a great burden removed from an administrator, who then doesn't need to constantly monitor the server's memory use and adjust

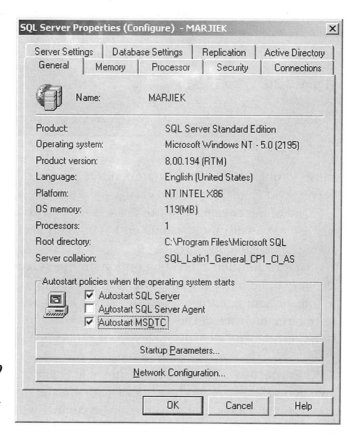

Figure 3.29
Server
Properties—
General

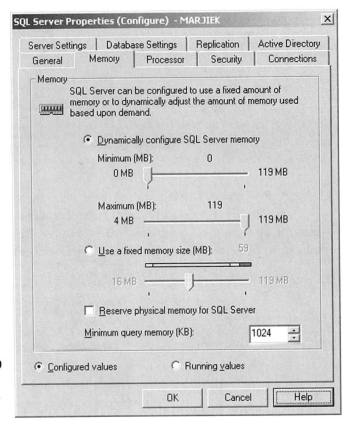

Figure 3.30
SQL Server
Properties—
Memory

those settings. Most administrators never set any memory options on a SQL Server 2000. Note that you *can* change these settings, but there's rarely a need to.

One of the changes you can make is to set a floor or ceiling on the memory use, even with the dynamic option on. This keeps SQL Server 2000 from taking all available memory.

There's another interesting option on this screen—it allows the server's memory to be set or frozen at the current running settings. You might use the automatic setting until you feel the server has reached an optimum performance level; then select this option. You'll see this option again in other tabs. I don't recommend a change unless your application directs you to change it.

CPU Properties   The next tab is shown in Figure 3.31. In this panel there are two items that we're interested in. The first is the option to set SQL Server to run using NT Fibers. You may already be familiar with what you thought was the lowest unit of operation for Windows NT, the thread. NT fibers allow even

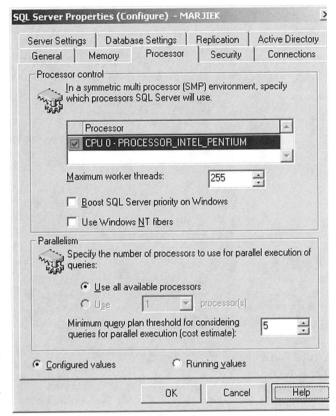

Figure 3.31
SQL Server
Properties—
CPU

more granularity when running a task. There can be performance benefits to selecting this setting, but you probably don't want to change it unless an application developer has told you to.

The other option of interest is the ability to set the processors that SQL Server 2000 uses. Normally, you should change this setting only if told to do so or for performance testing. Let's skip to the Server Settings tab next.

Server Settings   The Server Settings tab is shown in Figure 3.32. The area that we're concerned with in this tab is SQL Mail. SQL Server 2000 can use mail in two places: SQL Mail and SQL Server Agent Mail.

The mail setup for SQL Mail processes mail by SQL Server 2000—meaning that you can enable the server to send or receive e-mail, and process and return queries received by e-mail.

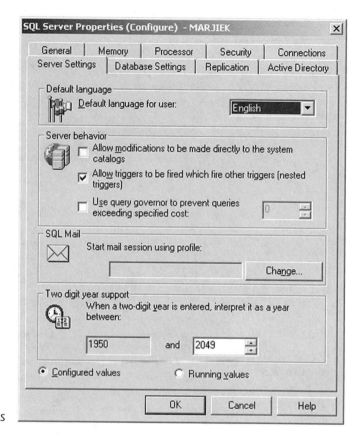

Figure 3.32
SQL Server
Properties—
Server Settings

To do this, see the next Graphical section for the steps you'll need to take. I'll cover SQL Server Agent Mail in Chapter 6.

Setting Up SQL Server Mail

The process for setting up SQL Server Mail for your server is as follows:

- Set up an e-mail account for SQL Server 2000 to use on your mail server.

- Set up a mail application programming interface (MAPI)– compliant e-mail program on the SQL Server 2000 (like Microsoft Outlook).

Figure 3.33
Mail profile
using Microsoft
Outlook 2000

- Set up an e-mail profile on SQL Server 2000. You can do this by right-clicking your e-mail program and selecting Properties, then Show Profiles. This is shown in Figure 3.33.

- Set up the MSSQLServer Service to log on as an NT/2000 account with rights to the previous mail account, using the Security tab in server Properties. This is shown in Figure 3.34.

- Select the Change button on Server Settings in server Properties, as shown in Figure 3.35.

Now that this section is configured, you're ready for SQL Server to start using mail.

Creating a Database Diagram

You can use the Database Diagram tool to design a new database or reverse engineer an existing one. Let's create a simple database diagram from an existing database.

From the Console root in Enterprise Manager, drill down to the Diagrams object following this path: Microsoft SQL Servers, SQL Server Group, (your computer

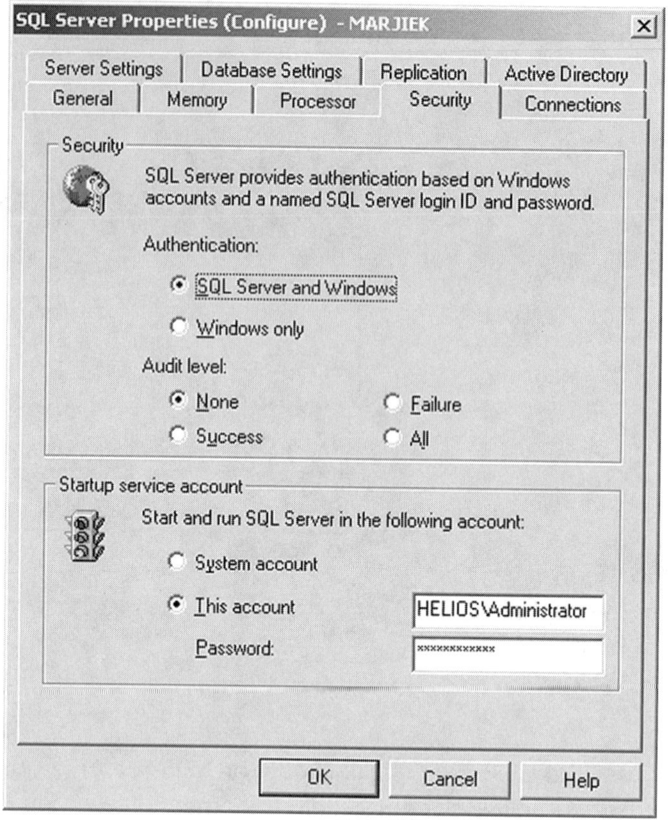

Figure 3.34
Setting the SQL
Server login

name), Databases, pubs, Diagrams. Right-click the Diagrams object and select New Database Diagram from the menu. The Create Database Diagram Wizard appears, as shown in Figure 3.36.

Select the Next button. You can now select the group of tables you want to work with. Notice that you can have the wizard select tables that have been related automatically. Next select the tables, as shown in Figure 3.37.

Add all the tables that do not start with the letters *sys* (they're system tables) and select Next. You're then given one last chance to hit the Back button. Select Finish to bring up the screen shown in Figure 3.38.

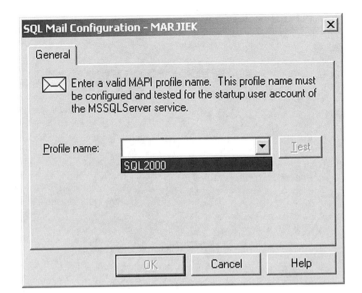

Figure 3.35
Setting the
mail profile
for SQL Server

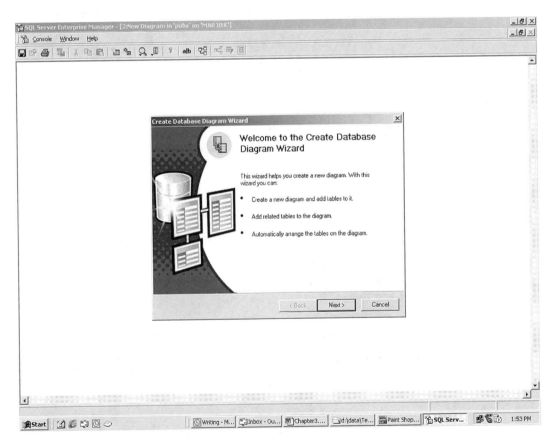

Figure 3.36 Create Database Diagram Wizard

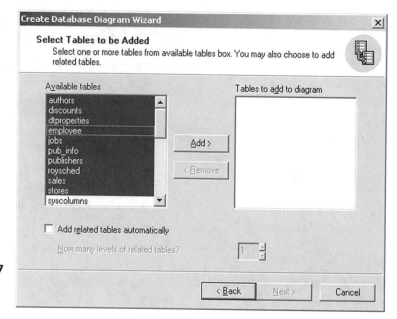

Figure 3.37
Selecting
tables

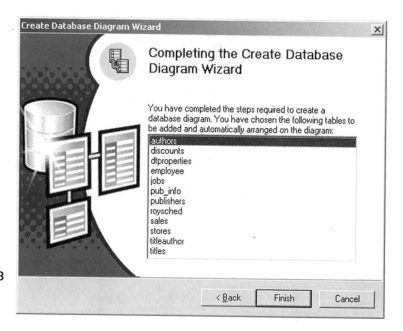

Figure 3.38
Wizard
completion

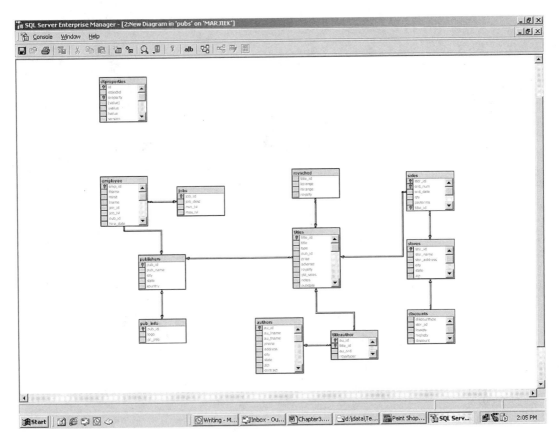

Figure 3.39 Completed Database Diagram

Now you're shown the completed diagram in Figure 3.39. You can right-click any object you see for a context-sensitive menu of the actions that can be performed on that item. You can even right-click the lines connecting the objects and select Properties to see the way that they are joined.

Use the magnifying glass icon to zoom in to 100%, and right-click the titles table. Once you've selected the Table View menu item, change it to Standard, as shown in Figure 3.40.

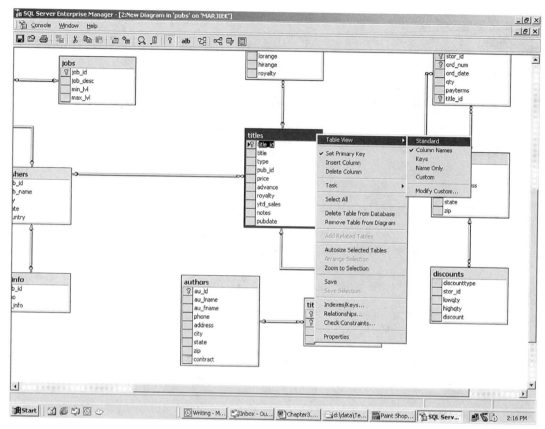

Figure 3.40   Changing the Diagram Table View

You can see the underlying structure of the table in Figure 3.41. This is an active diagram; so if you make any changes here, you'll be asked when you exit whether you want to save the changes to the database. You can also delay the changes by selecting the script button shown in Figure 3.42.

This button prompts for a location to save a SQL script that will make the change. You can run this script in any of the command-line tools.

You can save and print these diagrams, but you'll need a *bunch* of paper. The real value of this tool is altering a database and using the scripting feature,

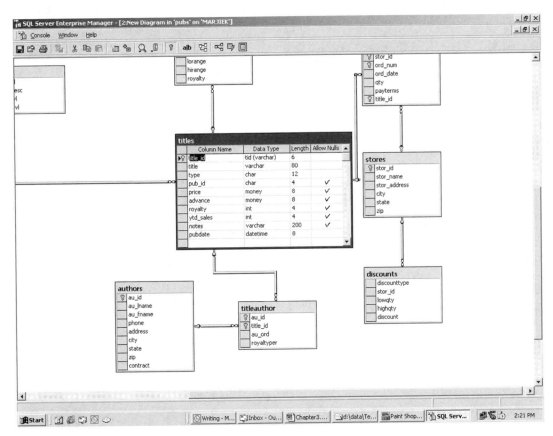

Figure 3.41   Standard Table View

or visualizing a relationship between tables, or even designing a new database graphically.

Accessing Tables
You may be asked to alter a table's structure, add a field, or look at data in a table. You can do all these tasks within Enterprise Manager.

From the Console root in Enterprise Manager, drill down to the Tables object following this path: Microsoft SQL Servers, SQL Server Group, (your computer name), Databases, pubs, Tables.

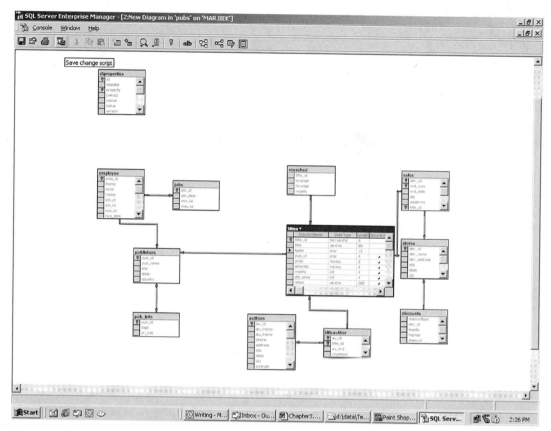

Figure 3.42 Save to Script

Altering a Table In order to alter a table, right-click the name of the table and then select *Design Table*. Now let's explore the *authors* table, as shown in Figure 3.43.

If you're familiar with Microsoft Access, Figure 3.44 will look familiar. In this screen you have the same ability that you did in the *Diagram* tool. You're able to save the changes directly to the database, or by selecting the script icon, you're able to create a script of the changes.

Querying Data from a Table Although using *Enterprise Manager* isn't the optimal way to look at data, it is an effective tool to quickly view and even edit

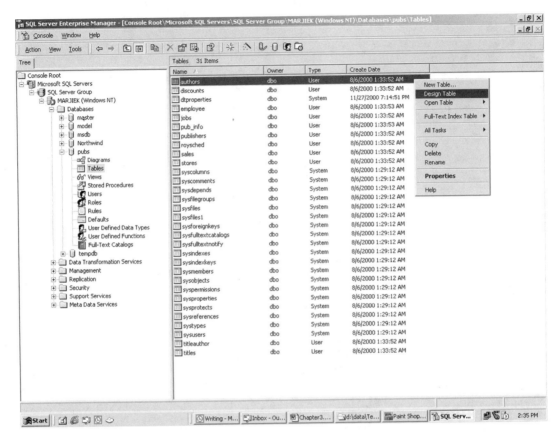

Figure 3.43 Altering a table

data. A word of caution here—be extremely careful editing data this way. When you move off of the field, the data is changed. There is no "Are you sure?" prompt for these changes.

From the Console root in Enterprise Manager, drill down to the Tables object following this path: Microsoft SQL Servers, SQL Server Group, (your computer name), Databases, pubs, Tables. Right-click the name of the table you want to look at, and select Open Tables and then Return All Rows.

Notice that you could have selected to retrieve only a certain number of rows (Return Top) or even create a query (Query) on the table. I'll get all the data for now, but keep in mind that if this were a production system, there

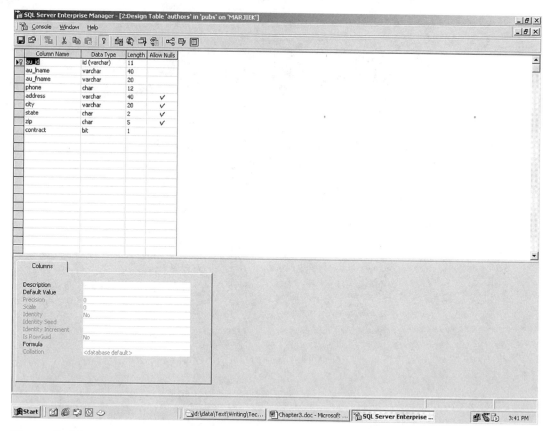

Figure 3.44   *Table designer*

might be millions of rows in a table. Retrieving that many rows takes time and takes CPU cycles from your users.

Once you do all that, the screen that is shown in Figure 3.45 appears. This brings up a spreadsheet-like view that contains the data from the table, as displayed in Figure 3.46. As I mentioned, it's active, and you should always remember to exercise caution here.

I'll select two icons from the icon bar. In Figure 3.47 you'll see one that looks like two squares that are joined by a line and the one with the letters SQL in it.

The top panel will look very familiar to you if you're a Microsoft Access user—and it works the same way. The second panel shows the SQL statements

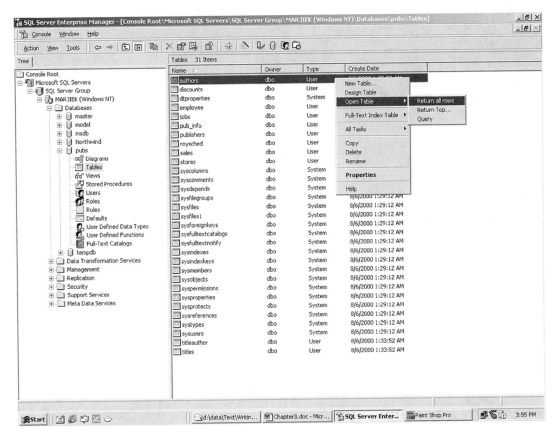

Figure 3.45 Open table

produced by the upper panel, and you can edit it and click the exclamation mark icon to rerun the statement. The SQL statements include those that modify or erase data.

Generating a Script   Another useful task *Enterprise Manager* can perform is the ability to generate SQL code that creates objects. This code, called a *script*, is just a text file, which can be opened in *Query Analyzer* or another command-line tool. Scripts are available for many objects, but I will stick with tables for now.

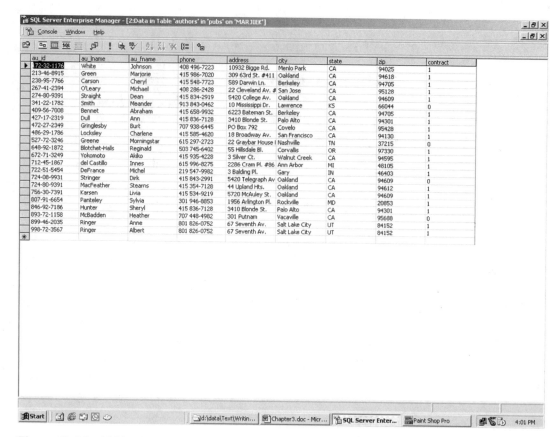

Figure 3.46 Table data

As displayed in Figure 3.48, from the Console root in Enterprise Manager, drill down to the Tables object following this path: Microsoft SQL Servers, SQL Server Group, (your computer name), Databases, pubs, Tables.

Right-click the name of the table you want, and then select All Tasks and Generate SQL Script from the menu, which gives you the screen shown in Figure 3.49.

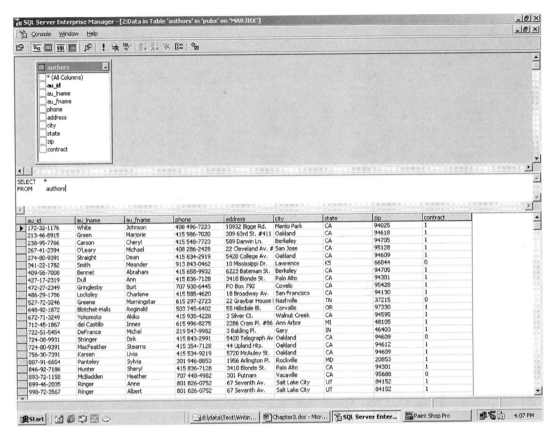

Figure 3.47 Table view variations

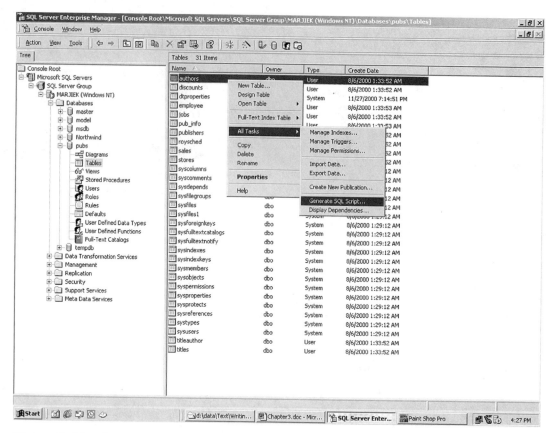

Figure 3.48 Generate SQL script

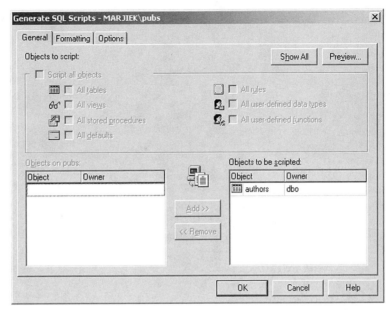

Figure 3.49
Script object
selection

The first screen you see in Figure 3.50 is the selection of the object(s) you want to script. Since you selected the command to generate from the table, this information is already filled out.

The Formatting tab shows the formatting options for the script. One important item to note here is the option Generate scripts for all dependent objects. This option finds all objects that are affected by this object and scripts those items too. This can make a big script and may affect things you didn't intend to change. Leave the settings as they are, and move to the next tab, shown in Figure 3.51.

The Options tab has three areas. The first involves creating the script to include the database and server security on the object. Selecting this option creates the commands in the script that you use to create users and permissions. The second area allows control of the ancillary objects for the table, such as indexes. The last section determines the file options for the script, as shown in Figure 3.52.

Return to the General tab and press the Preview button. This has the same effect as completing the script, but no file is created. Using this option, you can see the output in the window and even copy and paste it into another tool if you like.

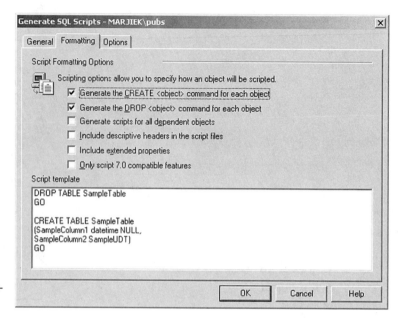

Figure 3.50
Script formatting options

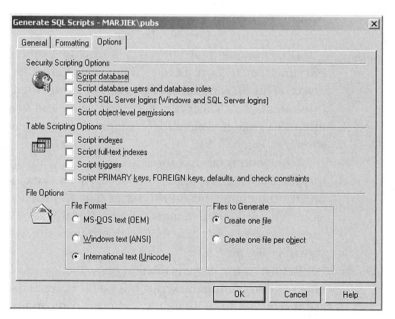

Figure 3.51
Script options

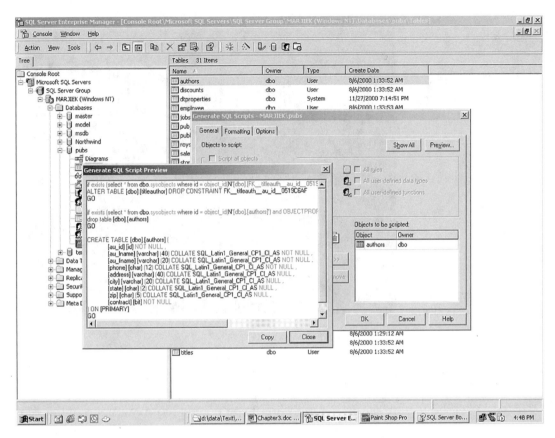

Figure 3.52   Completed script preview

Command Line

I've described the main command-line tool, Query Analyzer. Here, you'll see examples involving the other two, osql and bcp.

osql

The osql tool replaces the isql tool, which is still available, from previous versions of SQL Server. The osql tool is available at the operating system command line, and it gives command-line access to the database engine. You can use it against a local server or a remote server, run scripts, and save output to the screen or a file.

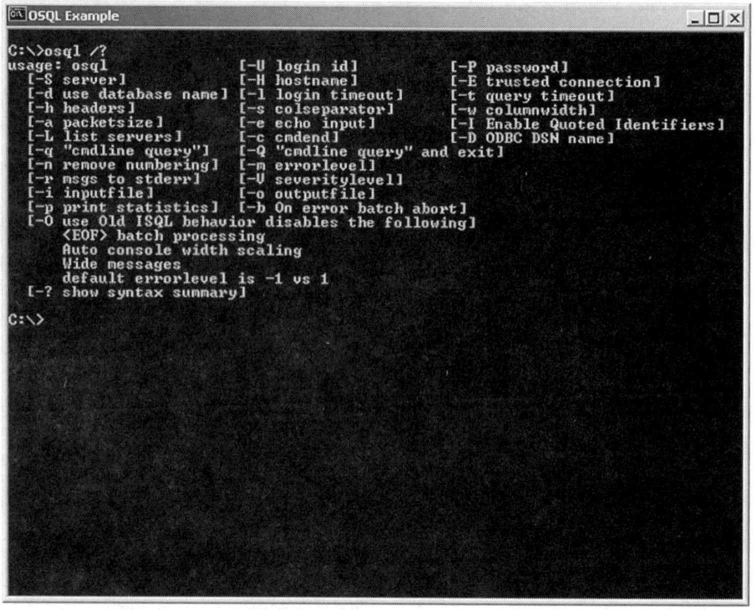

Figure 3.53
osql options

Enter the osql command with the /? switch to display all available options, as shown in Figure 3.53.

I show more of these options in Chapter 5 and more examples of this tool in Chapter 4.

Query Against a Local Server

The first example I'll demonstrate is the simplest use of osql. This example assumes that the SQL Server 2000 security allows Windows accounts to access the server and that the command is running on the server.

Let's ask SQL Server 2000 to give you, from the pubs database (-d), the first names in the author table (-Q) that begin with the letter A. Because you're running osql from the server, you won't need to specify the name of the server. You can use trusted authentication (-E) if your server is set to allow Windows authentication.

You can see the command output in Figure 3.54. Granted, this query is pretty basic, but keep in mind that the power lies not in simple examples like this one but in the ability to run scripts.

Earlier I showed you how to export a script to a file. This tool can be used to run that script. I'll show an example of that process in Chapter 4.

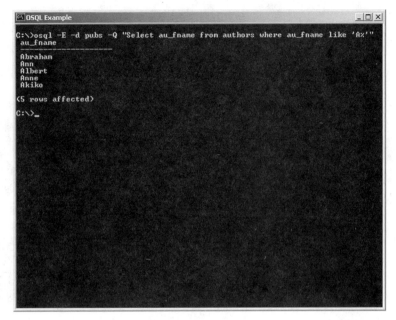

Figure 3.54
Simple osql
query

bcp

This acronym stands for *bulk copy program*, and it's used to move data into and out of a SQL Server. You'll use this command again in Chapter 5.

This example makes the same assumptions as did the osql example. You'll send the contents of that same table that you requested in the osql example to a file called out.txt.

I'll explain the switches later; for now, notice in Figure 3.55 that the file will be saved as a text file (the c switch) and will be separated by commas (the t switch). Just as with osql, you can type bcp /? and receive a list of the switches for the utility.

Figure 3.55
Exporting a
file with bcp

Rosetta Stone

There are a lot of database products out there, but I'll stick with showing just two of these, a large product (Oracle) and a smaller one (Microsoft Access).

The function of this section is to demonstrate the basic areas to locate the same items in all three products. This is more difficult to map at times than others; but if you're familiar with either of these two products, this section may help speed you along.

In this chapter, I've shown the tools that SQL Server uses. I try to map these tools as closely as possible to their counterparts in these other products.

Oracle

The version of Oracle that I'm comparing is Oracle 8 for Windows NT. If you're familiar with Oracle, you can map newer versions of it to Table 3.5.

Microsoft Access

The Microsoft Access version I use for this mapping is 2000. Not all commands map exactly, but the ones that do are listed in Table 3.6.

Table 3.5 Oracle and SQL Server 2000 Compared

SQL Server 2000 Tool	Oracle Tool
Books Online	Oracle documentation
Enterprise Manager	Enterprise Manager
Query Analyzer	SQL+ or SQL worksheet
Profiler	Performance Manager or Trace
osql	SQLPLUS
bcp	EXP80 and IXP80

Table 3.6 Microsoft Access and SQL Server 2000 Compared

SQL Server 2000 Tool	Microsoft Access Tool
Books Online	Help
Enterprise Manager	Primary interface
Query Analyzer	Queries tab
Profiler	*Tools	Analyze	Performance*
osql	MSACCESS.EXE /CMD (with an appropriate function in the affected database)
bcp	*File	Export*

Resources

These are some of the best resources I've found for using the tools (other than the best—Books Online).

Trying to use an old version of Enterprise Manager to connect to SQL 2000?
   http://support.microsoft.com/support/kb/articles/Q265/8/08.asp
More information on Query Analyzer:
   http://www2.itworld.com/cma/ett_article_frame/0,,1_2418.html
   http://www.mssqlserver.com/articles/sqlserver2000_p19.asp
More information on osql:
   http://support.microsoft.com/support/sql/content/70papers/sql7prep.asp
SQL 2000 options:
   http://www.sqlmag.com/Articles/Index.cfm?ArticleID=16362

Chapter 4

Accessing Data

Chapter at a Glance

This chapter introduces you to methods of accessing data, from both internal SQL Server 2000 tools and other programs. Read this chapter to understand the connection methods for SQL Server 2000.

The Resources section contains references for:

- Active Server Pages
- ODBC connections
- Visual Basic

Read Chapter 3 before reading this chapter.

Overview

As a database administrator, you're concerned about the tools that you use to *manage* SQL Server 2000. The users, however, are more concerned about the tools they use to *access* the data stored in SQL Server 2000. In this chapter I discuss the process for creating databases and the methods used to get at the data they store.

Databases can be restored, attached, or created manually using Enterprise Manager or command-line tools. Once they exist, user programs access the data remotely. The physical process for database operation involves write-ahead log technology, which means that all data is written first to a sequential log file, and then the logging process transfers the data to the database.

Once the logging process confirms the data to be in the database, a database-wide setting determines whether the data is removed or left in the log until a backup is taken. Data in the database is accessed by the SQL tools described in Chapter 3, through connections made with either ODBC or "DSN-less" methods. ODBC connections are created using a Control Panel applet at the client workstation, and ODBC is upgraded by the Microsoft Database Access Components (MDAC) version in SQL Server 2000. This upgrade may be necessary on each client machine that accesses the SQL Server if version-specific features are implemented in the client program. OLE-DB methods such as ActiveX Data Objects (ADO) often do not require a great deal of client configuration but may still require the MDAC upgrade on the client.

Detail

Before users can manipulate data, they need a database. You can get the database into your server in one of three methods:

- Create the database
- Restore the database from a backup
- Attach the database from a file

I'll explore the first method, leaving the other two for Chapter 8.

Databases

A database is just a collected set of information that can be stored, retrieved and modified. Every software vendor has its own way of dealing with storage and manipulation, and Microsoft is no exception.

Physical Storage Process

A single Microsoft SQL Server 2000 database physically consists of two parts: the *database* and the *log*. Each of these objects is stored as one or more files on the SQL Server using the File Allocation Table (FAT) or NT File System (NTFS).

Personally, I never use the FAT filesystem on Windows NT or higher because of security and speed issues, but you can store the files in that format if you want to. You can create one or more files to hold the database or logs, storing the individual tables or indexes on different files or even on different drives for performance reasons. You can also indicate that tables or indexes be placed in a particular file, which can be on different drives.

When data is modified, it is sent to a memory cache on the server, and then on to the log. The log stores all modified data, including adds, in a sequential fashion. There are exceptions to this rule; but in normal operation all data changes are logged.

Once data has been stored in the log, it is written to the database. When the data is verified to be in the database, the logging process makes a mark on that line of data indicating that the data is recorded. This marking process is known as a *checkpoint*. Settings on each database affect what happens after the checkpoint.

Database Recovery Settings

The setting that affects the logging behavior is called the Recovery model. This option is set using Enterprise Manager with the techniques I discussed in Chapter 3. There are three options for the Recovery model: Simple, Full, and Bulk Logged.

With Recovery set to the Simple option, the data is removed from the log once it has been successfully entered into the database. This is a common operation of a noncritical database and keeps the log file small as the data moves into the database.

With the Recovery model set to the Full or Bulk Logged option, the committed data is *marked* but not *erased*. In addition, the log file would grow until the disk ran out of space unless some other process removed the data from the log.

The process that removes the data that made it to the database is a backup of either the whole database or the log. Once a backup is successful, SQL Server 2000 is aware that it's safe to erase the data from the log. I cover backup techniques further in Chapter 8. The difference between the Full and Bulk Logged options involves the level of data that is logged.

Not all data additions are sent through the log when you're using the Bulk Logged Recovery model. The logging process accepts commands during data transfer that instruct SQL Server to bypass the logging process. This setting provides greater speed since the logging process requires more steps, but the data sent to the database is nonrecoverable. You must take a full backup of the database once the nonlogged event has completed.

The Full Recovery model, as the name suggests, sends *everything* through the log. This is the safest setting but can be much slower and can cause the log to grow quite large if backups are not taken frequently.

Database Growth Settings

SQL Server 2000 can handle the physical database and log files in one of two ways: You can either specify a size for the files, or you can allow them to grow automatically. Allowing files to grow automatically is a lot less to worry about, but the files can consume your entire drive if you're not careful. As part of this growth, you have the option to grow the files by a percentage or an amount.

Let's assume you've set the database to grow by percentage. The database starts with 10MB of space used and as such will grow by 1MB if you choose to auto-grow that file with a 10% setting. When that database is at 100MB, the next chunk that is taken is 10MB; and at 1GB, 100MB is taken, and so forth. The growth is exponential with this setting, like an adjustable mortgage on a house, and it can hurt at the worst possible time. If you choose this setting, you should monitor your system closely as the file becomes larger.

You can also limit the size the files can attain; otherwise the auto-growth settings can run your system completely out of drive space. If your databases happen to be on the same NT partition as the page file, which is not a wise practice, this space deficit can make the operating system unstable.

Other settings can have dramatic affects on your database, but the ones I just examined are the two you should be the most familiar with when looking at a new database.

To recap, you create a database and a log, which are stored on one or more files, which can be grow automatically or be limited to a certain size. You can set the log to remove entries when they are committed to the database or to keep them until they are backed up.

Accessing Data

Now that you have your database, you need to be able to access the data in it. There are several ways to do this, but the primary methods are broken into these three camps:

- SQL Server tools
- ODBC
- OLE-DB (sometimes referred to as DSN-less)

Users don't normally access the data using the SQL Server tools, so I won't spend a great deal of time on that method. The other two are used most often.

You'll see these other types as you work with applications written to use SQL Server 2000 as their database.

ODBC

Using Open Database Connectivity (ODBC) to access Microsoft SQL Server 2000 involves two parts: a program designed to use ODBC and a driver, located on each user's system. Sometimes you'll hear people refer to the driver as ODBC, but that's not technically right.

ODBC is a piece of software that is configured to connect to a specific server and database, using specific credentials. Each configuration within this ODBC driver is called a Data Source Name (DSN).

The ODBC program has a version, and you should always try to pair the proper ODBC program with the database it connects to. I'm using SQL Server 2000, so I'll use the MDAC setup that comes with the SQL Server 2000 CD.

The DSN is a collection of settings that access the database from a client. There are three types of DSN connections: User, System, and File.

A User DSN allows access only to the current user. If you set up this type of DSN on a system that is used by more than one person, you have to set up one per user. These settings are stored in the registry.

A System DSN can be used by anyone who can log on to the system. This is the most common type. These settings are also stored in the registry.

A File DSN is a file that contains the connection information. The problem with this type of DSN is that it requires the connection to make a trip to the filesystem each time that it is called. You won't see this type of a connection often.

What you need to set up on the client for access using ODBC are the ODBC drivers and a properly configured DSN. See the Examples section later in this chapter for more information on configuring a DSN.

OLE-DB

Microsoft has other ways to get to a SQL Server 2000 database. These other methods use Application Programming Interfaces (APIs)—code that programs use to get to the database. These APIs include things like ADO.

The impact to the DBA is that ODBC drivers aren't necessary on the user's system. Many times these DSN-less methods are used on server applications like Web-hosted databases and other server-side applications. They are becoming more common for programs used on the client side.

Usually, very little setup is required for OLE-DB. The developer of the program may include a configuration utility; or if it requires other parameters, it's usually specified in the documentation for that program. For Web pages or other server-side access methods, you don't need to place anything on the client.

In any case, the MDAC software may still be required on the client. Even the OLE-DB methods are dependent on the dynamic link libraries (DLLs) that access the server.

Programs and Database Access

Let's examine some of the applications you will encounter that connect to SQL Server 2000 and the access methods they use.

Microsoft Office   Virtually all of Microsoft Office can access data inside a SQL Server 2000 database using the ODBC or OLE-DB methods. Almost all the latest Office programs use OLE-DB, but many, such as Microsoft Access, still rely on ODBC for nonprogrammatic access.

In the Examples section, I show you how to set up an ODBC connection and use it in Microsoft Access. Once you've created that DSN, you could also use it in:

- Microsoft Word using Mail Merge
- Microsoft Excel using Query

You can also use a subset of Visual Basic called Visual Basic for Applications (VBA) in Microsoft Office products. You write VBA code in macros stored in the Office document, using OLE-DB.

Visual Basic   You can access SQL Server 2000 from many programming languages using either ODBC drivers or through the APIs I mentioned earlier. In the examples that follow, I use the OLE-DB method to access the server with Visual Basic to return data to a form.

Web Pages   More and more SQL Server 2000 data is accessed through Web pages. There are tons of ways to get at data using Web pages, including ODBC and OLE-DB.

You can also purchase programs that feed Web pages using ready-made controls. I use Microsoft's Active Server Pages using an OLE-DB connection to return data to a dynamic grid later in the chapter.

Command Line   Many Oracle users are familiar with managing a database without the advantage of graphical tools. Some are more used to this method than to using the new tools Oracle provides. Most novice Microsoft SQL Server users are usually less familiar with the command-line tools available to them, but at times you can benefit from using a nongraphical client.

Your servers may be located remotely, and you may have a slow link or even a dial-up connection as your only access. If so, a command-line tool can be perfect for accessing data.

The Examples section details using *Query Analyzer* and *osql*—the two main character-based tools at your disposal.

Graphical

As with many Microsoft products, there's a graphical way to do things and command-line way to do things. Let's look at some of the concepts I discussed in this chapter using the graphical tools.

Creating and Managing a Database

Many times a database is set up for you during a product's installation, but it's important to know how to create one yourself if need be.

Enterprise Manager

The simplest, quickest way to create a database in SQL Server 2000 is by using *Enterprise Manager.*

Creating a Database   First, click *Start, Programs, Microsoft SQL Server,* and then *Enterprise Manager.* Double-click *Microsoft SQL Servers,* then *SQL Server Group,* and then the server's name. Next, right-click *Databases,* and select *New Database* from the menu that appears. Figure 4.1 shows what you will see then.

In Figure 4.2 you're shown a panel that allows you to name the database and set other options. Just set the name as *TestDatabase* for now. Spaces are allowed, but they can cause difficulties later; so it's best to avoid that practice.

Select *OK,* and you'll see the new database in the right-hand panel of *Enter-prise Manager.* If you create a database using this method, you can navigate

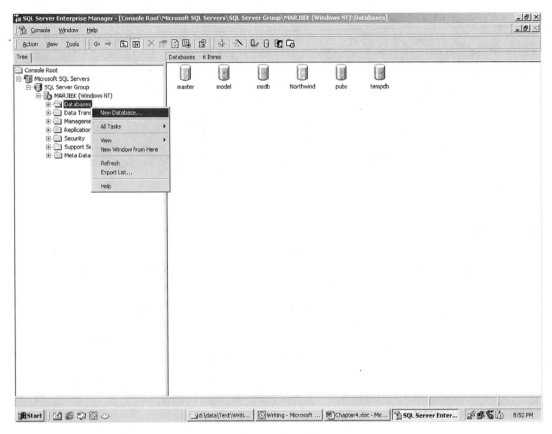

Figure 4.1 Creating a database using Enterprise Manager

through Enterprise Manager and see objects that you didn't create. Most of these are system objects, and some are there because they existed in the model template database.

Database Options Now that you have a database, you can control its options using Enterprise Manager. Let's drill down further in the left-hand pane

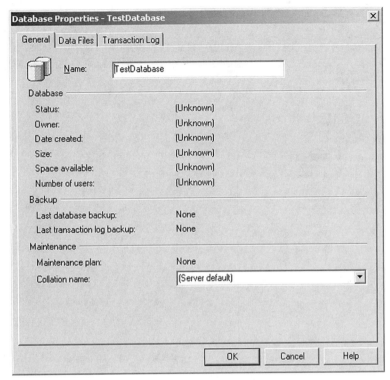

Figure 4.2
Naming the
database

to examine the current settings. Double-click Databases, then TestDatabase to
display the screen that is shown in Figure 4.3 on the next page.

Right-click the database and select Properties from the menu that appears.
That brings up the panels to check the current settings.

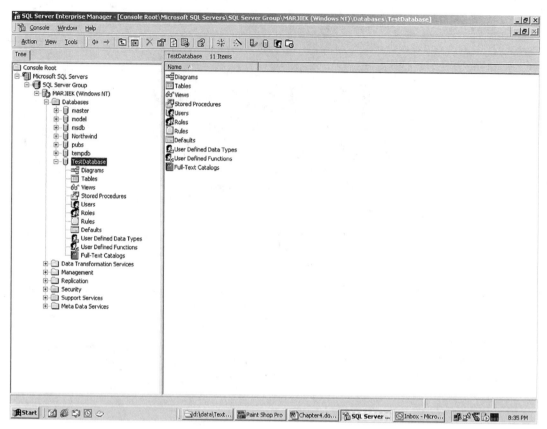

Figure 4.3 Selecting the database

File Settings In Figure 4.4 you see the Data Files tab, focusing on the growth options. Notice that the default is to automatically grow the files by 10% until they consume the whole drive. A prudent change on this panel, as well as on the Transaction Log tab, is to limit the amount of drive space that the file can take.

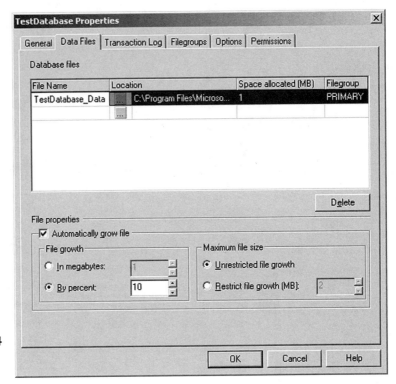

Figure 4.4
Data Files
options

Recovery Settings   In Figure 4.5 on the next page, you've selected the Options tab to modify options for the recovery mode. Select Simple for this database because you don't need to recover it to a point in time.

Those are the only options to change for now. I'll explore these options using the command-line tools a bit later.

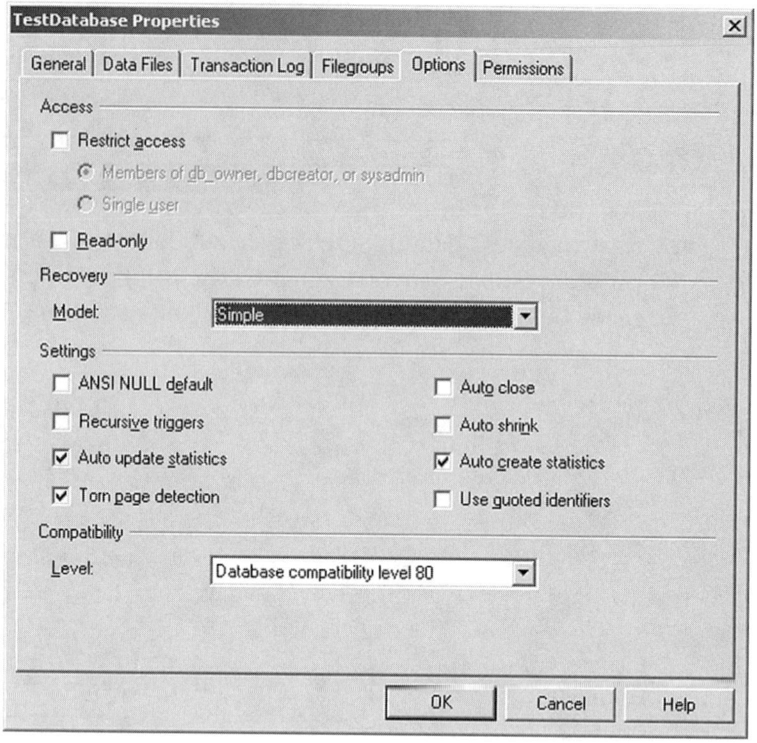

Figure 4.5
Options tab

Using the SQL Tools to Access Data

Enterprise Manager provides a convenient interface to access data. I'll discuss data access using Enterprise Manager as well as using an ODBC connection to access data using other tools.

I'll extend that process in the Examples section and use the ODBC connection to use other programs to display data from SQL Server 2000.

Enterprise Manager

Although not the optimal tool for regular data access, Enterprise Manager is a quick and easy method to access data. The process is to drill down to the table object and right-click the table name. Select Open Table and then Return All Rows from the menu that appears. I demonstrated using this tool to display data in Chapter 3. Remember the precautions for using this tool—it is deceptively easy to change or erase important data.

I'll discuss the Query Analyzer tool in the Command Line section.

ODBC

For the most part, you use tools other than Enterprise Manager or Query Analyzer to access data in SQL Server 2000. One of the older methods that many programs still use involves ODBC. The primary pieces of data you need to have ready before you set up your DSN are the names of the server and the database you want to access as well as the credentials to access the data.

Setting Up an ODBC Connection from a Client

It's fairly easy to set up an ODBC connection to SQL Server 2000. All Windows operating systems have an ODBC driver built in; but it's best to upgrade that version to the one on the SQL Server 2000 CD, using the setup program described in Chapter 2. Once the driver is installed, you can access the ODBC configuration program in the Control Panel of the client machine's operating system. Double-click the icon on your desktop shown in Figure 4.6 to display the three tabs I discussed earlier in the chapter.

Since we think that this DSN will be used by anyone who logs on to your system, select the System DSN tab, as shown in Figure 4.7.

Next, select the Add button to bring up the dialog box shown in Figure 4.8. This screen lets you pick the type of server you're connecting to. Pick SQL Server and then Finish. This doesn't *really* bring up the end of the configuration, just the end of making a server choice. Based on the type of server you choose, you'll see different information. Figure 4.9 on page 118 shows what you see when choosing SQL Server.

Notice the connection is named pubs, after the database. You're not required to do this, but it can come in handy to describe in the connection what it connects to. Notice also that I've pulled down the server name box. Select (local) because you are already on the same system as the SQL Server 2000 software.

Select Next to bring up the authentication method you'll use for this connection. The default setting is acceptable here because my server accepts requests from Windows security. But in order to demonstrate the configuration of a standard account, I will assume that there is no authentication from Windows.

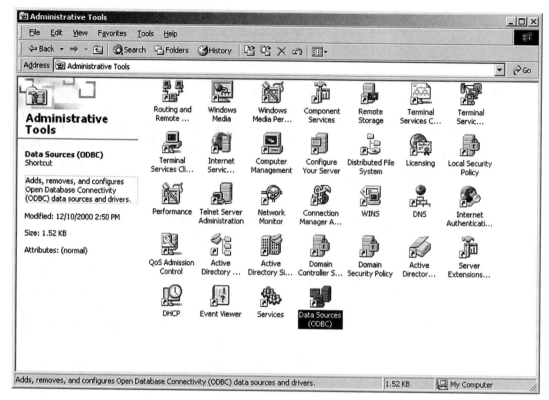

Figure 4.6 ODBC item in the Control Panel

Figure 4.10 shows that the option With SQL Server authentication . . . filled in the name and password that will be used to access the server. The password won't stick, but it will be used for the rest of this configuration. You have to supply the password each time this ODBC is used to connect to SQL Server. If you use Windows authentication, the connection just checks that the user who is logged on has been granted access to the database. I cover this choice further in Chapter 10.

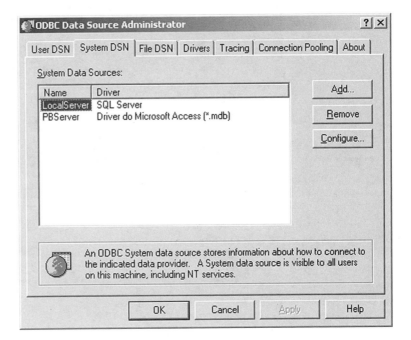

Figure 4.7
The System
DSN tab

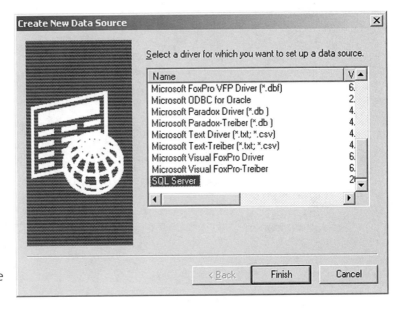

Figure 4.8
Selecting the
driver type

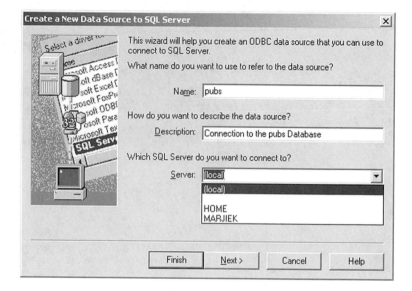

Figure 4.9
SQL Server
parameters

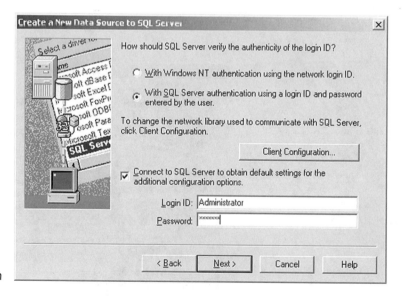

Figure 4.10
DSN
authentication

Also on this panel, using the Client Configuration button provides the ability to change the network parameters for this connection. You normally don't have to change this setting, but you can if need be.

Select Next to continue. Notice the box for selecting the default database. This connection can be used for any user, any password, and any database. Some programs require that the database you want to access to be specified here, so do that, as shown in Figure 4.11.

Now select Next. The screen you see in Figure 4.12 has even more options for connecting. One note of caution here: Do not select any of the tracing options on this panel. There are far more gentle tools you can use to monitor the statements that pass back and forth between the server and the client.

Select Finish to bring up the last panel, shown in Figure 4.13. This screen lets you test the connection from this client with the parameters you supplied—always a good idea.

Once the connection test is successful, press OK. The DSN is now configured and ready for use. I show that in the Examples section.

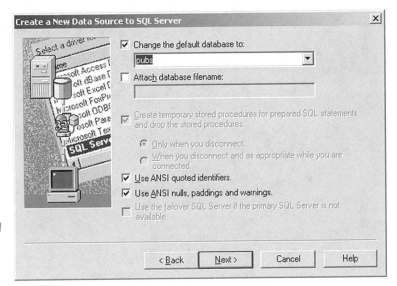

Figure 4.11
Selecting
the default
database

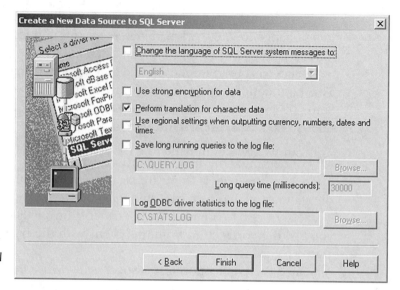

Figure 4.12
Ancillary DSN
settings

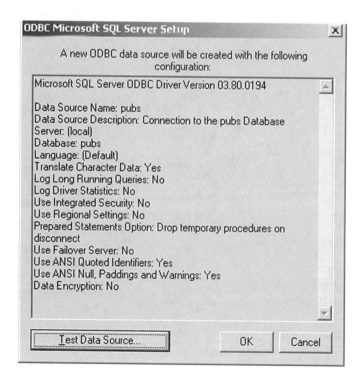

Figure 4.13
Completing
the DSN
connection

Command Line

You can use a command-line tool to do most anything that you can do graphically. Let's look at a few ways of using these tools to accomplish the same tasks as earlier in this chapter.

Creating and Managing a Database

You can use two command-line tools to run the following commands, but I focus on using Query Analyzer for this demonstration.

Query Analyzer

Select the Start button, then Programs, Microsoft SQL Server, Query Analyzer. You're asked to log in, and you do that. You're shown the screen in Figure 4.14.

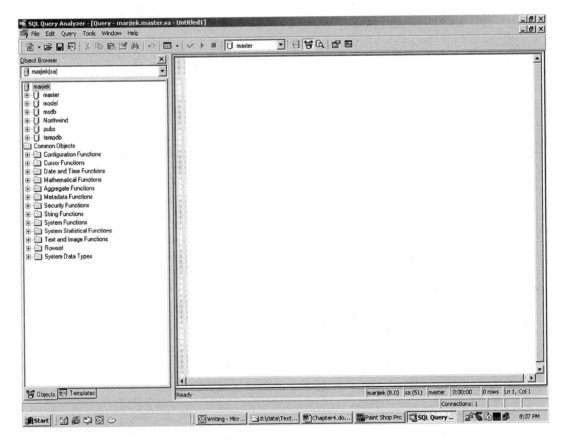

Figure 4.14   Query Analyzer

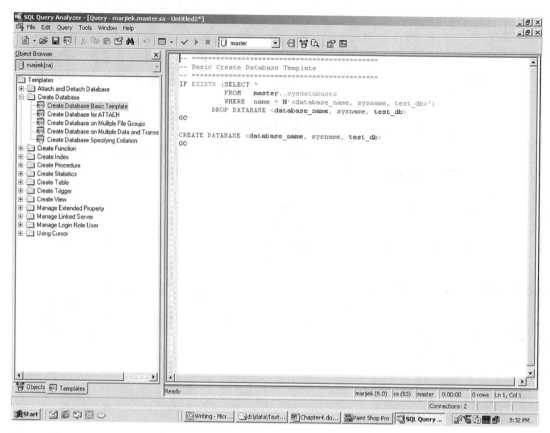

Figure 4.15 Create Database Basic Template

Creating a Database Select the *Templates* tab and then expand the *Create Database* object in the *Object Browser.* Double-click the *Create Database Basic Template,* and the code appears in the *command area,* as shown in Figure 4.15.

All you have to do now is replace the items within the brackets and run the code, as shown in Figure 4.16.

Remember, you could have added a lot more options for your database, such as file locations and sizes. If you'd like to see those, highlight the CREATE DATABASE command and press SHIFT+F1 to display the help on that topic from Books Online.

Database Options Once you have a database, you can use the command-line tools to view the same options you changed in the section on *Enterprise*

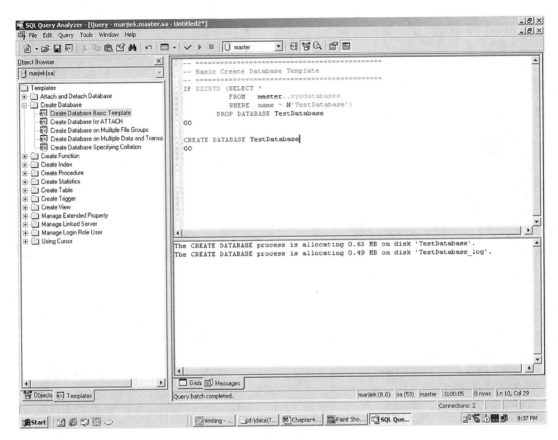

Figure 4.16   Running the code

Manager. The primary method for examining these options uses a stored procedure called sp_helpdb. Typing this stored procedure and supplying the name of the database you're interested in provides information about the current settings on the database.

Figure 4.17 shows the output. You have to scroll around a bit to see the options, or you could set the results to output to text rather than to the grid. Most of the current options are fine, but there are a couple of options I'd like to set for the database.

Log Settings   The first option you set is the Recovery model—and even though the default mode for a SQL Server 2000 database is Simple, we'll set your testing database to that again for demonstration. The command you use to do this is

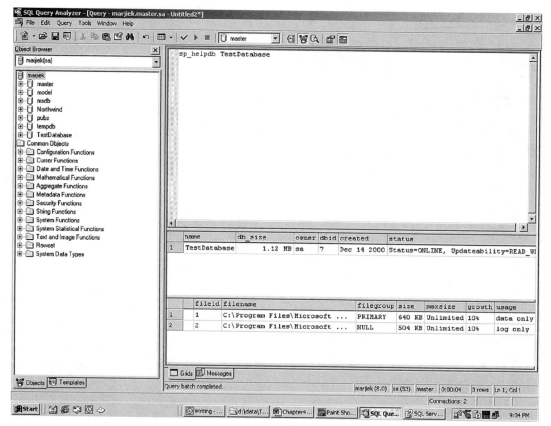

Figure 4.17   Current database options

ALTER DATABASE. Books Online has a full explanation for all the options you can set with this command. Type the command to change the option, as shown in Figure 4.18.

Notice the linefeed to separate the lines. As you'll recall, that's perfectly acceptable and can make your code a lot easier to read. Next press F5. Now that you've changed your Recovery model, we'll use the command-line tools to access data.

Using the SQL Tools to Access Data

Command-line tools are often the superior way to display data in SQL Server 2000. They provide more flexibility and control over the format, amount, and speed of data return than do graphical tools. Let's examine the two tools that ship with Microsoft SQL Server.

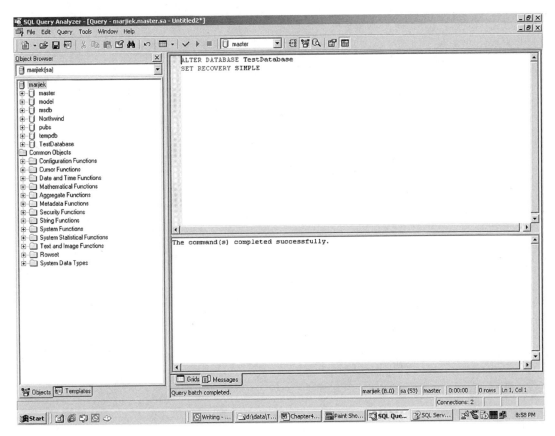

Figure 4.18   Recovery model setting

Query Analyzer

By far the most common method of data access used by DBAs is the Query Analyzer tool I explained in Chapter 3.

Let's connect to the server using Query Analyzer and access data from the authors table in the pubs database.

Figure 4.19 shows the drop-down database list from the toolbar, which sets the database that the command area will affect. There's also a command to do this, which is shown in Listing 4.1.

Listing 4.1   Selecting the database in code

```
USE pubs
GO
```

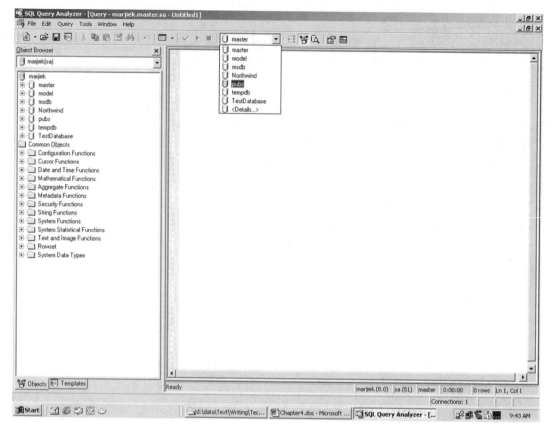

Figure 4.19 Selecting the database from Query Analyzer

This has the same effect as selecting the database name in Query Analyzer. I recommend that you get into the habit of using this command to ensure that your scripts run against the proper database.

Next expand the pubs database, User tables, and authors objects in the Object Browser. Right-click the authors table, and select Script Object to New Window As and then the Select option to see the screen in Figure 4.20. Press F5 and you see the data in Figure 4.21.

There are some excellent references for learning SQL, and if you're pressed into service to do that job, you should investigate those.

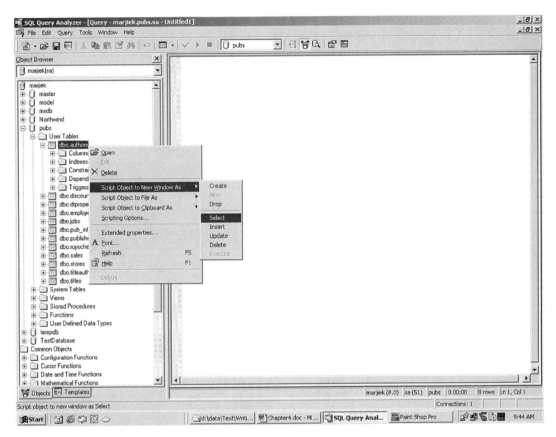

Figure 4.20   *Selecting data from a table*

Another handy use of Query Analyzer is to create a *script*, or a saved set of commands. To create the script, you select File, then Save As from the menu bar and give this file the name c:\temp\test.sql. Notice that your cursor must be in the top panel when you do this, or you'll save the results from the bottom panel instead. The process looks like the screen in Figure 4.22.

There is much more that you can do to manipulate data using Query Analyzer.

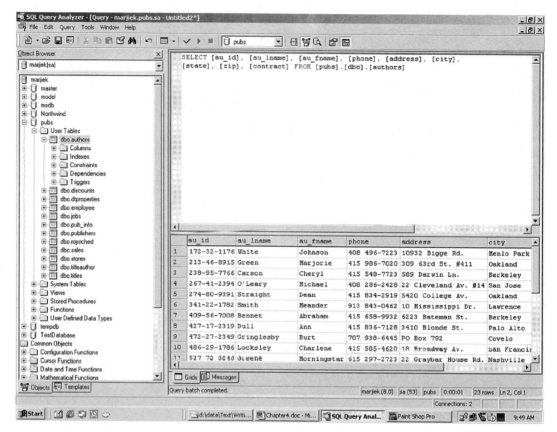

Figure 4.21 Data from the authors table

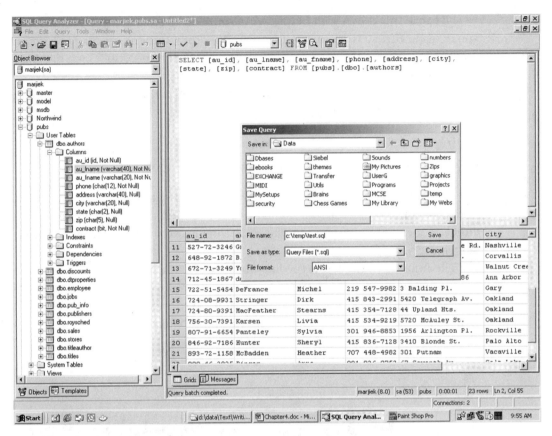

Figure 4.22   Saving the script

osql

One of the first things an Oracle administrator might ask on first glance at SQL Server is "Where is the operating system command-line access to the database?" It's here, in the osql tool.

The osql tool has three modes: interactive, query, and script. Let's take a quick look at all three.

To use the interactive mode, you have to specify only a few parameters. Using osql from the server and Windows authentication, the command is quite simple, as shown in Listing 4.2.

Listing 4.2   osql interactive mode

```
osql –E –d pubs
```

I'll break this down a bit before we go on. The –E (case matters) means that you're using a trusted account—meaning Windows authentication. I talk about security in Chapter 10. The –d parameter tells SQL Server 2000 which database to set for this connection.

If you want to access a server that requires SQL authentication, you use the command shown in Listing 4.3.

Listing 4.3   osql using SQL authentication

```
osql -S marjiek -U sa -P letmein -d pubs
```

The –S parameter sets the server you want to access, and the –U sets the user. The –P sets the password, and I've already described the –d parameter. Using either of these methods, you're placed in the *interactive* mode of osql. It looks like Figure 4.23.

The number to the left is the line number. The queries work the same as in Query Analyzer, and you can type commands on multiple lines, just as in Query Analyzer. The difference comes in the command to execute the query—you don't have the F5 key or a menu item for that. Instead, use the command GO and the Enter key, as shown in Figure 4.24.

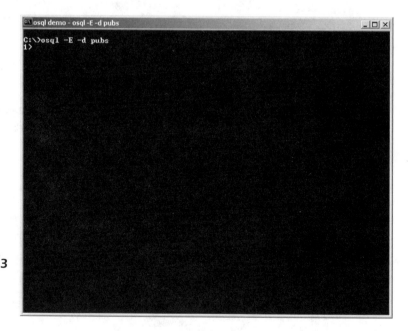

Figure 4.23
osql
Interactive
Mode

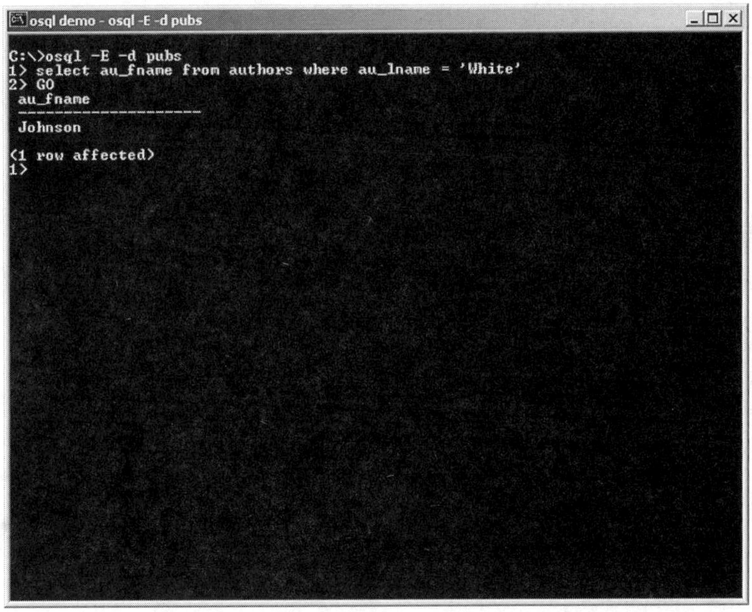

Figure 4.24
osql
interactive
query

When you're finished, you type `quit` to exit the tool. You can also pass a query directly to osql and then leave the tool, as shown in Listing 4.4. The uppercase -Q executes the query and then exits the tool.

Listing 4.4   Passing a query using osql

```
osql -E -d pubs "-Q SELECT * from authors"
```

The last function of osql you'll examine is to run the script you saved in Query Analyzer. Let's send the output of the script to a file for review later. I'll show the command, and then I'll break it down.

Listing 4.5   Using a script with osql

```
osql -E -d pubs -i "c:\temp\test.sql" -o "c:\temp\out.txt"
```

I've discussed the –E and –d parameters, so let's look at the other two shown in Listing 4.5. The –i parameter sets the input script file. The –o parameter sets the location of the output file.

There are some caveats to this command. You must separate all groups of commands with a GO statement if you're using an input script. Certain commands, such as creating a database, must be separated with this GO command and treated as a group.

I've done some interesting things with this tool, such as querying the database and creating a text file that can become the input to other commands in a batch.

ODBC

There's no easy way to create an ODBC DSN from the command line, but these are three general ways I've used:

- Directly accessing the registry
- Using a scripting language
- Using programming tools

I don't advocate accessing the registry directly because that's one of the fastest ways I've ever seen to trash a system.

The scripting languages you can use are as varied as Java, Perl, and CScript. I'm not a professional developer, so the code I'll demonstrate should be simple enough to follow, even if all you've ever done is install Visual Basic on your system. I've annotated the code in-line that follows.

Creating an ODBC Connection Using Visual Basic

Create a new form in Visual Basic, and create a button on called Command1. Type the code from Listing 4.6 in it.

Listing 4.6 Creating a DSN with Visual Basic

```
Option Explicit ' Always do this
'Declare some constants
Const ODBC_ADD_SYS_DSN = 4  'Adds data source
Const ODBC_CONFIG_SYS_DSN = 5 'Configures (edits) data source
Const ODBC_REMOVE_SYS_DSN = 6 'Removes data source
' This is the strDriver that does the work.
' Should be on Win95, NT and 2000 automatically
Private Declare Function _
SQLConfigDataSource Lib "ODBCCP32.DLL" _
(ByVal hwndParent As Long, ByVal fRequest As Long, _
ByVal lpszDriver As String, _
ByVal lpszAttributes As String) As Long
'Make a button on your form called Command1
Private Sub Command1_Click()
 Call Build_SystemDSN("NameYouWantToCallTheDSN")
End Sub
'This is the part that puts it all together
' Take one input - the name of the DSN
Private Sub Build_SystemDSN(DSN_NAME As String)
```

```
' Declare some variables
Dim lngRet as Long
Dim strDriver as String
Dim strAttributes as String
 StrDriver = "SQL Server" & Chr(0) ' Don't change
 strAttributes = "DSN=" & DSN_NAME & Chr(0) ' This is what's passed-don't Change
 strAttributes = strAttributes & "Trusted_Connection=no" & Chr(0) 'Don't change
 'Change to your database
 strAttributes = strAttributes & "Database=YourDataBase" & Chr(0)
 ' Change to your Server Name
 strAttributes = strAttributes & "Server=YourServerName" & Chr(0)
 ' Change to your Description
 strAttributes = strAttributes & "Description=YourDescription" & Chr(0)
 ' This is the command itself. Don't alter this!
 lngRet = SQLConfigDataSource(0, ODBC_ADD_SYS_DSN, StrDriver, StrAttributes)
 ' Let's do a bit of feedback
 If lngRet <> 1 Then
  MsgBox "DSN Creation Failed"
 End If
 If lngRet = 1 Then
  MsgBox "DSN Created Successfully. Press OK to continue."
 End If
End Sub
```

Remember to replace the names and passwords and the name of the server with your information. You can extend this project by modifying the input on the function to allow more parameters to be passed.

Examples

The examples that follow demonstrate ways in which to access SQL Server 2000 data.

Finding Information about a Database

If you need to find information about a database, you can use the *Enterprise Manager* as you did earlier in the chapter. You can also type the following command from Listing 4.7 using any of the command-line tools. You can also type the command shown in Listing 4.8 to get information on any object in the database.

Listing 4.7   Finding information about a database

```
sp_helpdb 'databasename'
```

Listing 4.8 Finding information about an object

```
sp_help 'objectname'
```

To find out the text that created a view or stored procedure, type the command shown in Listing 4.9.

Listing 4.9 Displaying the text that created an object

```
sp_helptext 'objectname'
```

Microsoft Access Linked Tables

You can use lots of products to access SQL Server data once you've created an ODBC connection. You can use Microsoft Word to create labels from SQL Server, and you can use Microsoft Excel to copy data from SQL Server 2000 into a spreadsheet. Another great tool to use ODBC is Microsoft Access. I'm using Access 2000, but the concepts presented here work equally well for Access 95 or 97. To access SQL Server 2000 data from Microsoft Access, create a new database, as shown in Figure 4.25.

When you've done that, open the File, Get External Data, Import menu items, as shown in Figure 4.26. In the Files of type area, select ODBC Databases (), as shown in Figure 4.27.

Next, select the pubs DSN you created earlier in the Machine Data Source tab, as shown in Figure 4.28 on page 138.

Next you're asked to pick the tables you're interested in. As shown in Figure 4.29 on page 139, select authors. You've now linked the table. By the way, the difference between *linking* a table and *importing* it is that the data in a *linked* table is live. The import feature is a copy of the data in the table at a point in time.

You can now access the table as if you had created it in Microsoft Access. The main limitation when linking a table is that you can't change the structure of the table. That's a small price to pay for the advantage of using the data in an interface many people are familiar with.

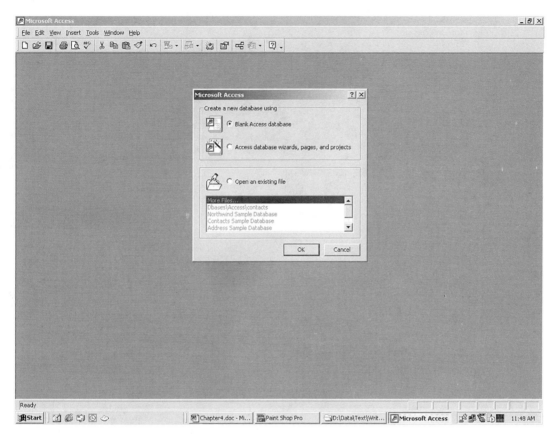

Figure 4.25 Creating a new access database

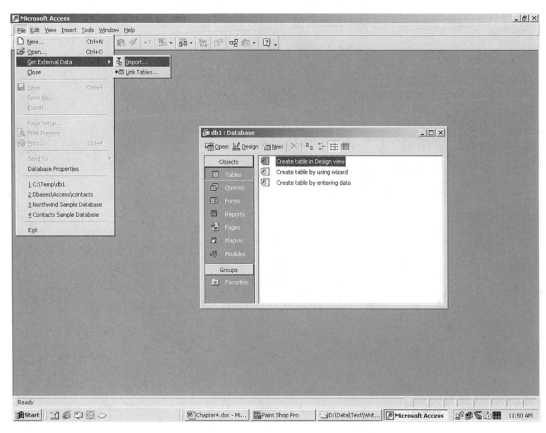

Figure 4.26 Getting external data

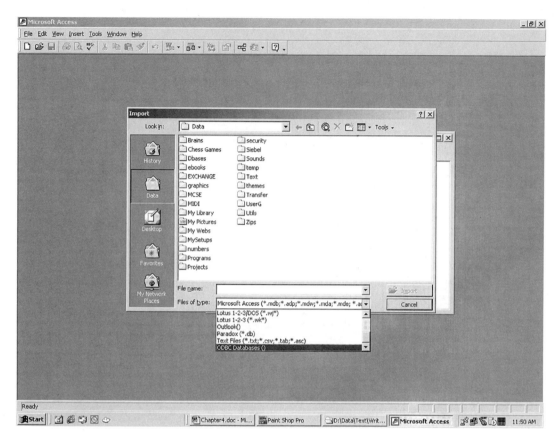

Figure 4.27 ODBC access

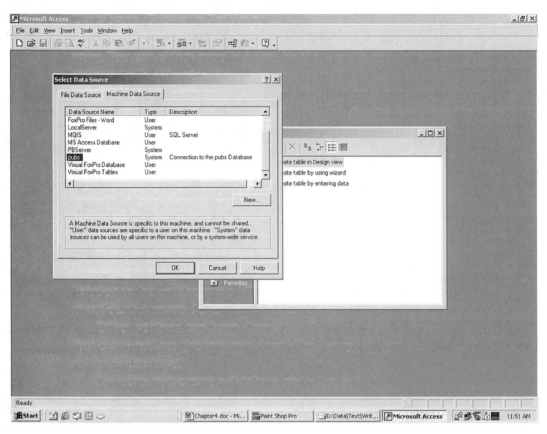

Figure 4.28   Selecting the pubs DSN

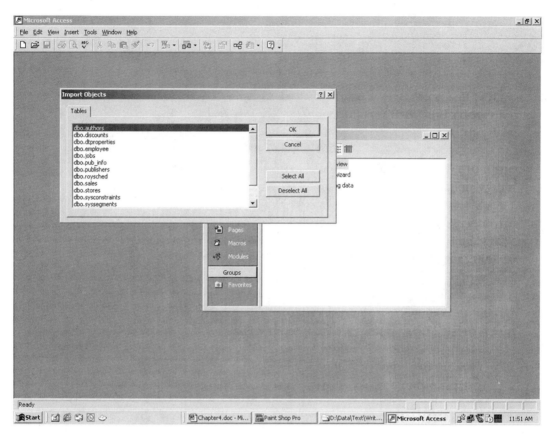

Figure 4.29 Selecting the authors table

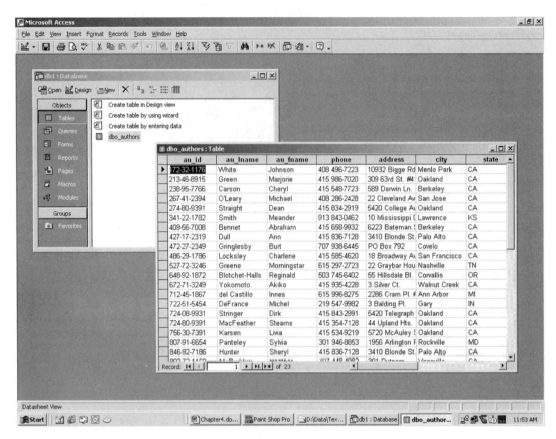

Figure 4.30   Accessing the authors table

Accessing the table is as easy as double-clicking it, as is shown in Figure 4.30.

The Web Assistant

Many people are used to examining data using a Web browser. You can use SQL Server 2000 to create these read-only pages automatically for you, using a wizard.

Start Enterprise Manager, and select *Tools* and then *Wizards* from the menu bar. As shown in Figure 4.31, expand the *Management* object and then highlight the *Web Assistant Wizard* item.

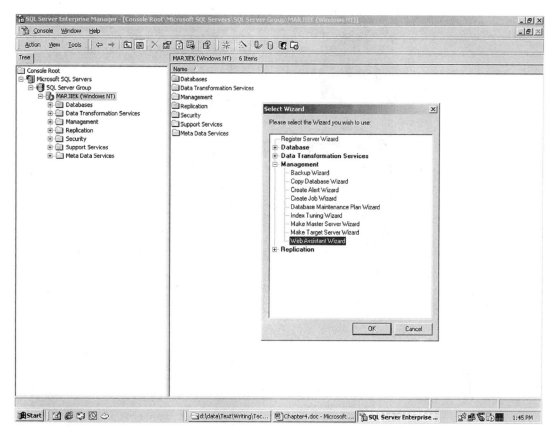

Figure 4.31   *Selecting the Web Assistant Wizard*

Select OK to start the wizard. Figure 4.32 shows a description of the wizard. The first item you need to take care of is where the data lives. As shown in Figure 4.33, pick the pubs database and then select Next.

Name your job, and in Figure 4.34 you see the real power of this wizard. You can pick a table, a stored procedure, or even type in a complex query to retrieve the data you want displayed in the Web page. Leave the default as your choice.

In Figure 4.35 choose the columns you want to show in the Web page. This panel would be different if you had picked the stored procedure or query option earlier. Notice the order here.

Now that you've vertically sectioned your data by specifying columns, you have the option of horizontally sectioning the data for your Web page by selecting matching criteria for rows, as shown in Figure 4.36 on page 144. Leave this set at the defaults for this demonstration.

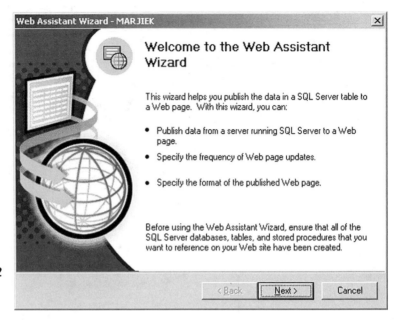

Figure 4.32
Wizard
description

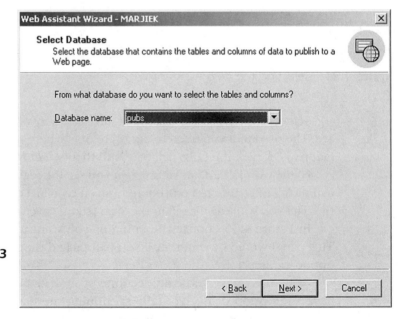

Figure 4.33
Selecting
the pubs
database

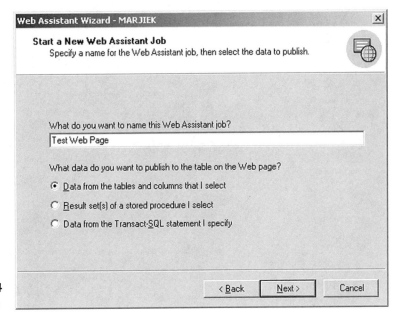

Figure 4.34
Data source

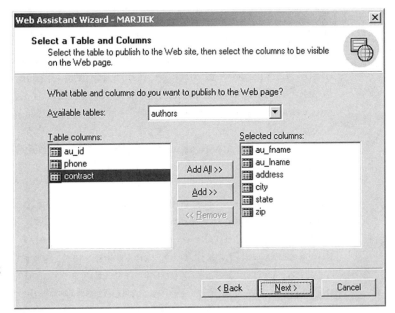

Figure 4.35
Column
selection

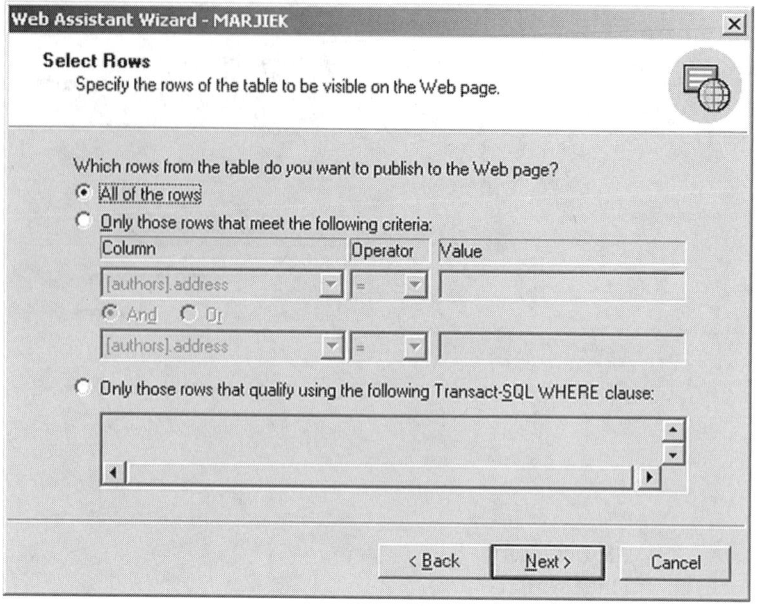

Figure 4.36
Row selection

Figure 4.37 shows that you can specify how often the Web page is created. Leave this at the Only one time setting, but you have the choice of creating the Web pages periodically.

The option to create the Web page when the data changes, however, is less useful than it looks. If the table is small and is changed infrequently, this option is appropriate. If the data changes frequently or the table is large, the load caused by running this task may be a bit much. You can save this task to run later.

Next set the location for your Web page. This can be anywhere the SQL Server 2000 startup account has access. Figure 4.38 shows what the display looks like.

Next you're asked if you need help formatting the Web page or if you'd like to use a template file. Leave the default as shown in Figure 4.39 and select Next. This brings up the display shown in Figure 4.40. Here you can specify the title for the Web page. Do that and press Next.

Next you're asked to format the table. Change the font as shown in Figure 4.41 and select Next. You can also add hyperlinks to your page automatically if you like or even find them in a table, as shown in Figure 4.42. Just take the defaults and move on.

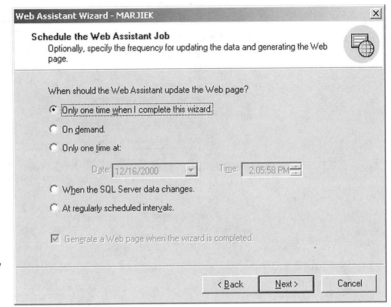

Figure 4.37
Web page
interval

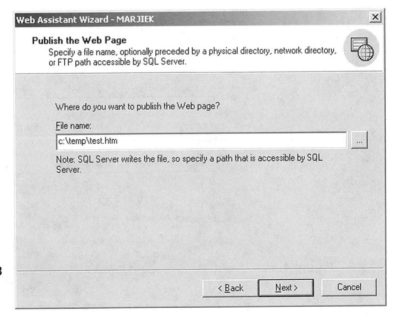

Figure 4.38
Web page
location

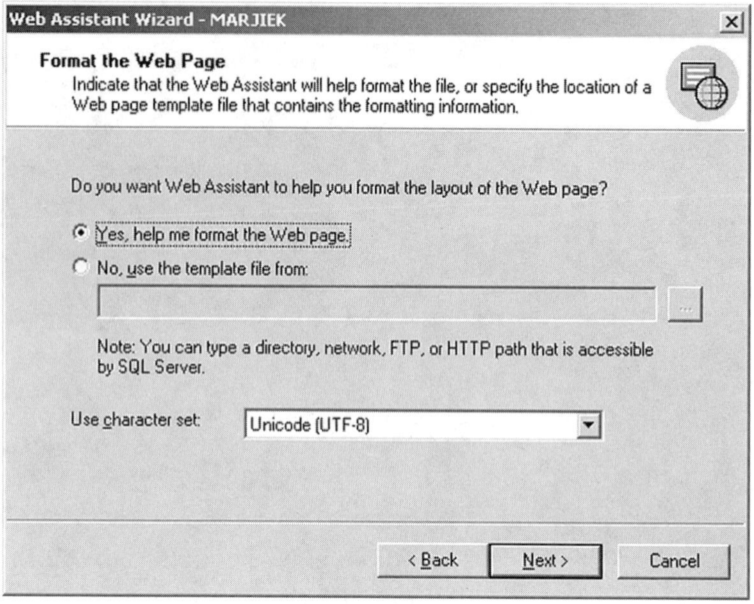

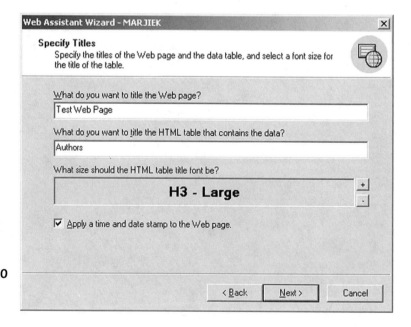

Figure 4.39
Web page
formatting

Figure 4.40
Web page
title

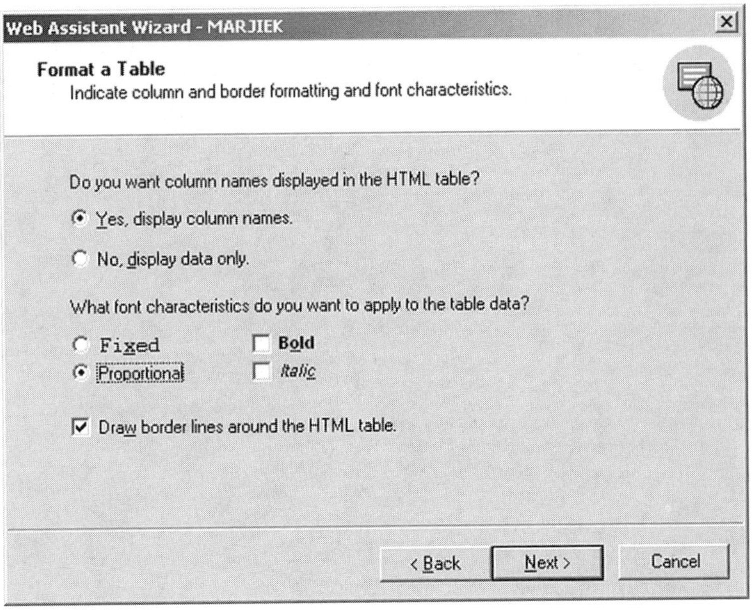

Figure 4.41 Table formatting

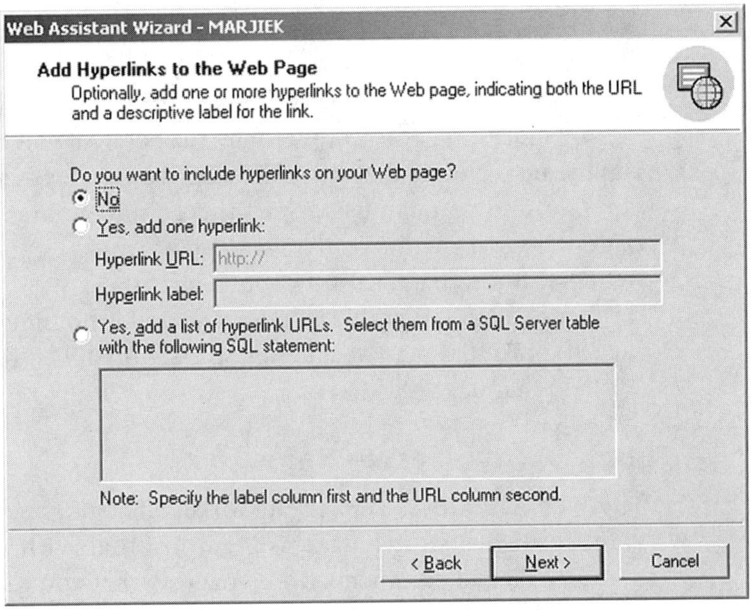

Figure 4.42 Adding hyperlinks

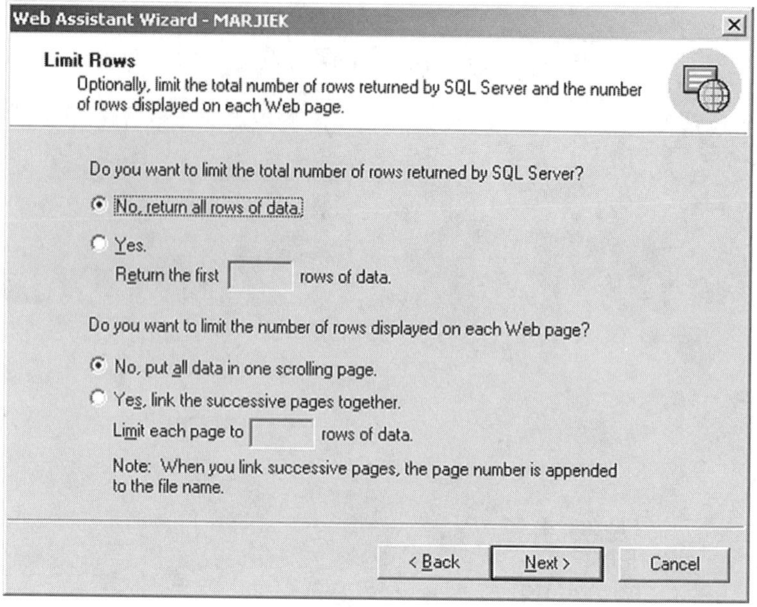

Figure 4.43
Data
limitation

If a result set is quite large, you may want to either limit the amount of data SQL Server 2000 returns or display it only a few items at a time. Figure 4.43 shows this panel. Leave the defaults here and move on.

In Figure 4.44 you complete the process. All you have to do at this point is run the task. Notice that you can also save a script that will perform this task if you like, and you can use any of the command-line tools to create the Web page whenever you like. The server informs you that the task is complete. Access the Web page, as shown in Figure 4.45.

Keep in mind that this is static data and is not linked to the database in any way. To have that kind of access, you'd set up a Web page that can access data. We'll do that next.

A Simple Active Server Page

The Web Assistant is very useful for small static pages, but many times you'll want to display active data. You can do that with the page shown in Listing 4.10. I'll add comments to the page so that you can tell what's going on.

There are some assumptions here. This page needs to reside on a Microsoft Internet Information Server (IIS) and must be accessed using HTTP, not as a file. That means you need to save the page as `test.asp` in the `inetpub\`

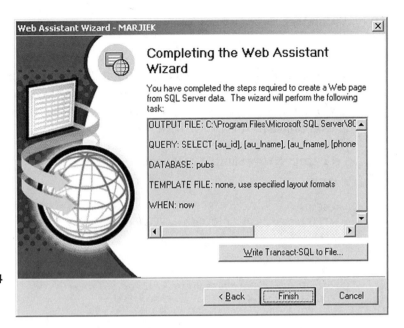

Figure 4.44
Fishing the
Web task

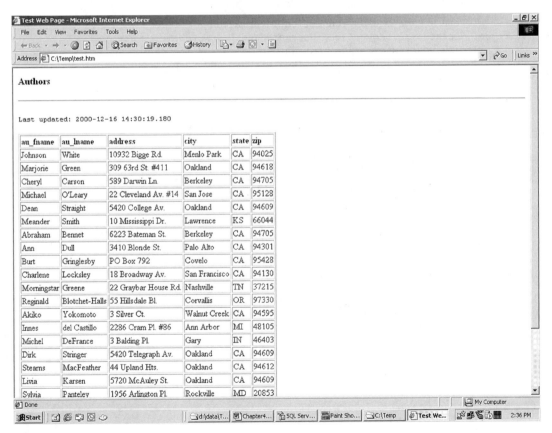

Figure 4.45 Completed Web page

wwwroot directory of a Microsoft IIS and then use a browser and type *http://myservername/test.asp* for this to work. This also assumes that the IIS has network access to the SQL Server. This is an OLE-DB connection method—you won't have to set up an ODBC driver first.

Listing 4.10 Sample ASP page

```
<HTML>

<HEAD>
<TITLE>Database Grid Demo</TITLE>
</HEAD>

<BODY BGCOLOR =#0000CC TEXT =#FFFFCC>

<H2> Dynamic Database Grid </H2>
<HR>

<%

' Here is the OLE-DB Connection Information
' Replace the Servername, Username and PasswordName
' with your information-this should all be on one line
' Name this file something like test.asp and save it on a
' Microsoft IIS web server.

Set MyConn=Server.CreateObject("ADODB.Connection")
MyConn.Open "PROVIDER=MSDASQL;" & "STRDRIVER={SQL Server};" &
"SERVER=ServerName;DATABASE=pubs;" & "UID=UserName;PWD=PasswordName;"

' Here is the SQL you want to pass to the server
MySQL="SELECT * FROM authors"

'The next line actually executes the SQL
Set MyRs=MyConn.Execute(MySQL)
%>

' Next you set up the table
<TABLE BORDER=1>
<TR>

<%
' Put Headings On The Table of Field Names
howmanyfields=MyRs.fields.count -1
for i=0 to howmanyfields
%>

<TD><B><%=MyRs(i).name %></B></TD>

<%
NEXT
%>
```

```
</TR>

<%
' Now get all the records
 do while not MyRs.eof
%>
<TR>

<%
FOR i = 0 TO howmanyfields
    thisrecord = myrs(i)
 ' And make sure to account for no data returned!
    IF ISNULL(thisrecord) THEN
    thisrecord = " "
END IF
%>

<TD VALIGN=TOP>

<%
' Put the data in each cell
Response.Write thisrecord
%>

</TD>

<%
' This is part of the next section
NEXT
%>

</TR>

<%
' Then iterate the loop
MyRs.movenext
loop
%>

</TABLE>

<%
'Make sure to clean up the connection when you're done with it.
MyRs.close
                Set MyRs= Nothing
                MyConn.Close
                set MyConn=nothing
%>


</BODY>
</HTML>
```

You could simply duplicate this information in a text file, replacing only the connection information, and the page will work. The better route is to dissect the page to understand what is going on and use the concepts to create your own pages.

You should know that just displaying the data is as simple as what you saw earlier. Adding, deleting, or modifying data is a bit more difficult. I've included a good site in the Resources section to help you with that.

The Sample Visual Basic Programs

You can also use Visual Basic to access a SQL Server 2000 database with or without an ODBC connection.

Books Online contains many sample database program references, from using simple connection methods to the techniques used to program the Enterprise Manager. Search on *Building SQL Server Applications* and then *Samples* to display this highly commented Visual Basic or Visual C++ source code as well as sample Web pages. This is yet another good use of *Books Online*.

Rosetta Stone

Many of the activities performed in this chapter have equivalents in Oracle and Microsoft Access.

Oracle

Table 4.1 shows the command equivalents for Oracle. Note that with Oracle you must start the database and its listeners. With SQL Server 2000, all databases are started and listening automatically.

Microsoft Access

The equivalent commands to use for Microsoft Access and SQL Server 2000 are shown in Table 4.2.

Table 4.1 Oracle to SQL Server

Task	Oracle Tool	Microsoft SQL Server 2000
Create a database	Oracle Database Assistant ORADIM80 and Server Manager (SVRMGR30) together CREATE DATABASE statement	Enterprise Manager CREATE DATABASE statement
Delete a database	Oracle Database Assistant ORADIM80 and Server Manager (SVRMGR30) together	Enterprise Manager DROP DATABASE statement
Delete a database service	Oracle Database Assistant ORADIM80	Not needed
Start a database	Instance Manager ORADIM80 and Server Manager (SVRMGR30) together SQL worksheet	Not needed
Shut down a database	Instance Manager ORADIM80 and Server Manager (SVRMGR30) together Control Panel SQL worksheet	ALTER DATABASE <*database name*> SET OFFLINE
Change internal database passwords	ORAPWD80 ORADIM80	Not needed
Create database objects	Schema Manager Server Manager CREATE <*object*> <*parameters*> statement	Enterprise Manager CREATE <*object*> <*parameters*> statement
Access data	Configure SQL*Net on server, install and configure SQL*Net on client, set up ODBC DSN if program requires.	If program does not require DSN, nothing. If program requires DSN, set up ODBC.
Create Web page from data	Web Page Assistant	Web Assistant

Table 4.2 Microsoft Access to SQL Server

Task	Access Tool	Microsoft SQL Server 2000
Create a database	*File, New* from the menu bar	Enterprise Manager CREATE DATABASE statement
Delete a database	Delete using operating system while database is not being accessed.	Enterprise Manager DROP DATABASE statement
Create database objects	Use the *Objects* bar or wizards.	Enterprise Manager CREATE *<object>* *<parameters>* statement
Access data	Install MS Access on client and share file location. If program allows, set up ODBC.	If program does not require DSN, nothing. If program requires DSN, set up ODBC.
Create Web page from data	Click the New button on the Database window toolbar. In the New Data Access Page dialog box, click Page Wizard.	Web Assistant

Resources

There are a lot of great references out there for programming, which is the primary method of accessing data from SQL Server 2000.

Using ODBC and SQL Server:
   http://www.microsoft.com/TechNet/sql/tools/sqldevkt/odbcwp.asp
ASP to Access Data:
   http://www.vallin.com/pub/1/asp1.asp
More ASP help:
   http://www.aspin.com/home/tutorial/database
Visual Basic help:
   http://www.cgvb.com/links/lpage.boa/BEGINNER

Chapter **5**

Importing and Exporting Data

Chapter at a Glance

This chapter covers the methods used to import and export data for SQL Server 2000. Read this chapter if you need to automate data transfer from existing sources such as text files or other databases to another destination.

The Resources section contains references for:

- Import and export
- DTS
- COM

Read Chapter 3 before you read this chapter.

Overview

Part of the DBA task is to bring in lots of data quickly and easily. I'm asked all the time to transfer large Oracle database information or a set of Excel spreadsheets into SQL Server 2000. The expectation is that the data will transfer in with a simple command, and often it's a difficult task to explain that date formats in Oracle and Excel are different than they are in SQL Server 2000.

In this chapter, I examine the ways you can get data from one place to another using SQL Server 2000, a task often called migration.

I separate my discussion of migration into importing data and exporting it. I further separate the import or export process by command or automation. All the processes I show in this chapter can be used either way, but some are a bit more complex to automate. I point out the ones that are more suited to the console method and that automate more easily.

The methods I use involve four tools:

- Data Transformation Services (DTS)
- The bulk copy program (bcp)
- The BULK INSERT statement
- The SELECT INTO statement

Some have included replication as a method to import and export data, but I treat that as a subject of its own in Chapter 11.

DTS is SQL Server's primary method for data transfer. DTS is a graphical tool that can transfer data into or out of many sources. DTS allows data transformations along with the transfer.

DTS settings are stored in a grouping called a package. Packages are made up of data sources and destinations (connections), instructions for transfer (tasks), and precedence constraints (workflow). Packages can be saved to databases, files, or even in the Microsoft Repository feature.

The bcp program is implemented from the operating system's command line. This program can import and export data from a text or SQL Server native format file.

The BULK INSERT command is a Transact SQL (T-SQL) command that can read a text file or native SQL Server file into an existing table or view.

The INSERT INTO command is a T-SQL command that reads data from a table or view and inserts it into a new table.

One final process to import data is the new XML software added as a patch to the XML features in SQL Server 2000. XML is becoming the primary choice for Microsoft's data transfer strategy, and in future releases you will see this technology emphasized. I cover XML in greater detail in Chapter 13.

Detail

You can use almost any of these methods to get data into or out of SQL Server 2000 with equal success, provided you have a text file or want one. The beauty of having a variety of tools is that you can migrate from many data sources, including text files, Excel files, Oracle databases, and Access databases, using a variety of methods as the situation dictates.

I'll describe the tools in detail, starting with the most flexible, DTS.

Data Transformation Services

By far the easiest method to import or export data, Data Transformation Services, can import and export data from many sources and transform the data along the way, based on logic you specify. You can use DTS to move data from an Excel spreadsheet into an Oracle database, changing every letter B to the number 5, if you want to. You can also write programs in Visual Basic, Visual C++, or C# that control DTS. Look up the subject Building SQL Server Applications, then DTS Programming in the Contents section of Books Online for information on writing these types of programs.

DTS can also store the results of the migration steps so that you can repeat the process either on command or on a schedule or condition. This collection of steps is called a package.

Packages contain all the elements necessary to perform the DTS operation. They contain the connections to the data sources and destinations and can be OLE-DB- or ODBC-driven. Packages also contain tasks, which are commands to transfer data, edit data, send mail, run SQL scripts, run other commands, and much more.

Also stored within each package is a workflow, which ties tasks together. The workflow constraint has three types: success, failure, and completion. For instance, you might define a task to send e-mail to an administrator. You might then use the workflow success constraint to execute that task when the transfer of data is successful. You might have another task that is tied by a failure constraint to perform some other action if the data transfer fails.

The bcp Utility

The bulk copy program (bcp) utility has been with Microsoft SQL Server since the beginning. This utility is available at the operating system command prompt, and it allows you to import or export data to a text file or a binary file that SQL Server 2000 Servers can read. The data you migrate can be a table name or an SQL query.

Its strength lies in the ability to use a format file, which bcp can create for you, to manipulate the data. Another advantage is its availability from the OS command prompt. It's also very fast. Its speed results from the fact that it can bypass the transaction log, and thus it can be a bit dangerous. Always back up your database before and after a bcp operation.

The bcp utility can be used in a sit-at-the-console mode, but most of the time it's an automated process.

BULK INSERT

The BULK INSERT statement is used inside a command-line tool such as Query Analyzer or osql. This command imports data into an existing table or a view from a text or SQL Server 2000 binary file. BULK INSERT can also use a format file, as the bcp utility can. This command is normally used at the console and can be saved to a script. The script can be automated with the osql command, as described in Chapter 4.

This command used to have the distinction of being the fastest method of data transfer, but bcp and BULK INSERT now use nearly the same process to transfer data. It's still a bit faster, though, because it doesn't have to start a session for each transfer. The same warning for bcp holds true here as well—make sure you back up the database after this operation.

SELECT INTO

The SELECT INTO statement brings data from one table to another. This table can be on the same SQL Server, another one using linked servers, or even on a different type of server using distributed queries.

The SELECT INTO statement is used at a command line, just like the BULK INSERT statement. It brings data into a table just like the BULK INSERT command, except it can't read an external file. SELECT INTO can also create the destination table automatically.

XML Bulk Insert

As I go to press, Microsoft is just releasing the latest version of its XML extensions to SQL Server. This technology is in the beta stage at this point, so I won't comment on it except to say that as XML becomes more ubiquitous, you should investigate this process. It's an add-on to the BULK INSERT command shown in this chapter.

Which Tool to Use?

With all these methods available, which one should you choose? Books Online contains an excellent chart for making this decision. Open Books Online, and go to the Contents tab. Expand Administering SQL Server, then Importing and Exporting Data, and then select Choosing a Tool to Import or Export Data. I'll demonstrate all the methods I've discussed in the sections that follow.

Graphical

In this section, I spend quite a bit of time on the Data Transformation Services tool. DTS is powerful, but it can also be simple to use. I'll begin my discussion with a simple export task using a wizard and then dig a little deeper into the structure of the DTS unit of work it creates.

Data Transformation Services

You can access DTS in three places: from the Import and Export Data menu item on the Start button, by right-clicking an object in Enterprise Manager, or by using the DTS Designer. We can begin by using the first method and exporting data from the authors table of the pubs database to a text file.

Start by clicking the Start button, then Programs, Microsoft SQL Server, and Import and Export Data, as shown in Figure 5.1.

Once you've selected this item, you see the screen shown in Figure 5.2. Just click Next here. The next screen, shown in Figure 5.3, appears.

In this panel, you're asked to select the source of the data. Since you're exporting data *from* your server, leave the selection set to Microsoft OLE-DB Provider for SQL Server, set the server name to (local), leave the authentication at Windows, and select the pubs database. Select Next button to bring up the screen that is shown in Figure 5.4. Here you're asked to set the destination for the data.

Notice that there are many types of destinations to choose from. Figure 5.4 shows the Text File driver and the location of the text file as c:\temp\authors. csv. Select Next, which brings up the screen shown in Figure 5.5.

Here you can choose whether to copy the whole table to the text file or to type a query against the table to limit the data you get. Leave the default and click Next to bring up the screen shown in Figure 5.6.

The wizard allows you to specify the way the data is saved in the file. Leave the defaults here, but choose that the column names be transferred with the

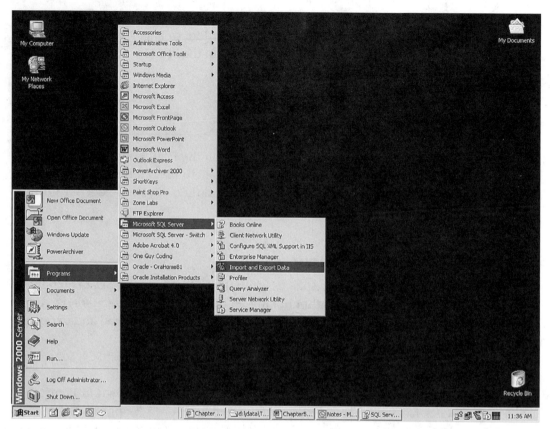

Figure 5.1   Import and Export Data menu item

data. Notice the Transform button on this screen. You'll use it later to manipulate the data on its way out.

Select the Next button to display the screen shown in Figure 5.7.

Another powerful feature of this tool is the ability to save the information so that it can run again or be edited. Let's do that, saving the package to a SQL Server 2000 database. This package will be stored in the msdb database I talked about in Chapter 4. You could also save this package definition to a file, a Visual Basic file, or SQL Server 2000's Meta Data services.

Select Next to continue, resulting in the screen shown in Figure 5.8.

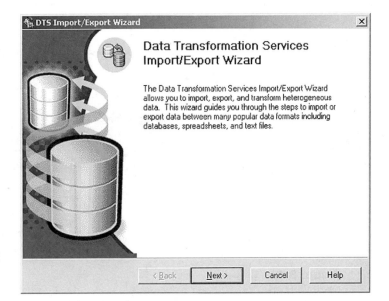

Figure 5.2
Welcome
screen

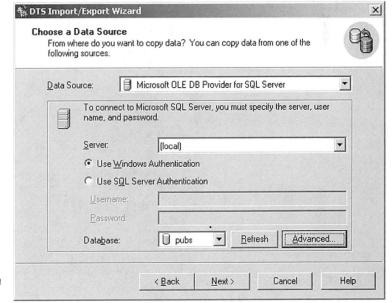

Figure 5.3
Choose data
source

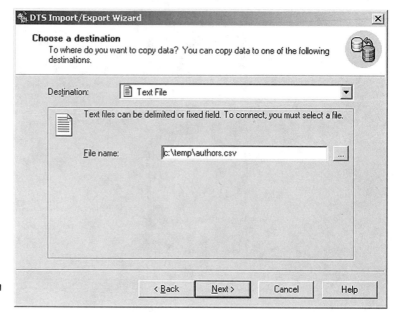

Figure 5.4
Choose data
destination

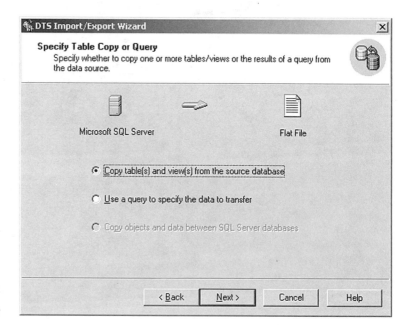

Figure 5.5
Choose
export type

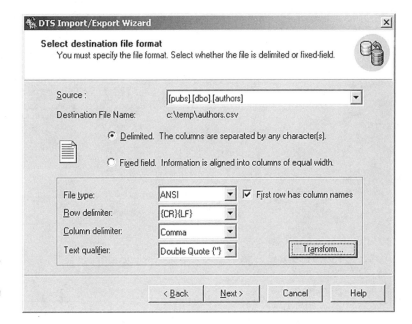

Figure 5.6
Choose
destination
file format

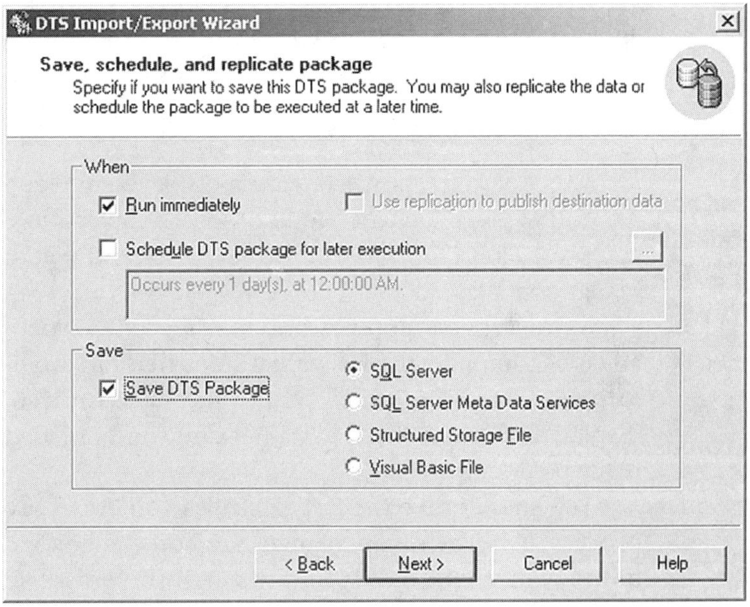

Figure 5.7
Save options

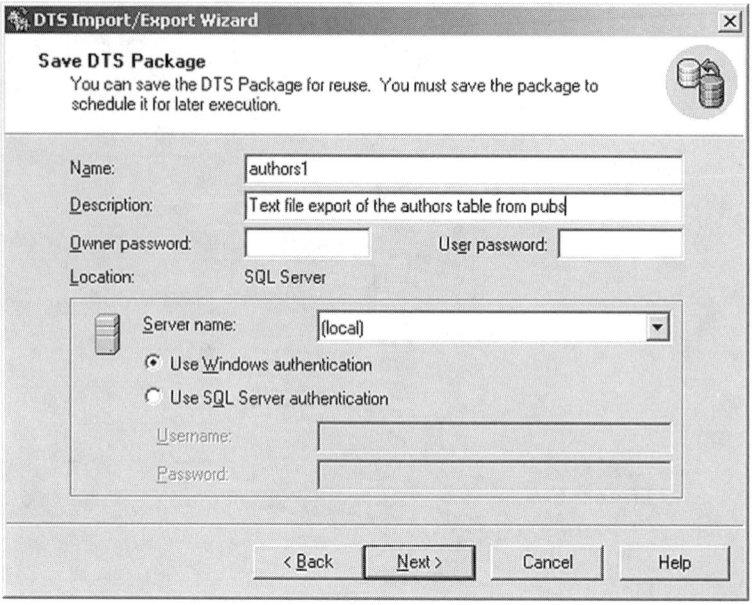

Figure 5.8
Save DTS
package
information

Give your test package a name and describe it to remind yourself what you've done here. Tell the wizard to store the information in the current SQL Server. You have the option of storing it on another server if you wish. Some shops do this to consolidate management of these types of things to a central server.

Select Next to show the screen displayed in Figure 5.9.

You're given a chance to use the Back button to change something, or you can press Finish to move on. Do the latter, and you're given the screen shown in Figure 5.10.

A progress bar appears, and the steps are displayed in the window. When all tasks complete, the individual steps that ran are displayed on each line. If a step fails, a red X appears next to the step. You can double-click that line to display the errors. You'll get a Back button here also, but the damage may already be done.

You should save the DTS packages you create, even if they are a one-time process. If you've saved the package, you can edit and then rerun it, but if you didn't, you might have to go through the entire selection process all over again.

Figure 5.9
Completing
the package

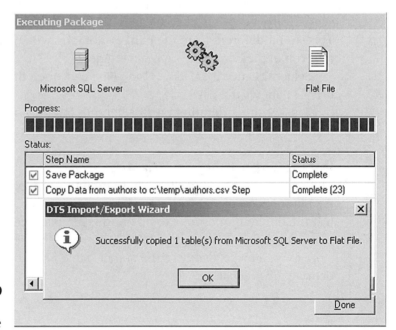

Figure 5.10
Executing
the package

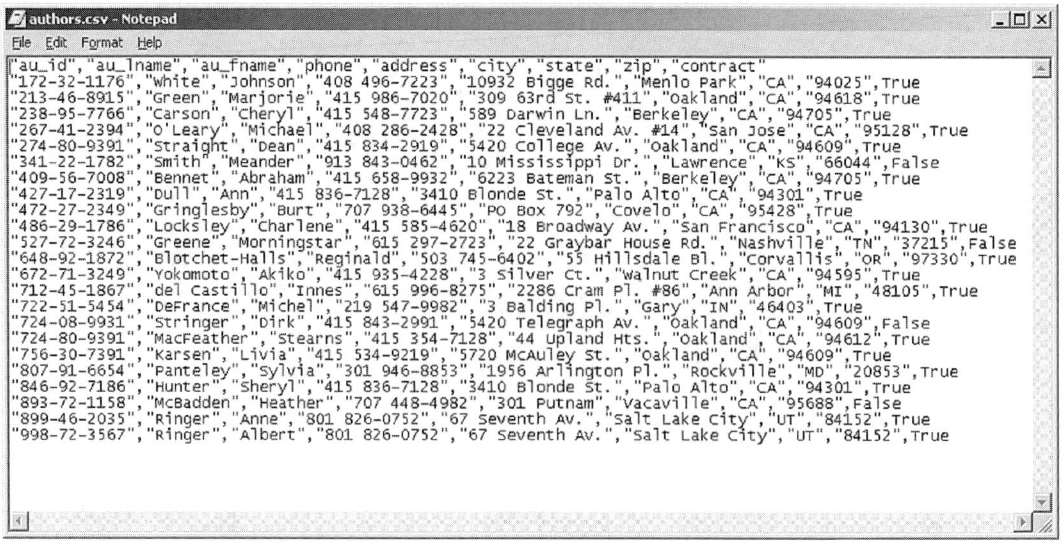


```
"au_id","au_lname","au_fname","phone","address","city","state","zip","contract"
"172-32-1176","White","Johnson","408 496-7223","10932 Bigge Rd.","Menlo Park","CA","94025",True
"213-46-8915","Green","Marjorie","415 986-7020","309 63rd St. #411","Oakland","CA","94618",True
"238-95-7766","Carson","Cheryl","415 548-7723","589 Darwin Ln.","Berkeley","CA","94705",True
"267-41-2394","O'Leary","Michael","408 286-2428","22 Cleveland Av. #14","San Jose","CA","95128",True
"274-80-9391","Straight","Dean","415 834-2919","5420 College Av.","Oakland","CA","94609",True
"341-22-1782","Smith","Meander","913 843-0462","10 Mississippi Dr.","Lawrence","KS","66044",False
"409-56-7008","Bennet","Abraham","415 658-9932","6223 Bateman St.","Berkeley","CA","94705",True
"427-17-2319","Dull","Ann","415 836-7128","3410 Blonde St.","Palo Alto","CA","94301",True
"472-27-2349","Gringlesby","Burt","707 938-6445","PO Box 792","Covelo","CA","95428",True
"486-29-1786","Locksley","Charlene","415 585-4620","18 Broadway Av.","San Francisco","CA","94130",True
"527-72-3246","Greene","Morningstar","615 297-2723","22 Graybar House Rd.","Nashville","TN","37215",False
"648-92-1872","Blotchet-Halls","Reginald","503 745-6402","55 Hillsdale Bl.","Corvallis","OR","97330",True
"672-71-3249","Yokomoto","Akiko","415 935-4228","3 Silver Ct.","Walnut Creek","CA","94595",True
"712-45-1867","del Castillo","Innes","615 996-8275","2286 Cram Pl. #86","Ann Arbor","MI","48105",True
"722-51-5454","DeFrance","Michel","219 547-9982","3 Balding Pl.","Gary","IN","46403",True
"724-08-9931","Stringer","Dirk","415 843-2991","5420 Telegraph Av.","Oakland","CA","94609",False
"724-80-9391","MacFeather","Stearns","415 354-7128","44 Upland Hts.","Oakland","CA","94612",True
"756-30-7391","Karsen","Livia","415 534-9219","5720 McAuley St.","Oakland","CA","94609",True
"807-91-6654","Panteley","Sylvia","301 946-8853","1956 Arlington Pl.","Rockville","MD","20853",True
"846-92-7186","Hunter","Sheryl","415 836-7128","3410 Blonde St.","Palo Alto","CA","94301",True
"893-72-1158","McBadden","Heather","707 448-4982","301 Putnam","Vacaville","CA","95688",False
"899-46-2035","Ringer","Anne","801 826-0752","67 Seventh Av.","Salt Lake City","UT","84152",True
"998-72-3567","Ringer","Albert","801 826-0752","67 Seventh Av.","Salt Lake City","UT","84152",True
```

Figure 5.11 Text file created by DTS

One important thing to remember when working with DTS packages is the security aspect. DTS packages run in the context of the client that runs them. This is a bit different from the behavior of jobs, which I'll discuss in Chapter 6. Jobs run in the context of SQL Server Agent.

Select OK and then Done. Using Notepad, open the text file you made. Figure 5.11 shows the data.

This process demonstrated selecting Import and Export Data from the menu. Next I'll cover the other two ways to use DTS.

Import/Export Object Wizards

All the methods you'll use from here until the command-line section are identical in function to the DTS wizard you just examined. The rest of the wizards just use different questions to fill out the DTS package.

You're going to import the text file you made earlier, but you need a place to store it. We'll make a copy of the authors table, and call it authors2 so you don't damage the original.

Open Query Analyzer and type the code shown in Listing 5.1 to create the table. The syntax isn't important at the moment; this is just a quick way of creating the table. You could also use the scripting capabilities I discussed in Chapter 3 to create this table.

Listing 5.1   Creating the authors2 table

```
USE pubs
GO
CREATE TABLE [authors2] (
        [au_id] [id],
        [au_lname] [varchar] (40),
        [au_fname] [varchar] (20),
        [phone] [char] (12),
        [address] [varchar] (40),
        [city] [varchar] (20),
        [state] [char] (2),
        [zip] [char] (5),
        [contract] [bit],
) ON [PRIMARY]
GO
```

Now close Query Analyzer and open Enterprise Manager. Drill down to the pubs database, opening the Tables object. Right-click this object to bring up the display shown in Figure 5.12.

Notice I've selected the menu items All Tasks, Import Data. You'll use this selection to import the data you exported earlier. After you select this menu option, you see the display in Figure 5.13.

This is the same screen from the Import and Export Data option from the Start menu. Select Next, and the screen in Figure 5.14 appears.

You need to choose the source of the data. This time you're *importing* data. So the text file that you created earlier becomes the source. Fill out the screen to reflect that, and then press Next to bring up the screen shown in Figure 5.15.

Notice that you're asked the format of the data—that's because you picked the Text driver and the driver specified that this file needs a format defined to import it. Select First row has column names because that's the way we created the file. Select Next to continue with the process and bring up the screen in Figure 5.16.

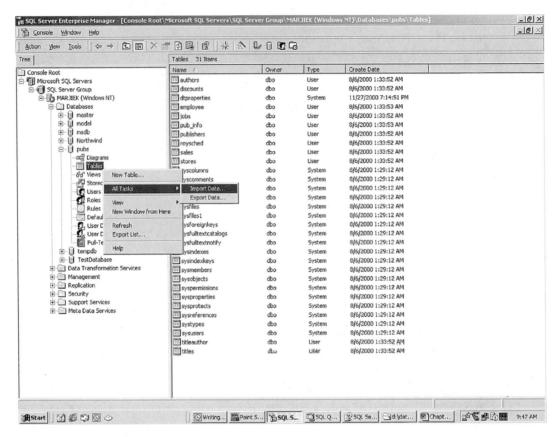

Figure 5.12 Beginning the import

You need to further define the format for the file, and at this point you're asked how to delimit the elements in the file. Leave the defaults and select Next to move on and display the screen shown in Figure 5.17.

Now you're asked to define the destination for the table. Because you began this process in the pubs database, the wizard has already filled that in for you. Select Next to bring up the display shown in Figure 5.18.

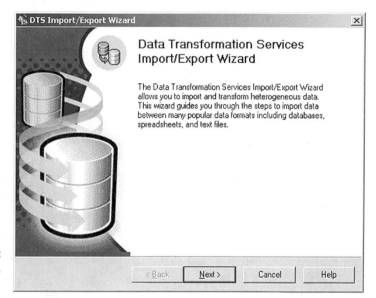

Figure 5.13
Welcome-to-
DTS screen

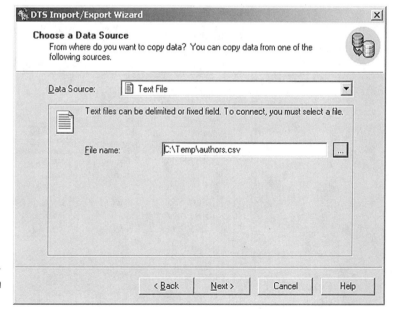

Figure 5.14
Choose data
source

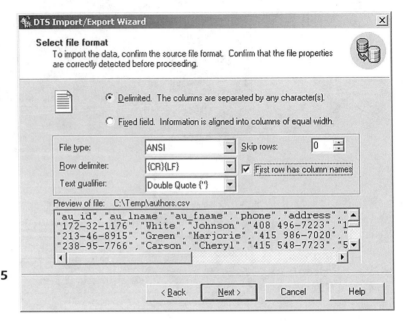

Figure 5.15
Data file
format

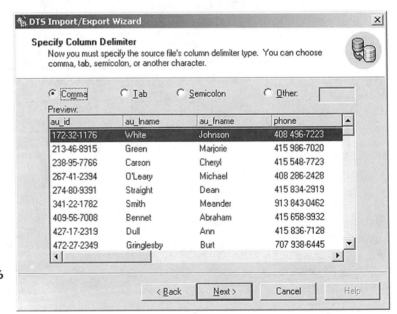

Figure 5.16
Column
delimiter

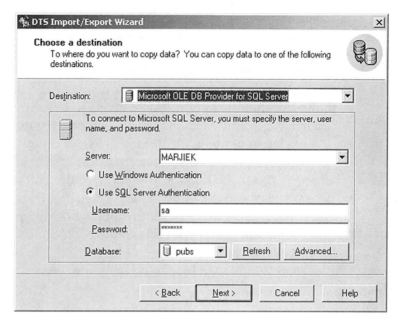

Figure 5.17
Choose
destination

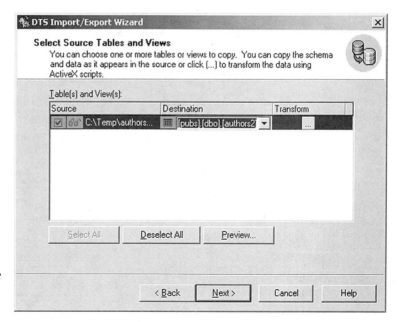

Figure 5.18
Selecting the
destination
table

Select the authors2 table you created earlier. Notice the Transform button on this screen. I'll take a little detour here to demonstrate this part of DTS. Select Transform to bring up a panel, shown in Figure 5.19, that allows you to change the data that will be placed into the authors2 table.

This panel allows you to manipulate the destination columns. This is useful if the layout of the import source differs from the destination table. We're not changing that, but we are interested in changing the data. Select the Transformations tab to bring up the display shown in Figure 5.20.

Select the radio button that transforms each row of data to reflect the changes you make here. Add + " T." to the end of the au_fname column, which will give every author a middle initial of T.

If you're a developer or know one who will help you, you can do some pretty amazing things with this feature. You can use ActiveX or JavaScript to make your changes.

Press OK and then Next to bring up the screen shown in Figure 5.21.

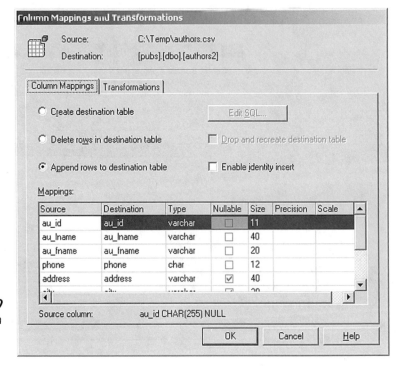

Figure 5.19
The Column Mappings panel

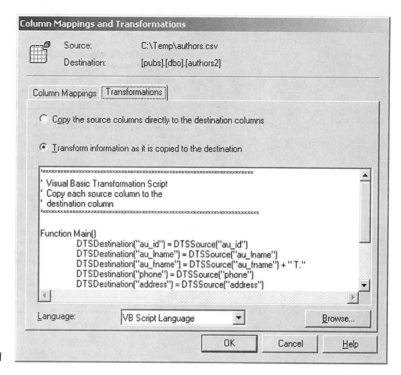

Figure 5.20
The Transformations panel

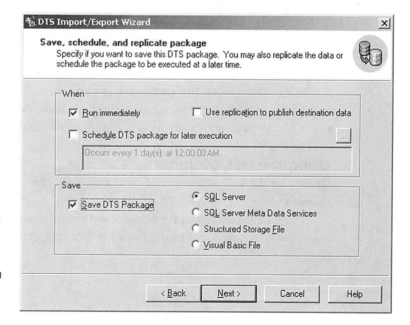

Figure 5.21
Save and run
the DTS
package

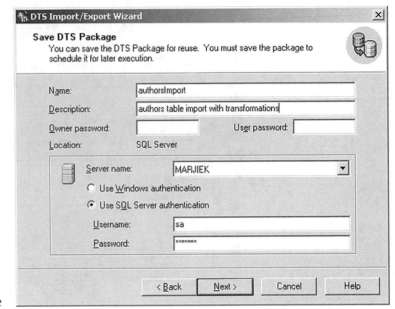

Figure 5.22
Naming the
DTS package

Once again you're asked if you'd like to save the package, so do that. Select Next to bring up the screen shown in Figure 5.22.

Name and describe the package, and then select Next. Figure 5.23 shows the final panel; select Finish there. The package runs, and you see the output in Figure 5.24.

Select Done once the package has run. To verify all this, I bring up Query Analyzer to make sure the transformations took. The result is shown in Figure 5.25. As you can see, everyone has the same middle initial.

Using the DTS Designer

Once the packages are saved, you can edit the choices and settings they contain.

You can also create the packages without the wizards. Staying in Enterprise Manager, you drill down to the Data Transformation Services object and then the

Figure 5.23
Completing the DTS package

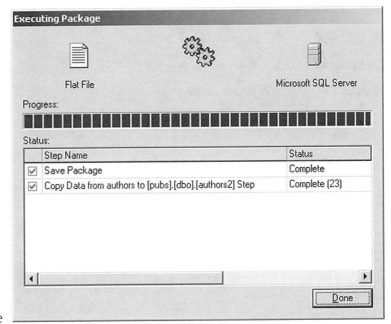

Figure 5.24
Running the DTS package

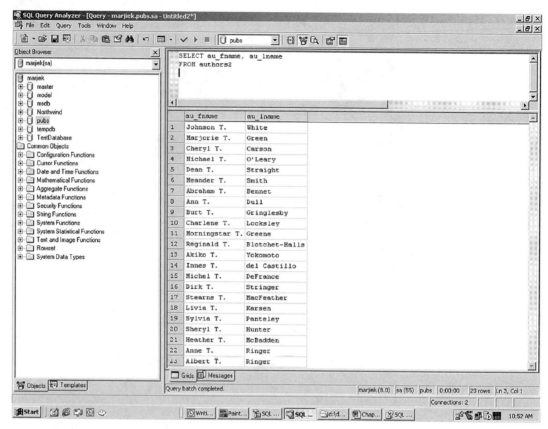

Figure 5.25 Query Analyzer output

Local Packages item. You'll see the two packages you saved earlier, as displayed in Figure 5.26.

This is the entry into the DTS packages and to the objects that you've been using.

Packages   The *package* is the total unit of work for DTS. It contains all the connections and tasks that you work with to import and export data.

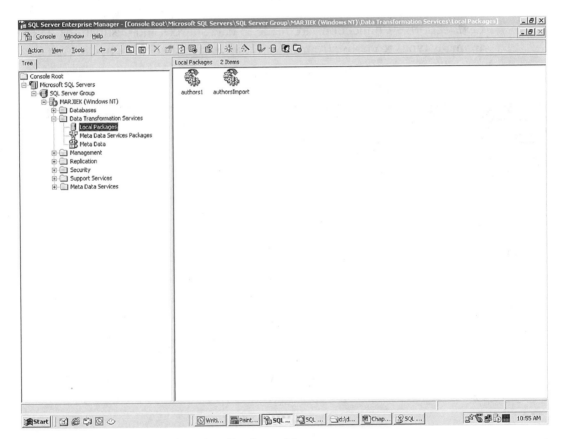

Figure 5.26   Data Transformation Services object

As shown in Figure 5.27, double-click your authorsImport package and you're placed in the *DTS Designer.*

Here you see the three elements in a package:

- Connections (Connection1 and Connection2)
- Tasks (contained inside the arrow)
- Workflows

The elements combine to allow you to process data in or out.

Connections Connections are made to data sources and destinations. There are many types to choose from as well as an "other" choice. Right-click the Con-

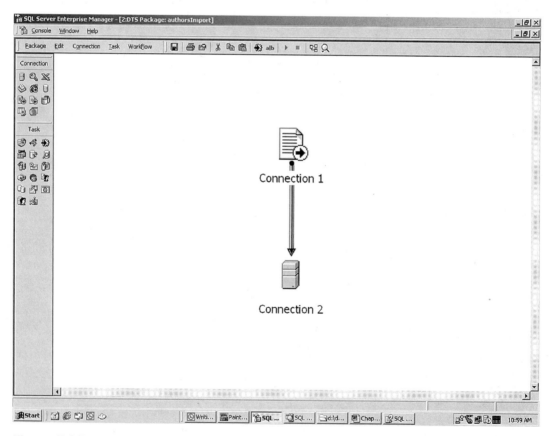

Figure 5.27 DTS designer

nection1 object in the Designer and select Properties from the menu that appears; you're shown the display in Figure 5.28.

Here you see all the information for the connection to the source text file. Rather than use the wizard as you did earlier, you could have added a source for the data directly by selecting the Connections item from the toolbar on the left and filling it out as displayed.

I'd like to direct your attention to one particular connection type. The Microsoft Data Link connection object is unique in that it allows you to set the source dynamically, so you can build extensible packages when you're not sure of the source or destination or both. If you're interested in doing that, look up Data Link Connection in Books Online for more information.

Tasks   Tasks are actions that the package takes. You build the migration operation layer on layer, such as copy the data, send an e-mail, transform the data, and then run a backup program. To see a task, you can right-click the big arrow in the DTS Designer (see Figure 5.27) and select Properties from the menu that appears. This will allow you to edit the Transform Data task.

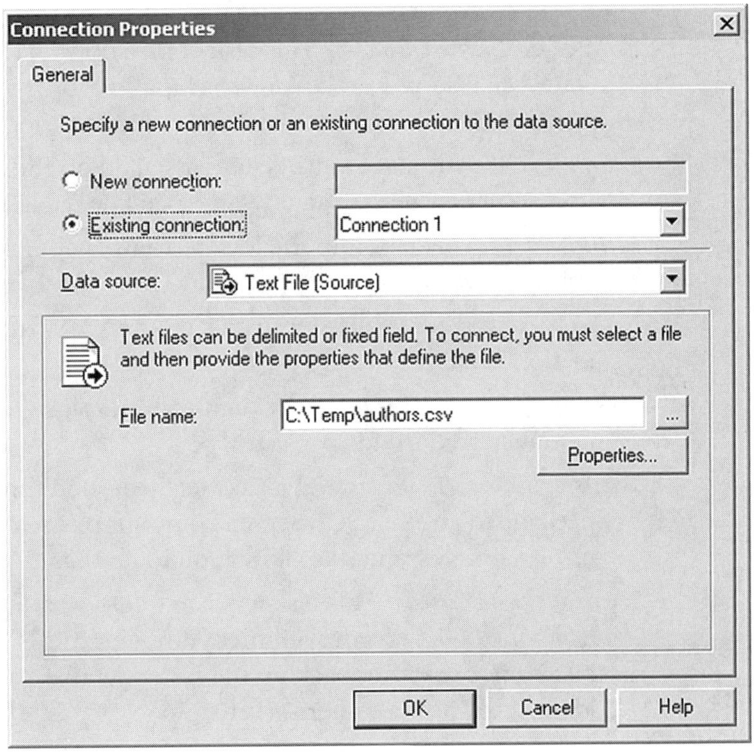

Figure 5.28
Connection1
properties

There are many more tasks you can perform with the DTS Designer.

File Transfer Protocol   With this task you can specify a location to copy the data from, whether it be on the Internet, a drive, or a network share.

ActiveX Script   This task gives a lot of flexibility in that you can program the system to do anything that ActiveX can do. For example, you can obtain the name of the currently logged on users and change the data appropriately.

Transform Data   This is the most commonly used task. You used this task in the earlier demonstration, and it allowed you to change the data on its way in.

Execute Process   This task allows you to run an operating system command.

Execute SQL This task executes an SQL command or set of commands.

Data Driven Query   This task is quite powerful, giving you the ability to affect data on the source side as you transfer it. For a more in-depth description of this tool, look up Data Driven Query Task in Books Online.

Copy SQL Server Objects   This task copies objects that SQL Servers understands, like stored procedures. For that reason, you can't use this task when the source or destination is anything other than SQL Server.

Send Mail   If you have a mail client installed on the server and SQL Mail set up, DTS can send mail at any stage you like using this task.

Bulk Insert   This task imports lots of data very quickly, but it sacrifices the ability to transform data for speed.

Execute Package   This task can call another DTS package, sending it information along the way.

Message Queue   This task lets Microsoft Message Queue data and variables be transferred to this package.

Transfer Error Messages   This task lets you send the errors generated by this package to another SQL Server. Some shops use one server for logs and error messages, and this allows you to do that.

Transfer Databases   This task lets you transfer an entire database instance from one SQL Server to another. Although this is a simple method, it's a bit simpler to either back up the other database and restore it, or detach it and copy it to another server.

Transfer Master Stored Procedures   This task copies stored procedures from one master system database on a SQL Server to another.

Transfer Jobs   This task copies jobs from one SQL Server to another. I'll cover jobs more fully in Chapter 6.

Transfer Logins   This task transfers SQL Server logins from one SQL Server to another.

Dynamic Properties   This is the other side of the Execute Package task. This part accepts the values from another package.

Workflows   Workflows are the items that tie the tasks together. You have a connection to data, and you have tasks you perform along the way—a workflow *is* that way. You attach a workflow to a task by selecting all the objects that define a state and right-clicking them to add a condition.

Let's use an example for a more clear explanation. Staying inside the DTS package you created, click the Send Mail task on the toolbar. You're shown the screen in Figure 5.29.

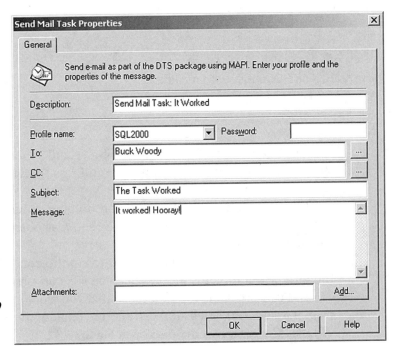

Figure 5.29
Adding a
mail task

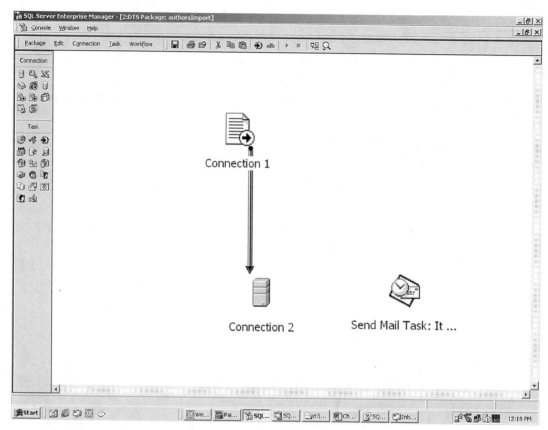

Figure 5.30 DTS Designer with mail task

Fill in the description, address, subject, and so forth, which define where the message will go and what it will say. Press OK and you're back at the DTS Designer screen, shown in Figure 5.30.

Click the Connection2 object, and holding down the Shift key, click the Send Mail task as well. Right-click the Send Mail object to bring up the menu shown in Figure 5.31.

Select On Success from the menu to set the condition. This means that if the final task completes successfully, you'll get an e-mail to that effect.

You can also set the condition so that you would know if the task failed or even if it just completed. You can set one or all of these conditions on one set of tasks. You're shown the display in Figure 5.32.

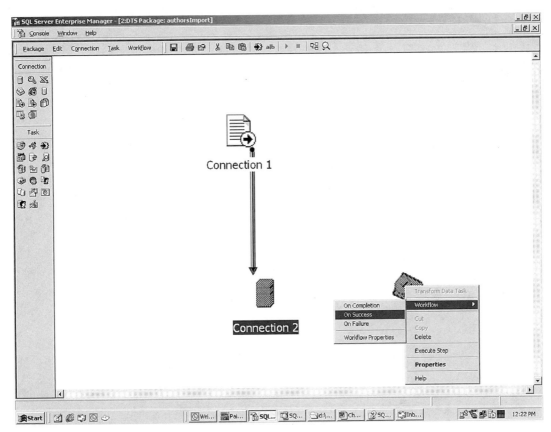

Figure 5.31 Workflow menu

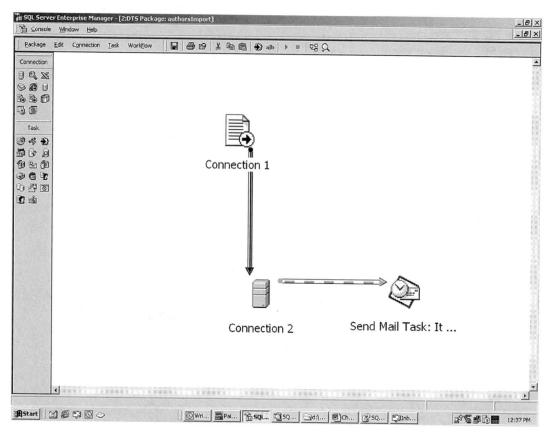

Figure 5.32 DTS Designer with workflow

Select Package and then Execute from the DTS Designer menu to run the package. You'll see the display shown in Figure 5.33. Check your e-mail, and there's the message. You now know the task ran successfully.

There's a lot more this tool can do, so be sure to experiment with your copy.

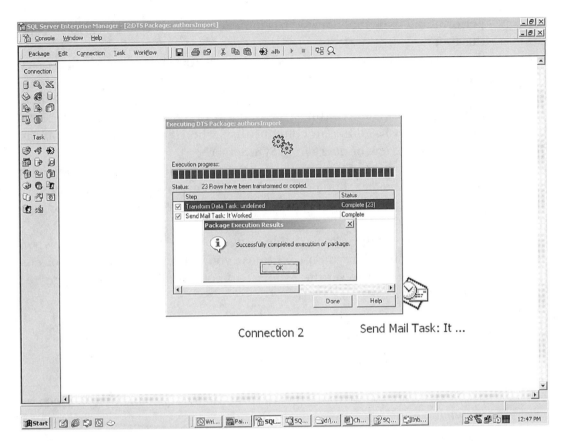

Figure 5.33　Completed package run

Command Line

The Data Transformation Service I just described is powerful and allows a great deal of flexibility. DTS packages can also be called from the command line with the dtsrun command and can be called using SQL statements.

There are three other command-line tools, one from the operating system and two from inside a command-line tool such as Query Analyzer or osql. Each has a distinct use and purpose. We'll use the authors2 table you created earlier for all the examples.

bcp

The bulk copy program (bcp) is an operating system command used to import and export data. It's a bit out of vogue these days because the DTS utility performs the same function and has more features, but I've still found uses for this tool.

Using bcp you can import a file of character data or a binary format called *native*. A *native* file is created with the bcp utility from SQL Server.

When you import data, you can use a format file that defines the field order, data types, and so forth. This is one way to get data into SQL Server 2000 from a file that has different columns than where you're putting it. You can export a table, view, or query from SQL Server.

There are quite a few switches for this utility, most of them dealing with the format of the data. I don't cover them all but show you the general use of the tool. You can look up the switches in Books Online for a more thorough discussion.

First, clear out the *authors2* table using *osql*. Type the command shown in Listing 5.2. Notice that you use –E to use your current NT administrator credentials, you use –d to set the database to *pubs*, and you use –Q to type in a query and leave the tool.

Listing 5.2   Emptying the authors2 table

```
osql -E -dpubs -Q"truncate table authors2"
```

Next, create your exported data from the *authors* table by using bcp, as shown in Listing 5.3.

Listing 5.3   Creating the text file

```
bcp "pubs.dbo.authors" out "authors2.csv" -T -c
Starting copy...
23 rows copied.
Network packet size (bytes): 4096
Clock Time (ms.): total    10
```

Let's look at this command a bit closer. The "pubs.dbo.authors" section indicates the *pubs* database, owned by the database owner (called dbo), and the *authors* table. The out command specifies this activity is an export. The words "authors2.csv" mean that this is the destination file. I didn't qualify the directory any further in this example, but you can if you wish. The –T means use the trusted connection. The –c means to export this file in character mode, which creates a text file.

Next, import that same data into the *authors2* table, as shown in Listing 5.4.

Listing 5.4   Importing data using bcp

```
bcp "pubs.dbo.authors2" in "authors2.csv" -T -c
Starting copy...
23 rows copied.
Network packet size (bytes): 4096
Clock Time (ms.): total     91
```

The options here are identical, other than the location for the destination and the in command. I create a format file for more complex import files in the Examples section.

BULK INSERT

The BULK INSERT command is used within a command-line query tool such as Query Analyzer or osql. It brings in data from a file, and you can use the files that bcp creates as well. It can read files of either text (character) or that ever popular native format. Its primary use is its speed—it's really fast!

Rather than go into a long explanation here, let's look at the self-annotated code in Listing 5.5. This code demonstrates the speed and simplicity of BULK INSERT.

Listing 5.5   Using BULK INSERT

```
-- Let's use the pubs database
USE pubs
GO
-- Now let's empty the authors2 table you made
TRUNCATE TABLE authors2
GO
-- Now you insert the data from the file you created
-- with bcp
BULK INSERT authors2 from "c:\temp\authors2.csv"
GO
-- Now you prove it worked
SELECT * from authors2
GO
```

SELECT INTO

The SELECT INTO command is used exclusively within SQL Server. It's not a utility like bcp but is a command like BULK INSERT. The difference in the two commands is that SELECT INTO pulls data from an SQL source to a table, and that table does not have to exist first. The SQL source can be a table, a table or view in another database, or even another table in another kind of server called a *linked server.* Linked servers are created to allow a query of a remote data source as if it were local to the server. Look up linked servers, described in Books Online, for more information on setting up a linked server.

The self-annotated code shown in Listing 5.6 is a simple example.

Listing 5.6   Using SELECT INTO

```
-- Let's use the pubs database
USE pubs
GO
-- Now let's delete the authors2 table you made
DROP TABLE authors2
GO
-- Now insert the data from the authors table,
-- creating the new one on the fly

SELECT * INTO authors2 FROM authors
GO
-- Now prove it worked
SELECT * from authors2
GO
```

Examples

I've covered many tools in this chapter, but you may have needs that the Graphical or Command Line sections didn't show you. I've put together a few real-world examples from things you do every day. I've kept the explanations to a minimum, except where things might not be obvious.

Creating a Scheduled Export of Data with DTS

One of the tables in my database at work is routinely imported into another application. The other application expects a text file, so we'll use a table in pubs for this example.

Open Enterprise Manager, drill down to the pubs database, and then right-click the tables object authors. Select All Tasks, Export Data from the menu, as

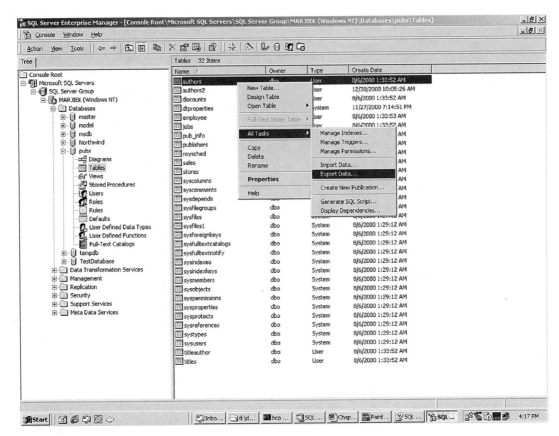

Figure 5.34   Beginning the export

shown in Figure 5.34. Click Next at the welcome screen to bring up the screen shown in Figure 5.35.

Set your source database and password, and select Next to continue. The screen in Figure 5.36 appears. Now set the destination as a text file, because that's what the other application expects. Click Next to show Figure 5.37.

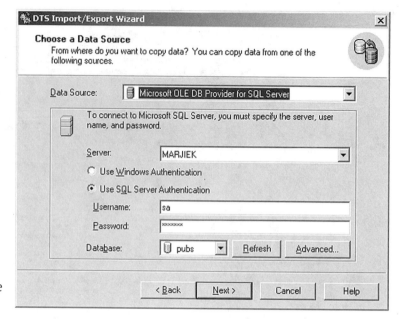

Figure 5.35
Selecting the
source

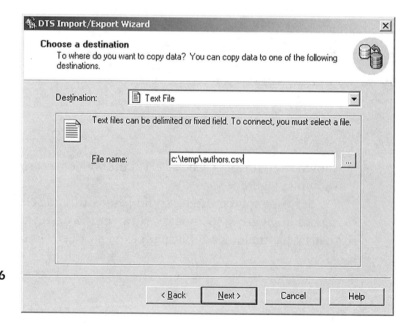

Figure 5.36
Setting the
destination

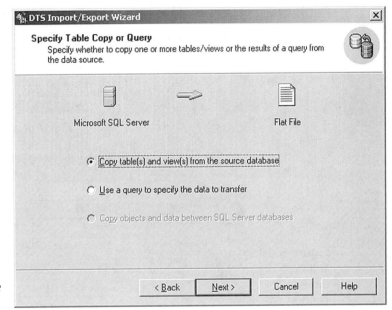

Figure 5.37
Selecting the
source type

Now select *tables and views* as your source option. After that, select Next, and the screen in Figure 5.38 displays. In this case, this other application does not expect the first row to have any headings, so leave all options at their defaults. Select Next to bring up the screen in Figure 5.39.

You're given the opportunity to set when the package runs. Select the *Schedule for later* option, and click the button to the right of the option to bring up the screen in Figure 5.40.

Set the frequency of the event. The other application expects the data by 4:00 A.M., so set this export to happen at 3:00 A.M. You'll need to test the speed of an export to set your own schedule, and be sure to allow for growth.

Once you've done that, select OK and then Next to bring up the screen in Figure 5.41. On this screen, name and describe the package. Select Next to move to the last screen, where you select Finish. The package is created and scheduled for you.

Using bcp to Export Data and Create a Format File

Sometimes when you use bcp to bring data in, the column types in the import file don't match the table or view where you're sending the data. To further

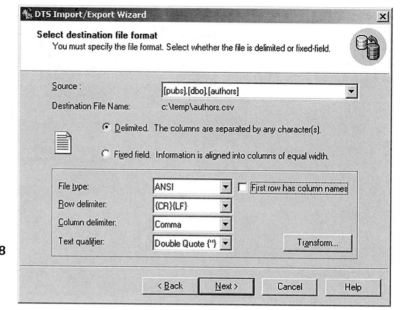

Figure 5.38
Setting the
table to
export

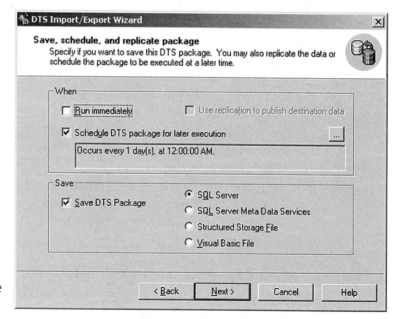

Figure 5.39
Save and
schedule the
package

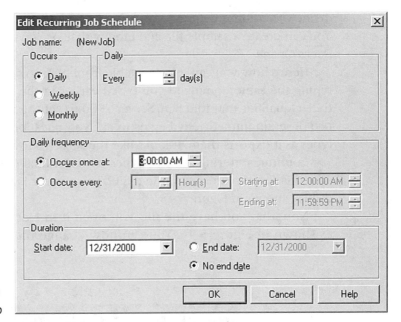

Figure 5.40
Schedule tab

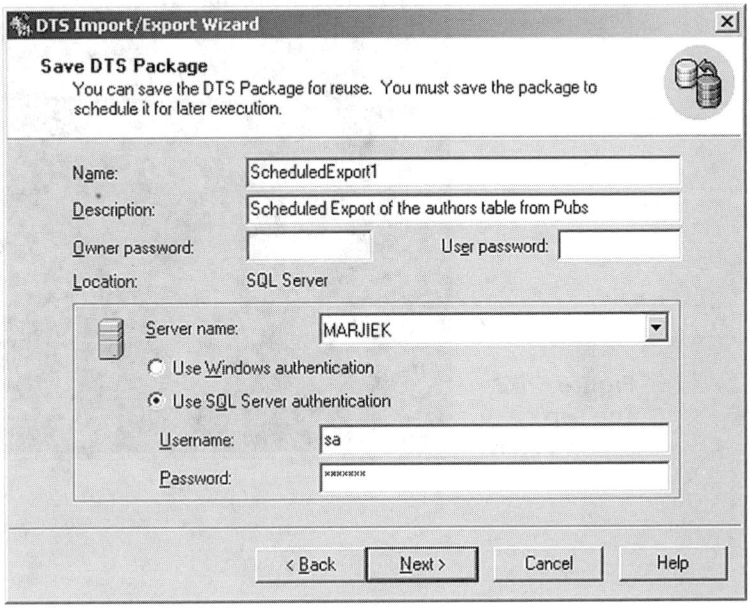

Figure 5.41
Naming the
package

define the column fields and placements, SQL Server 2000 wants a format file. You can create a sample file and modify that, or you can look up the format in Books Online.

Here's how you can export a table from pubs to see the format file. Start by typing the same command you typed earlier in the chapter, except leave off the -c qualifier that told SQL Server 2000 to set the format automatically. The bcp program immediately begins to ask you questions about each of the data types as it exports them. It looks like the screen shown in Figure 5.42.

Continue entering the data types until the final question: Do you want to save this format information in a file? The answer is yes, and you're given the display shown in Figure 5.43.

Now that you have the file, you open it in Notepad to see the options, as shown in Figure 5.44. You can now change the format options accord-

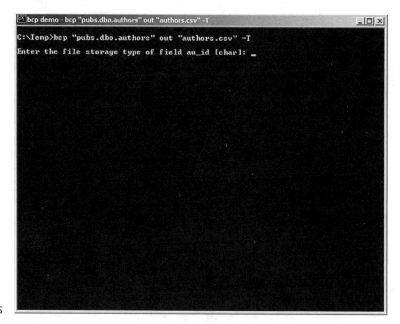

Figure 5.42
The bcp
export begins

Figure 5.43 Creating the format file

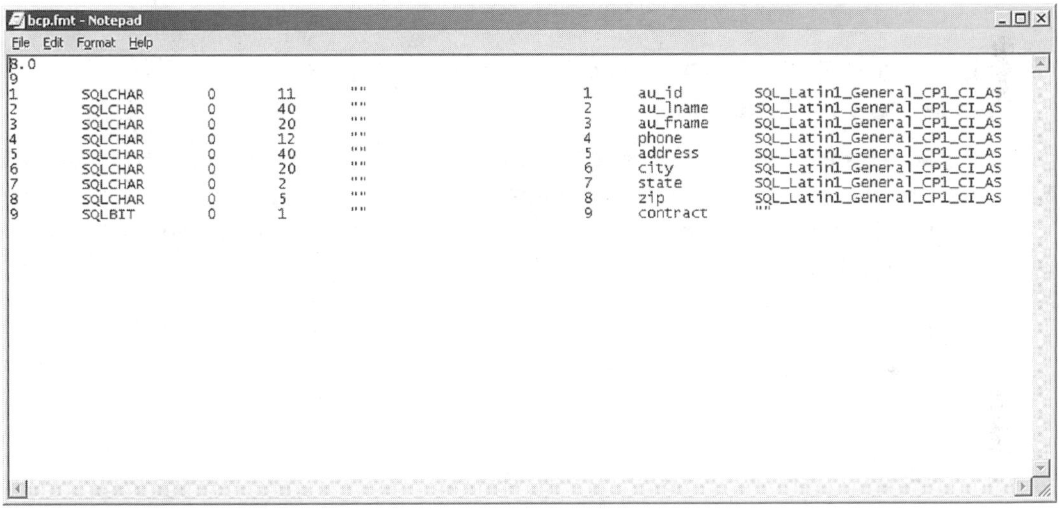

Figure 5.44   Contents of the bcp.fmt file

ing to your needs, even removing fields that don't exist in your destination table.

Now that you have the format file, you can use it to bring the data into the authors2 table, as shown in Figure 5.45.

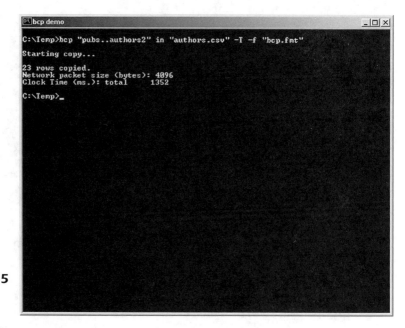

Figure 5.45
Using the
format file

Using SELECT INTO to Import from a Table Based on a Condition

Sometimes you need to create consolidated tables from existing data. You can do this with the SELECT INTO command. For this example we'd like a new table that shows an author's first and last names with the books the author has published. The commands shown in Listing 5.7 accomplish just that.

Listing 5.7 Creating a table with SELECT INTO

```
-- Let's set the pubs database
USE pubs
GO
-- and then do a query that gets two columns:
SELECT RTRIM(au_fname) + ' ' + RTRIM(au_lname) as Name, title
-- put that data into a new table called newtable, created automatically:
INTO newtable
-- and set up the criteria:
FROM authors a JOIN
titleauthor b ON a.au_id = b.au_id
JOIN titles c
ON c.title_id = b.title_id
```

Using BULK INSERT to Import Only Five Rows of Data

I'm limiting this example to five rows, but you could just as easily limit the rows to 10,000, if that's what your needs are. The code is shown in Listing 5.8. If for some reason you get a file error while trying this code, just reexport it with the bcp export example shown earlier in this chapter.

Listing 5.8   BULK INSERT

```
-- Let's use the pubs database
USE pubs
GO
-- And let's clean up any data that's still in the table
TRUNCATE TABLE authors2
GO
-- Here you get the data from the file you made earlier
BULK INSERT authors2 FROM "c:\temp\authors.csv"
-- and limit it to only five rows
WITH (LASTROW=5)
```

Rosetta Stone

Oracle and Microsoft Access have ways of getting the data into and out of their RDBMS.

Oracle

Table 5.1 shows the comparison for the Oracle system.

Table 5.1   Oracle Tools Comparison

Task	Oracle Tool	Microsoft SQL Server 2000
Transfer data using a GUI tool	Oracle Data Migration Assistant, but only between earlier versions of Oracle	Data Transformation Services
Import data from command line	Imp	bcp
Export data from command line	Exp	bcp

Microsoft Access

The tools for transferring data using Microsoft Access are compared in Table 5.2.

Table 5.2 Microsoft Access Tools Comparison

Task	Microsoft Access Tool	Microsoft SQL Server 2000
Transfer data using a GUI tool		Data Transformation Services

Resources

More information on import and export:
  http://www.microsoft.com/technet/SQL/manuals/admincmp/75517c02.asp
DTS and COM:
  http://msdn.microsoft.com/library/techart/unleash.htm

Chapter 6

Automation Using the SQL Server Agent

Chapter at a Glance

This chapter introduces you to automating tasks. Read this chapter to learn not only to automate SQL tasks, but also to use SQL Server 2000 to automate other tasks, from operating system commands to full-scale programming with conditional branching.

The Resources section contains references for:

- SQL Server Agent
- Scheduling
- Scripting technologies

Read Chapters 2, 3 and 4 before reading this chapter.

Overview

My view has always been that if there's a way to automate a repeatable process, you probably should. This view has saved me countless hours of work time and often eliminates the human error factor.

In this chapter, I describe automating tasks using SQL Server 2000. The tool used for automation and scheduling is the SQL Server Agent, and this feature can automate many tasks using SQL statements, operating system commands, and even programming. The SQL Server Agent is a service in the Control Panel of the SQL Server 2000 machine.

The SQL Server Agent is configured using Enterprise Manager, in the Management object. This object contains other items that work with SQL Server Agent: Operators, Alerts, and Jobs.

Operators are names and electronic contact information. These contacts do not require a SQL Server login. The notification methods are e-mail, e-mail pager, and the Windows NET SEND command.

Alerts are based on errors or SQL conditions. They can trigger messages to Operators or actions. Standard Alerts include those conditions that cause SQL Server to generate fatal errors.

Jobs are sets of instructions, schedules, and notifications. These individual operations are called Steps. Steps can have conditional logic. The Step types include T-SQL commands, operating system commands, and scripting language programming.

Detail

The automation facilities in SQL Server 2000 are all part of the same tool—the SQL Server Agent. In Chapter 2, during the setup process, I set this service to start with a user account, and I performed further configuration for SQL Server Agent in Chapter 4.

It is vital to carefully choose the account used to start the SQL Server Agent service. The two choices are the local system or a Windows account.

If you use a Windows account, the SQL Server Agent can do more things, like using mail and operating system commands, than if it is started with the local system account. This means that the SQL Server Agent can do anything that the account you use to start the service can do, so be aware that there *are* security implications.

SQL Server Agent contains the components Operators, Jobs, and Alerts. Let's look at each.

Operators

Operators are people who are notified of events that take place on the server. These notifications can be driven by an Alert or by T-SQL.

Anyone can be an Operator, not just IT people; so make sure you consider the choice of operators. Often a good choice for error notifications is the receptionist, because that station is usually staffed during operating hours. The receptionist also normally has access to cell phone and pager numbers and can notify you of a problem if you're away from your desk.

Notifications

Operators are people, and Notifications are the messages sent to those people. The notifications use any or all of three methods; e-mail, e-mail pager, and the Windows NET SEND command. Let's cover each of these in detail.

The e-mail notification method requires two things: that you've set up a mail client on your server and that you've set up the SQL Server Agent to use the mail profile associated with that client. Chapter 4 contains more information on setting up SQL Mail. Any MAPI-compliant system will do, Internet or local, but don't use offline folders, or your mail won't go anywhere. Once you've configured the e-mail profiles, you can set the e-mail of any person that this mail client can see as an Operator's address.

The e-mail pager notification is similar to regular e-mail but is a bit more useful when you have an e-mail address associated with your pager or cell phone. With this method, you can limit the times that the server will contact you. That's useful for "on-call" situations, when you don't want to get a page at 3:00 in the morning that the backups ran successfully.

The Windows NT NET SEND method is where the receptionist comes in. The name can be a person or computer name. I advise you to set this address to the computer name of the receptionist station, rather than that person's Windows account, because there may be more than one receptionist.

Jobs

The next component of the SQL Server Agent is the Job, which contains Steps, Schedules, and Notifications. Within the jobs, Notifications can be configured for the Operators.

Jobs can be called from SQL code, as I show in the Command Line section later in the chapter.

Steps

Steps are individual actions in Jobs. I'll discuss three types of Steps, which should cover most of what you need to automate.

First, there's an Operating System Command (CmdExec) type, which can start .com, .exe, .bat, and .cmd files.

The second type of Step you can run is a TransactSQL (SQL language) command. This type can in turn run complex SQL scripts.

The final type is the ActiveX Script. This type of Step can use VBScript or JavaScript programming commands. With this type of command, the sky's the limit. If you're a developer, you'll be right at home with this type of Step, and if you're not, it's worth learning a little code to do things you just can't get away with using batch files.

You can mix and match these Step types, having one type as Step 1 and another as Step 2, and so forth. I'll create a Job in the Graphical section later in the chapter that uses all three types.

When you set up your Steps, you can have one Step branch to another or even end the job based on a success or failure condition.

Scheduling

After you've defined your Steps, you can set up a schedule that can be set to one time, recurring, or not scheduled at all.

Notification

You can set the Notification to use any of the methods set up for the Operator, or you can send the notification to the NT event log based on the success condition of the Job or just the fact that it completed.

Alerts

An Alert is a condition in the SQL Server 2000 environment. There are two types. Alerts can be based on objects and counters from the Windows NT Performance Monitor, or Alerts can be based on messages from SQL Server 2000.

The general process to configure an Alert is to set up a name, determine a condition, and then choose a Notification or Job (or both) based on the Alert. We'll set up an Alert in the Graphical section.

I've ordered the discussion of the SQL Server Agent components this way on purpose. You normally set them up in this order. You need an Operator to notify for a Job, and Alerts are conditions that can cause a Job or notify an Operator.

Graphical

Now that I've shown a 50,000-foot view of the SQL Server Agent, let's set the parameters the service needs. We'll also set up an Operator, a Job, and an Alert.

Before you can use the SQL Server Agent, you need to set up its parameters. As shown in Figure 6.1, open Enterprise Manager and expand the object list down to the Management object. Although you can't see the colors on this

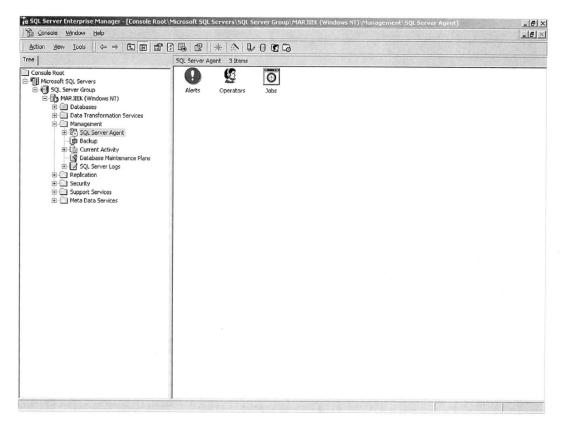

Figure 6.1   SQL Server Agent object

page, the SQL Server Agent object has a red circle on it, indicating that it's stopped.

The first thing to do, even before starting the SQL Server Agent, is to right-click the SQL Server Agent object and then select Properties from the menu item that appears. You're shown the display in Figure 6.2.

In my case, I've set the SQL Server Agent to run as my server's administrator account. You probably won't want to do this because of those security concerns I mentioned earlier. Select an account that can send mail, access network drives, and has whatever privileges your job steps will need.

Next, set the mail profile using the account you set up in Chapter 2 for SQL Mail. Finally, set the NET SEND recipient address of the account that starts SQL Server Agent. This isn't where Alerts are sent but is just the address that SQL Server 2000 uses if SQL Server Agent has an error.

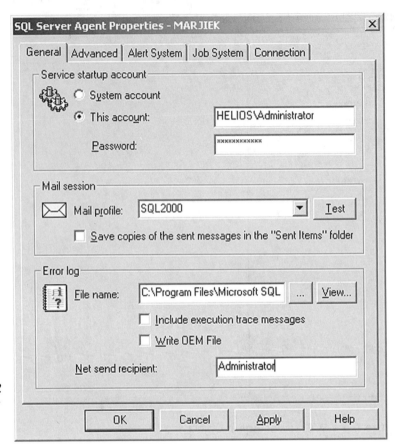

Figure 6.2
SQL Server
Agent
properties

Now select the Advanced tab to bring up the screen shown in Figure 6.3. This tab allows you to set whether the SQL Server Agent or SQL Server gets started again if it stops. I have no problem setting this for SQL Server Agent but not for SQL Server. You should usually take a peek at the event log if any process dies, before you try to restart it. In my experience, I've found that there are some pretty good reasons a server decides to terminate a process, and I like to investigate before I force the server to start again.

The SQL Server Agent is a different story. You do want it to restart because you won't know about a problem if it doesn't tell you. There's a bit of a catch-22 here because the SQL Server Agent uses the msdb database in SQL Server; so if they both die, and the settings are left as they are here, the Agent can't start.

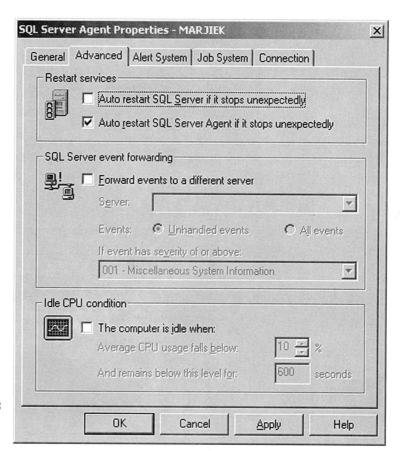

Figure 6.3
Advanced
tab

The worst that can happen in this situation is that the SQL Server Agent will not, in fact, be restarted.

Also on this tab is the ability to set the CPU idle condition. Steps in Jobs can be configured to happen when the server isn't busy, and this is where you set the number that SQL Server will consider idle. Normally, you don't change this setting.

Let's skip the middle box for now. Select the Alert System tab, as shown in Figure 6.4. The important part of this panel for your test system is to set a Fail-Safe Operator. This Operator is the one notified if SQL Server Agent can't reach anyone else.

Leave this one as-is for now, since we haven't discussed Operators yet. You'll come back to this once you've set up an Operator; then you can choose that person as the Fail-Safe. In this field it's important to have this Operator defined.

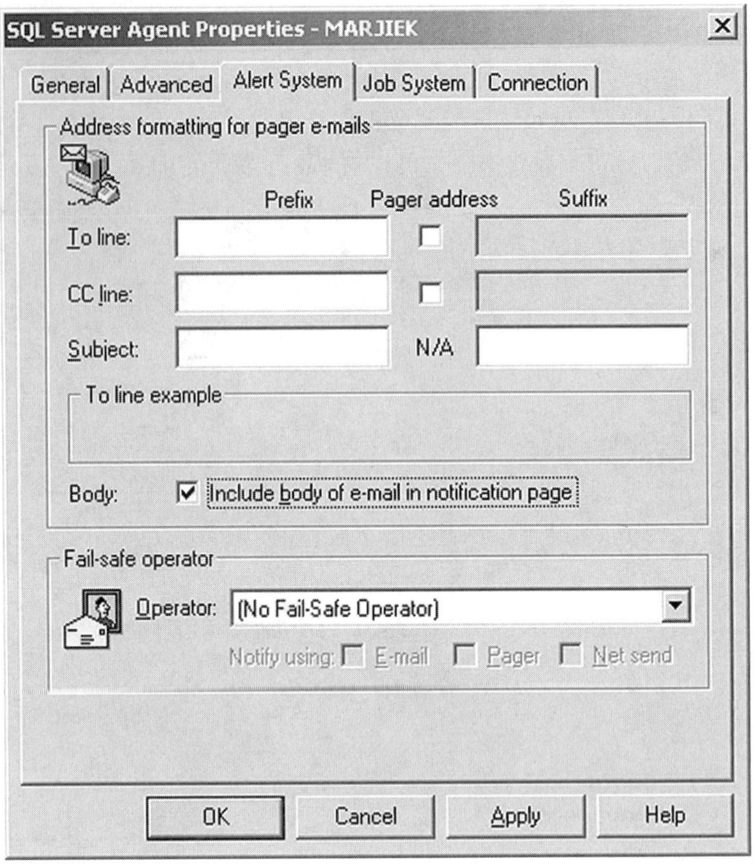

Figure 6.4
Alert System

Select the Job System tab, shown in Figure 6.5, next. Here you can set the account that CmdExec and ActiveX Scripting use. The default requires the user running the job to be a member of the SysAdmin account in SQL Server 2000 to run these Steps in a Job. I discuss security further in Chapter 10.

Select the Connection tab to bring up the screen shown in Figure 6.6. This tab sets the security that the SQL Server Agent uses to access SQL Server 2000 to do its work. If you've set up a server as I have here, you allow both NT accounts and SQL Server accounts to access the server. I'll assume you've done that, so you can leave this tab as it is. If you've set your server to allow SQL Server accounts to use the server, you can type in a SQL Server account and password so that the SQL Server Agent can access the databases on your server.

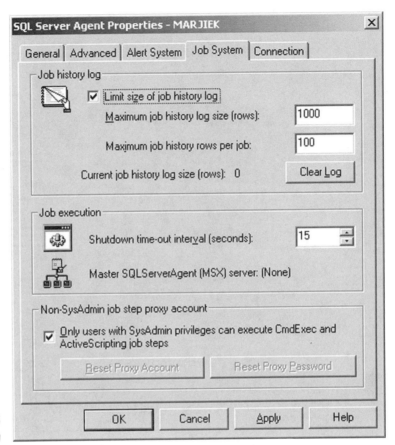

Figure 6.5
Job System

Select OK, and then right-click the SQL Server Agent object and select Start from the menu that appears. The SQL Server Agent is now started with the parameters that you just set up. The next step is to use the Windows Control Panel and double-click the Services applet. Look for the SQL Server Agent service (SQLSERVERAGENT in Windows 2000), and set the startup type to Automatic. If you don't do this, your automated processes won't be very automated if your server reboots.

One more note about services: if you're using more than one instance of SQL Server 2000, you'll have more than one instance of the SQL Server Agent service. The instance name will be part of the service name. Look for them all and set them to start automatically. I cover instances further in Chapter 15.

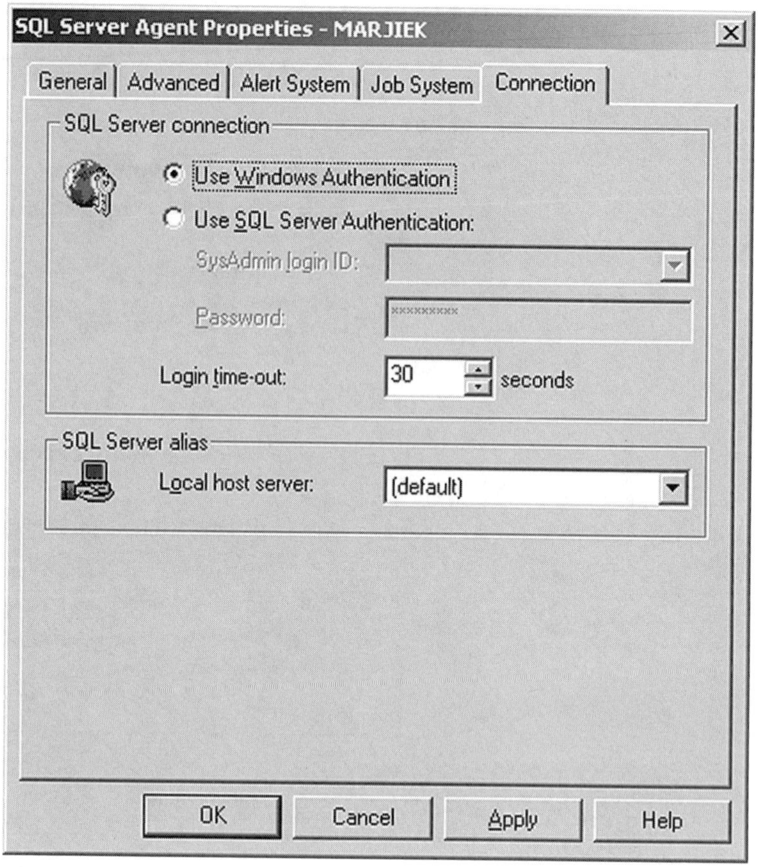

Figure 6.6
Connection
tab

Operators

Now that the SQL Server Agent is running, you can set up the first Operator. Double-click the Operator object and then right-click it. Next select the New Operator item from the menu that appears. The panel shown in Figure 6.7 displays the result.

In this panel you set up the identification of the Operator. This can be a user or a group of users. Place your name in the first box, and then enter your e-mail address. You can use Internet addresses as long as your mail client on the server can send mail there. If you don't have an e-mail pager system, don't fill in that option.

Use the name of your computer, not your username, as the NET SEND address method. That way, anyone logged on to your computer will be notified.

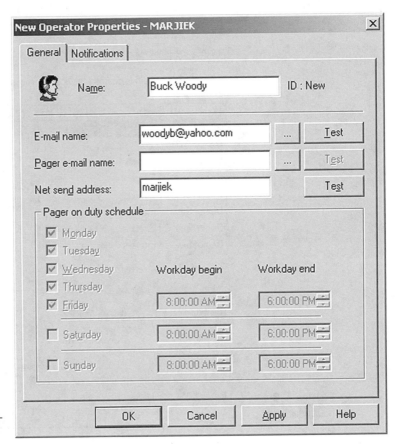

Figure 6.7
New Opera-
tor panel

That's my preference, but you can use either your username or the name of a computer here.

Select the Notifications tab to show the display you see in Figure 6.8. This tab allows you to set the Alerts this Operator will receive, although this can be changed in other places, such as in the Alert object.

There are a few predefined Alerts, and at least one person should get these particular messages through a NET SEND or pager method. These Notifications are for the nastiest errors that can happen to SQL Server, the ones that potentially involve terminated connections or cause the server to stop.

You can also select the Send E-Mail button here to let the Operator know that they've been targeted as an Operator. It's the polite thing to do.

Select OK, and the Operator is created. You can repeat this process for as many Operators as you like.

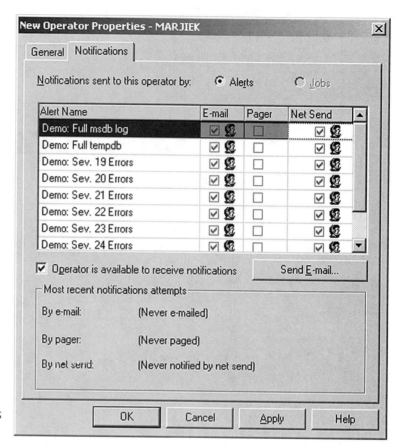

Figure 6.8
Notifications
tab

Keep in mind that this isn't just for IT staff. T-SQL code can send Notifications of various types. For examplee, a project manager can receive a message when the value in the budget column of the projects table reaches a certain number.

Jobs

To use these objects, set up a Job that has three Steps, one of each type, with a Notification and a Schedule. The criteria for this example are that you have an external program that stores files in the LOGS directory on your C: drive, you need to see data from a table, and you need to be notified of a deadline date. We'll create a Job that contains Steps that will tell you if that file exists, query the contents of a table, and calculate how many days exist until the deadline.

Drill into the Jobs object and right-click it, selecting New Job from the menu that displays. The screen shown in Figure 6.9 appears. You may already

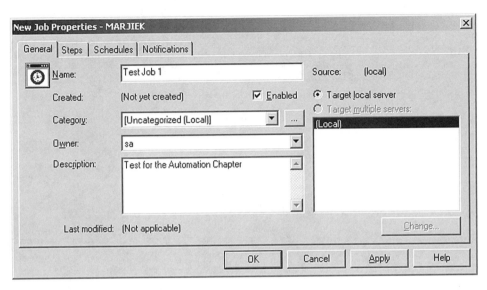

Figure 6.9 New Job

have a Job called "TestJob1." That came from the DTS wizard you followed in the previous chapter.

Set the name of the Job, give it a description, and take the defaults on everything else. You can categorize Jobs as the wizards do, but it isn't required. You can also set another server to run the Job, but you'll leave this set to Local.

Select the Steps tab to get the display in Figure 6.10. No Steps have been created yet, so select the New button to bring up the screen in Figure 6.11.

Here we do several things. First, name the Step. Next, set the type to Operating System Command (CmdExec). This means that the Step will use an operating system command as the function. Type the instruction DIR C:\LOGS in the Command box. Note that every command (even DOS commands) returns an exit code, which is just a number. The default is 0 for a successful run of the command. Leave it at the default.

You need to set the location for the output, so click the Advanced tab. This tab controls two objects: the flow of the Steps and any output files. Make sure to set the flow to move to the next Step if it succeeds, or to quit and notify if it doesn't. This flow feature can set up rather complicated branching logic effects when there are multiple Steps.

Set the output of your test to go to the C:\TEMP\ directory and to overwrite the file each time the Job runs. Select OK, and you're back to the Steps

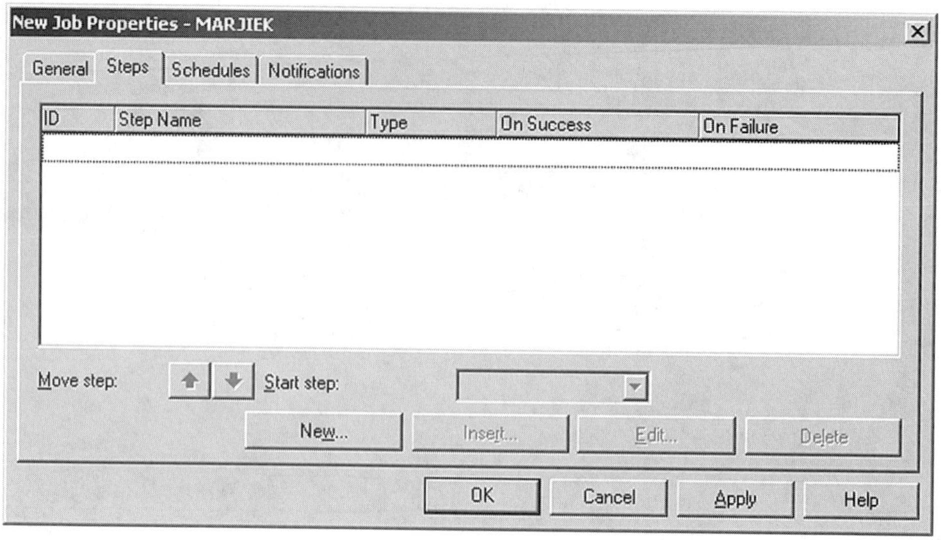

Figure 6.10 Steps tab

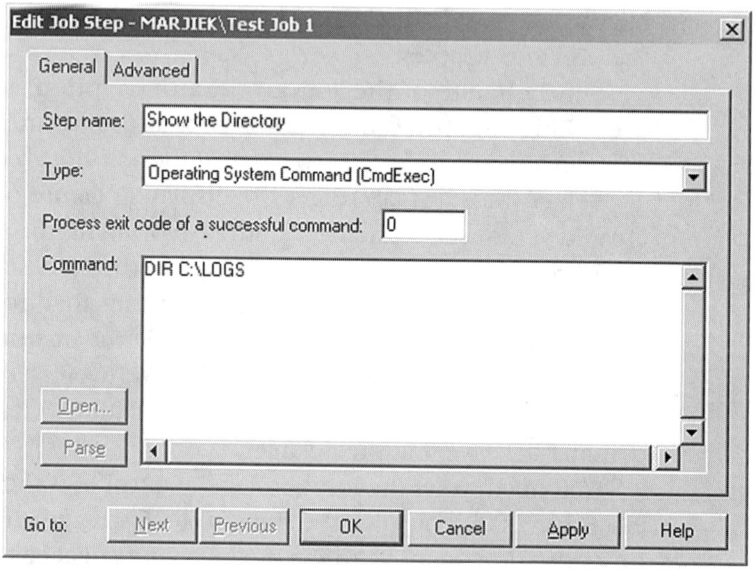

Figure 6.11 Creating a Step

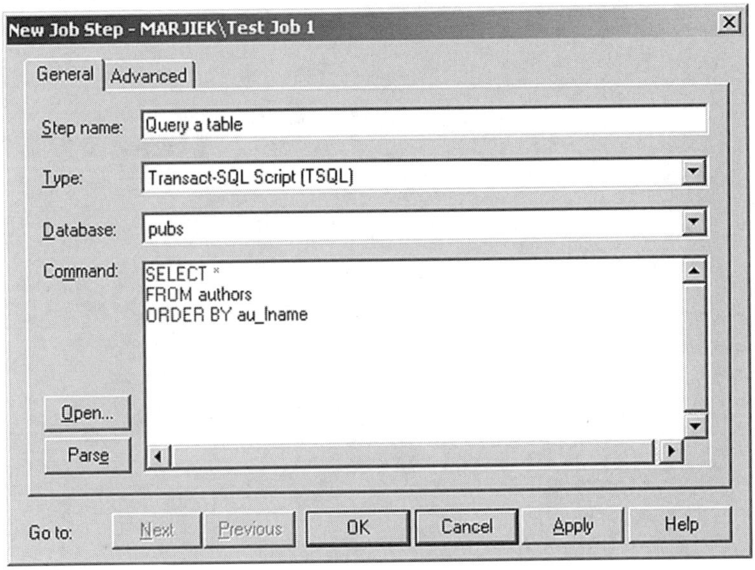

Figure 6.12
Adding the
SQL Step

screen (see Figure 6.10). You've met the first requirement of your criteria. Click New to add another Step, as shown in Figure 6.12.

Select the type as Transact-SQL Script (TSQL). Type in a very simple query as I have, but keep in mind that the commands can be as complex as necessary. A more complex query would be useful for an outside application that communicates with SQL Server and updates a table when it is through.

Select the Advanced tab to set the output of the file and the looping conditions, as shown in Figure 6.13.

Select OK, and then add your final Step. As shown in Figure 6.14, the Type on this Step is ActiveX Script. You're going to calculate the number of days between when the script runs and a set date. The output of this command isn't sent to a file, but it will be present when you run this Job and view its history.

Reproduce the code in Listing 6.1 in case you're not familiar with Visual Basic Script. This code could be modified to do something on that date rather than just tell you how many days are left.

Listing 6.1   ActiveX code

```
Rem Setup the now and later times
RightNow = #9/16/00#
Later = #12/01/2001#
Rem Do the Work
n = DateDiff("d",RightNow,Later)
Rem Show the Output
Print "There are " & n & " days until the deadline."
```

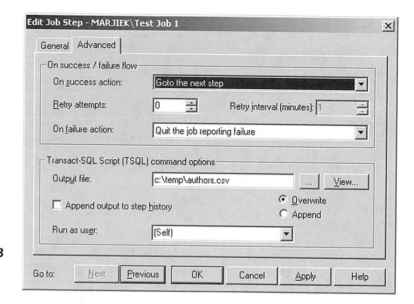

Figure 6.13
Advanced
options

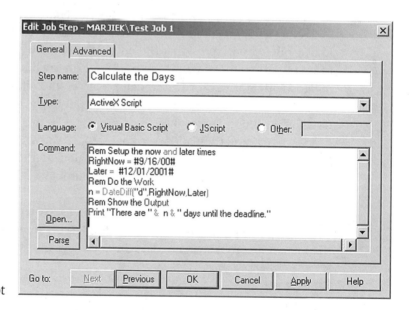

Figure 6.14
Adding an
ActiveX Script

The Advanced tab only allows for flow control on this type of command, so leave it at the default, and then select OK, which shows you the Steps that you see in Figure 6.15.

You can set the start Step, regardless of the order in which you created them. A Schedule isn't required—a Job can be fired from a command or even from an Alert. In this case, you want a recurring event, so let's set one up. Select the Schedules tab to bring up the display that is shown in Figure 6.16.

Select the New Schedule button; the result is shown in Figure 6.17. There are four conditions that you can use to set a Schedule. Some are self-explanatory, such as One time. The two that are interesting are "when the CPU is idle," which is affected by the settings for the SQL Server Agent I described earlier, and the Recurring setting.

Pick Recurring, and then select the Change button to bring up the display shown in Figure 6.18. Set your Job to run each night at midnight. Now select OK, and then select OK again. You have a completed Schedule. You probably want to be notified when this Job completes. Click the Notifications tab, shown in Figure 6.19, to set that up.

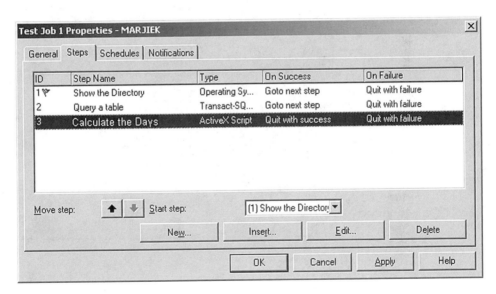

Figure 6.15   Completed Steps

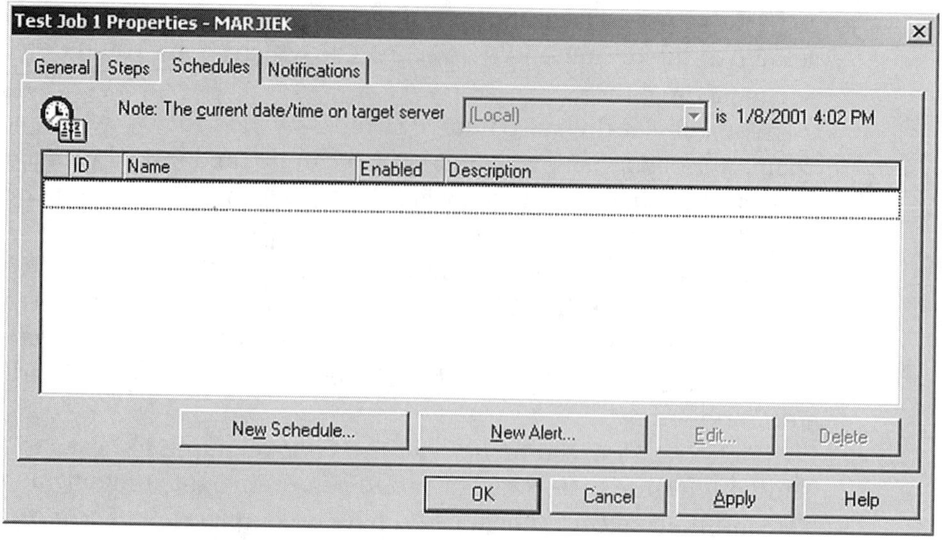

Figure 6.16 The Schedules tab

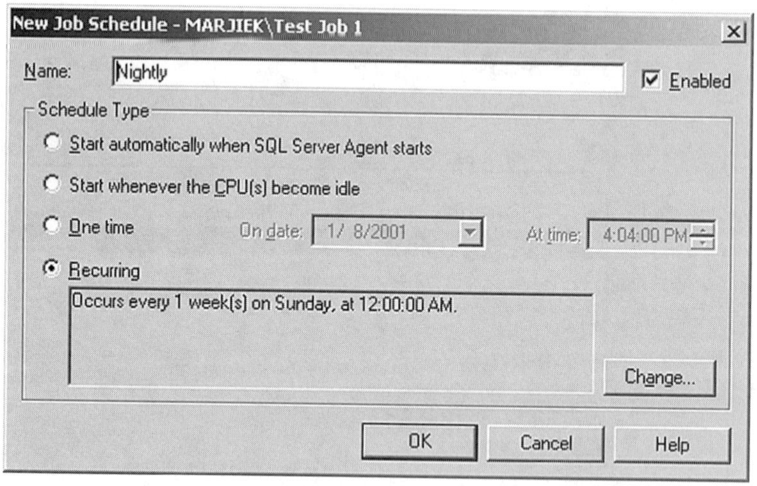

Figure 6.17
Setting the
Schedule

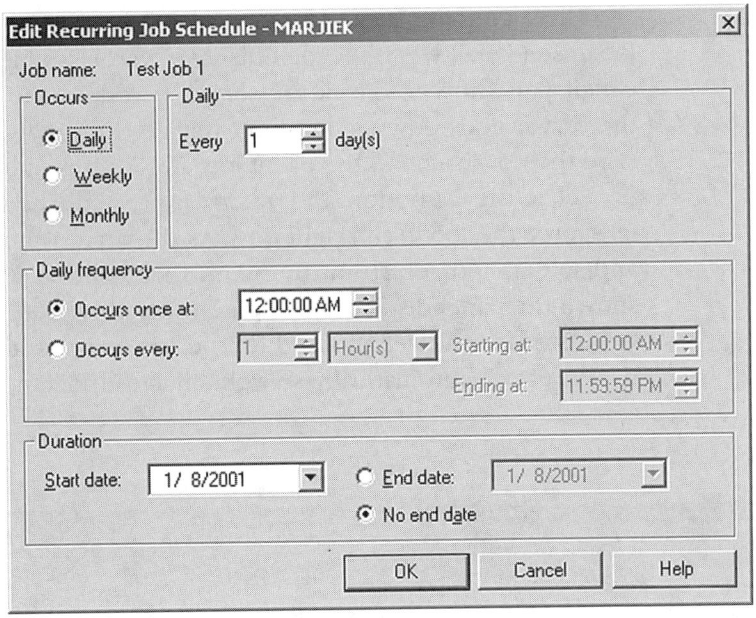

Figure 6.18
Changing
the Schedule

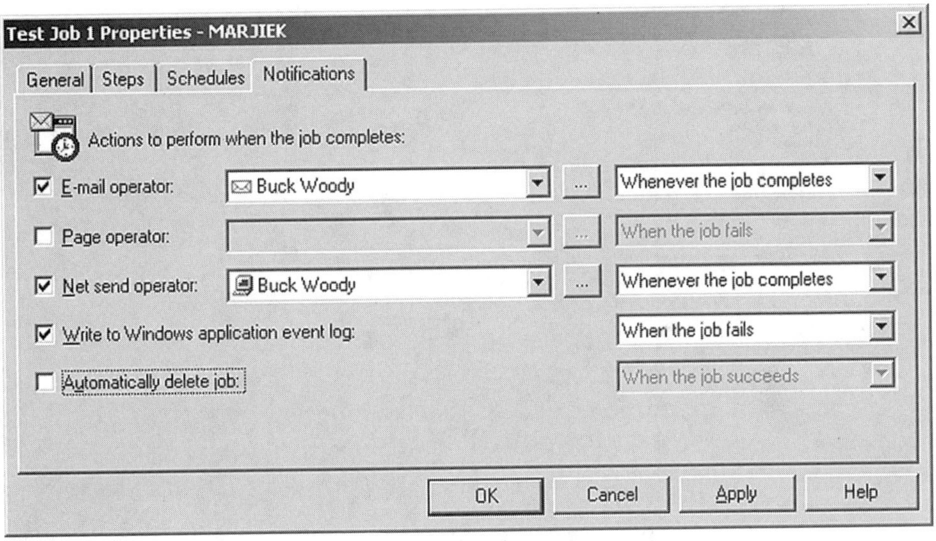

Figure 6.19   The Notifications tab

Three conditions can trigger the notification. The best practice is to set the job to send mail when the job finishes, regardless of its state. If you don't get an e-mail, you know to check the server. If you set the condition for failure and the server goes down, you won't realize there's an error. Note that you can send the notification to the event log, and for this one you use the failure logic.

Select the OK button, and the Job is created. The schedule is functional, but let's force the Job to run right now. As shown in Figure 6.20, right-click the Job and select Start Job from the menu that appears. Once you do that, you're shown the panel displayed in Figure 6.21.

Just leave the defaults and let the Job spin. As it does, Enterprise Manager won't refresh automatically, so right-click the Job and select Refresh to see the

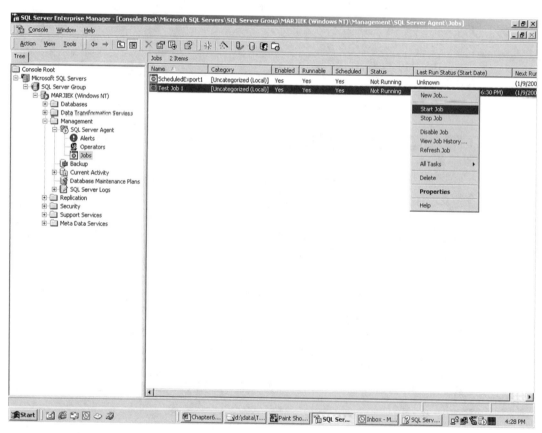

Figure 6.20 Starting the Job manually

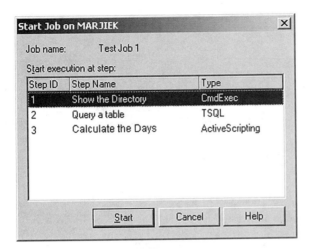

Figure 6.21   Job start options

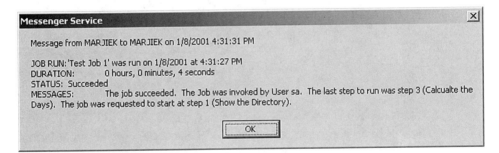

Figure 6.22   NET SEND Pop-up

status. As the Job progresses, you get the NET SEND pop-up that is shown in Figure 6.22.

Once the Job completes, right-click it again and select View Job History from the menu to bring up the display shown in Figure 6.23. Select the Show step details box so that you can click the line for the Calculate the Days step to see that there are 441 days left until your deadline. Also check the output files for verification, and check your e-mail. The Notification should have arrived successfully.

You'll see how to fire off this same Job from a command line later in the chapter.

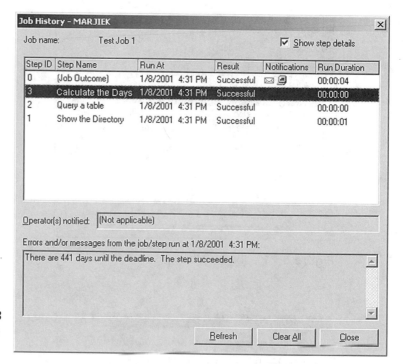

Figure 6.23
Viewing the
Job history

Alerts

Alerts are Notifications or Jobs that are triggered in one of two ways. The first way is by watching for errors that SQL Server knows about, including the ones you create. There are many errors that SQL Server knows about, but only the ones that are reported to the Windows application log are monitored. By default, the errors that are given a severity lower than 19 are placed in the application log, but you can create your own errors and force them to be placed there. When you do, the Alert will fire if it's configured to.

The performance objects and counters in the NT Performance Monitor tool can also fire Alerts. You can set the Alert to be fired on this condition, and the Alert can run a Job or notify when the condition is met. We'll create one of each as a way of introduction.

Open the Alerts object in Enterprise Manager, as shown in Figure 6.24. Notice that several Alerts are already defined. Right-click the Alerts object and then select New Alert from the menu that appears. The result is shown in Figure 6.25.

Give your test Alert a name, and then change the type of Alert from an error message to a performance counter. Select the SQL Server:General Statistics

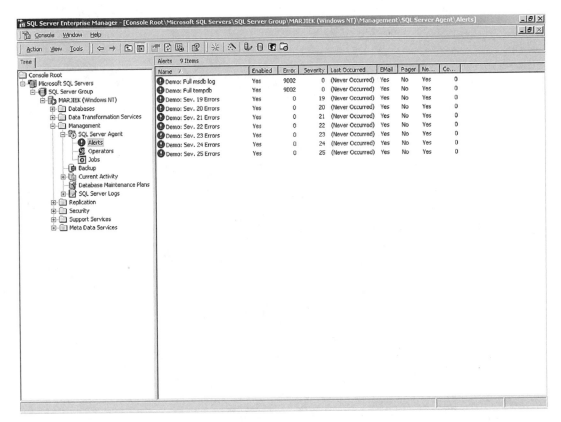

Figure 6.24   Alerts object

object and then the User Connections counter. Because you would like to be notified when the count of this item rises above three, set that condition accordingly.

Select the Response tab for this condition, shown in Figure 6.26. In this tab, you should choose to receive a message, but you could just as easily execute one of the Jobs you created earlier.

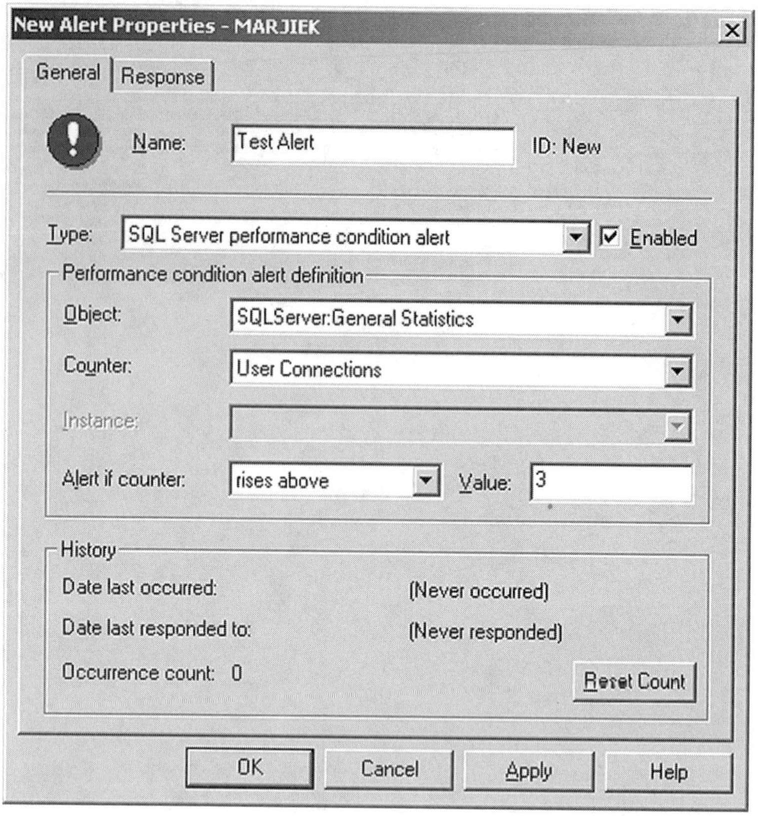

Figure 6.25
Creating a
new Alert

Tell the Alert to give you the full error message in the text as well as some more information. The delay setting is the testing interval for the Alert. If you set this too short, you'll be paged every minute. Click OK, and then wait one minute. The screen shown in Figure 6.27 should appear.

We've set the threshold this way on purpose to show the message, but we set more useful counters to monitor in Chapter 9.

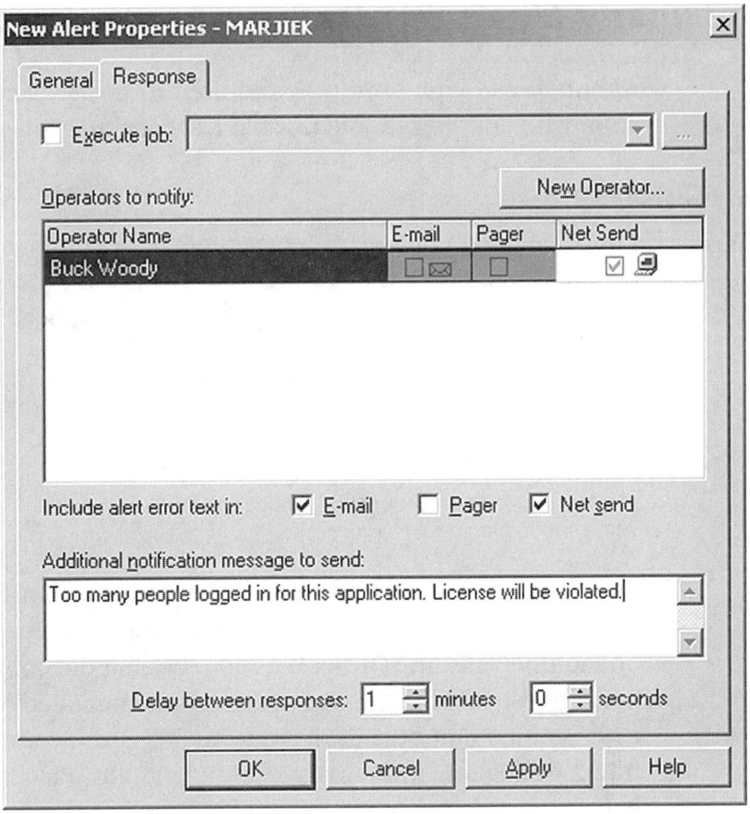

Figure 6.26
Setting the
response

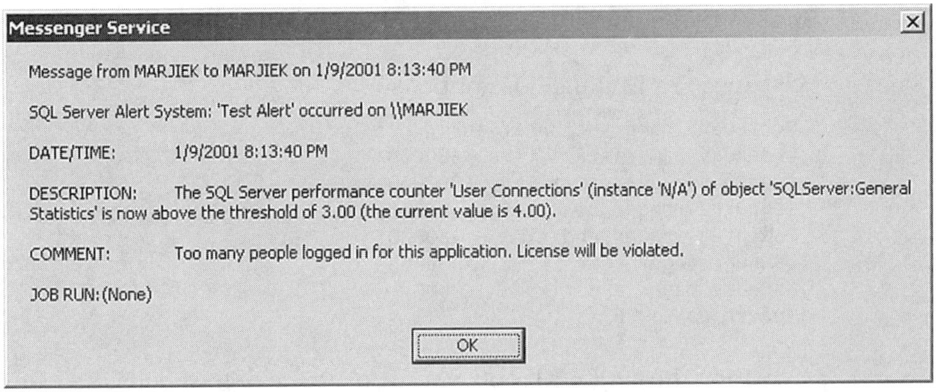

Figure 6.27   Getting the message

Command Line

Although you won't often be required to create Alerts or Operators using the command line, you should be able to create and trigger Jobs.

Operators

I don't recommend creating Operators with commands, but at times this may be necessary. Using the script shown in Listing 6.2, you can create the same Operator you made earlier using Enterprise Manager.

Listing 6.2   Creating an Operator

```
EXECUTE msdb.dbo.sp_add_Operator
@name = 'Buck Woody'
,@enabled = 1
,@email_address = 'woodyb@yahoo.com'
,@netsend_address = 'marjiek'
```

There are a couple of interesting things to notice about this script. The first is where I've placed the commas. Remember that you can type commands on multiple lines in SQL Server 2000. Placing the commas at the *beginning* of the line instead of at the end prevents a common error. When you're typing an extensive amount of code, it's easy to forget the comma placement and spend hours debugging an embarrassing oversight. Placing the commas this way helps you spot the proper places for commas.

You might have also noticed that the pager schedule, along with a few other items, isn't in the script. If you want to add that, append the code in Listing 6.3 to the one in Listing 6.2.

Listing 6.3   Adding more options

```
,@category_name = '[Uncategorized]'
,@weekday_pager_start_time = 80000
,@weekday_pager_end_time = 180000
,@saturday_pager_start_time = 80000
,@saturday_pager_end_time = 180000
,@sunday_pager_start_time = 80000
,@sunday_pager_end_time = 180000
,@pager_days = 62
```

Using the graphical tools, you were also able to specify the Alerts this Operator would receive, without leaving the Operators panel. Let's see how to do that in code as well. The code in Listing 6.4 shows how to add one of the standard errors that come with SQL Server 2000 to the Operator you just created.

Listing 6.4 Adding the Alert

```
EXECUTE msdb.dbo.sp_add_notification
@Alert_name = 'Demo: Full msdb log'
,@Operator_name = 'Buck Woody'
,@notification_method = 1
```

Alerts

I explain Alerts next, saving Jobs for last. Let's create the same custom Alert you made using the graphical tools. The code shown in Listing 6.5 creates the Alert you made earlier and adds the Operator that will be alerted.

Listing 6.5 Creating an Alert

```
EXECUTE msdb.dbo.sp_add_Alert @name = 'Test Alert'
, @message_id = 0
, @severity = 0
, @enabled = 1
, @delay_between_responses = 60
, @notification_message = 'Too many people logged in for this
application.'
, @performance_condition = 'SQLServer:General Statistics|User
Connections||>|5'
, @include_event_description_in = 5
, @category_name = '[Uncategorized]'

EXECUTE msdb.dbo.sp_add_notification
@Alert_name = 'Test Alert'
, @Operator_name = 'Buck Woody'
, @notification_method = 1
```

You won't normally create Alerts this way, but it is possible. The easiest way to create a script like this is to right-click a graphically created object and script it to file, using the methods detailed in Chapter 4.

Jobs

As opposed to Alerts and Operators, you can create Jobs and trigger them using the command line. Listing 6.6 shows a script that creates the Job we created earlier in the Graphical section. This listing is a bit long but reads quickly.

Listing 6.6 Creating the Job

```
-- First you'll add the Job
EXECUTE msdb.dbo.sp_add_Job
@Job_name = 'Test Job 1'
,@owner_login_name = 'sa'
,@description = 'Test for the Automation Chapter'
```

```
,@category_name = '[Uncategorized (Local)]'
,@enabled = 1
,@notify_level_email = 0
,@notify_level_page = 0
,@notify_level_netsend = 0
,@notify_level_eventlog = 2
-- The line below sets whether the Job will be deleted
-- after it runs
,@delete_level= 0

-- Next you'll add the Job Steps
EXECUTE msdb.dbo.sp_add_JobStep
@Job_name = 'Test Job 1'
, @Step_id = 1
,@Step_name = 'Show the Directory'
,@command = 'DIR C:\LOGS'
,@database_name = ''
,@server = ''
,@database_user_name = ''
,@subsystem = 'CmdExec'
,@cmdexec_success_code = 0
,@flags = 0
,@retry_attempts = 0
,@retry_interval = 1
,@output_file_name = 'c:\temp\dir.txt'
,@on_success_Step id = 0
,@on_success_action = 3
,@on_fail_Step_id = 0
,@on_fail_action = 2

EXECUTE msdb.dbo.sp_add_JobStep
@Job_name = 'Test Job 1'
,@Step_id = 2
,@Step_name = 'Query a table'
,@command = 'SELECT * FROM authors ORDER BY au_lname'
,@database_name = 'pubs'
,@server = ''
,@database_user_name = ''
,@subsystem = 'TSQL'
,@cmdexec_success_code = 0
,@flags = 0
,@retry_attempts = 0
,@retry_interval = 1
,@output_file_name = 'c:\temp\authors.csv'
,@on_success_Step_id = 0
,@on_success_action = 3
,@on_fail_Step_id = 0
,@on_fail_action = 2

EXECUTE msdb.dbo.sp_add_JobStep
@Job_name = 'Test Job 1'
,@Step_id = 3
,@Step_name = 'Calculate the Days'
```

```
,@command =
'Rem Setup the now and later times
RightNow = #9/16/00#
Later = #12/01/2001#
Rem Do the Work
n = DateDiff("d",RightNow,Later)
Rem Show the Output
Print "There are " & n & " days until the deadline." '
,@database_name = 'VBScript'
,@server = ''
,@database_user_name = ''
,@subsystem = 'ActiveScripting'
,@cmdexec_success_code = 0
,@flags = 0, @retry_attempts = 0
,@retry_interval = 1
,@output_file_name = ''
,@on_success_Step_id = 0
,@on_success_action = 1
,@on_fail_Step_id = 0
,@on_fail_action = 2

-- Now you'll set the Step order
EXECUTE msdb.dbo.sp_update_Job
@Job_name = 'Test Job 1'
,@start_Step_id = 1

-- Add the Job schedules
EXECUTE msdb.dbo.sp_add_Jobschedule
@Job_name = 'Test Job 1'
,@name = 'Nightly'
,@enabled = 1
,@freq_type = 4
,@active_start_date = 20010108
,@active_start_time = 0
,@freq_interval = 1
,@freq_subday_type = 1
,@freq_subday_interval = 0
,@freq_relative_interval = 0
,@freq_recurrence_factor = 0
-- this date code means never!
,@active_end_date = 99991231
,@active_end_time = 235959

-- And now add the Target Servers
EXECUTE msdb.dbo.sp_add_Jobserver
@Job_name = 'Test Job 1'
,@server_name = '(local)'
```

For the most part, the script explains itself, and where it hasn't, I've added some comment lines that start like this: `--`. Creating Jobs with a script can be a bit daunting. It's a lot easier to run these Jobs with a command. Look at Listing 6.7 for an example of initiating the Job you just created.

Listing 6.7 Firing the Job

```
USE msdb
EXEC sp_start_Job @Job_name = 'Test Job 1'
```

You'll notice a couple of things about this command. First, it started by setting a different database to run the command. This may be the first time you've
had to change databases to run something, but keep in mind that everything in
SQL Server 2000 is stored somewhere. It's sort of like the commands you run
on the command line of your operating system. Some are "intrinsic" or part of
the running operating system; others are files stored on your hard drive.

In the case of the operating system, to run a command that isn't intrinsic,
you need to be in the directory that houses the command or at least preface
the command with that location.

The same concept holds true for SQL Server 2000 commands. You can
either change to the database, as in Listing 6.7, or reference the database where
the command is stored, as in Listing 6.8.

Listing 6.8 Referencing the database

```
EXEC msdb..sp_start_Job @Job_name = 'Test Job 1'
```

The representation of all this is in the following format:

```
server.database.owner.object
```

But you can leave out the first part of any command as long as you're in that
server and database and you're the owner of the object. You can also leave off
any part of the four-part name as long as you include the periods it requires
and it doesn't violate anything.

For example, I left off the owner name in Listing 6.8; but since I am the
owner of that object, it's OK. Don't let all that bog you down for now; just
know that the sp_start_Job command lives in the msdb database.

Look at the output shown in Listing 6.9.

Listing 6.9 Error message

```
Server: Msg 2812, Level 16, State 62, Line 2
Could not find stored procedure 'sp_start_Job'.
```

If you see something like this, either you've spelled the command incorrectly,
or you're in the wrong database. Use the trick of highlighting the command
and pressing Shift+F1 for help. Jump down to the examples section displayed
in the help, and you'll see right away where the command lives.

There are some other parameters to this command; they involve the server name and the Step to start with. There are a couple of "cousins" to this command, which are fairly obvious. See Listing 6.10 for a few.

Listing 6.10   Other Job commands

```
sp_delete_Job
sp_help_Job
sp_stop_Job
```

Examples

Automation is a wonderful thing. You may have already extrapolated the previous information to create your own ideas about what you need to do.

Since I've covered the setup of the agent, I focus on two areas in the examples: creating a performance Alert and creating a Job to back up a database and copy it to a location after zipping it.

Finding Out When You Need More RAM

A good real-world use for Alerts is to let you know when the server is running low on resources. I focus on RAM here, but this monitor could be configured for any of the bottlenecks your server might have as far as SQL Server 2000 goes. I won't focus on the objects and counters right now because I cover that in Chapter 9.

I won't re-cover the ground I've already explained. At this point it might be helpful to refer to Figure 6.25, shown earlier in the chapter. Repeat the steps you performed there, and all you need to do to monitor the RAM instead of the user connections is to change the type of object you used.

Change the object from SQL Server:General Statistics to SQL Server:Buffer Manager and then change the User Connections counter to Buffer cache hit ratio. Specify to be alerted if this counter falls below 80%. This may not *necessarily* mean that the server needs more RAM, but if you get multiple alerts after SQL Server has been running for a while, it's worth knowing about.

This counter tells you how many times the server had to go to the hard drive to look up data instead of getting it from the cache, which is much faster. If you don't have much RAM, the server can't store things there, and it must go to the hard drive for data.

Back Up a Database, Zip It, Copy It

Not long ago, a client brought me a problem. They wanted to be able to trigger a backup whenever they wished and to save every backup forever. The server didn't have a lot of room on the hard drive, and backing up to a tape drive was problematic because the server was in a remote office and no one was available to change the tapes.

They also wanted to compress the backup file and then copy that much smaller file to a network share. And they wanted to automatically store those backups on a CD periodically.

The main difficulty I encountered was that I needed to uniquely identify each zip file. I couldn't use the backup wizard, which automatically stamps the date and time on the file, because the clients wanted to be able to trigger the backup whenever they wished.

I divided the solution into four parts:

1. Create a batch file for the users
2. Back up the database
3. Compress the backup file, naming it with a unique identifier
4. Copy the file

I could have written the process in Visual Basic, but I wanted to keep the entire process, other than the first Step, in SQL Server 2000. I accomplished this with a Job. Rather than show the screens, I'll cover the process and the commands I used to do this.

For Step 1, I created a batch file that connects to SQL Server 2000 and starts a Job. I explained earlier how to kick off a Job from the command line, and I discussed how to use the osql command in Chapter 3. I put both of those concepts together and create a batch file with the commands shown in Listing 6.11. In this batch file, I use a trusted connection (so that no one runs the file who isn't supposed to) and then execute a Job. This part was pretty simple.

Listing 6.11   BackMeUp.cmd file

```
@echo off
cls
osql –E –d master –Q"EXEC msdb..sp_start_Job @Job_name = 'Zip Files'"
```

Next, I created a Job that has three steps. The first Step is a Transact SQL-type Job, and it contains the command shown in Listing 6.12.

Listing 6.12 First Step

```
BACKUP DATABASE pubs to disk = 'c:\temp\pubs.bak' WITH INIT
```

I haven't explained the BACKUP command yet, but the command shown in Listing 6.12 backs up the pubs database to a file called 'c:\temp\pubs.bak'. The WITH INIT part overwrites a backup file if it exists; otherwise, SQL Server adds each backup to the same file. Sometimes you want that; this time you don't.

Next, I created another *Transact SQL Step* using the commands shown in Listing 6.13.

Listing 6.13 Creating the zip file

```
-- Zip up the backup file
DECLARE @ZIPME char(255)
SET @ZIPME = 'c:\batch\pkzip -add=incremental c:\temp\pubs' + (SELECT
-- Get the date in yymmdd format and set the copy command to use that name
CONVERT(char(6),GETDATE(),12))+'.zip c:\temp\pubs.bak'
-- Run the operating system command with the parameters just created
EXEC master..xp_cmdshell @ZIPME
```

If you're not a T-SQL developer, you can just replace the parameters I explain next to use this code.

First, I set aside some memory space in SQL Server 2000 for the command by declaring a variable, @ZIPME, to hold the command. Next, I ran the pkzip compression program to create a compressed file with the date as part of the name. This keeps the backups different by date. To get that date, use the Transact SQL command CONVERT(char(6),GETDATE(),12)).

I next interrupted the filename with this command (watching the quotes) and then continued with the syntax from pkzip to include the file. This creates a unique filename, with the date embedded.

I then created one more *Step*, which you can probably make without my help. It's an *Operating System Command* type, shown in Listing 6.14. You can see here that I've copied the test file from temp to holder, but that can be changed to anywhere, even to a network drive or an FTP location.

Listing 6.14 Copying the file

```
copy c:\temp\*.zip c:\holder
```

If you try this example, you can change the *Job Steps* to do things such as deleting the .bak file when the *Job* is done and adding a *Notification* or *Schedule*.

You can also change the logic you used to add a date to the filename into logic that creates a numerically sequential version stamp or any other scheme you need. The point is that this Job can be scripted, modified, and added to any other server.

Rosetta Stone

I couldn't locate a base-product tool in Oracle that equates to the SQL Server Agent. There are external tools that can work the way SQL Server Agent does, but most Oracle DBAs I spoke with use operating system commands to automate Oracle tasks. Keep in mind that Oracle runs on many platforms, and many of those, such as UNIX, have a far richer set of automation tools than Windows NT.

This is also true for Microsoft Access. The difference is that most Access automation is done within programs that use Access as a back end.

Resources

Another good explanation about SQL Server Agent, even if it is version 7:
   http://www.mssqlserver.com/articles/sqlagent_p1.asp
A little more about scheduling, version 7 again (it still applies, though):
   http://www.microsoft.com/technet/sql/admovw.asp
Scripting languages, tutorials, and samples:
   http://msdn.microsoft.com/scripting/

Chapter 7

Maintenance

Chapter at a Glance

This chapter focuses on the maintenance of your databases. This is the most important chapter in the book.

The Resources section contains references for:

- Jobs
- Tasks
- Other maintenance

Read Chapters 2, 3, and 6 before reading this chapter.

Overview

The most important and least glamorous tasks a DBA performs are those that involve maintenance. It's the kind of thing that if you do, nobody notices; but if you don't, *everybody* knows.

There are two types of maintenance tasks: tasks that keep the database going and tasks that keep the database going *fast*. I explain both types of tasks in this chapter, with a heavier focus on the first. The fast part I examine more closely in Chapter 9.

If you're already a DBA using another platform, you'll be pleased with how easy it is to maintain a database in SQL Server 2000. In fact, it's one of the main selling points for the product. Wizards are provided for almost everything you need to keep the database in shape.

The primary tool I'll describe for database maintenance is the Database Maintenance Wizard. This graphical tool walks you through setting up a scheduled plan that can include integrity checks, optimizations, and backups. These plans can be edited at any time.

The second set of tools are the T-SQL Database Consistency Check (DBCC) commands. They perform maintenance tasks on a database or an index, as well as on filegroups. There are four categories of DBCC commands: maintenance, miscellaneous, status, and validation statements. This chapter focuses on the maintenance commands.

Detail

You must understand the physical structure of the database engine to understand why you need to perform maintenance.

Physical Structure

Data is stored in files on the hard drive. Because the data is constantly modified, SQL Server 2000 sets aside an entire area of the hard drive to work with. Within this space, the engine places data in smaller sections called pages, which are 8K long.

As an illustration, you can act as a database engine. Think of a piece of paper eight lines long. You write information on the piece of paper as you take orders. Some orders are small, only a few lines long; and others are longer, perhaps several pages. After you enter an order, it can be modified.

Let's assume you've entered order number 1 on page 1, and it's two lines long, as shown in Table 7.1.

Next you enter order number 2, which is seven lines long. Looking at your order sheets, you now have two pages of information. On page 1 you have two lines from one order and six lines from order 2. The second page contains one line from the second order, as shown in Table 7.2.

Table 7.1 First Order, First Page

Order 1	Item 1	Client 1
Order 1	Item 2	Client 1

Table 7.2   Second Order, Second Page

Order 1	Item 1	Client 1
Order 1	Item 2	Client 1
Order 2	Item 1	Client 2
Order 2	Item 2	Client 2
Order 2	Item 3	Client 2
Order 2	Item 4	Client 2
Order 2	Item 5	Client 2
Order 2	Item 6	Client 2
Order 2	Item 7	Client 2

The client from order 1 calls back and adds two more items to her order. You dutifully record the items on the second page, where you have room, as shown in Table 7.3. RDBMS systems really work like this, and I'll use this description throughout the rest of the chapter.

Making a database fast is often a function not only of maintenance but also of design. Because you probably can't redesign your database, I'll focus on maintaining the internal structures of SQL Server 2000 to optimize the database.

The two primary tools for maintaining your databases are the *Maintenance Wizard* and the DBCC commands.

Table 7.3   First Order, Second Page

Order 1	Item 1	Client 1
Order 1	Item 2	Client 1
Order 2	Item 1	Client 2
Order 2	Item 2	Client 2
Order 2	Item 3	Client 2
Order 2	Item 4	Client 2
Order 2	Item 5	Client 2
Order 2	Item 6	Client 2
Order 2	Item 7	Client 2
Order 1	Item 3	Client 1
Order 1	Item 4	Client 1

The Maintenance Wizard

I've taught several classes on SQL Server, and I always tell my students about the SQL Server Maintenance Wizard. I've visited some of these same students' offices later, and in a few I've been shocked to see that even the simple step of setting up a maintenance plan using a wizard has been ignored. Invariably, after the wizard has been set up and run, the users see a dramatic difference in the speed of database access.

The Maintenance Wizard creates a group of Jobs and Schedules called a plan. This plan can be edited after you create it. You should set up one plan per database—even though you can choose more than one database in a single plan. If you create the plans separately, each of them can have separate schedules and tasks.

You should also create a plan for the system databases, especially master and msdb. You may recall from earlier chapters that the information in these databases involves logins and server configuration information (master) and the SQL Server Agent information (msdb). You should protect this information, and the wizard provides an easy way to do that.

The Maintenance Wizard automatically performs tasks in the following areas:

- Optimizations
- Integrity
- Backups
- Reporting

Let's look at the optimizations step first.

Optimizations

As data is entered into and deleted from the database, the defined space mentioned earlier becomes a bit fragmented, much like the files on your hard drive. The optimizations portion of the wizard examines three things in your database that affect this storage. The first item the wizard examines and changes is fragmentation. You also can select how much free space for new data will be left when the wizard is done defragmenting. How much space should you choose, and why? The explanation goes deeply into whether your database is data-entry-more-often versus read-more-often.

If your database is used primarily for data entry, it's best to leave a bit more space at the end of each page so that data stays together. This largely prevents the mixed data pages displayed in Table 7.3 earlier in the chapter.

If your database is composed of data that's read more often than it's written, such as a report server, leave a lower percentage of the page space free. In this case fewer pages have to be read into memory, thus saving time.

Both of these recommendations are a bit broad, but there's a good treatment on this topic in *Books Online* under DBCC SHOWCONTIG that explains how to monitor your database to determine a good fill factor. You can usually take the default on most of the questions asked when using the wizard, if you're not sure which value to select.

The second item the optimizations step performs for you is to update database statistics. Statistics are samples of data that assist the SQL Server 2000 search engine in locating data quickly. As data is added and deleted, these statistics become outdated.

You can keep statistics updated in two ways: by selecting this item while using the wizard or by setting a database option that automatically updates them. I explained this option in Chapter 4.

You pay a small performance penalty when the server takes time to update the statistics on the fly, and some programs have a problem with it. See the owner's manual for your software to see if it is mentioned. As a rule, I normally leave this option on for the database; and the wizard grays that item out, indicating that it's not necessary to check the statistics.

The last thing the optimizations step does is to remove any free space from the database. Recall that SQL Server 2000 allocates space in an operating system file and then uses space within that file. When data is deleted, space in the file isn't automatically reclaimed. This setting in the wizard handles shrinking the database at a specific recurring time. A database option can be set to auto-shrink the database. The same caveats from earlier apply.

The next step in the wizard checks the integrity of the database.

Database Integrity

For the most part, SQL Server 2000 is one of the most stable RDBMS platforms you'll ever encounter. It's designed to recover from just about anything all by itself. Even so, it's always prudent to check the integrity of a database from time to time. This step offers to correct any minor errors for you, which means that only checks that don't change data are performed. This is normally a safe option to set.

The next step involves backing up the database and potentially the logs.

Database Backups

You can back up your database or logs to tape or hard drive. The hard drive location can be broken into different directories for each database, and the wizard deletes backups from the hard drive that are older than a certain age.

The final step in the wizard involves recording all these activities and sending Notifications. The reports can be sent to disk, to a central server, to a history table, and to an operator, or all the above.

In a word, the Maintenance Wizard performs all the maintenance most systems need.

DBCC Commands

The next set of tools at your disposal are the DBCC commands, which are typed at the command line. As a matter of fact, the Maintenance Wizard uses many of these commands to do its magic. There are several maintenance commands, many of which can fix issues in addition to reporting them.

The DBCC commands I'll discuss are:

- DBCC CHECKDB
- DBCC CHECKTABLE
- DBCC DBREINDEX

The DBCC CHECKDB command examines an entire database for corruption. I'll describe the switches used with this command to indicate errors and perform various levels of repair.

DBCC CHECKDB

DBCC CHECKDB is the primary command that Microsoft recommends because it checks all the tables and indexes in a database. Although you can run this command in a diagnostic mode while people are using the system, the database must be set to single-user mode to correct any problems. I do that in the Examples section.

DBCC CHECKTABLE

The DBCC CHECKTABLE command does the same thing that DBCC CHECKDB does except against just one table. You can also use this command while people are using the system unless you're using the repair functions.

DBCC DBREINDEX

The DBCC DBREINDEX command updates the indexes on a server. Indexes point to the location of data, which speeds things up. Think of looking for the subject "backups" in this book without using the index in the back. How quickly could you find all the references to that subject?

Indexes are just as important in a database. They point to locations of data, and they are stored just like data in pages. These pages become fragmented over time, and the DBCC DBREINDEX command defragments them.

You should be aware that this defragmentation process can be quite long, depending on the number of indexes, the size of the index, and the load on the server at the time the command runs.

Graphical

The Maintenance Wizard is the primary tool for maintaining your databases. It is so simple and takes so little time to implement that there is no excuse for not performing the steps on each of your databases.

The Maintenance Wizard

We examine this tool by setting up a live maintenance plan that you can leave in place on your test database. I have to steal a little thunder from the Examples section to describe the process.

Begin by opening Enterprise Manager, opening your server's name, and then drilling down to Maintenance, Database Maintenance Plans. Right-click that object and select New Maintenance Plan from the menu that appears. You'll see the screen shown in Figure 7.1. The introduction screen tells you what the wizard can do. Select Next, which brings up the screen in Figure 7.2.

Select your test database, but also notice the other choices. You have the option for the wizard to perform the same tasks on all databases. I don't like this choice because I often need different options per database, and a reported failure in one part of the wizard might be hard to spot. Notice as well that you can select just the system databases or all databases except the system databases.

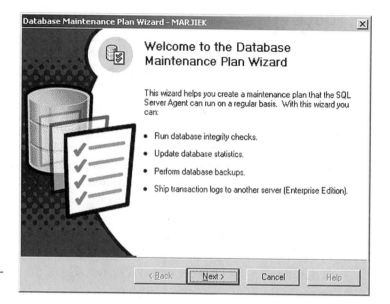

Figure 7.1
Creating a
new mainte-
nance plan

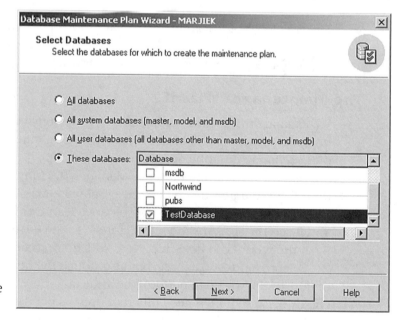

Figure 7.2
Selecting the
databases

As I mentioned earlier, you should make one plan per database, although you should create a plan for at least the two system databases *master* and *msdb*.

Select the test database you created. Then select Next to bring up the screen shown in Figure 7.3.

This panel sets the optimizations tasks. Notice that I've taken the defaults here, but you should change the schedule for this task. To do that, select the Change button to bring up the panel shown in Figure 7.4. In this panel you can see that the schedule is changed from a weekly recurrence to a nightly one. You shouldn't necessarily copy me in this choice; this part requires a little planning.

The issue involves the time it takes to perform the optimizations, as well as any other impacts, such as when users log in. On a small database, this isn't a big deal; but on a larger one, you need to monitor the time each step takes.

The other issue is how long the task takes to run. The logic goes like this: If the task runs once a week, it has a lot to do, and it takes a long time. If it runs more often, it doesn't have as much to do, and it doesn't take as long.

My suggestion is to set your schedule to your offpeak time and change it to offpeak days if the users are impacted. Make the changes and select OK to bring back the previous panel; then select Next to bring up the panel shown in Figure 7.5.

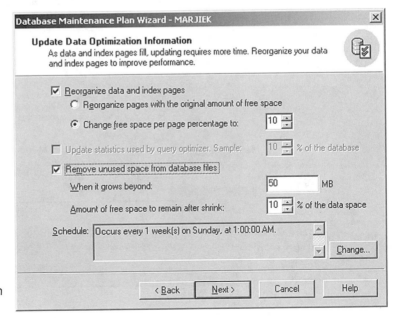

Figure 7.3
Optimization
options

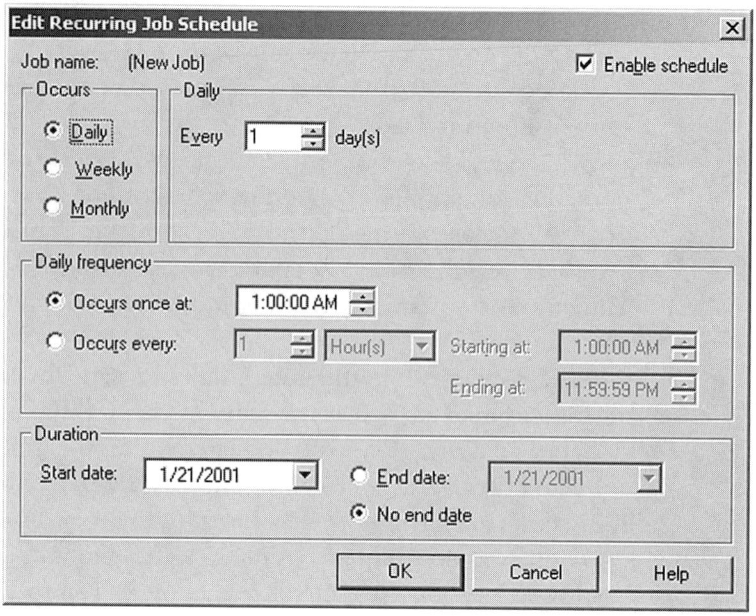

Figure 7.4
Changing
the schedule

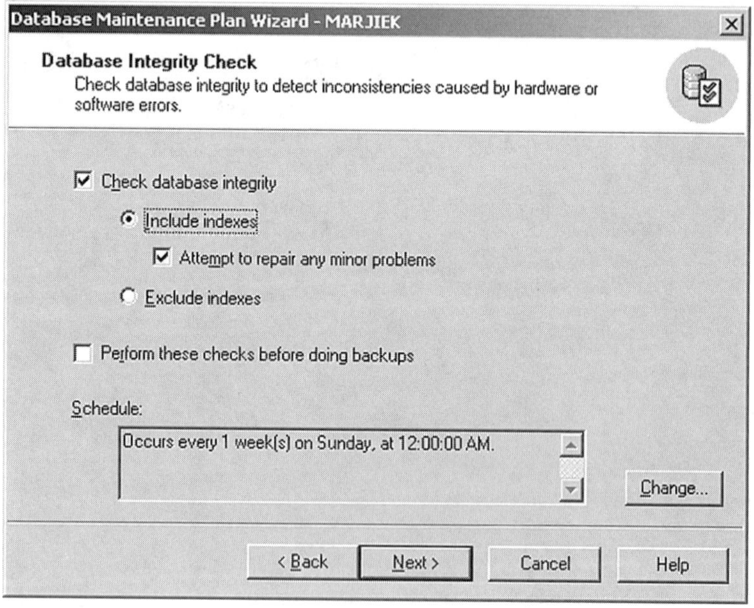

Figure 7.5
Database
integrity
checks

Here you select the integrity checks to run, which includes checking the integrity of indexes. You should tell the wizard to fix any minor problems it finds. Set this process to happen after the backups take place. This preserves a "pre-fixed" copy of the database in case the problem-correcting causes a problem. Change the schedule to happen each night rather than weekly. Now select OK and return to this panel; then select Next to move to the screen shown in Figure 7.6.

Here you select the backups to be placed on disk and that they will be verified when complete. I explain backup strategies fully in Chapter 8. This verification process just rereads the backup file and makes sure that the file is viable. This part takes a bit more time. Change the schedule to nightly, which brings you back to this panel. Select Next to bring up the panel that is shown in Figure 7.7.

Select the C:\TEMP directory for the backups and set the backups to be erased after one day. Why do this? If you can afford the space, it's nice to have the backup on a drive in case you need it quickly. Many sites send their tapes offsite each day for protection, so it takes time to get them back when needed. Leaving the file on the hard drive allows you to restore the database without

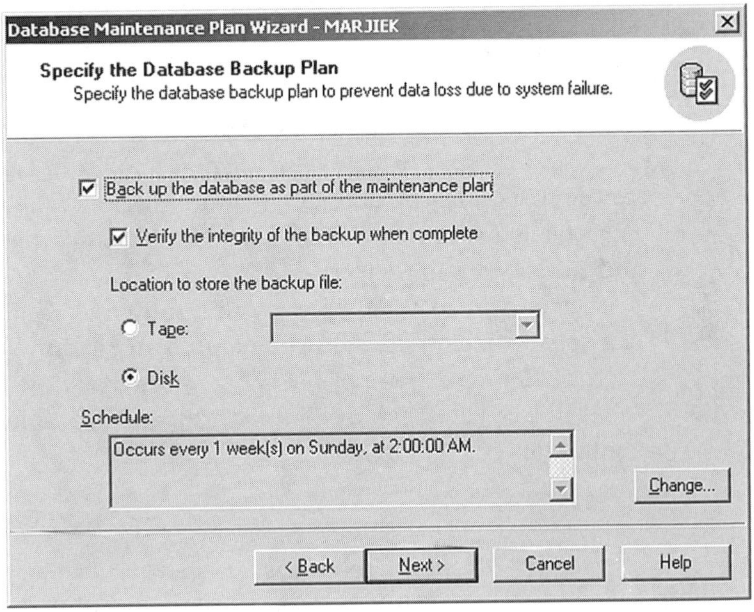

Figure 7.6
Database backup

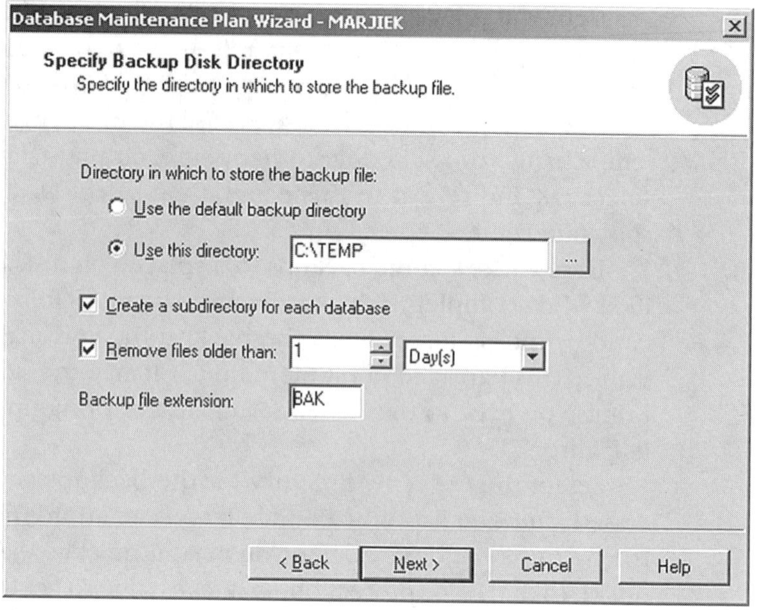

Figure 7.7
Backup
location

the tape. Notice also that you should select that the backups be placed in their own directories. This keeps things nice and tidy.

Select Next to bring up the panel shown in Figure 7.8. In this panel you can select the backup for the logs. Because your database is set to the Simple recovery model, you can't back up the logs; so changes are needed here. For more information on this setting, see Chapter 3.

Select Next to bring up the display shown in Figure 7.9. Here you select text reports, and you should have those deleted daily. You can have those reports mailed to you every day, because you set up that Mail profile in Chapter 2 and an Operator in Chapter 6.

Select Next to bring up the panel shown in Figure 7.10. In this panel you can select the activities of the maintenance plan to record to a table on the server. Later in the Examples section, I show you how to access this table to see the status of each step in the plan. You can also send this data to a table in a central server.

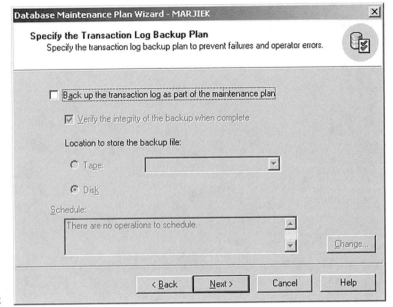

Figure 7.8
Transaction
log backups

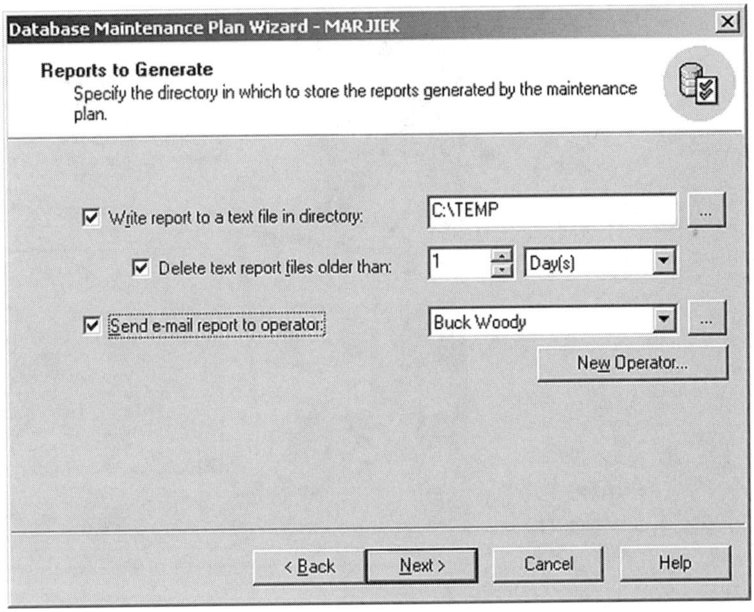

Figure 7.9
Reports

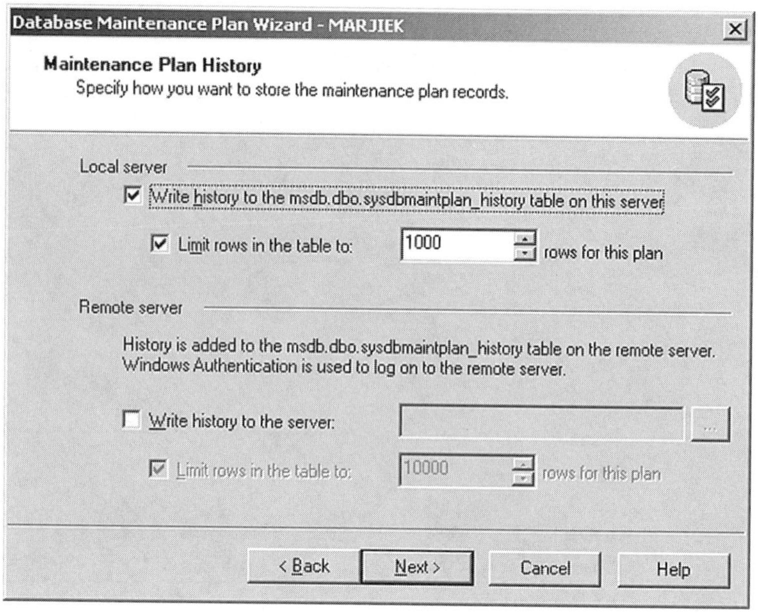

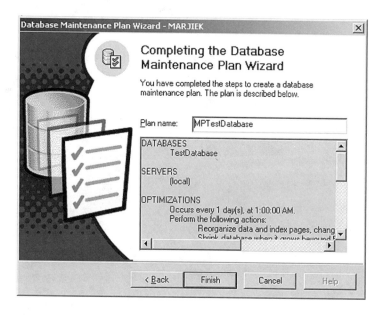

Figure 7.10
Maintenance
plan history

Figure 7.11
Saving the
plan

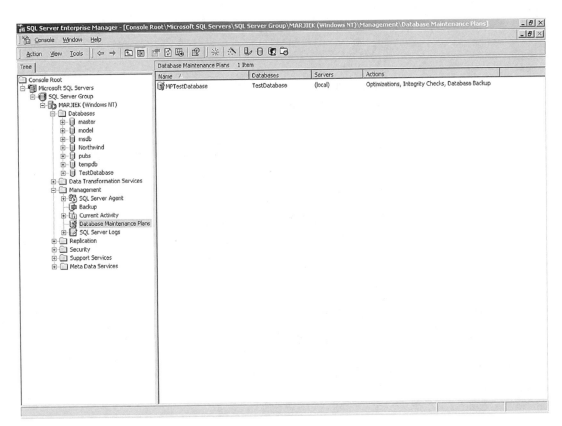

Figure 7.12   Maintenance plans object

Pick Next to bring up the display shown in Figure 7.11. Name the maintenance plan, and then click Finish. To demonstrate the capability to edit the plan once it's complete, drill back down to the Maintenance Plans object, as shown in Figure 7.12.

Double-click the maintenance plan you created, and the display shown in Figure 7.13 appears. You can use the tabs to edit any of the items set up earlier. Once you've made your changes, select OK to save them. SQL Server 2000 takes care of the rest.

Set your plan to run in a few minutes from now; we'll display the history of the plan a bit later.

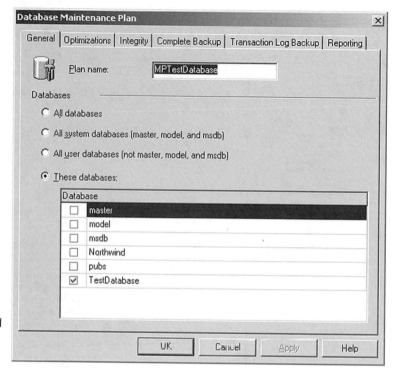

Figure 7.13
The completed
maintenance
plan

Command Line

Although the Maintenance Wizard is the way to proactively maintain your database, sometimes running reactive commands may be necessary.

Recovering a Suspect Database

You'll run into these situations sometimes if a database server is shut down incorrectly or if there is some hardware failure on the server. I've not run into a lot of these errors, but they can happen.

Sometimes a database just gives up the ghost on its own. You'll see a grayed-out icon next to your database's name and the word "suspect" tacked on next to it in Enterprise Manager.

If this happens to you, don't panic. The first thing to do is to locate the last good backup and have it handy. This is a good reason for having the backups on a hard drive.

NOTE: If this is a mission-critical, time-sensitive database, it might be prudent to initiate a service call to Microsoft.

You can employ one of two fixes to correct a suspect database. The first is simply to make sure that your drives have enough space. If they don't, clear some space. It's the most common error you'll see.

The second thing to do is to reboot the server, or at least stop and start the SQL Server 2000 services. The reason for this is that when SQL Server 2000 starts, it automatically attempts to fix any problems it can.

The problem may have been caused by an OS error rather than an SQL one, so rebooting is often a good shotgun method to fix things. If that doesn't do it, your database may need more drastic corrections.

The complete list of emergency tactics to take against a problem can be found in *Books Online* under the topic *Troubleshooting*. We'll examine a couple of those involving the DBCC commands. You definitely should open the manuals and delve a little further into this topic before you experience this problem; then plan on paper the steps to take.

DBCC Commands

Many problems can be checked and even corrected by using the DBCC commands. These commands are the primary tool to use at the command line to diagnose and correct your ailing database. I'll focus on two of them.

DBCC CHECKDB

The DBCC CHECKDB command checks every object in a database for what SQL Server 2000 calls "structural" integrity. This means that everything is where SQL Server 2000 expects to find it and responds correctly. It does not mean that your data is OK—just that the database is *structurally* OK. Because this command affects everything in the database, it's not a good idea to run it in the middle of the day or when the server is in heavy use. You can—it's just not a good idea. Let's look at running this command in several flavors against your test database.

First, open Query Analyzer and run the simplest form against the database, as shown in Listing 7.1. Here I've told the DBCC CHECKDB command to display the results of checking the database. Listing 7.2 shows the long output of the command. It's worth reading at least once.

Listing 7.1 Simple DBCC CHECKDB

```
DBCC CHECKDB ('TestDatabase')
GO
```

Listing 7.2 DBCC CHECKDB output

```
DBCC results for 'TestDatabase'.
DBCC results for 'sysobjects'.
There are 21 rows in 1 pages for object 'sysobjects'.
DBCC results for 'sysindexes'.
There are 31 rows in 1 pages for object 'sysindexes'.
DBCC results for 'syscolumns'.
There are 256 rows in 4 pages for object 'syscolumns'.
DBCC results for 'systypes'.
There are 26 rows in 1 pages for object 'systypes'.
DBCC results for 'syscomments'.
There are 92 rows in 4 pages for object 'syscomments'.
DBCC results for 'sysfiles1'.
There are 2 rows in 1 pages for object 'sysfiles1'.
DBCC results for 'syspermissions'.
There are 18 rows in 1 pages for object 'syspermissions'.
DBCC results for 'sysusers'.
There are 12 rows in 1 pages for object 'sysusers'.
DBCC results for 'sysproperties'.
There are 0 rows in 0 pages for object 'sysproperties'.
DBCC results for 'sysdepends'.
There are 196 rows in 1 pages for object 'sysdepends'.
DBCC results for 'sysreferences'.
There are 0 rows in 0 pages for object 'sysreferences'.
DBCC results for 'sysfulltextcatalogs'.
There are 0 rows in 0 pages for object 'sysfulltextcatalogs'.
DBCC results for 'sysfulltextnotify'.
There are 0 rows in 0 pages for object 'sysfulltextnotify'.
DBCC results for 'sysfilegroups'.
There are 1 rows in 1 pages for object 'sysfilegroups'.
CHECKDB found 0 allocation errors and 0 consistency errors in database 'TestDatabase'.
DBCC execution completed. If DBCC printed error messages, contact your system administrator.
```

The rows in the pages that you see in the display conceptually correspond to Tables 7.1 through 7.3 that I showed earlier. Notice from the output that all the tables are checked. These include database system tables that SQL Server 2000 uses to track itself.

If the DBCC CHECKDB command finds a problem, you'll need to take steps to correct it. My standard operating procedure is to perform the less risky corrections first and then move to a more drastic command if that's necessary.

To do that, the server needs to be in single-user mode so that the users aren't able to access data. Notify your users to log out. If they don't or can't, you can use the T-SQL command `kill` to forcibly disconnect them. The process ID it needs can be derived from *Enterprise Manager* in the *Current Activity* object. Use the *Properties* menu item, *Options* tab, on a database using *Enterprise Manager*, and set the database to *single user*.

I recommend the command shown in Listing 7.3 in *Query Analyzer*. This method is a bit safer than using *Enterprise Manager* because *Enterprise Manager* can take multiple connections to the database.

Listing 7.3   Setting the database to single-user mode

```
ALTER DATABASE TestDatabase
SET SINGLE_USER
GO
```

Now that you've done that, you can go a bit further and allow the server to correct minor errors that it finds. The command to do this is shown in Listing 7.4.

Listing 7.4   DBCC CHECKDB with Repair Fast

```
DBCC CHECKDB ('TestDatabase', REPAIR_FAST)
GO
```

I won't bog you down with the output, which is the same as the output you saw in the earlier listing. The important thing is that the REPAIR FAST qualifier does the least amount of damage. As a matter of fact, this command is made to not lose any data. If that doesn't work, you escalate the DBCC routine to the command shown in Listing 7.5.

Listing 7.5   DBCC CHECKDB with Repair

```
DBCC CHECKDB ('TestDatabase', REPAIR_ALLOW_DATA_LOSS)
GO
```

This command is the most harmful but could save the overall database. When you run this command, SQL Server 2000 takes the gloves off and fixes the data any way it can. You get messages based on what was fixed, and you should print those so you can do a postmortem on the results. I recommend using this command only on a database that you're willing to restore from an earlier backup.

When you're finished, you need to put the database back in multiuser mode, or no one will be able to get in. The command to do that is shown in Listing 7.6.

Sometimes you don't need to fix a problem; you just want to update the indexes on a database. You do that with the next DBCC command, DBREINDEX.

Listing 7.6   Setting the database to multiuser mode

```
ALTER DATABASE TestDatabase
SET MULTI_USER
GO
```

DBCC DBREINDEX

The DBCC DBREINDEX command updates the indexes on any or all of the indexes in a database. In Listing 7.7 I've lifted the example from *Books Online* to demonstrate this command, since we didn't create any indexes on your test database.

Listing 7.7   DBCC DBREINDEX from *Books Online*

```
DBCC DBREINDEX ('pubs.dbo.authors', UPKCL_auidind, 80)
GO
```

In this example, I've selected the *authors* table in the *pubs* database and then specified a particular index on that table. All indexes have names that you can set; but if you don't, SQL Server 2000 sets them for you.

The number on the right specifies how full the index will be, which in turn indicates how much room is left for new index information. There's a whole section on choosing this number in *Books Online*; I cover that topic a bit more in Chapter 9.

Examples

As I mentioned earlier, I stole a little thunder from this section by placing an example of creating a plan in the Graphical section. Because your time is valuable and you've already seen the process once, I won't repeat that process here.

I discuss a neat query that shows the success of a maintenance plan, and I also show an example of correcting a corrupt database.

Checking the Success of a Maintenance Plan

Recall that you created a maintenance plan earlier in the chapter and you selected that the history of the plan be stored in a table in the local server. You can now use the query shown in Listing 7.8 to see the results of that history table. The output is shown in Listing 7.9.

Listing 7.8   Query to show the maintenance plan history

```
SELECT plan_name
, activity
, succeeded
, Duration
FROM
msdb.dbo.sysdbmaintplan_history
```

Listing 7.9   Maintenance plan query output

```
plan_name        Activity                       succeeded  duration
MPTestDatabase   Rebuild Indexes                1          1
MPTestDatabase   Shrink Database                1          1
MPTestDatabase   Check Data and Index Linkage   1          3
MPTestDatabase   Backup database                1          3
MPTestDatabase   Verify Backup                  1          0
MPTestDatabase   Rebuild Indexes                1          1
MPTestDatabase   Shrink Database                1          0
```

The "duration" column is in minutes. Notice also the column called "succeeded." This column returns a 1 for each successful part of the plan and a 0 for those that were not. Knowing that, you can tack on the line WHERE succeeded = 0 at the bottom to display just the parts that didn't work. Combine this script with the Web page you created using the *Web Assistant Wizard* in Chapter 4, and you have an automatically updated Web page that shows the status of your maintenance plans.

Correcting a Suspect Database

This section demonstrates the correction steps I talked about earlier in the chapter. To do this, I had to run scripts to corrupt my database, but I won't show those here. The database I corrupted is called *pubs2* and is a mirror copy of the *pubs* database. You'll learn how to make a mirror copy of a database in Chapter 8.

In this example, the situation is that your users began to complain that a program that uses a SQL Server 2000 database has suddenly stopped working. You investigate the problem, and it seems that everyone is getting the same errors in the same location, making you suspicious that something endemic is wrong. You check the user's program files and middle tier, and everything seems to be in order. You begin to suspect that the database may have a problem.

The first step is to diagnose the error rather than blindly attempting to correct it, so you type the DBCC CHECKDB command and receive the output, both shown in Listing 7.10. I've removed the nonerror parts to save you some reading time.

Listing 7.10 Detecting a corrupt database

```
DBCC CHECKDB('pubs2')
GO
-------------------
DBCC results for 'pubs2'.
DBCC results for 'roysched'.
Server: Msg 7965, Level 16, State 2, Line 1
Table error: Could not check object ID 213575799, index ID 0 due to invalid
allocation (IAM) page(s).
Server: Msg 8968, Level 16, State 1, Line 1
Table error: IAM page (53764:0) (object ID 213575799, index ID 0) is out of the
range of this database.
Server: Msg 8996, Level 16, State 1, Line 1
IAM page (53764:0) for object ID 213575799, index ID 0 controls pages in filegroup
0, that should be in filegroup 1.
Server: Msg 2576, Level 16, State 1, Line 1
IAM page (0:0) is pointed to by the previous pointer of IAM page (1:110) object ID
213575799 index ID 0 but was not detected in the scan.
Server: Msg 2575, Level 16, State 1, Line 1
IAM page (53764:0) is pointed to by the next pointer of IAM page (0:0) object ID
213575799 index ID 2 but was not detected in the scan.
Server: Msg 7965, Level 16, State 1, Line 1
Table error: Could not check object ID 213575799, index ID 2 due to invalid
allocation (IAM) page(s).
Server: Msg 8968, Level 16, State 1, Line 1
Table error: IAM page (53764:0) (object ID 213575799, index ID 2) is out of the
range of this database.
Server: Msg 8996, Level 16, State 1, Line 1
IAM page (53764:0) for object ID 213575799, index ID 2 controls pages in filegroup
0, that should be in filegroup 1.
Server: Msg 2576, Level 16, State 1, Line 1
IAM page (0:0) is pointed to by the previous pointer of IAM page (1:134) object ID
213575799 index ID 2 but was not detected in the scan.
There are 0 rows in 0 pages for object 'roysched'.
CHECKDB found 5 allocation errors and 4 consistency errors in table 'roysched'
(object ID 213575799).
CHECKDB found 5 allocation errors and 4 consistency errors in database 'pubs2'.
DBCC execution completed. If DBCC printed error messages, contact your system
administrator.
```

Now that you've determined that the database has a problem, you check to determine what it is. Reading from Listing 7.10, you see that you have both allocation (structural) and consistency (data-related) errors.

You try the least harmful fix first, using the DBCC CHECKDB command with the REPAIR_FAST option. Before you do that, you need to get everyone out of the database, and make a backup. You also need to set the database to single-user. You can do that with the commands shown in Listing 7.11.

Listing 7.11   Setting the database to single-user mode

```
ALTER DATABASE pubs2
SET SINGLE_USER
GO
```

Now that you've done that, try the gentle fix. The commands are shown in Listing 7.12. I won't bore you with the output I got, but I can tell you it wasn't good!

Listing 7.12   DBCC command with least amount of damage

```
DBCC CHECKDB ('pubs2', REPAIR_FAST)
GO
```

Since we now know you could lose data, we make sure you have a current good backup. Type the next command, shown in Listing 7.13.

Listing 7.13   DBCC command with possible data loss

```
DBCC CHECKDB ('pubs2', REPAIR_FAST)
GO
```

You glance at the screen and notice that there are still errors in the output. You count them, and there are fewer. Repeat the command in Listing 7.13. This time you have no errors. You then check the data, and nothing is lost.

The method used was a bit of a "shotgun." We used the DBCC CHECKDB command instead of some of the other, more focused DBCC commands, which might have been more advisable. We were looking for the fastest solution to the problem, and the DBCC CHECKDB command checks the entire database. If this command doesn't fix the problem, you can always restore the backup you made before you began. You can then attempt to fix the database using the other DBCC commands. This approach isn't as useful if the database is large or time is of the essence. In that case, I would advise that call to Microsoft.

Notice also that we repeated the DBCC command. This is a common practice if the first run corrected some, but not all, errors. At other times, you'll run one type of DBCC command and then another type to fix the errors you'll get. If you get into that predicament, look up the DBCC commands in *Books Online* before you try your corrections.

Once you're done, comb through the logs, both Windows and SQL, to do a postmortem to find out how you got here. You should also document what happened so you (or someone) will know what to do if the problem reoccurs.

I've covered a very basic problem with databases. Countless problems can occur, but most are correctable. On the whole, SQL Server 2000 is incredibly stable, and I've not experienced any corruption problems with the 30-plus large databases I manage on as many servers. As a matter of fact, I had to go through quite a few gymnastics to corrupt a database for this example!

Rosetta Stone

You'll find that the commands for solving database problems are the one area that diverges the most in database platforms because each deals with that based on how it's put together. Therefore, the commands I parallel are fairly broad.

Oracle

Oracle doesn't have an automatic maintenance wizard in the 8i version I have, although there are some after-market products available to do the job.

Some tasks, such as backups, can be accessed through the graphical tools, but most of Oracle's tools for maintaining the database are command-driven. You can see these Commands compared with SQL Server 2000 in Table 7.4.

To be sure, there are many more commands in Oracle (and SQL Server, as you've seen) to maintain a database. Because of the difference in architectures, the two systems are maintained in ways that suit their particular physical implementation of an RDBMS. This isn't a cop-out for the lightness of the comparison, but the commands so distinctly diverge beyond what I've shown here that it's difficult to map them directly onto each other.

Table 7.4 Oracle and SQL Server maintenance commands

Task	Oracle Tool	Microsoft SQL Server 2000
Physical integrity check	DBVERIFY	DBCC commands
Reindex a current index	ALTER INDEX *index_name* REBUILD;	DBCC DBREINDEX
Back up and recover databases and logs	See Chapter 8	See Chapter 8

Redo Logs, Key-Compressed Indexes, and other Oracle constructs are simply not correlated in SQL Server 2000.

Microsoft Access

With Microsoft Access, there aren't many maintenance or recovery commands. The closest thing you have in Access to all the commands involving maintenance is the Compact and Repair Database menu item.

Resources

SQL scripts involving maintenance:
> *http://www.swynk.com/sqlhome/maintenance7.asp*

More on automating maintenance tasks:
> *http://www.microsoft.com/technet/SQL/manuals/admincmp/75517c06.asp*

Jobs:
> *http://www.sqlmag.com/Articles/Index.cfm?ArticleID=5492*

Chapter 8

Backing Up and Restoring

Chapter at a Glance

Read this chapter to find out about backing up and restoring SQL Server 2000 databases to and from disk or tape. This chapter also explains the recovery models SQL Server uses for its databases and how they affect backups and restoration.

The Resources section contains references for:

- More backup and recovery information
- Backing up databases to another server's tape drive

Read Chapters 4 and 7 before you read this one.

Overview

As I pen this chapter, I'm winging my way over the Atlantic to the United Kingdom. Because it's tough to land a plane on the ocean to correct any problems the crew might encounter, they explained to me that this aircraft is built with lots of redundant systems (I'm happy about that). The same concern holds true for database systems. Just in case *you* need to make an unexpected water landing, you should understand the various backup strategies available in SQL Server 2000. Specialized packages such as *Backup Exec* or *Arcserv* can also back up SQL Server 2000 databases with special agents. In this chapter, I concentrate on the native methods available in SQL Server 2000.

In addition to using the *Maintenance Wizard*, described in the last chapter, you can take backups from *Enterprise Manager* or with T-SQL commands.

There may be active connections while backups run but not while the restore process is in operation. You can back up the complete database (full backup), the transaction logs (log backup), or the changes since the last full backup (differential backup).

Recovery models were covered fully in Chapter 7 and apply to backups taken using the methods in this chapter as well. These recovery models are Simple, Bulk Logged, and Full.

The Simple recovery model removes data from the transaction log once it is moved to the database. With this model, the database can only be recovered to the last full backup, because these transactions are removed. Log backups cannot be taken with this model.

The Bulk Logged recovery model leaves each transaction in the log once it is moved to the database until a full or transaction log backup is taken. In this model, certain bulk activities are not fully passed through the logging process, so although the logs are fully available, not all information is in those logs. Because of that, the database can be recovered to the last transaction log backup but not to a specific point in time.

The Full recovery model leaves each transaction in the log once it is moved to the database until a full or transaction log backup is taken. With this model, the database can be recovered to the last transaction log backup or even a specific point in time. If the device the logs are stored on is available, there may be no data loss.

You can recover a database using Enterprise Manager or Query Analyzer. If the recovery is set to the Simple model, the recover process restores the last full backup, leaving the database usable. If the recovery model is set to Full or Bulk Logged, the recovery restores the last full backup, leaving the database nonoperational but able to restore log backups. The rest of the process restores the logs, in order, from earliest to last, leaving the database operational in the last log restoration.

Detail

In the last chapter, you used the Maintenance Wizard to create scheduled backups. There are reasons that you might want to take a separate backup, such as securing the database before an upgrade. Backups are taken not only for security but also to freeze a data set or to move a database from one server to another.

In its simplest form, the database backup and restore procedure for SQL Server 2000 is incredibly easy. One command or just a few clicks in Enterprise

Manager perform a backup or restore one. You can make these backups to disk, network shares, or tape. If you need a test database to play with, you can easily get one by backing up the current database and restoring it with another name. You don't have to create a set of special files first or make any other changes to your database server to do this.

As a matter of fact, the users don't even have to be out of the database during the backup, although that's usually a good idea. Both the backup and the user activity will be slightly slower.

Once the database is backed up, it's an equally simple matter to restore it, even to another server. During a restore, the users cannot access the database. Backups can be taken graphically or with the command-line tools, and they can also be scheduled.

The backup and restore process isn't difficult and usually is quite fast. Even so, for large databases, in the multigigabyte range, the process can take more than a few hours to complete. You might wonder what data is stored in the backup file if the backup starts at midnight but doesn't complete until one o'clock in the morning, and people are still entering data in the database. The answer is the last piece of data that makes it into the database at one o'clock in the morning.

Backing Up Databases

Even though backing up a simple database is easy, rarely are things in their simplest form.

One of the primary variables that affects your backup is the size of the database. Obviously, a bigger database means a longer, larger backup. If a database is quite large, it may not fit on a single tape or one drive location. This longer backup may also take more time than is available to complete the backup.

To deal with these size and time issues, SQL Server 2000 provides the ability to stripe backups across multiple tapes or disk devices so that several devices can be combined. You can also structure your backups such that only the changes since the last backup are included.

Recovery Models

The next factor that affects your backups is the recovery model.

In most cases, when data is written to SQL Server 2000, it is written not to the database but to a separate file called the *log*. This log file contains all the individual data transactions, and a logging process writes those changes to the database. The committed data items are then marked to indicate they made it into the database, a process called a checkpoint. The recovery model determines what happens next.

If the database has been set to the Simple recovery model, after the change is written successfully to the database, the marked data is erased from the log file. In that way, the log shrinks and expands automatically if the database option auto shrink is on.

If the Bulk Logged model is selected for the database, changes are not erased after they make it to the database until you back up the database or log. Certain bulk-load operations are not completely logged, so all data may not make it to the log backups. Recovery can be as recent as the last log backup.

If the Full model is selected for the database, the changes are not erased from the log after they make it to the database and are erased only when you back up the database or log. In this model, all operations are logged, so all data makes it to the log backups. This slows the process of bulk-load operations but is safer. Recovery can be as recent as the last log backup or to a specific point in time.

Full Backups

As an example, imagine a database set to the Simple recovery model. You perform a full backup at midnight, when no one is using the database, and people start to enter data again at 7:00 in the morning. At 11:01 your server catches on fire, and after it is replaced, the backup you restore brings the database to a current state as of midnight the night before.

Log Backups

Next imagine the database is set to use the Full recovery model. You make that same midnight backup, and then every two hours, starting at 7:00, you make a separate backup of the log. A fire breaks out again at exactly 11:01. This time, however, you restore that midnight backup, making the database current as of midnight. Next you apply the 7:00, 9:00, and 11:00 log backups in that order. You've now lost only one minute's work.

Large Backups

The recovery model affects not only the level of recovery you can achieve but also the time it takes to create the backup.

With the database set to Simple recovery, you must perform a full backup of the database (there is an exception), which may take a while if the database is huge, in the multigigabyte range.

With the database set to the *Full* or *Bulk Logged* model, you perform that long full backup only periodically, and you perform periodic log backups that take very little time because they contain only the changes.

To restore the database to a good state, you restore the full backup and then each log backup in order, starting from the earliest. The other side of that coin is that it takes a bit longer to restore under the latter model because you have to do all the log restores in order.

Differential Backups

I mentioned an exception earlier. The exception involves something called a *differential* backup. This is sort of like an extended log backup (except in the *Simple* model), in that it backs up just the changes, but they are all the changes since the last full backup. This type of backup can be used with any of the recovery models.

Let's return to the combustible server example to illustrate. In the *Simple* recovery model, you back up the database at midnight as before. This time, however, you take a differential backup at 10:00, intending to do so every four hours thereafter. The server is again well engulfed in flames by 11:01, but this time, you are safe as of 10:00. What you have to do at this point is restore the full backup of midnight and then the differential one from 10:00.

In the *Full* and *Bulk Logged* models, assuming a large database, the strategy is that a full backup is taken on the weekend, which gets all data. Logs are backed up every two hours as usual, but because the database is so large, you would have to apply the full restore and then far too many log backups to be comfortable.

The answer to this dilemma is to perform a differential backup each night, which gets all the changes since the last full backup. You now don't need the log backups between the time you took the full and differential backups, because the differential backup is a kind of combined log backup. This strategy allows you to restore the full backup, the differential backup, and then only the log backups *since* the differential backup. The restore time in this model takes a lot less time. The trade-off here is that the differential backups can become quite large.

Backup Locations

Assuming that you've installed the required tape hardware and drivers on your NT or Windows 2000 system, you can send your backups there.

The first tape drive is referred to as \\.\TAPE0, replacing the 0 with the next number (1, 2, 3, etc.) for the other tape drives you have on your system.

The tape drives must be physically located on the server to do this, so you can't use remote tape drives with SQL Server 2000's native backup commands.

SQL Server 2000 backups can exist on the same tape as a Windows NT backup made with the NTBACKUP command, but you should put the SQL Server backup on first and set the backup switch that doesn't rewind the tape. I don't use this feature; I always feel a bit insecure about how much room will be left on the tape for either backup.

The other option is to send the backup directly to disk, specifying the path and filename directly. Your NT backup program can then back up these files because they aren't in use. In this model you should carefully monitor your drive space, and a good compression utility can bring the size of the .bak file to less than 25% of its original size. If you're going to do this, it usually makes sense to put the backup files on a drive other than the hard drive where the SQL databases are stored, for both speed and safety.

Backup Devices

Not only can you send the backup file directly to tape or hard drive paths, you can also specify a friendlier name by creating a logical device. I'll explain those a bit later.

Recovery Process

You can recover a database using Enterprise Manager or Query Analyzer. The types of commands depend on the recovery model of the database.

If the recovery is set to the Simple model, the recovery process restores the last full backup, leaving the database in a usable mode. This effectively closes the database and allows connections from users.

If the recovery model is set to Full or Bulk Logged, the recovery restores the last full backup, leaving the database nonoperational but able to restore log backups. To complete the backup, you restore the logs, in order, from earliest to last. At the last log restore, you leave the database operational.

Graphical

The first operation in this section is to create a backup device on your test system and then use that device to take a full database backup, finishing with a log backup directly to a physical disk device. We'll restore the database with a different name and then set that copy of the database such that you can perform a log backup.

Creating Backup Devices

First, we'll create a backup device—in this case, a disk device that you can use for your backup. Open *Enterprise Manager*, and open the *Management* item. Next, right-click the *Backup* item, as displayed in Figure 8.1. This brings up the panel shown in Figure 8.2.

Here you name the device and specify that the device go to a file on the hard drive. Keep in mind that the device you're creating here is just a name; whatever you specify is what you refer to during a backup. It's just a redirector used to make the backup process easier. It's also useful to create portable scripts, because

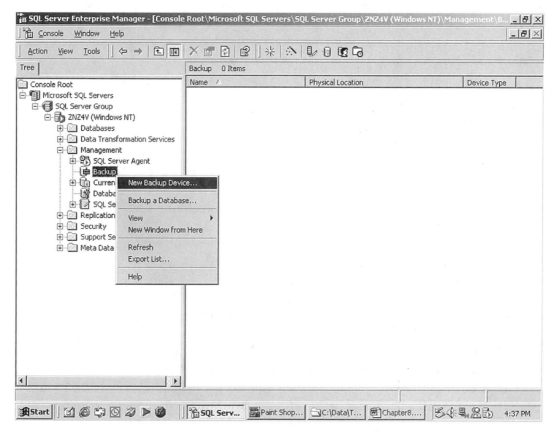

Figure 8.1 Creating a backup device

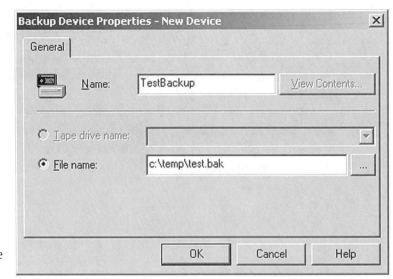

Figure 8.2
Naming the
device

that allows other administrators to create their own file or tape locations. If they follow the naming scheme, the script will work on just about any system.

Click OK to complete the creation of your device.

Backing Up a Database

To back up the database, simply right-click the database name—in this case, pubs—to bring up the floating menu, as shown in Figure 8.3. Select the item All Tasks and then Backup Database. Once you've done that, you get the panel shown in Figure 8.4 on page 268.

This action brings up the General tab, where you indicate the database that you wish to back up and the name of the backup. Notice the section that defines the type of database backup you can take. Here you can set the full or differential type of backup. You may have also noticed in the graphic that the option to back up the transaction log is grayed out, because the database is set to the Simple recovery model.

As the graphic shows, the backup will append to the device you've created, so you must be careful about that. You can add as many backups as the device has space for, but they will pile up in the file, and it's a bit less intuitive to extract a particular backup from it. You'll make the change in a moment to overwrite the device so that this backup is the only thing in it.

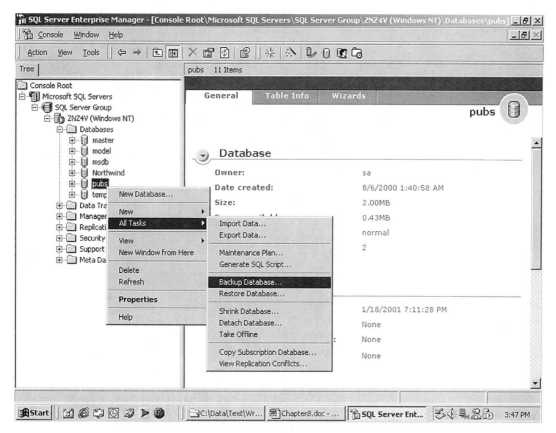

Figure 8.3   Beginning the backup

For now, click the *Add* button to select your backup device, which displays the screen shown in Figure 8.5. Select *Backup device*, and use the pull-down list to select the device you created earlier. Notice that you could have directly specified the filename.

Next select *OK*, and you'll see the screen in Figure 8.6.

Now you see the backup device listed in the *Destination* box. You can add other devices or files to that box, and if you have multiple tape drives connected directly to the system, you can specify them here. The backup stripes across all the tapes or file locations in parallel, but keep in mind that they'll

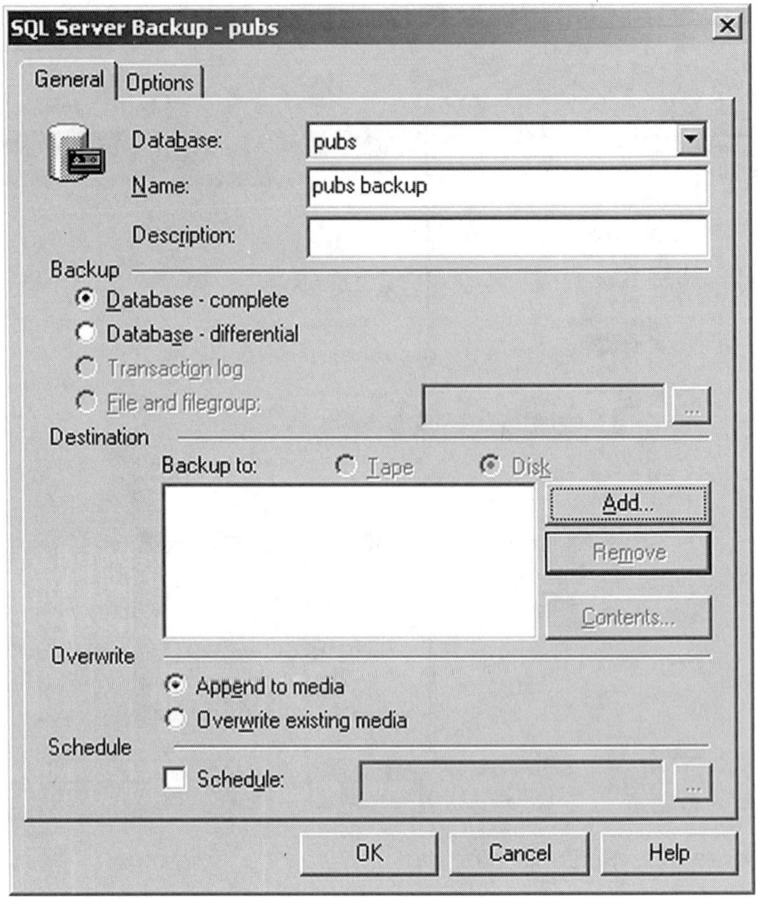

Figure 8.4
General tab

need to be available to restore the database. If you use this feature, make sure you experiment with it a bit.

You should also set the backup to overwrite the device so that you have only one backup in the file. As shown, don't set the backup to happen on a schedule. You're already using the Maintenance Wizard to do the repetitive backups; you're doing only a discrete backup here so that you can restore the database with a separate name.

Figure 8.5
Selecting
the backup
device

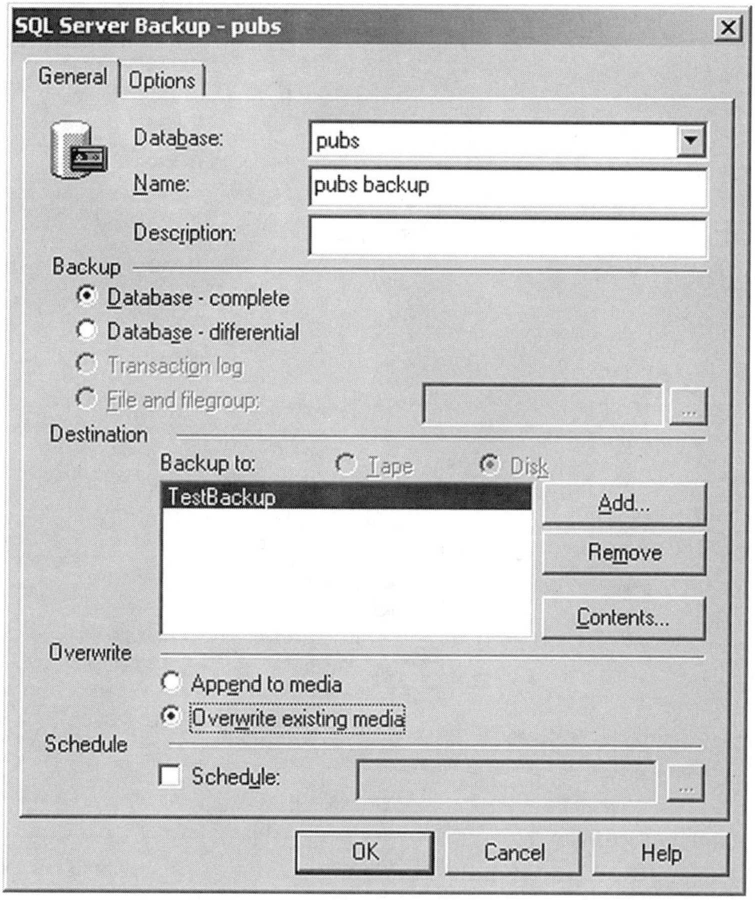

Figure 8.6
Setting
Overwrite

Now select the Options tab and bring up the panel shown in Figure 8.7. In this panel, you can select that the database backup be verified once it's complete. This process reads the backup to make sure it's valid. Unless the backup takes a long time, this is a usually a good option to select.

You can select an expiration for the backup, just in case this data is catastrophically time sensitive. In other words, you set a date for expiration if overwriting this backup could be harmful until after a certain date.

If you back up to tape, then you can initialize that media to format it. Select OK, and the panel in Figure 8.8 appears briefly.

It's always amazing to me how fast the backup runs in SQL Server 2000. Even fairly large databases perform the backup in a short time. After one second, the screen shown in Figure 8.9 appears. You may have had a screen be-

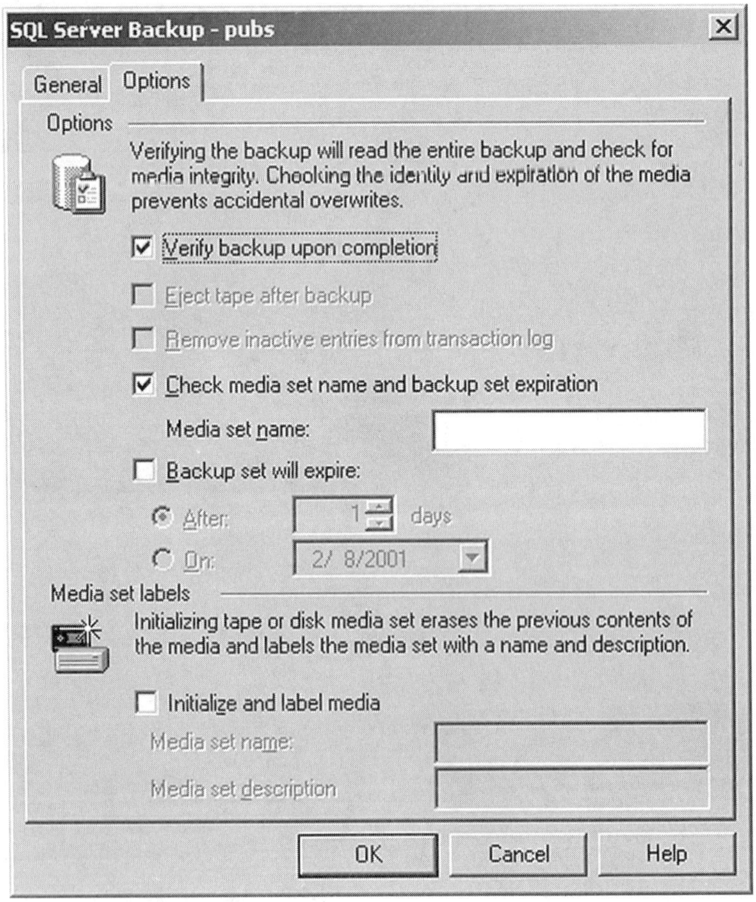

Figure 8.7
The Options
tab

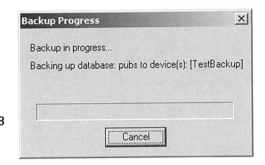

Figure 8.8
Backup
progress

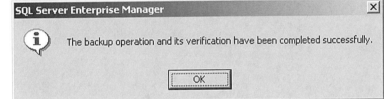

Figure 8.9
Database
backup
completion

fore this one, stating that the verification was being performed, but it was simply *way* too fast for me to capture.

Restoring a Database

Now that you have the backup safely stored in the file defined in your backup
device, let's restore from the file. Remaining in Enterprise Manager, select the
Databases object.

You can restore right over an existing database so long as no one's in it. See
Chapter 4 for information on how to set the database to single-user mode if
that's your goal.

Right-click the Databases object to bring up the same menu you did earlier,
but this time, under All Tasks, pick the Restore Database option, as shown in
Figure 8.10. Once you've selected that item, you'll see the panel shown in Figure 8.11. Change the database to be restored to a new database, pubs2, which
does not exist.

Select the pubs database name from the Show backups of database pull-
down list to demonstrate that you could use the backup you just made. With a
simple click of the OK button, you could create your new database.

Instead, select the radio button marked From device to demonstrate
another feature of SQL Server 2000. Not only can you restore a backup from
another database to create a new one, you can also restore a backup created on

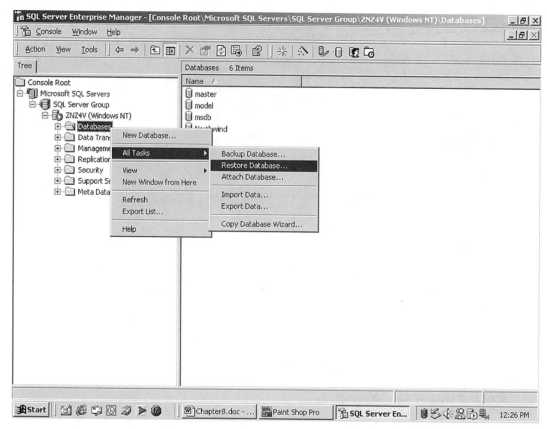

Figure 8.10 Beginning the restore

another server. This makes SQL Server 2000 databases highly portable. You can see the change in Figure 8.12.

The backup needs to read a device to see what to restore, so you need to select that device. Click the Select Devices button, which displays the screen shown in Figure 8.13.

Here you can add the device used for the backup. Notice that the tape option may be grayed out on your system because you may not have a tape drive. Select the Add button to bring up the panel shown in Figure 8.14 on page 274.

Now select the backup device to add to the list of places to restore from. Select OK, which brings up the screen in Figure 8.15. And now the place you're restoring from is defined. You may just have one location, but you can have several locations to back up to; if so, you need to select them all here. Select the OK button to bring up the screen in Figure 8.16.

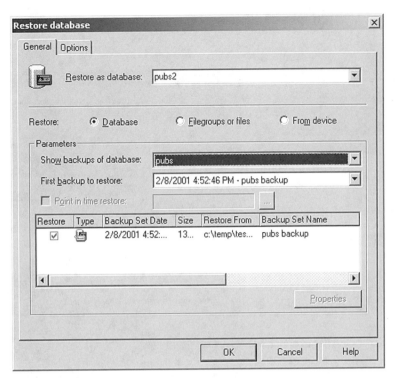

Figure 8.11
The General
tab

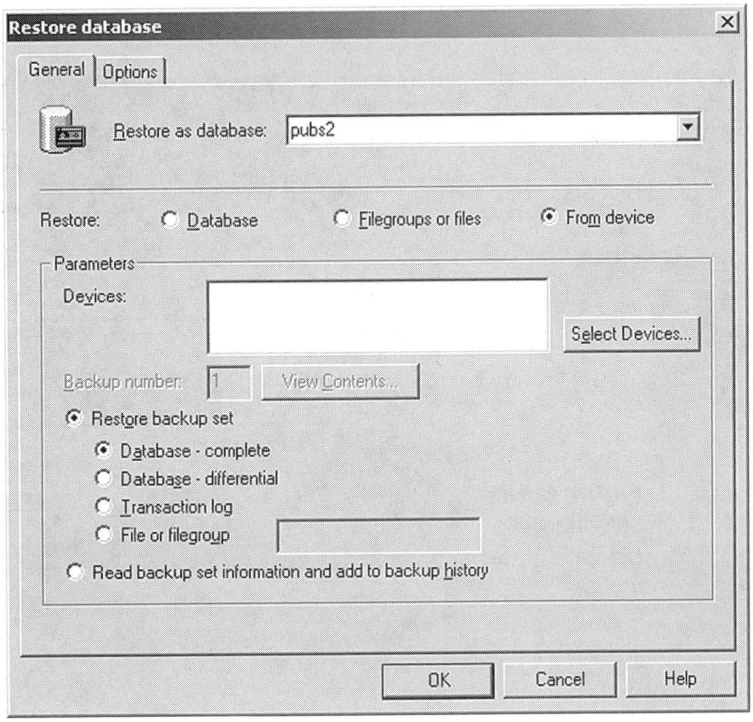

Figure 8.12
Changing
the restore-
from type

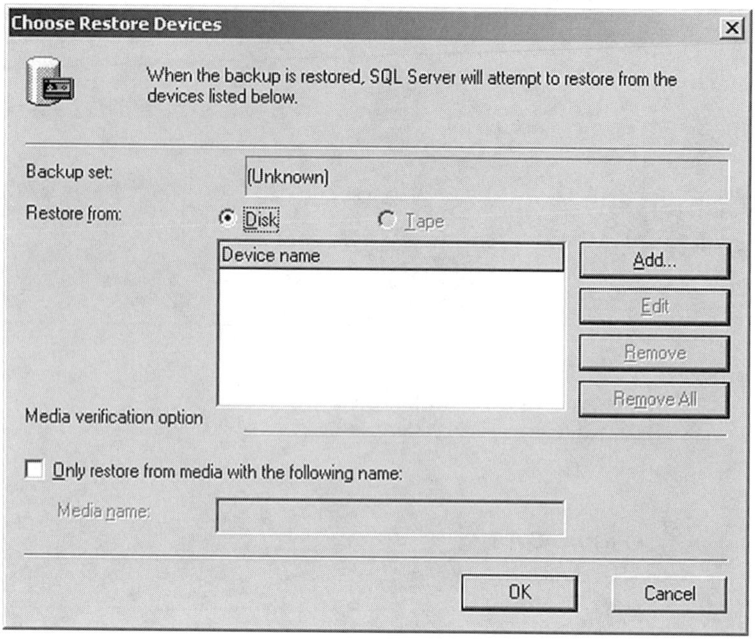

Figure 8.13
Adding the device

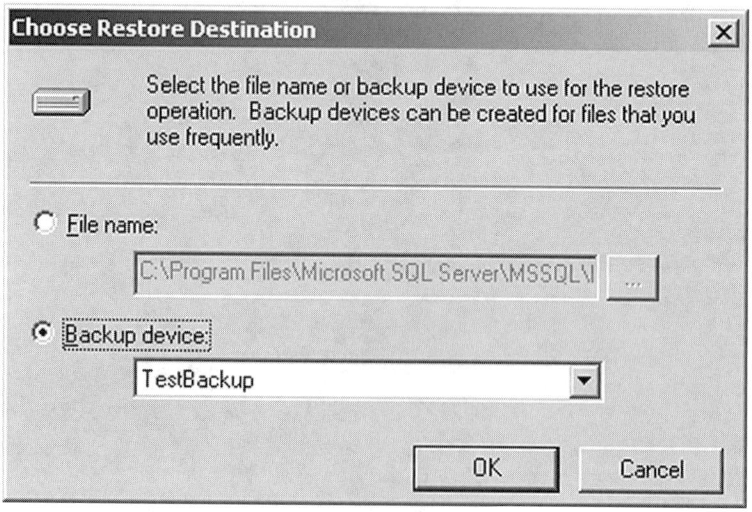

Figure 8.14
Selecting the device

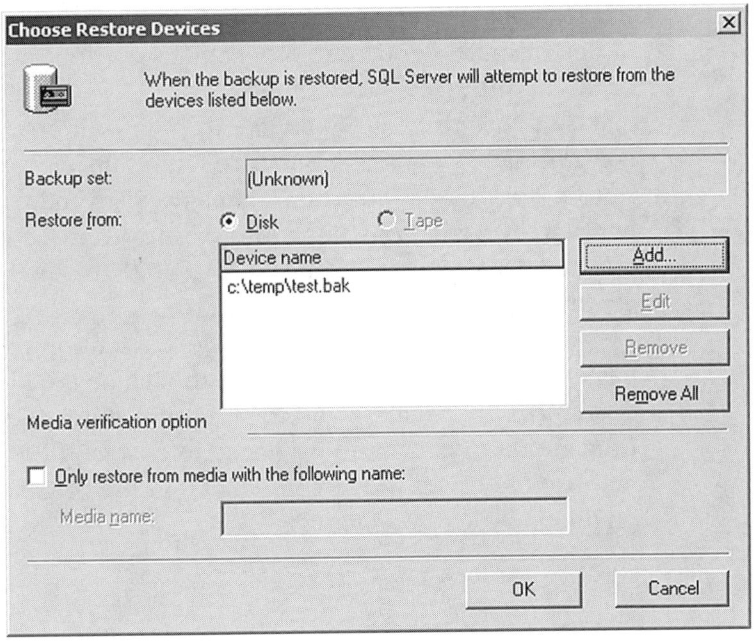

Figure 8.15
The selected
device

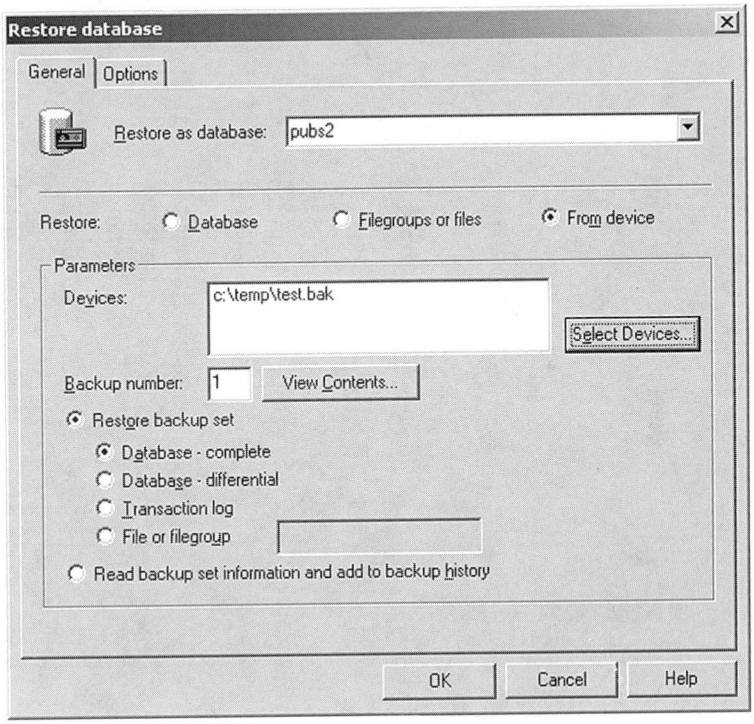

Figure 8.16
Completing
the selection

The filename within the device is displayed. You're done here, but I'd like to demonstrate a couple of other things on the Options tab. Click that, which brings up the screen in Figure 8.17.

There are three areas I'd like to point out on this panel. The first is the Force restore over existing database radio button. I said earlier that you could restore a database even when it already exists, and you can, but before that can happen, everyone has to be out of the database and this button must be selected. Don't worry if you forget to do that—the backup will fail, and you'll get the opportunity to rectify your error.

Second, you may need to pay close attention to the Move to physical file-name boxes. These boxes are used to change the location of the physical file that stores the database and the one that stores the log. If you've backed up from another system, you may need to change these boxes when you restore, because the drives they existed on from the originating server may not exist on the one you're using now.

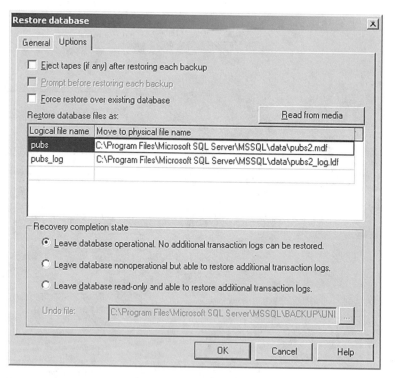

Figure 8.17 The Options tab

The last set of boxes deal with the log file recovery, which I'll demonstrate in a moment. If you have logs to restore, you select the last option, which prevents anyone from using the database until you're done restoring it. You then perform the restore process again for each of the logs and then select the first option (as I have here) on the last one. As a matter of fact, if the database is being restored where the backup was taken, SQL Server is intelligent enough to determine the backups and check them for you.

You can now press the OK button to begin the restore. Once you do that, the screen in Figure 8.18 displays very briefly for this small restore.

After a moment, you see the screen in Figure 8.19. Press OK here, which brings up the screen in Figure 8.20. And that completes the process.

There is one further detail to note here: The restored database is a duplicate of the one that was backed up. That means that all the settings, including the recovery model and growth options, are transferred with the restore. The security settings in the database are also transferred, although the logins to the server are not. I explain this a bit further in Chapter 10.

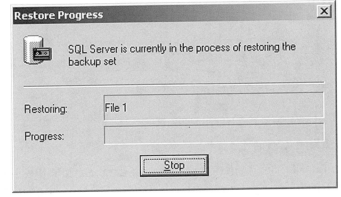

Figure 8.18
The restore
status screen

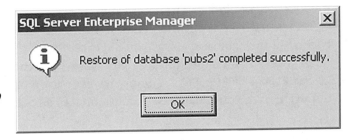

Figure 8.19
Completed
restore

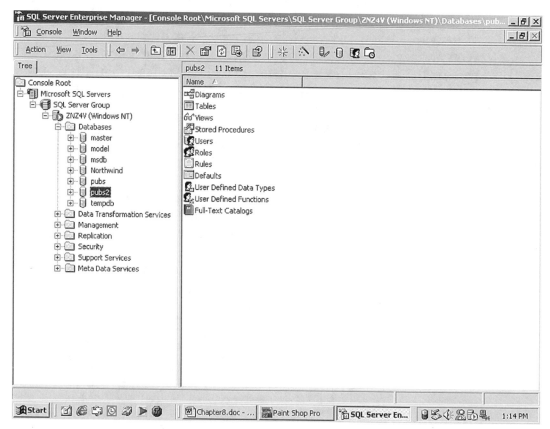

Figure 8.20 The pubs2 database

Backing Up a Log

Recall that you need to have your database in either the Full or the Bulk Logged model of recovery to back up the log. Set your pubs2 database to the Full model by right-clicking the database, selecting Properties from the menu that appears, and then selecting the Options tab. Next select the Full option under the Recovery section, as shown in Figure 8.21.

Now that you've set the database to the Full model, you'll perform a full backup of the database, just as you did earlier, with the exception that you will need to use a filename rather than a device. Send the backup to the file C:\TEMP\FULLBACKUP.BAK. You now have a copy of all the data, which is just a duplicate of the pubs database, safely stored in a backup file.

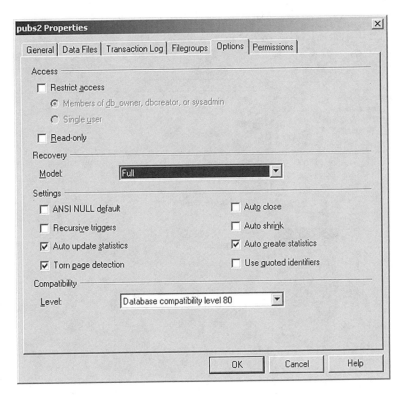

Figure 8.21 *Setting the recovery model*

Now, you need to enter some data in the database so that you have something in the log to back up. You could use some fancy scripts to populate a particular table with lots of valid data, but since this is just a demo, we'll cheat a little and enter data directly from *Enterprise Manager*.

Let's pause for a minute and consider what you've done. Your database is set to the *Full* recovery model, which keeps the data entered since the last backup in the log file, even after it makes it to the database file. Your full backup is good as of a couple of minutes ago, and you're about to simulate entering data. You need to consider the fact that processes other than users can enter data as well. If you perform a full backup only every night, you might lose all the data entered during the day if you have a meltdown.

Right-click the *Jobs* table and enter five lines of data. Now you can proceed to back up the log file. Right-click the *pubs2* database and select *All Tasks*, then

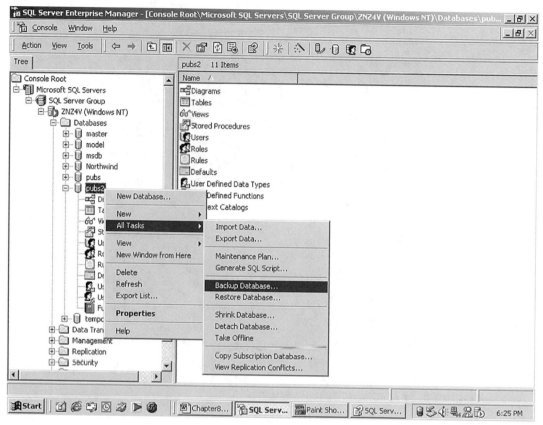

Figure 8.22 Beginning the log backup process

Backup Database from the menu, as shown in Figure 8.22. This brings up the panel shown in Figure 8.23.

Notice that a backup file already exists for this database because you performed a full backup. SQL Server 2000 remembers that and fills out the Destination panel for you. In this case, you don't want that, so highlight that file and

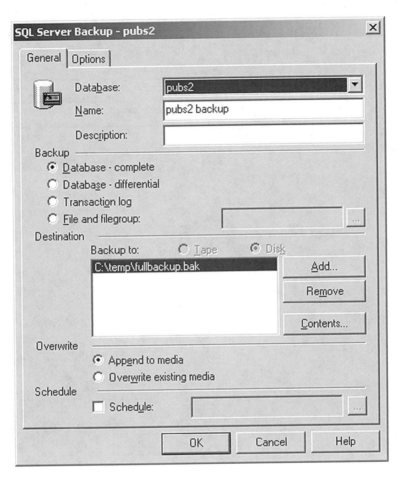

Figure 8.23 General backup tab

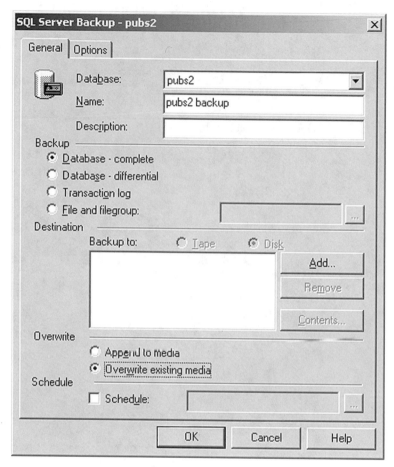

Figure 8.24   Changing the backup options

press the Remove button to take it out of the list. Set the backup to overwrite the file when you create it, as shown in Figure 8.24.

As before, select the Add button to set the destination for the backup, and then press OK, as shown in Figure 8.25. You can see from the graphic that you've set the filename to C:\TEMP\LOGBACKUP.BAK. Set the option for the

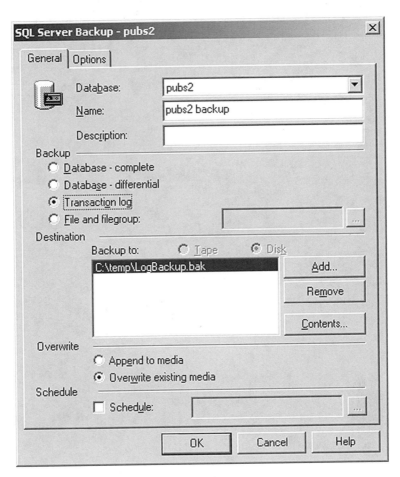

Figure 8.25   The log file backup destination set

recovery—in the Backup section, select the radio button for the Transaction log option. All that is left is to select the OK button, and off the backup goes. The only things in the transaction backup are the five lines in the jobs table.

Next you'll recover the database to the latest possible moment using these two backup files.

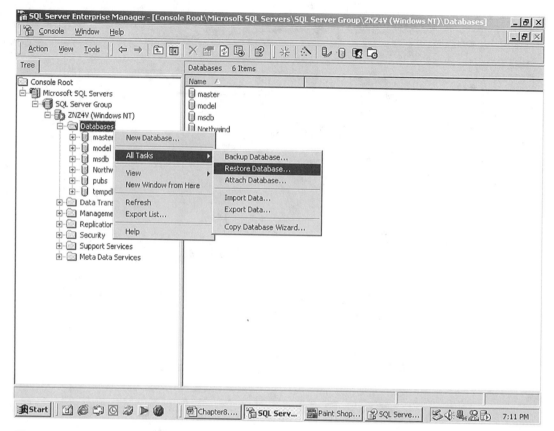

Figure 8.26 Beginning the database restore

Recovering a Database Using a Log Backup

Right-click the pubs2 database and delete it, simulating a meltdown. Right-click the Databases object, and select *All Tasks* and then *Restore Database* from the menu, as shown in Figure 8.26.

Type in the pubs2 name, and then set the restore to use a device. Now choose the *Select Devices* button and then the *Add* button; then select the C:\TEMP\FULLBACKUP.BAK file to add it to the restore. You can see the result of all this in Figure 8.27.

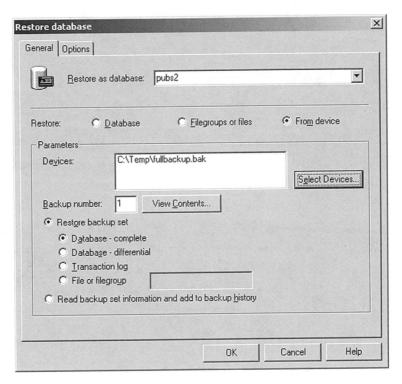

Figure 8.27   The completed restore selection

Select the Options tab, change the backup type to keep everyone out of the database, and leave the database open to more restore operations, as shown in Figure 8.28. Now select OK to see the panel shown in Figure 8.29. When you return to Enterprise Manager, the database object has turned a different color, and the word (Loading) has been tacked on to it. Figure 8.30 shows this screen.

At this point, the data in the database is current as of the full backup—that is, minus the five items you entered—but no one can use the database. Right-click the pubs2 database, and select All Tasks, then Restore Database from the menu that appears. Next select the From device button, and set the location to

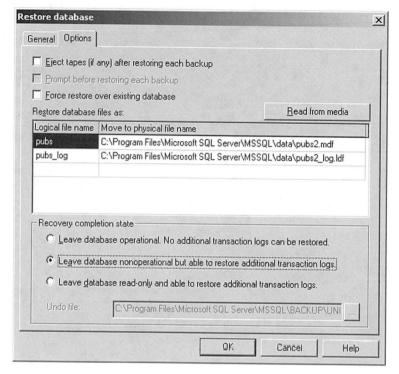

Figure 8.28 The Options tab

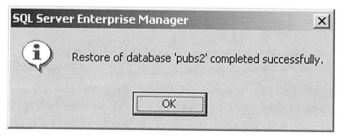

Figure 8.29 The completed first step

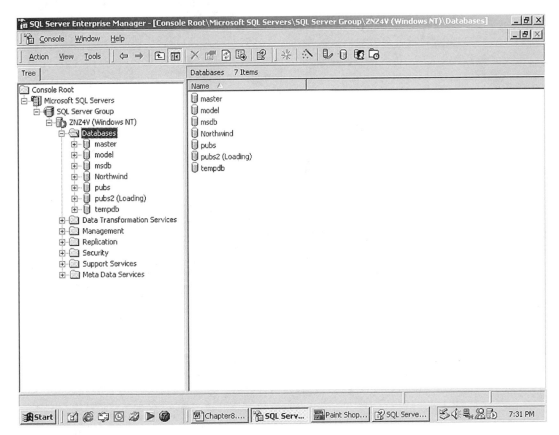

Figure 8.30   *Database in loading mode*

the `C:\TEMP\LOGBACKUP.BAK` file with the same process you've been following, as shown in Figure 8.31.

Set the type of restore to *Transaction log.* Now select the *Options* tab to finalize this restore. Look at Figure 8.32. The only change you need to make here is to select the *Leave database operational...* radio button. This effectively closes the restore operation and lets users into the database. Select OK, and the database is ready to use.

If you have multiple log file backup files, just restore the earliest to the most recent, in order, leaving the database open until the last log. That's all there is to it.

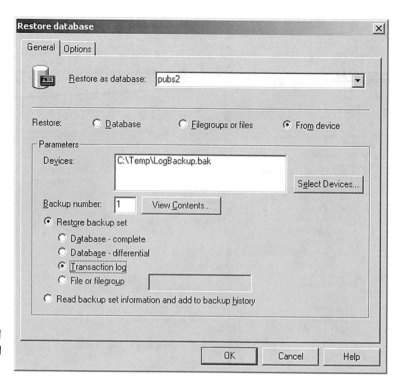

Figure 8.31
The General
tab

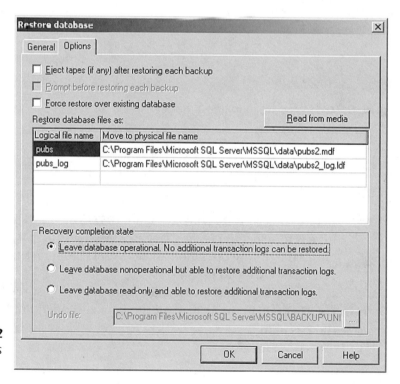

Figure 8.32
The Options
tab

Command Line

The act of backing up systems and restoring them is one of the most important set of commands to learn. At countless times you'll be pressed to use the command-line tools to back up the database, so we'll perform the same backups that you did with the graphical method, starting with creating a backup device.

Creating a Backup Device

You don't normally create backup devices using the command line, but you can. We'll use Query Analyzer for this demonstration. Listing 8.1 shows the commands used to create the same backup device you did earlier, using a file location to store the backup.

Listing 8.1   Creating a backup device

```
USE master
EXEC sp_addumpdevice 'disk', 'TestBackup', 'c:\temp\test.bak'
```

The first parameter specifies the type of device (you could have used 'tape' instead), and the second parameter the name. The third parameter sets the location. If you had set the type of device to tape, the third parameter would be something like '\\.\tape0'.

Now that you've created the backup device, use it to take a backup of the *pubs* database.

The Backup Command

This command is simple. It is shown in Listing 8.2. Run that command, and the database is sent to the device you made. You can change the line TO TestBackup to read TO DISK = 'c:\temp\test.bak' to do the same thing without creating a device. This is the way you normally perform backups.

Listing 8.2   A simple backup

```
BACKUP DATABASE pubs
TO TestBackup
GO
```

The Restore Command

The RESTORE command is a bit more complicated without the backup device in place. We'll use the device to create the *pubs2* database. Listing 8.3 shows the way.

Listing 8.3 Restoring a database using a backup device

```
RESTORE DATABASE pubs2
FROM TestBackup
GO
```

The process becomes a bit more complex if the database was backed up on a server using different drive letters than you may have on your system. As an example, let's assume that the database was backed up on a server where the files were stored on the E: drive, and you want to store it on drive C:. The commands in Listing 8.4 do that.

Listing 8.4 Moving the file locations

```
RESTORE DATABASE pubs2
 FROM TestBackup
 MOVE 'pubs' TO 'C:\MyData\pubs_data.mdf',
 MOVE 'pubs_log' TO 'C:\MyData\pubs_log.ldf'
GO
```

Notice that you need to know the logical filenames that the database and logs use. Once you do, you can place the files anywhere. The command shown in Listing 8.5 lists the information you need for the last command to work. That command shows you the particulars of the backup device, including its contents.

Listing 8.5 Displaying the logical filename

```
RESTORE FILELISTONLY
FROM TestBackup
GO
```

A Backup and Restore with Logs

Now that you've done all this, you've got a second copy of the pubs database to work with. First, you need to set this copy of the database to the Full recovery model. Listing 8.6 shows the commands to use. Next, back up the database, as shown in Listing 8.7.

Listing 8.6 Setting the database to full recovery

```
ALTER DATABASE pubs2
SET RECOVERY FULL
GO
```

Listing 8.7   Backing up the database

```
BACKUP DATABASE pubs2
TO TestBackup
WITH INIT
GO
```

The WITH INIT qualifier ensures that the backup overwrites the file during the process.

Now you have a clean copy of the database with the current data in it. With the database in the Full recovery model, you can begin to enter data into the database. We do that in Listing 8.8.

Listing 8.8   Entering some data

```
USE pubs2
GO
INSERT INTO jobs (job_desc, min_lvl, max_lvl)
VALUES ('Test', 10, 15)
GO
```

Press F5 five times, entering those lines into the database five times. That data is now in the log. Back up that log, just as you did in the Graphical section. The commands to do that are shown in Listing 8.9.

Listing 8.9   Backing up the log

```
USE master
GO
BACKUP LOG pubs2
TO DISK = 'C:\temp\LogBackup.bak'
GO
```

In that log backup you have the five lines you entered earlier. Now you simulate the meltdown, as shown in Listing 8.10.

Listing 8.10   Deleting the database

```
USE master
GO
DROP DATABASE pubs2
GO
```

And the database is gone. Now you can put it all back. Start with the full backup you took earlier, using the commands in Listing 8.11.

Listing 8.11 Restoring the full backup

```
USE master
GO
RESTORE DATABASE pubs2
FROM TestBackup
WITH NORECOVERY
GO
```

Notice the WITH NORECOVERY qualifier at the end of the RESTORE command. You apply that qualifier to each log restore until the last one, where you type the commands shown in Listing 8.12.

Listing 8.12 Restoring the log backup

```
USE master
GO
RESTORE LOG pubs2
FROM DISK = 'c:\temp\LogBackup.bak'
WITH RECOVERY
GO
```

The WITH RECOVERY qualifier is optional, but I like to include it so that I can visually identify the last restore in a script. You might have other restore operations to do in a single script, and this helps identify the end of this one.

Examples

I've shown most of the primary uses of the backup and restore commands and procedures, but you have one database that needs to be archived every day to CD. This process is an extension of the example detailed in Chapter 5.

Backing Up a Database to a Network Share

Look at the script in Listing 8.13. Remember, you could create this process as a Job Step and schedule this whole process to happen on a recurring basis. On line 4 you back up the database to a network share. You need to replace \\ServerName\ShareName\ with the name of a valid server and share name. Be sure to allow for the additional time for copying over the wire.

Listing 8.13 Backing up a database to a network share

```
USE master
GO
BACKUP DATABASE pubs2
TO DISK = '\\ServerName\ShareName\Test.bak'
WITH INIT
GO
```

An alternative that I use is to back up the database to a drive, zip it, and then copy it to a network share.

Rosetta Stone

Oracle

The backup of most RDBMS programs is similar. The differences show up mainly during a restore. I've done the best comparison I can for these functions, as shown in Table 8.1.

The differences in log backup strategies are not covered in this table, so pay close attention to the section in this chapter about the recovery model.

Table 8.1 Oracle and SQL Server Backup Commands Compared

Task	Oracle Tool	Microsoft SQL Server 2000
Backup/restore of databases and logs	Enterprise Manager	Enterprise Manager
Command-line backup and restore	RMAN utility, or ALTER DATABASE BACKUP command	BACKUP and RESTORE commands
Duplicate a database	RMAN utility	Enterprise Manager or BACKUP/RESTORE

Microsoft Access

Not worthy of a full table to compare the processes, the backup and restore for Access involve copying a file.

Resources

Back up a SQL Server to another server's tape drive:
   http://www.mssqlserver.com/faq/backup-remotetape.asp
SQL Server 2000 can set marks to restore to:
   http://www.mcpmag.com/members/00nov/fea1main.asp

Webcast on the new recovery models:

http://support.microsoft.com/servicedesks/webcasts/wc120500/wcblurb120500.asp

More backup and restore information:

http://www.win2000mag.net/Channels/SQLServer/TopicResults.cfm?TopicID=10

Chapter **9**

Monitoring and Optimization

Chapter at a Glance

Read this chapter to learn how to tune SQL 2000 Server, with both hardware and the nondesign options you can set.

The Resources section contains references for:

- SQL Server Profiler
- A webcast from Microsoft
- An optimization Web site
- A white paper from Microsoft on the Index Tuning Wizard

Read Appendix B before you read this chapter.

Overview

The best career booster I know of for IT professionals is to do something that has a large "wow" factor and is very visible. A good example is to make something that is running slowly run faster.

SQL Server 2000 is amazingly self-tuning; you don't need to adjust dozens of memory or database parameters to optimize the server. SQL Server 2000 watches database activity and adjusts itself automatically, greatly simplifying your job as a DBA. This isn't to say that you're *completely* off the hook, because there are things to watch and things to tune.

In this chapter, I detail the hardware you need to run your database and the software settings that affect performance.

On the hardware side, four main areas can be addressed. Refer to Appendix B for more information.

- CPU
- Memory
- Storage
- Network Interface Card (NIC)

In this chapter, I discuss what you can look at on these hardware issues and some ways to affect them.

On the software side, you normally tune the following items:

- Queries
- Indexes
- Locking

There are database and server settings, but SQL Server 2000 manages these automatically. They can be overridden, but it's not often wise to do so.

Windows Performance Monitor contains objects and counters that provide performance information. Hardware and SQL Server 2000 software objects are available using this tool.

Enterprise Manager provides a view of current activity in all databases.

The SQL Server Profiler is another tool that shows activity to a greater degree and can be used to observe locking, resource use, and much more.

Several commands provide access to performance counters—in particular, the `sp_monitor`, `sp_who`, and `sp_lock` stored procedures.

Detail

It's important to define exactly what needs to be tuned. There are things that a maintenance DBA doesn't normally change. Design is one of those—databases can have a really poor design that can negate the best hardware and database engines ever created. Many books, Web sites, and magazines can teach you to design a proper database, so in this chapter, I focus on the factors that the maintenance DBA normally changes. The major factor that affects the server performance is how it is used.

There are two main types of applications: applications that write more transactions (OLTP, for Online Transaction Processing) and applications that read more often from the database (OLAP, for Online Analytical Processing). Many applications often demand both activity types from the database. Each of these types of databases has diametrically opposed factors to be optimized. This often negates any blanket tuning and requires a generic tuning mode.

Among the items you can tune for all application types are three main software areas:

- Queries
- Indexes
- Locking

Many settings at the server or database level also can affect performance, but for the most part you never have to touch them. As a matter of fact, almost *no one* ever touches them, because SQL Server 2000 is simply much better at tuning itself dynamically.

We begin the process of optimizing your server with those hardware configurations I mentioned. I'll then run through the major software settings to tune.

Hardware Optimizations

I'll begin by discussing the hardware perspective on performance. Whether the database is used more for OLAP or for OLTP, these hardware suggestions hold true.

CPU

The faster the CPU, the faster the work is done, but more isn't necessarily better. Windows NT uses more than two processors in a less than beneficial way. Windows 2000 does this much better, and in both cases SQL Server 2000 takes great advantage of multiple processors. The various editions of NT and Windows 2000 have limits on the number of CPUs they support. Microsoft's Web site states the number of processors each OS supports.

Regardless of whether you're using NT or 2000, SQL Server 2000 can split a query to the various processors to be worked on in parallel. It does this for a variety of things, not just queries. So as far as CPUs go, more is better, to a point.

To keep your server fast, keep everything else off. Having other software use the hardware does nothing but slow the database down.

As explained in Appendix B, you should have a large L2 cache on those processor(s) or as much cache as they can handle. For a SQL Server that's busy, 2MB of cache on the processor isn't excessive at all.

Memory

This time, more *is* better. Windows NT 4 Server can use up to 2GB of physical RAM, and up to that point, more is better. Windows 2000, depending on the flavor, can handle more. The type of RAM is not usually selectable, but faster ECC RAM is better.

Storage

More is better here too, but not for performance. Giving your server lots of disk isn't a performance factor, but it beats putting it in later.

More important to performance is the speed of the drives you select. Your hard drive subsystem is a mechanical device and as such is one of the slowest subsystems you have, so you should have the fastest drives you can afford. Drives are normally specified in revolutions per minute (rpm), enabling you to choose the faster models.

You also should use Redundant Array of Independent Disks (RAID) (level 1 or 5; see Appendix B) and hardware RAID only—software RAID shouldn't be used under any circumstances. Software RAID must calculate each storage bit, and hardware RAID handles this with its own onboard processor.

There's also the issue of caching on the controller. This caching is memory right on the card that tells the CPU that the data made it to the drive, even when it hasn't left the card. This makes the drives seem faster.

There's a danger here in that if SQL Server 2000 thinks data is on the drive but it isn't, and if you lose power, you could corrupt a database. For this reason, Microsoft says you shouldn't use a caching controller at all. I don't go that far, because the newer controllers come with batteries that keep the memory on the card alive and roll that data forward onto the hard drives when the system restarts. If you trust this process, make sure you use a reliable vendor.

Since data is written first to the log and then to the database, it makes sense to locate the log files and the database files on separate drives. As the system writes to the log file on one drive, the separate drive is free to provide data to queries. This helps with those OLTP/OLAP hybrid databases I mentioned earlier.

Although you should keep the log files and database files separate, you can also locate tables and indexes on different drives. This process involves creating filegroups, which are created when the database is created or altered. Tables and indexes can be placed on separate filegroups, which can be on different drives. In this manner, a heavily used table and its equally heavily used index can gain the same performance advantage as I described for the log and database files.

It's not just the drive *letters* I'm talking about; it's the *physical* drives that matter. Splitting one physical drive into five drive letters does no good whatsoever. It's still the same spindle and the same heads that have to do each seek.

Always use NTFS as your filesystem for SQL Server. NTFS uses a far superior algorithm to store and access data and is more secure. It's also self-healing and supports journaling.

Keep the OS and the database files on separate drives, because the heads that are making OS calls won't take time away from the database calls.

NIC

Although some systems can combine multiple network cards, these are often vendor-specific. If you have that option, use it. You should have at least one card, however, that is 100MBs, connected to a switch. If your network has a 10MB architecture, having a 100MB switch and card on your server uses bandwidth far more effectively than a single 10MB card in the server connected to a simple hub.

Keep in mind as well that the fewer routers between your server and its intended audience, the better. If your network uses only one protocol, make sure that's all you have installed on the server. Install and use only the protocols you absolutely have to.

Windows Performance Monitor

Performance tuning is often a matter of dealing with bottlenecks. By using Windows NT *Performance Monitor*, you can determine which factor is the current bottleneck. This tool can monitor, log, and alert you about categories called *Objects* and items called *Counters*. *Counters* have values, and that's what you measure.

You may have already used this tool. If you don't have much experience with *Performance Monitor*, see the demonstration of it in the Graphical section.

Several *Counters* detail SQL Server 2000's operation, including those that monitor the hardware. Table 9.1 shows the hardware *Counters* to watch in SQL Server 2000.

Table 9.1 Hardware Counters

Thing Being Measured	Object	Counter	Value to Watch For	What to Do
CPU	Processor	% total processor time	Above 80% for 15 minutes or so	Add processors or tune the software.
CPU	System	Processor queue length	Above 2 for 10 minutes or so	Add processors or tune the software.
Memory	Memory	Pages/sec	Above 0 for any significant period	Add RAM—soon.
NIC	Network interface	Bytes total/sec	Need a baseline	Tune network— hardware and drivers.

You need to do a few things before you set up Performance Monitor to observe these settings. For one, if you want to monitor network parameters, you need to install the Simple Network Management Protocol (SNMP) services in Windows NT or 2000.

If you want to measure the *physical* (not logical) hard drive object, you need to run the command perfmon /y at the command line and then reboot. Unless you know that you need to do that, don't. Most people forget to turn the Counters off (using perfmon /n), and these Counters affect server speed. Although there are times to monitor the hard drive in this way, most of the time it simply isn't necessary.

Not only are there hardware Counters to monitor, but there are some interesting SQL Server 2000 Counters to monitor as well. Table 9.2 shows these SQL-specific Objects and Counters.

There are many more Objects and Counters you can monitor. Books Online details these Counters in the Performance Tuning section. If you know what's happening to your server, you stand a better chance of fixing any problems that might arise.

Index Tuning Wizard

Now that I've discussed the hardware a bit, let's consider the software issues you might deal with.

The primary reason a query runs slowly is because it's tough for the server to locate the data. An index is an object that solves this problem because it points to the physical location of the data.

Table 9.2 *SQL Server 2000 Counters*

Thing Being Measured	Object	Counter	Value to Watch For	What to Do
Caching	SQL Server buffer manager	Buffer cache hit ratio	Under 95%	Add RAM or tune database.
Locks	SQL Server locks	Number of deadlocks/ sec	More than 10 a second using SQL Profiler.	Monitor deadlocks
Indexes	SQL Server access methods	Page splits/ sec	Varies—need to base- line	Monitor indexes using SQL Profiler.
Users	SQL Server general statistics	User con- nections	Varies—need to base- line	If there's a dramatic increase in users, add RAM or monitor other hardware factors.

Without an index, SQL Server has no quick way to locate a particular piece of data. It's similar to your finding the word "server" every time it appears in this book, without looking in the index. The difference is that in the database's case, the "book" is being rewritten constantly.

Indexes help a great deal with read operations, but because they are written to when data is added or removed, they impose a cost on write operations. Because of that, you need to maintain your indexes.

The developer DBA creates indexes, usually on just a few important columns in a few tables. Sometimes the database is missing indexes that may be useful. SQL Server 2000 comes with a wizard that monitors your database activity and proposes changes to the indexes based on what it sees.

There is a big caveat here: Don't change the indexes on your database until you speak with the developer in charge of the product. You can seriously impact the performance of your database by placing the indexes in the wrong places. This is especially true for the types of applications that put more data in the database than they read out, because the indexes have to be updated when the data is inserted. Databases that do more reading (like those heavy on reports) usually benefit more from using this tool.

The important thing to remember with the *Index Tuning Wizard* is that you should make sure there is a representative amount of activity going on against your server to accurately measure the indexes, or the lack of them.

Check the Resources section, and look up the Microsoft white paper on this tool.

SQL Server Profiler

The primary internal view for SQL Server 2000 activity is the SQL Server Profiler. This tool not only finds performance issues on your server, it also can glean huge amounts of information about what's going on in your server. It's a good idea to become familiar with this tool.

The process for using the tool involves gathering information (called a Trace) about Event Categories, which are descriptions of items that are monitored, called Event Classes. Within these Event Classes are Events. You can get specific information about the Event, such as how long it took to complete or who ran it, depending on what the Event describes.

I'll describe a recent experience using Profiler to diagnose a problem I had with a database. Around lunchtime each day, several people complained that they couldn't open a particular screen in an application. The problem seemed to be caused by a block, which is a condition caused when two processes want the same piece of information exclusively.

Using Profiler, I set up a Trace to monitor an Event Class of Locks, and the Events of Locks:Acquired and Locks:Released. I started the Trace a little before lunch and ran it until the users told me the problem stopped. I then checked the columns displayed from that Trace of LoginName, StartTime, and EndTime.

Using this information, I found that a user was leaving for lunch with the program set to modify a piece of data crucial to the rest of the application. Modern programs rarely have this problem, but this one did. I demonstrate this further in the Graphical section.

Look up Administering SQL Server, Monitoring Server Performance and Activity, Monitoring with SQL Profiler in Books Online for a full, if a bit disjointed, explanation of this powerful tool.

Current Activity

The Enterprise Manager also has a section that can tell you what's going on with your server. This tool can display the activity, locks, and even the queries that are running on the server. I take a closer look at this panel in the Graphical section.

sp_monitor

You can run a few commands to observe the performance of your system. One of these, sp_monitor, displays some rather broad statistics about your server's activity. The command can also track the last time it was used and give you long-range specifics. In the command-line section, I'll run this command to show the type of information it can provide.

sp_who

The sp_who command shows the users connected to your server. It can also show the users who are blocking each other—I could have used this tool instead of using Profiler earlier.

sp_lock

As a user looks at or modifies a piece of data, it can be very important that another user not look at or modify that particular piece of data. SQL Server 2000 allows the user to lock that data, at the database, table, or row level, so that the changes are guaranteed to be sequential.

SQL Server 2000 can automatically pick out what it thinks is the best kind of lock to take (database, page, table, or row), or when writing the code, the developer can specify the lock to take. You can examine which process has what kind of lock by using the sp_lock command.

Graphical

The graphical tools are well suited to displaying performance data. Often it's not enough to use one tool to diagnose an issue. Combining the graphical tools I demonstrate can help you pinpoint a performance bottleneck.

Windows Performance Monitor

Windows Performance Monitor provides you with hardware and software Objects and Counters so that you can check the health and performance of your server.

If you're using Windows NT, Performance Monitor is a selection from the Administrative Tools menu item. If you're using Windows 2000 Server (as I am here), the tool has been moved into a Microsoft Management Console (MMC) console but is still located in the Administrative Tools area.

Start the tool, as shown in Figure 9.1, and you're presented with a blank screen. The first panel is the Chart panel or, in Windows 2000, the Current Activity panel. This panel displays trend data—things that change over time. There

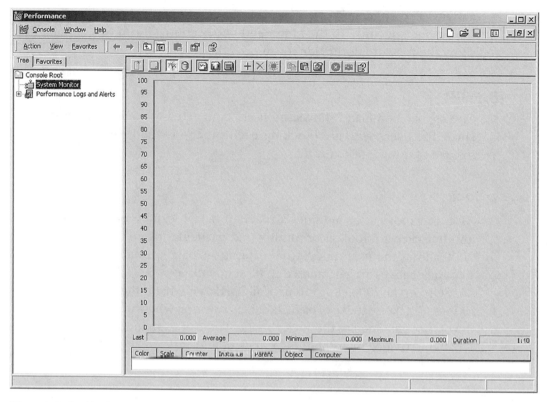

Figure 9.1 Performance Monitor

are other views, which you'll see in a moment, but certain Counters require certain views.

Click the big plus sign on the toolbar in Performance Monitor to bring up the selection panel shown in Figure 9.2. Notice here that you can select Objects from other computers, assuming you have the NT or Active Directory (AD) rights to do so.

This panel is where you pick the object you wish to monitor. The first Object that pops up is the CPU, and that covers the base for one of the objects I've already pointed out as a potential bottleneck.

Once you select the Object, you can select the Counters that the Object exposes. There's an Explain button on this panel, but some of the explanations are more useful than others.

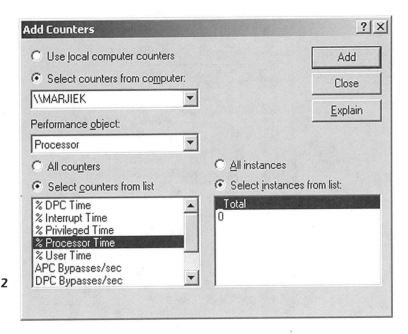

Figure 9.2
Selection
panel

Add this default Counter to your test by pressing the Add button. Next press the Close button to bring up the screen in Figure 9.3.

Allow the Counter to run for a couple of minutes under load. You'll notice from this display that the CPU isn't the problem in this system. It hovers around an 11% average for the time monitored.

This Counter alone isn't good enough to completely diagnose the condition of this server. More hardware than just the CPU could be a bottleneck, so let's add a different Counter the same way you did a moment ago. This time pick the Memory Object and the Pages Per/Sec Counter.

Table 9.1, earlier in the chapter, details the Counters you're monitoring. In that table, you see that the threshold to watch is anything above 0 for significant periods of time. As you can see in Figure 9.4, it is obvious this system needs more RAM.

I've shown only one Counter at a time since this book isn't in color. You would set up all the counters I've mentioned in the tables on one monitoring session to watch them all. Although this is a fairly trivial example, it mirrors a serious exercise you should perform on your servers at work.

If you're using Windows NT, you can use the menu to save the data you've been collecting as either a comma-separated-value or a tab-separated-value file.

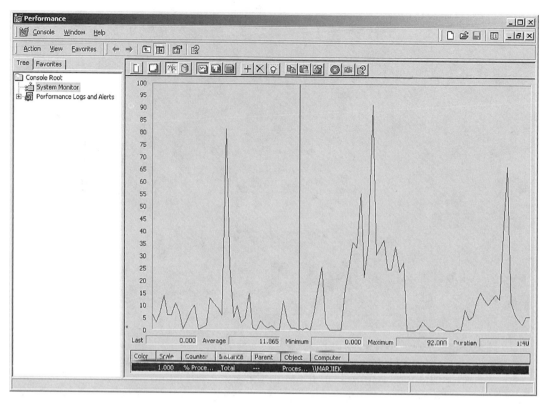

Figure 9.3 Viewing the Counter

These files can be imported into Excel for graphical study later. In Windows 2000, right-click inside the Counter space, and you can save the output as either the tab-separated file or an HTML page.

The most important thing to do with Performance Monitor is to take a baseline. You can't gauge whether a particular Counter is good or bad until you know what you started with.

Enterprise Manager

Enterprise Manager can also be used to some good effect to show you the activity that's happening in your server. Open Enterprise Manager and drill down to the Management, Current Activity, Process Info object, as shown in Figure 9.5.

You can see that I'm running a query against the pubs database using Query Analyzer. You can't tell from the picture here, but the globes beside each item are in various colors. The depth of color and the level of detail on the

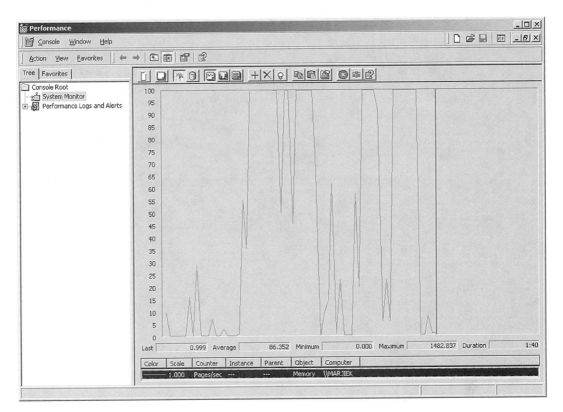

Figure 9.4 *Memory Counters*

globe indicate the "freshness" of the information. This is a like a Web page in that the information you see here is a snapshot in time. The information doesn't refresh itself automatically; you need to right-click the Current Activity and select Refresh to make the view current again.

There's a lot of useful information on this screen if you scroll to the right—especially the time a command took to run (CPU) and the RAM the item consumed (Memory Usage). This should be the first place you come to see information about your server activity.

SQL Server Profiler

Profiler is very useful to help you find out what's going on during a SQL Server 2000 session. I'll demonstrate with a simple Trace session. You can extrapolate this simple demonstration into other uses, and I encourage you to do so.

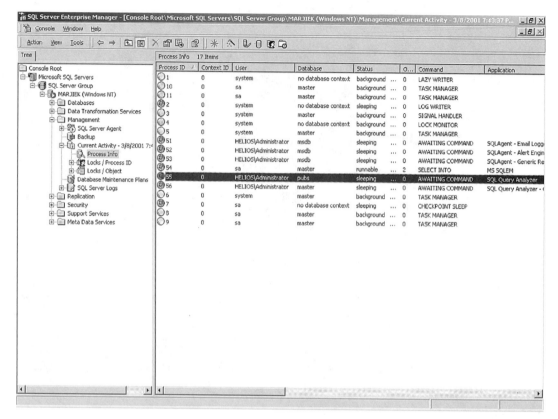

Figure 9.5 Process information

Remember: You can't hurt anything (other than a little bit of performance) by using this tool.

Open the SQL Profiler by selecting Start, Programs, Microsoft SQL Server, Profiler. You'll see the display shown in Figure 9.6.

The first thing you need to do is tell Profiler to begin your session, called a Trace. Do this by selecting File, New, Trace from the menu bar, as I've done in Figure 9.7.

Figure 9.6   SQL Profiler

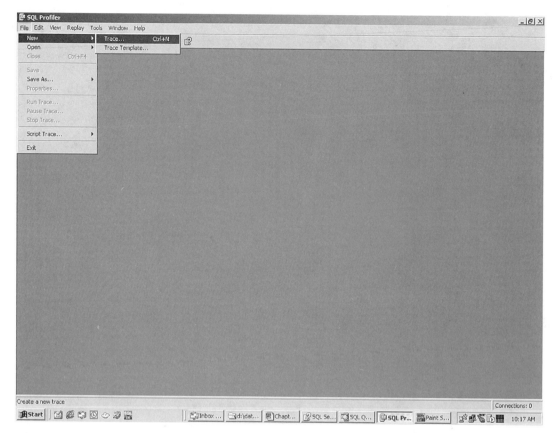

Figure 9.7 Beginning a new trace

The next item is the connection to a server to monitor. Leave the settings as shown in Figure 9.8, and select the OK button.

After you connect, the panel shown in Figure 9.9 appears. Name your test Trace, and you can see from Figure 9.9 that you can save the Trace session to a file or a table in SQL Server. The table option is useful for running queries against later to see time spreads, individual parts of a Trace, and so forth.

You can also save a Trace to play back the same SQL statements against another server if you want. You'll need to include some specific Events to do that, which you can look up in Books Online.

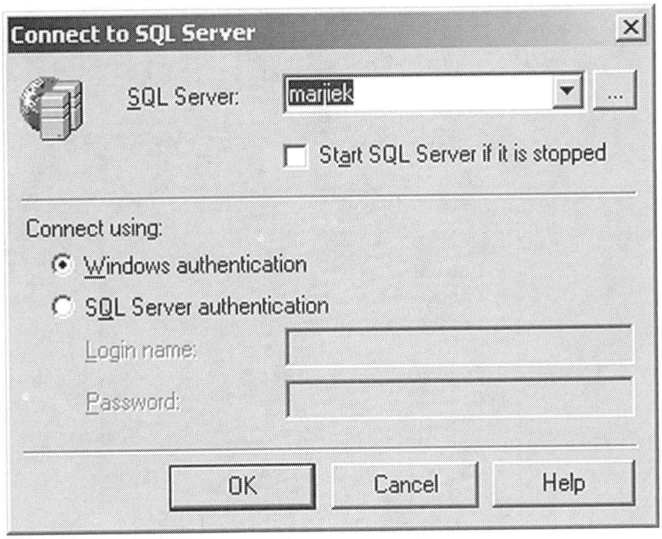

Figure 9.8
Connection parameters

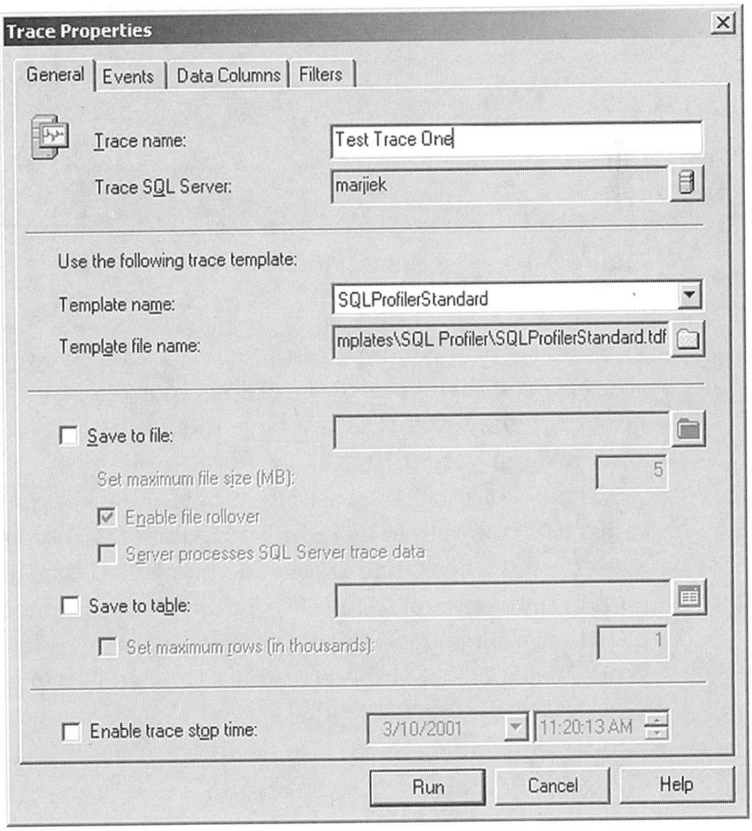

Figure 9.9
The General tab

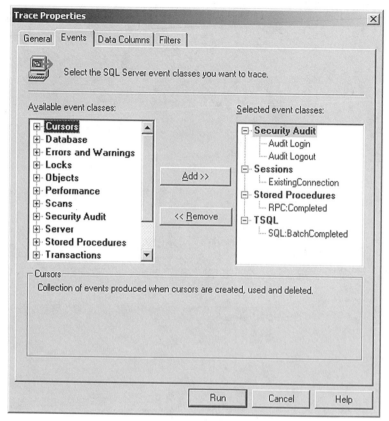

Figure 9.10 The Events tab

You can also choose from Templates, which have items already set up for you. You can save your own settings to a Template for later if you wish. For now, leave the settings as you have them here and move on to the Events tab, as shown in Figure 9.10.

This is a busy tab, but basically it involves picking the Event Classes I discussed earlier that you want to monitor. The Template we used has preselected the Event Classes you see here, but you can add or take away anything you like. Leave these for now, and move on to the Data Columns tab, as shown in Figure 9.11.

There's some good information here, but it's a bit much. Let's remove the Reads, Writes, CPU, and Client Process ID and add End Time as a column to watch.

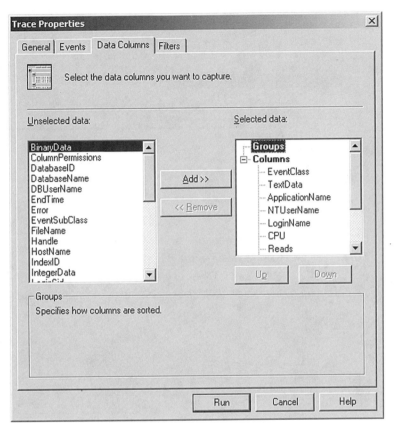

Figure 9.11   Data Columns tab

This is just for brevity, because you're interested in finding out who's running what and how long it took to run it.

Once you've made these changes, select the Filters tab to bring up the display shown in Figure 9.12. This tab allows you *not* to trace certain things. For one, notice that the Template has removed the Profiler tool itself; otherwise you'd get tons of lines that the monitoring tool generates. Next, select the box Exclude system IDs; otherwise, you'd see all the things the server is doing behind the scenes.

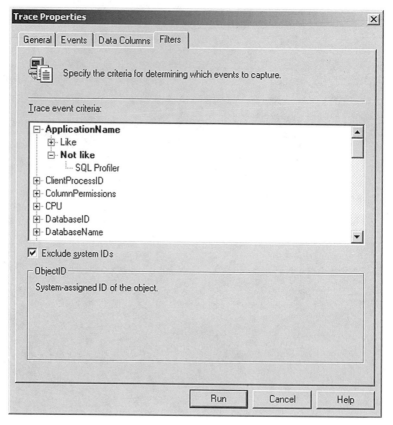

Figure 9.12 Filters tab

Select the Run button and begin your collection, as shown in Figure 9.13. You'll see some information rolling across, but not much is happening on this test server. Start Query Analyzer, connect to your server, and run the query shown in Figure 9.14.

Now that you've run a query, switch to the Profiler screen to see what's happening, as shown in Figure 9.15. Notice that you see the command that was run in Query Analyzer. I don't have it expanded here, but there is a column that displays who ran the command. You'll also see that it took 100% of the CPU for 2,363 milliseconds or so.

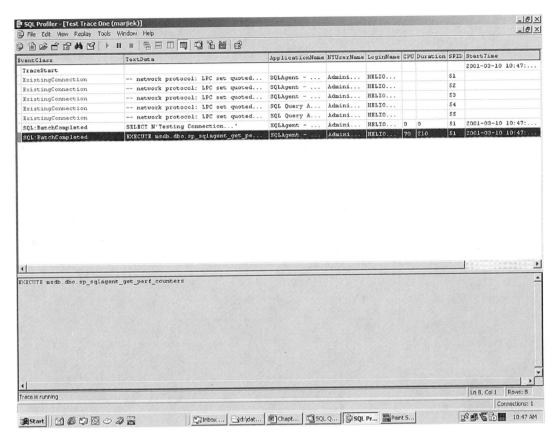

Figure 9.13 Trace begins

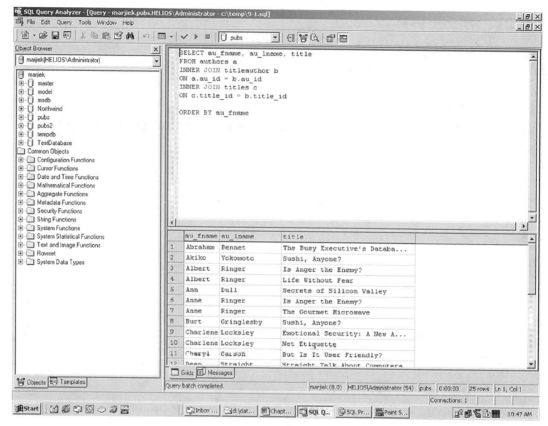

Figure 9.14 Query Analyzer

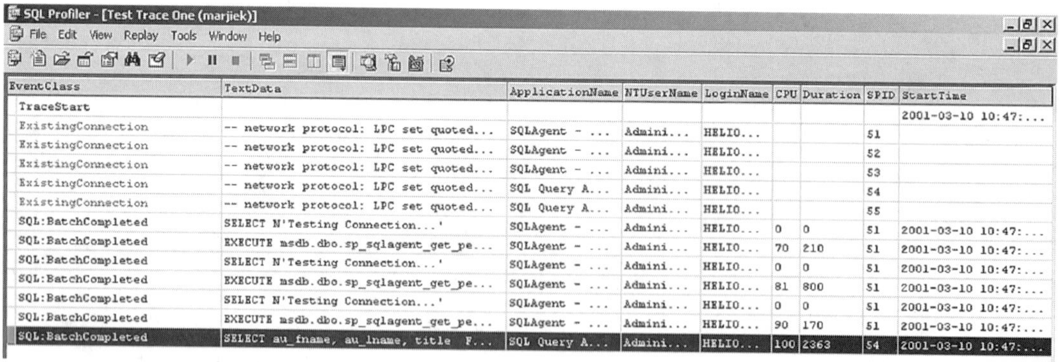

Figure 9.15 Profiler Trace

Command Line

Seasoned DBAs often use the command-line tools as well as the graphical tools to view the server activity. It's often useful to have both graphical and command-line tools in your repertoire.

Query Analyzer

Query Analyzer has several options that display the statistics, query plans, and Trace information while you're using the tool for queries. Setting one (or more) of these options from the menu bar before you run the query gives you information about that query, as shown in Figure 9.16. Most of the time, however, you'll be concerned with what *other* people are doing, not the quick queries you'll create in Query Analyzer.

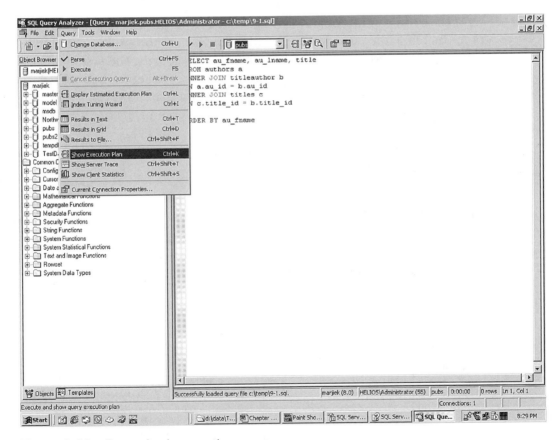

Figure 9.16   Query Analyzer options

Query Analyzer—sp_monitor

A command you can use is `sp_monitor`. This command gives you information on many of the *Counters* your server tracks. Run the command to get the output shown in Listing 9.1. I've changed the format of the output a bit to get it all on one page. The order is what's important, not the layout.

Listing 9.1 sp_monitor output

```
last_run              current_run         seconds
2001-03-08            2001-03-08          14
20:36:47.403          20:37:01.767
cpu_busy              io_busy             idle
25(0)-0%              3(0)-0%             3919(13)-92%
packets_received      packets_sent        packet_errors
816(3)                838(3)              0(0)
total_read            total_write         total_errors      connections
925(2)                214(1)              0(0)              45(0)
```

The first bit of information you get back from this command is the last time you ran it, the current time, and the time it took to run. The next bits of information provide a snapshot of the computer's activity. The first number is the current value of that particular *Counter* since SQL Server was started (or restarted); the second number (the one inside the parentheses) is the value since the command was last run. I like to run this command once a month on my servers.

The important parts of the *Counters* are the "busy" items and "errors" items. You should keep an eye on them.

Query Analyzer—sp_who

The `sp_who` command is similar to the *Current Activity* display in *Enterprise Manager*.

Run it to get the return shown in Listing 9.2.

Listing 9.2 sp_who output

spid	ecid	status	Loginame	hostname	blk	dbname	cmd
1	0	background	Sa		0	NULL	LAZY WRITER
2	0	sleeping	Sa		0	NULL	LOG WRITER
3	0	background	Sa		0	master	SIGNAL HANDLER
4	0	background	Sa		0	NULL	LOCK MONITOR
5	0	background	Sa		0	master	TASK MANAGER
6	0	background	Sa		0	master	TASK MANAGER
7	0	sleeping	Sa		0	NULL	CHECKPOINT SLEEP

8	0	background	Sa		0	master	TASK MANAGER
9	0	background	Sa		0	master	TASK MANAGER
10	0	background	Sa		0	master	TASK MANAGER
11	0	background	Sa		0	master	TASK MANAGER
51	0	sleeping	HELIOS\ Administrator	MARJIEK	0	msdb	AWAITING COMMAND
52	0	sleeping	HELIOS\ Administrator	MARJIEK	0	msdb	AWAITING COMMAND
53	0	sleeping	HELIOS\ Administrator	MARJIEK	0	msdb	AWAITING COMMAND
54	0	runnable	HELIOS\ Administrator	MARJIEK	0	master	SELECT
55	0	sleeping	HELIOS\ Administrator	MARJIEK	0	master	AWAITING COMMAND

The interesting parts here are the blk and cmd columns. The blk column tells you if another process is blocking the one on that line, and its number. The cmd column tells you the SQL Server owner process that's doing the work on that line.

You get a bit more information than you normally care about, but I show a better use of this command in the *Examples* section.

Query Analyzer—sp_lock

The sp_lock command details the locks being taken on various things in the database, as discussed earlier. Locks aren't necessarily bad things; it's just that they can get out of control. It's important to know what's going on in the databases.

Run the command to produce the output shown in Listing 9.3.

Listing 9.3   sp_lock output

spid	dbid	ObjId	IndId	Type	Resource	Mode	Status
51	4	0	0	DB		S	GRANT
52	4	0	0	DB		S	GRANT
53	4	0	0	DB		S	GRANT
54	1	85575343	0	TAB		IS	GRANT

We don't have a lot of locking going on here, as you can see. The first column is the spid—the same one as in the sp_who command. I show a way to combine the two in the *Examples* section. The dbid column shows the database that's being locked, or more accurately, its number. This number can be found by typing the following command:

```
SELECT name FROM master.dbo.sysdatabases where dbid = 1.
```

Table 9.3 Types of Locks

DB	Database
FIL	File
IDX	Index
PG	Page
KEY	Key
TAB	Table
EXT	Extent
RID	Row identifier

Replace the 1 with the number of the database you're interested in. The ObjId is the number of the thing that's being locked—the table, the index, and so on. The mapping of the Type is shown in Table 9.3.

The Mode column in Listing 9.3 indicates the kind of lock. The three most important are Shared, Update, and Exclusive. If the mode is Shared, other processes can read but not change the data that's being locked. In other words, if the Type column is TAB (Table) and the Mode column is S (Shared), no one can change anything in that table until the lock releases. Other processes can read the data, but they can't change it.

If the lock mode is X (Exclusive) no one else can change it or read it. The U (Update) mode is used to prevent a deadlock situation, so that other processes cannot claim the same Exclusive lock on an Object.

Examples

I have a few examples here of finding information about the server activity. All of these use the command-line tools, because the graphical tools were dealt with earlier.

An interesting combination with these examples is to include them in a Web Assistant Wizard (see Chapter 6) to create a page that you can allow anyone to access to see the state of the server.

Who's Logged On

We'll begin with a simple script to show who's logged on to the server and what database they are using. Keep in mind that this query doesn't take into account any processes that are sleeping or not doing anything. If you want to see those, remove the line that reads `WHERE a.status = 'runnable'`, shown in Listing 9.4.

Listing 9.4   Who's using what database

```
SELECT 'SQL Name' = loginame
, 'NT Name' = nt_username
, 'Using Database' = b.name
FROM master.dbo.sysprocesses a
INNER JOIN master.dbo.sysdatabases b
ON a.dbid=b.dbid
WHERE a.status = 'runnable'
ORDER BY b.name
```

This script uses the system tables that I spoke about in Chapter 2, so there's no guarantee that it will work in the next version of SQL Server. Microsoft does not want you to use system tables, but often it's the only way to get certain kinds of information.

Kill a Process

You might have heard another DBA mention that she's going to kill a user. Normally (although not always) that means that she is going to terminate the process of a user who is either blocking another user or has a runaway query.

To do this, you use the `sp_who` command discussed earlier, to find the `spid` of the offending user. Then, simply type the command `kill` and that number. Don't take this method lightly, because it is a very ungraceful way to end a process.

How Busy Is My Server

The `sp_monitor` command is useful to help you watch your server. Sometimes, however, in places such as in code or on a dynamic Web page, you'd like to have a simple display of how busy the server is and whether the CPU or the I/O is the issue at the moment. You can do that with the simple query in Listing 9.5.

Listing 9.5   Quick and dirty system stats

```
SELECT
'CPU:' = @@cpu_busy
, 'you/O:' = @@io_busy
, 'As of:' = GETDATE()
```

You may have noticed that I didn't include a table in this `SELECT` statement. I used a special set of system variables that SQL Server 2000 keeps about itself.

There are many of these, and you can look in Books Online under Functions to find more of the kinds of things you can learn with these queries.

Rosetta Stone

Oracle

Oracle includes a few interesting ways to get information from its query engine. There are fundamental differences in the way you tune Oracle, depending on the hardware and OS you're using, but Table 9.4 shows the mappings between SQL Server 2000 and Oracle.

Microsoft Access

As you can imagine, the tools to monitor what's going on inside a database don't exist in Microsoft Access. Many people upgrade a Microsoft Access database for that very reason, to improve performance in a multiple-user environment. Built-in tools to see the locks being taken simply don't apply to Microsoft Access.

Table 9.4   Oracle and SQL Server Compared

Task	Oracle Tool	Microsoft SQL Server 2000
Performance information	Expert	Profiler
Index tuning	Index Tuning Wizard	Index Tuning Wizard
Who's on the server	SELECT username FROM v$session;	sp_who
Lock information	UTLLOCKT.SQL Script;	sp_lock
I/O statistics	SELECT * from V$SESS_IO;	sp_monitor
CPU statistics	SELECT (busy/ (busy + idle)) * 100 "% OF TIME BUSY" FROM v$dispatcher;	sp_monitor
General monitoring	SELECT * FROM V$SYSSTAT ;	sp_monitor

Resources

Webcast from Microsoft on using SQL Server 2000 Profiler:
*http://support.microsoft.com/servicedesks/webcasts/wc111400/
WCT111400.asp*
Showing execution plan using Query Analyzer:
http://www.swynk.com/friends/mcgehee/sql_2000_tools.asp
Profiler SQL for database design issues:
http://www.swynk.com/friends/smirnov/sqlprofiler.asp
http://www.swynk.com/friends/Vartanyan/DBOptim2000.asp
Excellent optimization and tuning site:
http://www.sql-server-performance.com
White paper from Microsoft on the Index Tuning Wizard:
http://msdn.microsoft.com/library/techart/itwforsql.htm

Chapter **10**

Security

Chapter at a Glance

Read this chapter to understand the security in SQL Server 2000. You'll need to know this information if your application has SQL Server or Windows logins to the server.

The Resources section contains references for:

- A great security white paper from Microsoft
- A discussion about "broken" logins
- A discussion on permissions inheritance

Read Chapter 2 before you read this one.

Overview

One of the toughest things I had to learn about administering a large database system was how the security works. Most every large Relational Database Management System (RDBMS) implements its security in a highly granular way, which can be a little frustrating at first. In this chapter, I peel back the security layers one at a time, starting with server authentication and moving all the way down to object permissions.

The process to allow all this is simple. You create a server *login* and then allow that login to access a database by creating a corresponding database *user*. You can create a SQL Server 2000 server login by graphical means or by commands. Using *Enterprise Manager*, you can tie the server login you create to a database, automatically creating a database user account. These database user accounts can be created separately as well. The primary commands used to create a new login and database user are `sp_addlogin` and `sp_grantdbaccess`, respectively.

Once the logins and users have been created, they can be grouped into roles. Roles are logins or users grouped by like security. There are several predefined server roles, which provide an easy way to allow logins to manage various aspects of the server's operation. There are also predefined database roles, which provide management permissions or access to objects in the database. You can create more database roles.

If you're working with an application, it may use an application role. This is a special type of permission that requires no users at all—the application provides security credentials to the server and database, and the data is available only to the program.

You can create roles by using graphical means or with the command `sp_addrole`, and add users to roles with the command `sp_addrolemember`. To create an application role, you can use the command `sp_addapprole`. Once created, the application role is activated with the command `sp_setapprole`.

There are two types of permissions: object and statement. Statement permissions are granted on items in the database such as tables and views, and allow you to create or modify these objects. They are the CREATE verbs. Object permissions are granted to allow access to the objects. Permissions are granted on each object in the database and are layered to allow or deny access. These permissions include the verbs SELECT, INSERT, DELETE, UPDATE, EXECUTE, and REFERENCES.

If the same user creates all objects, that user only has to grant access to the higher object, such as a view, that calls the other objects.

Detail

SQL Server 2000 is light-years ahead of many other large-scale database servers in ease of management, but all this management may be a bit more work than you are used to if you're coming from a smaller database system such as Microsoft Access. Because of the complexity of this security arrangement, I'm going to spend a bit more time on theory than I normally do.

I'll divide my discussion into two main parts. First, I'll discuss authenticating to a database, and second, I'll talk about permissions on objects and statements in that database. If you're familiar with network security, this is similar to user accounts and file rights concepts. Dealing first with authenticating to a database, I'll break *that* subject down further into two parts as well.

Because SQL Server 2000 can contain multiple databases, it logically follows that all the people allowed to use a particular server aren't necessarily allowed to use all the databases on that server. To facilitate this process, SQL Server 2000 allows users to log in to the server, called a *server login,* and allows server logins to access databases, called *database users.*

You can allow a Windows account or group to act as a server login, which means that you don't have to create or track a separate password. SQL Server 2000 looks to Windows or Active Directory for the name and password.

In case the user doesn't have a Windows or Active Directory account, you can create a separate name and password for a user to authenticate to the server. To do that, you need to make sure the database is in the mode that allows both NT *and* SQL Server accounts to be created. See Chapter 2 for more information on this server setting, called mixed mode. In most of the examples, I use the mixed mode settings we set up in Chapter 2, but I explain both kinds of logins in this chapter.

Once you create a server login through Windows or by creating a new SQL Server 2000 login account, you'll create a database user. This ties the login to the user name. You perform this step in each database you want the user to access.

In Chapter 15, I look at how security is affected when you are set up to use multiple instances of SQL Server 2000 on the same server.

The next part of SQL Server 2000 security involves permissions. You grant or deny permissions on *objects* and *statements*. Objects are nouns, like tables and views; statements are verbs indicating what you can do to those things, like creating or destroying them.

If you want to allow a user to *access* a noun, you grant *object* permissions. If you want to allow a user to *create* a noun, you grant *statement* permissions. Permissions are granted in a database system on each object—that's what can make security complex.

The verbs you use to grant or deny permissions are GRANT and DENY. Object permissions you grant or deny include SELECT, INSERT, DELETE, UPDATE, EXECUTE, and REFERENCES. I'll detail all these permissions further in a moment.

You grant or deny these permissions against objects, like tables or views. By combining the permissions and objects, you come up with a usable security map for your application. If the developers of the application use stored procedures to access all data, they simplify the security model. This is because of something Microsoft calls an *Ownership Chain*. As long as the same login account creates all database objects, that account can grant permissions on the stored procedure alone, without needing to grant permissions on all the objects the stored procedure touches.

Another way that Microsoft helps simplify security is by using a special SQL Server 2000 group called an *application role*. This special group is active only when it is called from within a program. In other words, you can't use the application role with a tool such as Query Analyzer.

Permissions are granted to the role and activated by the program. If the program is developed correctly, you'll not need to store any users in SQL Server 2000. Security in this model is normally handled by the application.

I begin my explanation of SQL Server 2000 security with an examination of the security types and then move on to logins, users, and roles. I then describe the permissions for each object and statement.

Security Types

As I mentioned earlier, the basic idea behind SQL Server 2000 security is to create a server login and tie that login to a database user, which might be placed in a role, either of which is granted or denied permissions on objects and statements.

Server Logins

People must be allowed to access the SQL Server 2000 server before they can access a database. This can be accomplished by creating a user in SQL Server 2000, or by leveraging a Windows or Active Directory account. You do this by using one of three methods:

- Create the server login using a wizard
- Create the server login using Enterprise Manager
- Create the server login using command-line tools

In this chapter's Graphical and Command Line sections, I look at the specific process to add or edit a server login.

Server Groups (Roles)   Logins can belong to a serverwide group, called a *fixed server role*. These roles and what they can do are displayed in Table 10.1, which I got directly from Books Online. Server logins can belong to more than one role. You can't create any new server roles.

Database Users

Once you've created a login, you tie that login to a user account in a particular database. You can do this graphically or by using a command. To tie that account, you create a database user with the login name you created in the last step.

Table 10.1   Fixed Server Roles

Role	Rights
Sysadmin	Can perform any activity in SQL Server.
Serveradmin	Can set serverwide configuration options, shut down the server.
Setupadmin	Can manage linked servers and startup procedures.
Securityadmin	Can manage logins and CREATE DATABASE permissions, also read error logs and change passwords.
Processadmin	Can manage processes running in SQL Server.
Dbcreator	Can create, alter, and drop databases.
Diskadmin	Can manage disk files.
Bulkadmin	Can execute BULK INSERT statements.

Database Groups (Roles)   Just as you can assign logins to predefined *server* roles that have built-in rights, there are predefined *database* roles as well. The difference is that you can add your own database roles and then grant rights to those roles. Table 10.2 shows the fixed database roles, once again from Books Online.

The rights and permissions from roles and users are cumulative. If you add a user to a role that has INSERT permissions on a table and add her to another role that has DELETE permissions, then she has both INSERT and DELETE permissions.

Table 10.2   Predefined Database Roles

Fixed Database Role	Description
db_owner	Has all permissions in the database.
db_accessadmin	Can add or remove user IDs.
db_securityadmin	Can manage all permissions, object ownerships, roles, and role memberships.
db_ddladmin	Can issue ALL DDL, but cannot issue GRANT, REVOKE, or DENY statements.
db_backupoperator	Can issue DBCC, CHECKPOINT, and BACKUP statements.
db_datareader	Can select all data from any user table in the database.
db_datawriter	Can modify any data in any user table in the database.
db_denydatareader	Cannot select any data from any user table in the database.
db_denydatawriter	Cannot modify any data in any user table in the database.

This isn't true, however, if a user or role has specifically been *denied* access to a noun. This works just like many types of network security.

Permissions

After you create a server login and a database user and set up the roles, you grant or deny those users or roles permissions. If you're a member of the sysadmin role, you can grant any permission in any database on the server. If you're in the db_owner or db_securityadmin role, you can grant permission on all statements or objects in the database you own. Regardless of your group, you can usually grant permissions for objects that you own.

You set permissions with the verbs GRANT, DENY, and REVOKE. GRANT gives the permission, and DENY takes it away.

The REVOKE verb removes the permission from the user but doesn't specifically deny them that right. If I was REVOKE'd the SELECT permission on table TEST, but I belonged to a *role* that had the SELECT permission, I could still access the table. If I was DENY'd that SELECT permission, I couldn't access the table even though the role I'm in could.

Remember that permissions are layered—if you create a view that looks up values in a table you didn't create, you need to make sure the user gets permissions for both the table *and* the view.

This doesn't hold true, though, if you created both the table and the view. All you have to grant there are permissions to the view. That makes things much more simple. The user won't need access to the table, but he does have access to the view that looks at only certain data in the table. In that manner, you control what the user sees with just a little bit of security work.

To put a fine point on it, you can even grant or deny permissions down to the column level. You probably won't do that very often, because it's easier to use a view for something like that.

Object Permissions

The first object-level permission I discuss is SELECT. This permission gives the user the ability to get data and display it. It's a bit like READ permissions on a filesystem. The INSERT permission lets the user insert data into the object. The DELETE permission lets the user delete something from the object. The UPDATE permission lets the user change data. You need to grant this permission if the user has to change data that already exists in the object.

Once again, remember that the permissions are layered. If you grant a role the INSERT permission but not the SELECT permission, the role can insert data but not see it.

The next permission, EXECUTE, is granted on stored procedures, those Transact SQL (T-SQL) code programs that run on SQL Server 2000. To allow a user to run a stored procedure, you need to grant the EXECUTE permission on that stored procedure to the user or the role.

You'll probably see this a lot, and it may be the only permission the developer asks you to grant to your users. That's because as long as one person creates all the tables, views, and other objects, that person can create a stored procedure that accesses them and that follows those rights all the way through. Let's look at an example.

You create a table, called TEST. You then create a stored procedure called usp_test that selects data from that table. You then grant the user the EXECUTE permission on usp_test, which allows him to look at the table, even though he can't directly use the SELECT command against the table.

The last object-level permission I examine is REFERENCES. This is a fairly unusual permission, but you may still run into it.

Database designers can create relationships between data so that data in one table must exist in another to be valid. To place data in that second table, you'd normally need permissions on the other table as well, because the first item must look up the second. Since the developer might not want the user to have permissions in the second table, the REFERENCES permission allows the user to enter data in the second table without having rights in the first.

Statement Permissions

Statement permissions allow users to create or modify objects like tables. The commands are:

- CREATE DATABASE
- CREATE DEFAULT
- CREATE FUNCTION
- CREATE PROCEDURE
- CREATE RULE
- CREATE TABLE
- CREATE VIEW
- BACKUP DATABASE
- BACKUP LOG

The CREATE variety of permission does pretty much what you think. By granting this statement-level permission, you allow a user to create an object.

What might be a bit less obvious is the BACKUP permission. When you think about it, you're allowing a user the same level of access to back up a database as to create one, which is why you need this special right.

Graphical

By far the easiest method to work with logins, users, and permissions is to use the wizards or Enterprise Manager. That isn't to say it's the fastest method for bulk operations, but it can be the fastest way to alter a single permission or to create one user or login.

We'll do all of our graphical work from Enterprise Manager, so go ahead and open it now.

Working with Server Logins

We'll create your first user, MrBasicNT, as a Windows 2000 user who is allowed to select data from one table in the pubs2 database. We'll create your next user, MrNormalUserSQL, as a SQL Server 2000 user who can use all the tables and objects in pubs2. The next login we'll create is MrsDboNT, an NT user who is the database owner of the pubs2 database.

We'll then create a user called MrsDeveloperSQL as a SQL Server 2000 user who can create objects in the pubs2 database.

To create all these users, you need to create the server logins first. You then tie those logins to users in the database and assign them to the proper groups.

Begin by using the Create Login Wizard to make your first login, MrBasicNT. Create this user in Windows 2000 and assign him a password of password. As shown in Figure 10.1, open Enterprise Manager and click on Tools and then Wizards.

Next expand the Database wizard selection box, as shown in Figure 10.2. Select the Create Login Wizard. Press OK, which brings up the opening panel in

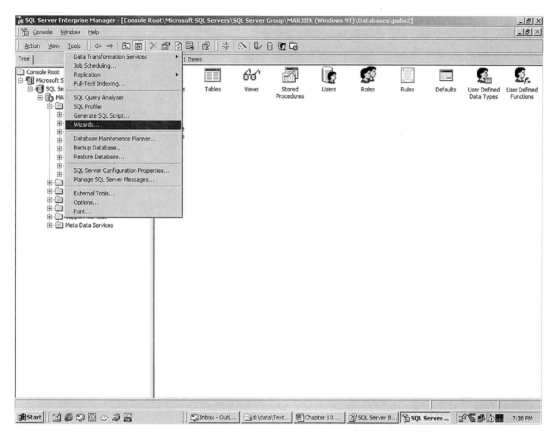

Figure 10.1 Enterprise Manager

the wizard, shown in Figure 10.3. This wizard allows you to not only create the login, but also assign the user to a server role and log in to a database. Press Next to bring up the screen in Figure 10.4.

Next select Windows authentication and then Next to bring up the panel in Figure 10.5.

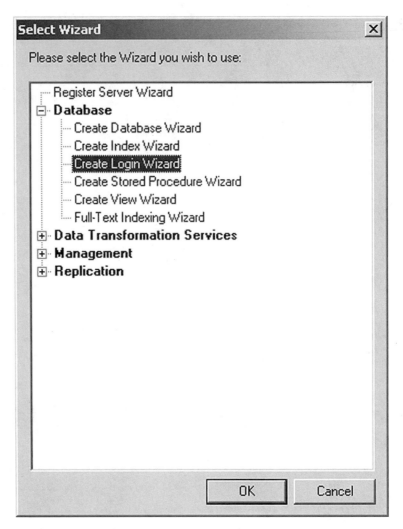

Figure 10.2   *Selecting the wizard*

Type in the domain and name of the user as shown and then select the Next button to bring up the panel in Figure 10.6. In this panel, you assign this login to fixed server roles if you need to. You're not going to do that; just select Next to bring up the panel in Figure 10.7.

Figure 10.3
Starting the
wizard

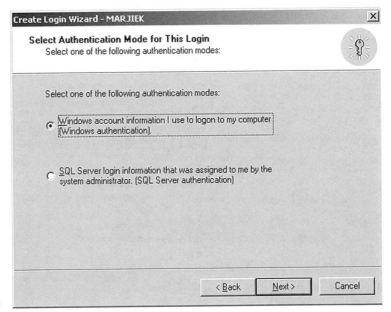

Figure 10.4
Selecting
authentication

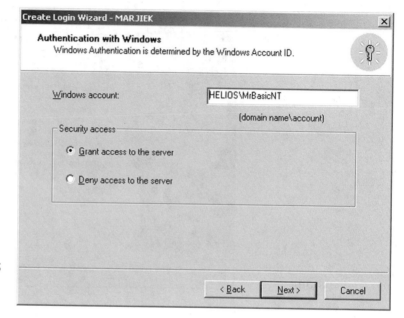

Figure 10.5
Naming the
user

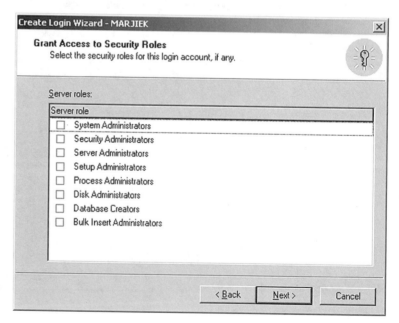

Figure 10.6
Granting the
security roles

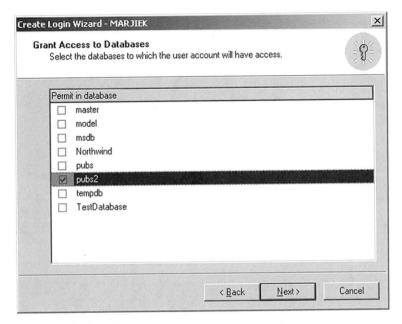

Figure 10.7 Granting database access

Because you selected the pubs2 database, the login will be created in the database with the same name. This is the easiest way to create a database user from a login. Select Next to bring up the final panel, shown in Figure 10.8. And you're done. This panel just displays the fact that the user will be created.

As shown in Figure 10.9, expand the Security and then Logins objects to show the login that you created. Next you'll create the MrNormalUserSQL login. Let's not use the wizard this time; just right-click in the Logins object in Enterprise Manager and select New Login from the menu that appears. That action brings up the panel shown in Figure 10.10.

As you can see, we need to do a few things here. First set the name, and then change the login type from Windows to SQL Server Authentication. This ensures that SQL Server 2000 will track the username and password instead of looking to Windows to do it.

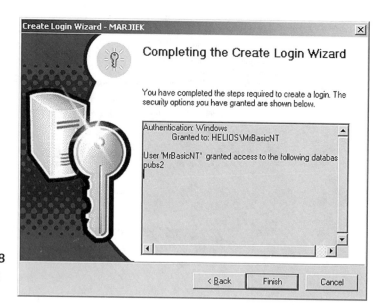

Figure 10.8
Completing
the wizard

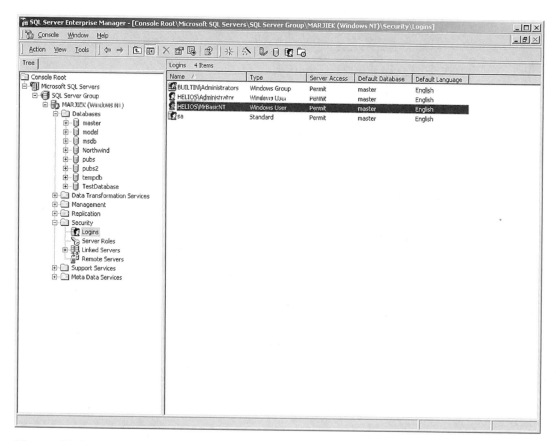

Figure 10.9 The Logins object

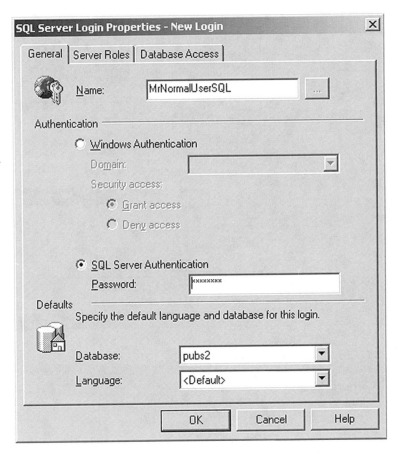

Figure 10.10   Creating a SQL Server 2000 login

Enter the password (it's password), and set the default database for this login to pubs2. If you *had* picked Windows Authentication, you would get a button that allows you to select the user from a list. Select the Database Access tab to bring up the panel shown in Figure 10.11.

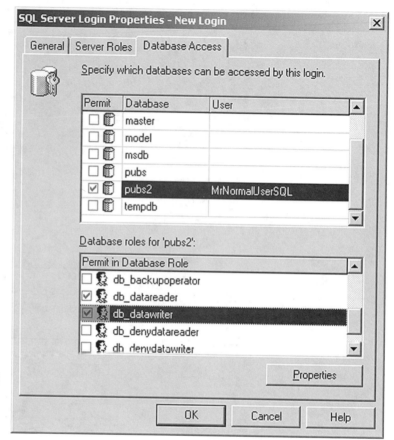

Figure 10.11
Setting the
database
access

Here you're creating the database user. You'll tie him to the pubs2 database and then add him to two special roles. These roles, db_datareader and db_datawriter, allow this user to read and write data in all objects in your database. If there were more objects that you *didn't* want him to access than objects that you *did*, you wouldn't use these roles at all. In that case, you would grant the user or another role individual rights on individual objects.

Click OK and then confirm the password you created for this login. Create the other two logins I mentioned the same way, except you won't tie them to a database this time. Because the process is the same, I won't show those screens here.

Working with Database Users

Now that you've set up the logins MrsDboNT, an Active Directory account, and MrsDeveloperSQL, a standard or SQL account, tie them to a database, since you didn't do that on login creation. As shown in Figure 10.12, drill down to the Databases, pubs2, Users object to show the users you already have.

Here you see the logins you created earlier and two users you *didn't* create. These users are dbo and guest. The dbo user isn't real—it's mapped to the sa account, which is the login that owns the server and, in particular, is a database owner. This is a throwback to a long time ago when this database user was an *alias* for another, all-powerful user.

If a database has a guest account, logins not mapped to this database are able to use its privileges to access the database. Whatever you grant this account, everyone without a database user account gets. This is a fairly large security hole, so you may wish to remove this account from the database or

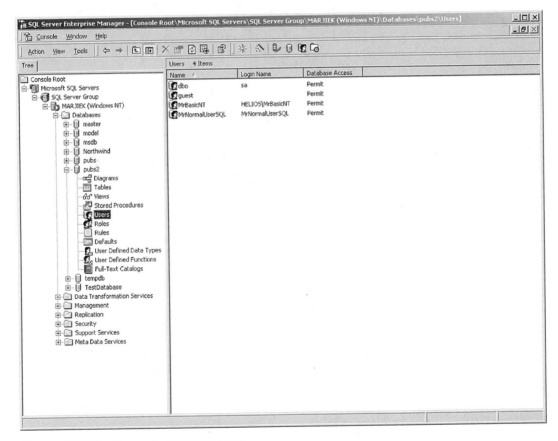

Figure 10.12 Current database users

even from the *model* system database so that it doesn't get created in all new databases by default.

To continue with tying a server login to a database user, right-click in the right-hand panel and select New Database User from the menu. You're shown the panel in Figure 10.13.

You can see here that the first database user you're creating is MrsDboNT. Pull down the menu and select that user, and you're shown the panel displayed in Figure 10.14.

Set this user to a special role, db_owner. This role owns all the objects in this database. We'll come to all that in a moment. Repeat the process without assigning a role for the MrsDeveloperSQL login.

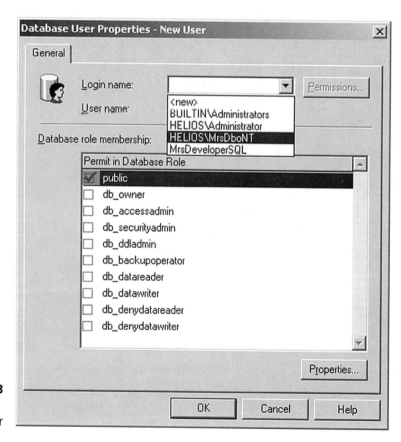

Figure 10.13
Creating a database user

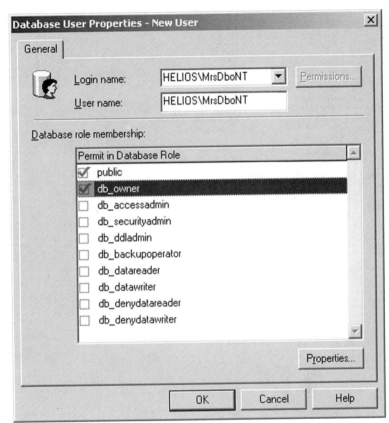

Figure 10.14
The database
user

Working with Roles

Next you'll start assigning users to database roles. You're going to use a couple
of roles to your advantage to bypass granting individual permissions on each
object.

Earlier you assigned the MrsDboNT account the db_owner role, so now you
assign the MrsDeveloperSQL user the ability to do her job. As shown in Figure 10.15, select the Roles object.

All users belong to the public role, so you don't have to add any of them there.

Next set up the permissions for the MrsDeveloperSQL database user. This
user needs standard read, write, and delete permissions on each object in the
database. These are called Data Manipulation Language (DML) statements. The
user also needs to have the ability to create new objects in the database, called

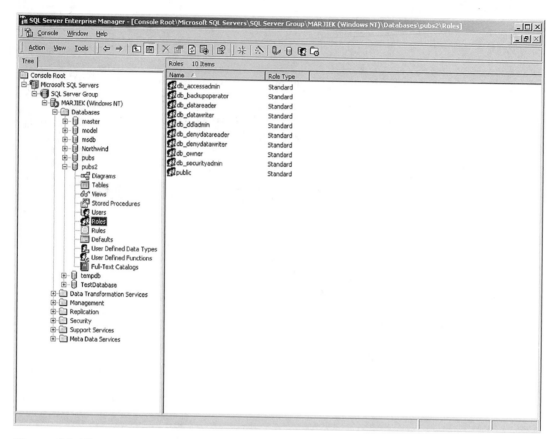

Figure 10.15   The Roles object

Data Definition Language (DDL) statements. Combine these three roles—db_datawriter, db_datareader, and db_ddladmin—to give this user the DML and DDL rights.

As shown in Figure 10.16, double-click the db_ddladmin role. Next click the Add button to select your user. This is shown in Figure 10.17. Next select OK and then OK again, and the process is complete. Repeat all this for the db_datawriter and db_datareader roles.

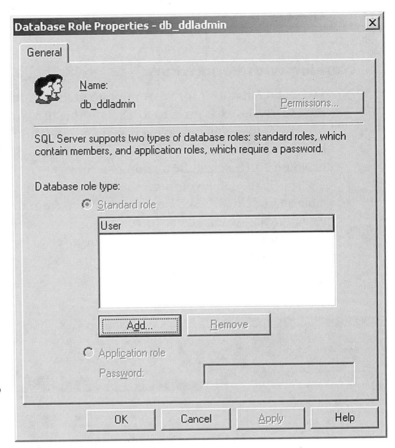

Figure 10.16
The
db_ddladmin
group

Figure 10.17
Adding the
user

Working with Permissions

I've saved MrBasicNT for last, opting to give him permissions one object at a time to display that process. Let's limit this user to being able to select data from two tables and modifying data in only one. You don't do that in here; you have to move to the objects that you want to grant or deny access to. As shown in Figure 10.18, select the *authors table* object.

This is the table you want the user to read and update, so right-click the table and select *All Tasks, Manage Permissions* from the menu that appears. The results are shown in Figure 10.19.

Grant the permissions you want this user to have by clicking the proper boxes. Leaving the box blank allows the user to inherit rights from any of

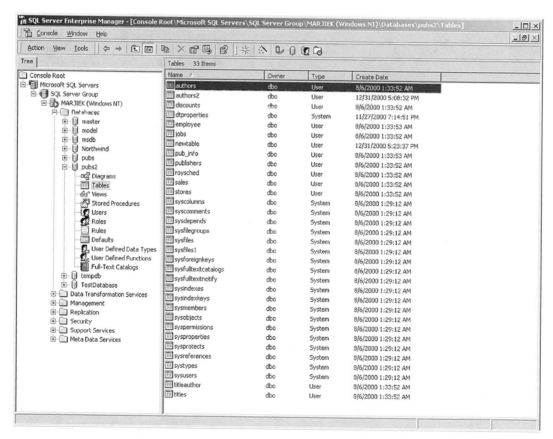

Figure 10.18 The authors table

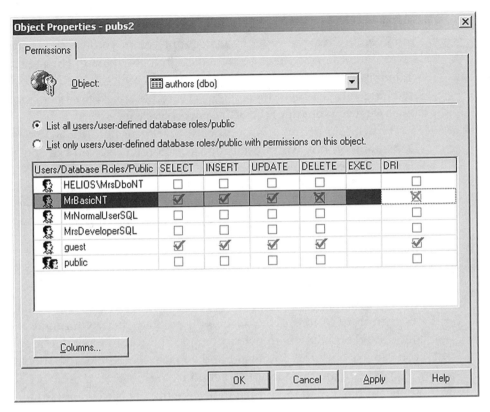

Figure 10.19   Managing permissions

the roles he might be a member of. Clicking the box multiple times until a red X appears denies the user the right to use that verb, regardless of the role membership.

Repeat this process for the other two tables you want this user to access, titles and titleauthors, with the exception that he'll only get SELECT permissions there.

Command Line

For creating logins and users, the graphical method works well as long as you don't have a lot of them to enter. If you do, it makes a lot more sense to use commands. A trick I use is to create a spreadsheet containing the commands and then type the users' names in the proper cells. I then save the result as a text file and open it in Query Analyzer to run the commands.

Working with Server Logins

You need to create a server login account before you can tie a user to a database or grant her permissions to objects in that database. The logins and users end up in system tables, but you don't have to remember the tables or the SQL statements to put them there. SQL Server 2000 provides lots of stored procedures (SQL Server code) that do the work for you.

Two kinds of login authentication are possible for SQL Server 2000. Depending on how your installation was configured, you can allow Windows or SQL Server authentication. The commands change slightly based on the type of authentication you select.

The primary command you'll use for creating SQL Server 2000 logins is `sp_addlogin`. The format looks like the one shown in Listing 10.1.

Listing 10.1   sp_addlogin

```
sp_addlogin 'MrsDeveloperSQL', 'password'
```

The first argument is the name of the user, and the second is the password. As with most stored procedures, you enclose the text arguments in single quotes and separate them with a comma. There are a few other arguments that you can use with this command, and you can look them up in *Books Online*.

Next, create a Windows account login. The command for that is `sp_grantlogin`, and the format looks like the one shown in Listing 10.2.

Listing 10.2   sp_grantlogin

```
sp_grantlogin 'HELIOS\MrsDboNT'
```

Notice that this time you don't need to specify a password, because SQL Server 2000 allows Windows or Active Directory to track the password.

There are a few other commands to help you with server logins, as detailed in Table 10.3. You can look in *Books Online* for more information on each of these if you're interested in finding the exact syntax.

Working with Database Users

Now that you have those server login accounts, you can tie them to the database with the `sp_grantdbaccess` command. The format looks like Listing 10.3.

Listing 10.3   sp_grantdbaccess

```
USE pubs2
GO
EXEC sp_grantdbaccess 'HELIOS\MrsDboNT', 'MrsDboNT'
GO
```

Table 10.3 Working with Server Logins

Command	What It Does
sp_helplogins	Displays information about a login
sp_droplogin	Removes a login
sp_revokelogin	Revokes a login
sp_denylogin	Denies a login
sp_password	Changes a login's password
sp_defaultdb	Sets a login's default database
sp_validatelogins	Shows "orphans" in the database. These are logins that exist in SQL Server but no longer exist as a Windows account.

This command is a bit different. Notice first of all that it's necessary to use the database that you want to grant access to. The first two lines of code do that. This is called "setting the database context."

Notice also that the stored procedure is prefaced with the word EXEC. You have to do that if a stored procedure isn't the first command on the line, and it's a good practice to do all the time.

Next set the name of the server login. Because this is a Windows user, you need to include the domain the user is assigned to. You wouldn't have to do that if the login belonged to SQL Server; you would just type the name in ticks or single quotes.

The second argument is the name of the user in the database. This name is the same as the server login account. Table 10.4 shows the other commands you can use to assist with these accounts. Now that you have the database logins and users in place, you can work with the roles.

Working with Roles

There are several sections to this part of the command discussion. You will often need to add and remove logins from the server roles, add and edit the

Table 10.4 Working with Database Users

Command	What It Does
sp_helpuser	Displays information about a database user
sp_revokedbaccess	Removes a login from the database

Table 10.5   Working with Server Roles

Command	What It Does
sp_helpsrvrolemember	Displays who belongs to a server role
sp_dropsrvrolemember	Removes a login from a server role
sp_srvrolepermission	Displays what a role can do
sp_helpsrvrole	Displays the fixed server roles

database roles, and add and remove users from those database roles. We also examine application roles.

Server Roles

First I'll explain adding members to server roles. The command you use for this function is sp_addsrvrolemember. The code in Listing 10.4 adds the SQL Server 2000 user SuperUser to the sysadmin group.

Listing 10.4   sp_addsrvrolemember

```
sp_addsrvrolemember 'SuperUser', 'sysadmin'
```

There are a few other commands that you can use to work with server roles, as shown in Table 10.5.

Database Roles

There are two parts to this topic: the roles themselves and the users you put into the roles. I'll describe both.

Let's examine the commands to add a new database role. The stored procedure is sp_addrole, and the syntax is shown in Listing 10.5.

Listing 10.5   sp_addrole

```
sp_addrole 'Developers'
```

You can use another argument that specifies the owner of the role. This allows a database user or another role to manage the users for that role. Table 10.6 shows other commands for working with the database roles.

The next part of the database role discussion involves moving database users in and out of those roles with the stored procedure sp_addrolemember. The syntax shown in Listing 10.6 adds the database user MrsDeveloperSQL to the role of Developers.

Table 10.6   Working with Database Roles

Command	What It Does
sp_droprole	Removes a role
sp_helprole	Displays information about a role
sp_helpdbfixedrole	Displays what rights the fixed roles have

Listing 10.6   sp_addrolemember

```
sp_addrolemember 'Developers', 'MrsDeveloperSQL'
```

As before, a few other commands can assist you with working with the role members. These are shown in Table 10.7.

Application Roles

Application roles give permissions to a program—no user is ever assigned to the role; it's just a role that gets a password and rights. The process for using an application role involves creating the application role, giving it a password, granting it some permissions, activating it through code, and using the role through code.

To create the role, use the `sp_addapprole` command. The syntax shown in Listing 10.7 creates an application role called *TestApplication* with a password of *password*.

Listing 10.7   sp_addapprole

```
sp_addapprole 'TestApplication', 'password'
```

Now that you have the role and the password, you can assign permissions to it just as you would for another role or user. Normally, you would assign permissions next, but I'll save that discussion for the permissions section later. For now we'll pretend it already has rights, so you'll activate the role next.

Table 10.7   Working with Role Members

Command	What It Does
sp_droprolemember	Removes a member from a role
sp_helprolemember	Displays information about membership in a role

Table 10.8 Working with Application Roles

Command	What It Does
sp_approlepassword	Changes the password for an application role
sp_dropapprole	Removes an application role

This is done in code passed to SQL Server 2000 using the sp_setapprole command. The command shown in Listing 10.8 activates the *TestApplication* application role with the password you assigned it earlier. The developer's code sends this command to SQL Server 2000, which grants it the proper security.

Listing 10.8 Activating an application role

```
sp_setapprole ' TestApplication ', 'password'
```

Two other commands are used when working with application roles, as shown in Table 10.8.

Working with Permissions

Now that that the logins, users, and roles are created, we'll focus on the permissions. For clarity, we'll work with users here, but know that you can use the same commands for roles or application roles as well.

The commands you'll use were discussed in the Detail section—GRANT, DENY, and REVOKE. Keep in mind that these permissions are *layered*—meaning that if a view accesses a particular table, you need to grant permissions on *both* objects if they aren't owned by the same person. If the same person owns them, only the higher object needs the permissions granted. You can see that, from a security perspective, one database user should create all the objects in a database.

Another thing to remember about permissions is that they are set for the verbs SELECT, INSERT, UPDATE, and DELETE on tables or even particular columns in a table. You might not know your users are using those verbs, and your users are unaware of it, but if they look at data using a program, something is using a SELECT verb. If they change data, they are using the UPDATE verb, and so forth.

If a program uses stored procedures, they might be using EXECUTE permissions. In this case, as long as one user created the objects in the database, only the stored procedures get the permissions, and that makes life pretty easy. To make life truly easy, the program would use an application role and might not even need logins or users.

GRANT

The GRANT verb allows access to an object. Listing 10.9 shows the syntax.

Listing 10.9   Granting SELECT access to a table

```
GRANT SELECT
ON authors
TO MrsDeveloperSQL
GO
```

To build a permissions "sentence," first you use the verb (GRANT), then you set the direct object (SELECT), then you set the preposition (ON authors), and finally you set the indirect object (TO MrsDeveloperSQL).

Notice that the direct object(s) are what you want the user to be able to do. If you want them to have more than one privilege, such as INSERT and SELECT, include them but separate them with a comma.

A special adjective, called ALL, gives all permissions to the object. Replace SELECT with ALL in Listing 10.9 to see how that works.

The GRANT command can be used with the statement permissions, like CREATE, and with object permissions, like SELECT. The person granting the permissions has to have the rights to do so. You can also add as many users or roles as you like in one statement by separating them with commas.

If you want more information and examples of the GRANT command, type GRANT, GRANT (described) in the Index panel of *Books Online*.

DENY

To remove the permissions a user or role has on an object, use the DENY verb. Listing 10.10 shows an example. Notice the brackets around the Windows username, which is required because it has a \ character in it. As with GRANT, you can remove permissions to objects and statements.

Listing 10.10   Denying INSERT access to a table

```
DENY INSERT
ON authors
TO MrsDeveloperSQL, [HELIOS\MrAverageNT]
```

If you want more information on this topic, look up DENY in *Books Online*.

REVOKE

The previous two commands affect permissions regardless of the role a user is in, and that might not be the exact effect you're after. You may not want a user to have permissions in an item unless she exists in a role that grants her the permission. For this, you use the REVOKE verb. Listing 10.11 shows an example.

Listing 10.11   Using the REVOKE Verb

```
REVOKE SELECT
ON authors
FROM MrsDeveloperSQL
```

The same caveats involving multiple users or objects and so forth apply to this command. The REVOKE verb can be a little confusing—if you're thinking about situations in which you might use this verb, search for REVOKE in *Books Online*.

Examples

Since I've described logins, users, roles, permissions and the like, I'll show an example of a simple database permissions schema. I'll also include a *very* useful example of an "orphaned" database user. This condition occurs because of the design I've been talking about—the fact that *logins* are stored at the server level in the server system tables, and the *users* are stored at the database level in the database system tables.

You can see that if you back up a database on one server and then restore it to another, the *users* in the database tables no longer belong to the *logins* in that new server's tables. It's a common problem and can be a sticky wicket if you don't know what to do.

Setting Up a Database Permissions Schema

Let's take a real-world example: an application that houses a contact management database. You have several users that are grouped by department, and the departments need varying access to different objects in the database. You're asked to manage the database as part of the application, and you're getting a new SQL Server 2000 server.

You've done the sizing, installation planning, and so forth, and the company has provided you with the ODBC DSN settings for each workstation that will connect to the database server.

Planning the Users

The first step is to plan the security model. Can you use Windows security, or do you need to create logins using SQL Server 2000? The answer to this question usually depends on the network you have.

Are you using Linux or NetWare? Are the NT domains the users are in non-trusted? Is the Active Directory (AD) tree foreign to your forest? You'll have to use the SQL Server 2000 authentication model and manage passwords for your users.

Do you have an NT domain or trusted domains? Is your AD schema such that you're all in one forest? If you have Windows authentication available, it's best to leverage that. Let's assume for this example that you have to use SQL Server 2000 authentication.

Planning the Roles

Next, plan the roles. Group users by function, not by department. Just because a user works in accounting doesn't mean that he has the same application requirements that another accounting worker does. It's best to lay out a grid with all the functions in the application and then write the users' names to the left of the grid. Check off each function next to a user's name, and then group the users by checkboxes.

These groups will be the roles. For instance, if five users need to add data but not change it in a particular function in the application, make that a role.

Be conservative, but make sure you check with the user community to ensure that you allow them to do their jobs.

Planning the Permissions

Finally, decide what permissions the roles need on each object. If the same person created all the objects, you'll only need to grant permissions to the higher object, such as the view that references a table.

If the application uses stored procedures, that's even better. You can just grant the proper EXECUTE permissions and be done with it. This assumes that the developer laid out the stored procedures such that you *can* do that. When that happens, you'll often notice an almost one-to-one correlation between roles and stored procedures.

Now that you've completed those processes, you have a choice of using all this information to create the logins, users, and roles with the graphical tools or the command-line versions.

What I've found is that if you have just a few things to do, graphical methods are quicker, but if you have a bunch, it's quicker to create a spreadsheet with the commands and save that data as a text file. You then run that file with the command tools to do the work.

There's one other way you can manage this task. You can create a table for the users, with a column each for the username, password, and role. Let's assume you've done that, and the table is stored as CreateUsers. You can now use SQL Server itself to do the work of creating a list of users for you. Listing 10.12 shows the command and the output.

Listing 10.12 Creating logins and users with SQL statements

```
SELECT
'EXEC sp_addlogin ''' + UserName + ''', ''' + Password + ''''
+ CHAR(13) + 'GO' + CHAR(13)
+ 'EXEC sp_grantdbaccess ''' + UserName + ''', ''' + 'pubs2' + ''''
+ CHAR(13) + 'GO' + CHAR(13)
+ 'EXEC sp_addrolemember ''' + UserName + ''', ''' + Role + ''''
+ CHAR(13) + 'GO' + CHAR(13)
FROM CreateUsers

EXEC sp_addlogin 'Tom', 'password1'
GO
EXEC sp_grantdbaccess 'Tom', 'pubs2'
GO
EXEC sp_addrolemember 'Tom', 'db_owner'
GO

EXEC sp_addlogin 'Dick', 'password2'
GO
EXEC sp_grantdbaccess 'Dick', 'pubs2'
GO
EXEC sp_addrolemember 'Dick', 'db_select'
GO

EXEC sp_addlogin 'Harry', 'password3'
GO
EXEC sp_grantdbaccess 'Harry', 'pubs2'
GO
EXEC sp_addrolemember 'Harry', 'db_insert'
GO
```

Take a good look at this script; it shows one way to embed single quotes (ticks) in the output of a SQL Server 2000 query. The CHAR(13) reference puts a linefeed in the output. Here you've included only three users in the table, but it would work just as well with hundreds. I've used this method to handle most all the repetitive tasks I've had to do. After the command runs, you simply cut the results from the Results pane, and paste and run them in the command window of Query Analyzer.

This trick of using SQL Server to write other SQL statements is used a great deal by DBAs, and I even use it to create script files for Linux and NT. There's even a way to make the script not only generate the statements but also run them, but since I use this same method for operating system commands and so forth, I don't do that.

Re-create Permissions after a Move

Re-creating the link between a database user and a server login after you copy a database is quite a problem. This happens when the database, with its associated users, is restored to a server where the *master* database has different login information. In this situation the link between the *master..sysxlogins* and the *datbasename..sysusers* table is broken.

This doesn't hold true if you're just replacing a server, because you can back up the *master* database that has the server logins table and then restore that along with the affected database. The database users and server logins will then match on your new server, and all is well.

If you do have the problem of a database backup and these orphaned users, there is a simple fix. The command to use is `sp_change_users_login`. There are three parameters to this command:

- Action
- Username
- Login Name

Let's take a couple of examples. In the first one, you have backed up the database *pubs*, to which you've granted access to three logins on a server called SQLServerOne. Now restore that backup, as described in Chapter 8, to another server, SQL ServerTwo. You'll have different logins there, but you don't want to map the permissions all over again.

The action you use in this case is `Update_One`. The command shown in Listing 10.13 allows the current user `MrsDeveloperSQL` in the *pubs* database to be used by the login `MrsCurrentLogin` on SQLServerTwo.

Listing 10.13   Linking logins and users one at a time
```
USE pubs
GO
EXEC sp_change_users_login 'Update_One', 'MrsDeveloperSQL', 'MrsCurrentLogin'
```

Now let's take a second example. You have that *pubs* database again, but this time you have the same logins on SQLServerTwo that you had on SQLServerOne. Won't that work? Nope. It's not the name that matters; it's a number in the system tables in each database that is linked.

You can use the `sp_change_users_login` command to have SQL Server 2000 update those numbers based on the name. As always, check everything after you finish to make sure that what you wanted to happen, did. Take a look at Listing 10.14.

Listing 10.14   Linking logins and users in bulk

```
USE pubs
GO
EXEC sp_change_users_login 'Auto_Fix'
```

This command just looks in the database tables and server tables and does a best match.

There's one final action you can qualify on this verb: the Report action. You should run this action to find out the "orphans" in the database.

Rosetta Stone

The mechanisms for security are vendor-specific, but there are more corollaries here than you might think.

Oracle

You'll not have many problems mapping the idea of restricting and granting access to objects if you're familiar with Oracle, because there are many similarities in the concepts behind object security between Oracle and SQL Server 2000.

Oracle security has two parts: a security domain that contains privileges and roles, drive space, and resource limits (called a Profile, a concept you really like); and the rights and privileges granted to database objects for that user. Security can be accomplished through graphical or command means, and the commands are often similar to those in SQL Server 2000. The REVOKE command from SQL Server 2000 has, as I understand it, no equivalent in Oracle, although the same effect can be achived through other commands.

Table 10.9 compares the two products.

Microsoft Access

Microsoft Access can protect a database at the primary level by setting a password. You can create groups and users, but the permissions are not quite as granular as they are in SQL Server 2000. See Table 10.10 for a comparison of the products.

Table 10.9   Oracle and SQL Server 2000 Compared

Task	Oracle Tool	Microsoft SQL Server 2000
Manage users and roles graphically	Security Manager	Enterprise Manager
Manage rights and privileges graphically	Security Manager	Enterprise Manager
Grant rights from the command line	GRANT	GRANT
Remove rights from the command line	REVOKE	DENY
Audit a user	Security Manager	Profiler

Table 10.10   Microsoft Access and SQL Server 2000 Compared

Task	Access Tool	Microsoft SQL Server 2000
Manage users and roles graphically	Tools…Security…User and Group Accounts	Enterprise Manager
Manage rights and privileges graphically	Tools…Security…User and Group Security	Enterprise Manager

Resources

Excellent white paper on SQL Server 2000 security from Microsoft:
http://www.microsoft.com/technet/sql/technote/sql2ksec.asp
Another way to fix broken logins:
http://www.swynk.com/friends/boyle/fixingbrokenlogins.asp
Permission inheritance behavior between Windows 2000 and Windows NT 4:
http://www.microsoft.com/technet/support/kb.asp?ID=287024

SQL Server 2000 Advanced Features

In the chapters that follow, I cover some of the more advanced features of SQL Server 2000. You may never be asked to manage a replication scheme or run multiple instances, but maybe you're just curious about what SQL Server 2000 *could* do—if so, these chapters are for you.

These chapters may be a bit heavier on theory than previous chapters, but there is still a practical approach to each topic. I continue to provide graphical and command-line tasks.

Although the information in these chapters won't make you an expert on any of the topics presented, they will provide a clear introduction and are intended to be as simple as possible. As always, if you're going to need further help with any of these topics, review *Books Online* and the other references I mention at the end of each chapter.

I have removed the *Rosetta Stone* section from these chapters, because there's no clear map between these advanced features and the base features included with the other products.

The chapters that follow assume that you've read and understand the information in the first part of this book.

Now, let's look at some of the advanced features built into SQL Server 2000.

Chapter **11**

Replication

Chapter at a Glance

Read this chapter to understand replication, and to see a simple replication schema put into place.

The Resources section contains references for:

- Using SQL replication through proxy server
- Understanding distributed transactions versus replication
- Replication server tuning
- A reference to a great publication about SQL Server replication

Read Chapters 2, 3, and 6 before you read this one.

Overview

Defining replication is pretty easy. The basic idea is that you want to copy data from one place to another, automatically. SQL Server 2000 can do that for you. In this chapter, I cover the processes and procedures you can use to set up replication between one or more SQL Servers.

Although the concept of replication is simple, several functions are involved, such as collecting the data, defining the conditions for moving the data, and moving the data. These functions can be installed on different servers or on the same system, but the processes they use are the same regardless of where they are installed.

The following functions and terms are used in replication:

■ Publisher

■ Publication

■ Article

■ Distributor

■ Subscribers

■ Subscription

The Publisher is the server that has the data you want to replicate. It makes the data available in a package called a Publication. You can set this server to "push" the data out to the receiving server, or you can have the receiving server "pull" the data in.

A Publication is made up of the various pieces of data you can replicate, such as tables and views, each called an Article.

The Distributor is the next function in the transfer. This function does the work of transferring the Publication, and its job changes a bit based on the type of replication you are doing.

The system that receives the data is called the Subscriber. This server can request to "pull" the data from the Publisher rather than the Publisher "pushing" the data.

The Subscriber server, then, has the information required to get the data from the Publisher, called a Subscription. It's important to note that a Subscription is to a Publication, not an Article. In other words, the Subscriber doesn't pick and choose the data that is sent to it; it receives all the data. That can become an important distinction.

SQL Server 2000 uses services called *Agents* that watch the various pieces of data and schedules to perform the replication.

To summarize, a Publisher makes a group of information (the Publication, composed of Articles) available for replication. The Distributor transfers the data to a Subscriber, which has a Subscription for that Publication.

There are three types of replication: snapshot, transactional, and merge. Snapshot replication takes an entire set of data and replicates it to another database. Transactional replication also takes a snapshot but replicates only the changed data from then on. Merge replication compares two databases and transfers the data differences between them.

There is an excellent treatment of replication in *Books Online*, which I recommend you read after this chapter if you're asked to set up replication at your site.

Detail

There are two parts to setting up replication: planning and implementing. Never skip the planning step; this simply isn't one of those things that you can follow a wizard and expect to work. This planning is normally done in the order I describe here, but you are likely to move back and forth through the steps as each decision affects the others.

The first thing you need to plan is the type of replication—snapshot, transactional, or merge. The type of replication has a great deal to do with how you'll set up the rest of your plan.

Snapshot replication takes an entire set of data and replicates it to another database. This type is the most straightforward and the easiest to set up but usually has the largest data size. Because of its size, this type is not always the best choice for disconnected remote clients. It's normally better suited to static data sets, such as lists and catalog items.

Transactional replication takes an initial snapshot of data as well but then tracks the changes that have been made at the Publisher and sends them to the Subscriber. This type of replication is typically smaller and is often used for remote clients.

Merge replication allows updates from both the Publisher and the Subscriber of the data. This is very useful for remote clients that make changes in a disconnected fashion in the field to keep the office data set current and that receive changes from the office as well. This type can be a bit more involved to implement because of conflict resolution.

Once you've decided on the type of replication, you also need to decide on the physical layout. At this step you decide which server will be the Publisher and which will be the Distributor. Often these are the same machine, but the load placed on your server from each function has a performance impact.

Another impact in the physical layout choice is the network position of the server. If the Publisher is behind a firewall, you may need to have the Distributor on the other side of the firewall so that your remote clients can access the Distributor.

The next step in the plan is selecting the data that you want to replicate. You can replicate many forms of data, from a complete table to only parts of it, stored procedures or their output, views or their output, and even a user-defined function or its output. Often you may want just a small subset of your data at another site, and sometimes you need an entire database to be sent to the Subscriber. The factors to consider here are the size of the data, the speed and quality of the connection, and the use of the data.

The next decision is whether the Publisher sends the data along at a defined point, called a push subscription, or whether the Subscriber goes to get the data at a specified point, called a pull subscription.

If users are using laptops, you may not know when they are online, so you'd want a pull subscription. If you have a constant-connected link to the Subscriber, you normally set up a push subscription.

Not only are the requirements a factor in this decision, setting the replication timing is vital, especially on push subscriptions. If the links to the Subscribers are constant-connected but very slow, the data should be transferred more often so that it doesn't pile up. This timing aspect is probably one of the most difficult parts of planning.

Now that you have your functional planning done, you set up your replication schema by defining all the pieces in the list of terms mentioned earlier. The Publisher, Subscribers, Articles, and the rest are all detailed at this stage. The rest of this chapter helps you do that.

Finally, you set the monitoring in place to make sure your replication works. Whenever you set up a process to happen automatically, whether it is a backup or any other server process, you don't let it run blindly. Although you do have a feedback mechanism (via e-mail) to monitor maintenance plans, that process is a bit more hands-on with replication.

Let's begin the planning process by exploring the types of replication.

Types of Replication

The three types of replication are snapshot, transactional, and merge.

Snapshot

Snapshot replication, which copies the data you want to move in its entirety, to another server, is well suited to users who need an offline copy of some data. Suppose your sales force has a price list that should be updated daily. You might set the database at their site to pull data early in the morning and then use the data in a static mode throughout the day. Because you're copying an entire data set that might be quite large, you should limit how often you set this replication to happen.

Transactional

In transactional replication, the changes on one server are replicated to another. This means that each time your users insert, select, update, or delete data in the Publisher, the Distributor sends it on to the Subscriber. This can happen instantly or pile up to go at a certain time.

One important thing to keep in mind with this type of replication is that it's an all-or-nothing proposition. If one of the changes in a transaction fails to go to the Subscriber for whatever reason, none of the changes will go. Because of that, this is the most difficult type of replication to monitor, although it's often one of the most useful types.

Use transactional replication when you need to keep two data locations in sync or when the data just gets too big to replicate with snapshot replication.

Let's look at another example. Headquarters records sales all day long and inventory is reduced. Field offices need to know the new inventory counts instantly so that they don't sell what they don't have. With these requirements, you'd set up transactional replication with the data pushing from the Publisher at headquarters out to the Subscriber servers at each office as soon as the changes occur. This process assumes that you have a constant connection to each office.

An interesting feature is the ability of the Subscriber to make changes based on received data and send those changes back to the Publisher, called two-way replication. Although you can use transactional replication over disconnected or dial-up methods, it requires a bit more monitoring.

Merge

Merge replication allows two copies of a data set to be synchronized. The toughest thing to decide is how to handle conflicts, but if your data lends itself to this type of replication, you shouldn't encounter that too often.

The process sends an initial snapshot to the replication partner, and at synchronization, the two systems accept each other's data. If there is a conflict, you have a lot of options on how to handle it, including setting default options (like Server A always wins) or having the system prompt you for what to do.

Let's look at another example. The sales force tells you that although they enjoy having a copy of the inventory, what they'd really like is to be able to record sales information on the spot. To do this, they need to reduce inventory by the sales amount and bill the customer.

To fulfill this requirement, you'd set up merge replication between a database on their laptops and the server. You could replicate only the data from their region if you wish, guaranteeing that they wouldn't see each other's customers.

One thing to keep in mind is that merge replication is the most restrictive type—you can't merge-replicate the results of a stored procedure or an indexed view.

Replication Topology

Now that you've picked the type of replication you want, you need to do a little infrastructure work. A database must be configured to allow replication. Configuration is done through a wizard or with commands. This process is performed for all the databases within the replication scheme, such as the Distributors, Publishers, and Subscribers.

SQL Server 2000 uses system-level objects to perform replication, and it stores this information in tables in either the user databases or a separate database. If you use the wizard to set up your replication, you can also specify this separate database.

I'll detail the physical process in the Graphical section. Let's continue with a little more theory.

Distributors

The first function to set up is the Distributor, which is the machine that distributes data. The Distributor makes the Publication available to the Subscriber. You set the Distributor with a wizard or with a command.

This machine stores the data to be replicated on tables and files that it creates, so you should ensure that you have enough room for that. The Distributor makes a copy of *all* the data that's replicated, so take that into account when determining the drive space impact. SQL Server 2000 can place the snapshot type of replication's data on another location and even compress the data to a CAB file.

This machine also needs to be able to "talk" to the Subscriber, so make sure you take into account the bandwidth, firewall placement, and other network issues.

There are often a lot of benefits from moving this function to its own server, such as improved space distribution and security.

Publishers

Publishers are the servers that have the data you want to replicate. The Publisher server takes the heaviest load, depending on the type of replication you select. For instance, snapshot replication that is scheduled for late at night when no one is on the server has less of an impact than does constant transactional replication.

You set a server to be used as the Publisher by using the replication wizard or a stored procedure.

Now that you've decided on the Publisher and Distributor, you need to define the Subscribers.

Subscribers

The Subscribers are the databases that get the data. They need to be able to access the Distributor, unless you're using the snapshot offline option I mentioned earlier.

The configuration of the Subscriber depends a great deal on the type of replication that you choose. If you pick a push-snapshot, you configure the Subscriber differently than if you pick merge-pull.

I detail the pull type of Subscriber in the Graphical and Examples sections, but it's imperative that you read about replication in *Books Online* if you're going further than I do in this chapter.

Now that you've planned the machines that will house the various functions, let's explore the data you'll replicate.

Articles

Articles are the base-level objects you replicate. Here's a list of what you can include, direct from *Books Online*:

- Tables
- Stored procedures—definition
- Stored procedures—execution
- Views
- Indexed views
- Indexed views as tables
- User-defined functions

You'll see exactly how to add these items to the Publication in this chapter's Graphical and Command Line sections a little later on.

Publications

Publications are the Articles you wish to send. You could select a table as one Article and a view as another, and then combine those Articles as a Publication.

Remember that the Subscriber always subscribes to a Publication, not an Article. Even if you select just one Article, you need to make it a Publication to transfer the data.

Subscription

The Subscription is the function that receives the Publication. This is often another SQL Server but can include other types. You can replicate to databases such as Oracle and Microsoft Access. The Subscriber database is set by using the wizard or commands.

I've given a wide description of the replication pieces, and next I'll bring those pieces together to create a simple replication.

Graphical

I'm going to stick with the replication wizard for this demonstration. This is one of the fastest ways to set up replication, and it's often used by experienced DBAs to do the legwork for the initial schema. You can always modify the process later.

Setting Up Replication Using the Wizard

Open Enterprise Manager, and drill down to the Replication object. Right-click the object and select Configure Publishing, Subscribers, and Distribution from the menu that appears, as shown in Figure 11.1

The wizard is going to do all the work necessary for setting up the entire schema. Once you select the menu item, you will see the screen that is shown in Figure 11.2.

As the screen indicates, the wizard is going to do the work of setting up this server as a Distributor and a Publisher. Select Next and you're shown the display in Figure 11.3.

You could specify that another server operate as the Distributor, but leave this server with that function for this example. Select Next and you're shown the display in Figure 11.4.

The server will take a baseline of the data, known as a snapshot, which will serve as the initial transfer of the data to the Subscriber. It has to store this in a folder on the hard drive, and you specify that folder here. Leave this selection alone, but normally you don't. You'll see why in a moment.

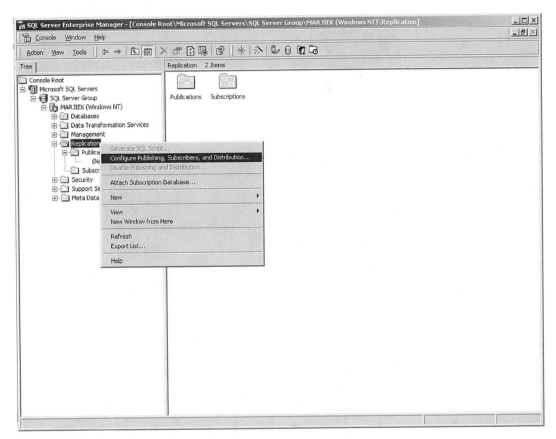

Figure 11.1   Starting the wizard

Select Next to bring up the panel shown in Figure 11.5.

Because the location is pointing to the C$ administrative share, the wizard warns that users without admin rights to this server won't be able to get there. You should create another share, grant the rights to the proper accounts on the Subscriber, and use that for the replication share. Leave the setting alone for this demo, and continue by answering Yes to the warning. You'll see the display shown in Figure 11.6.

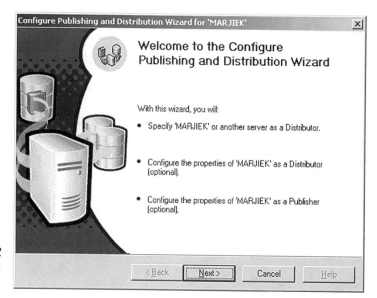

Figure 11.2
Introduction
screen

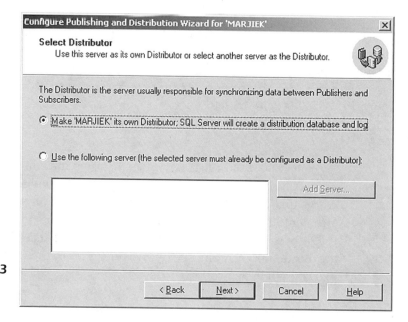

Figure 11.3
Setting the
Distributor

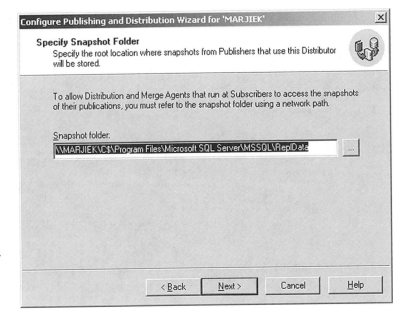

Figure 11.4
Setting the
snapshot
folder

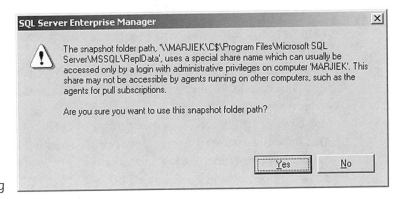

Figure 11.5
Path warning

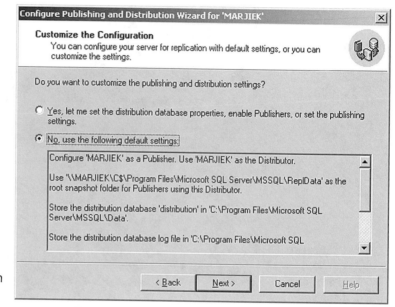

Figure 11.6
Configuration
options

Here you're allowed to set other options for the Distributor and Publisher. Don't change anything yet; just press Next to continue. You're shown the screen in Figure 11.7.

You need to give SQL Server 2000 a database to store all the information it needs to run the replication. Take the defaults, and select Next to bring up the screen shown in Figure 11.8.

Now set the Publishers that can use this Distributor. Only the servers that the system is aware of from a network perspective show up automatically, but you can select New to add more. Leave the defaults as shown and select Next to bring up the screen in Figure 11.9.

Now pick the databases you want to replicate, and set the type of replication you want. Notice the Transactional selection. Select Next to bring up the panel shown in Figure 11.10.

Here you set the Subscriber information. You can add Subscribers, and clicking the three dots in the button on the right sets the login information

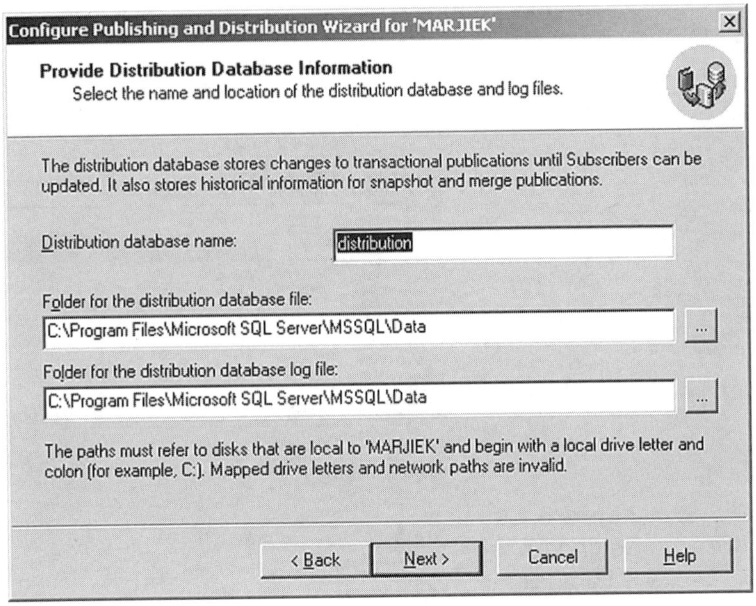

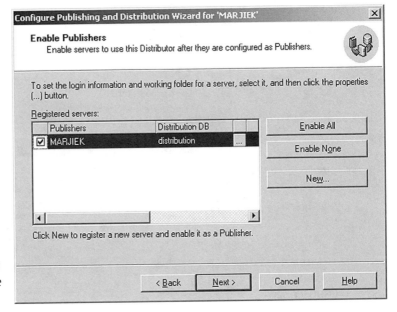

Figure 11.7
Setting the
distribution
database

Figure 11.8
Enabling the
Publishers

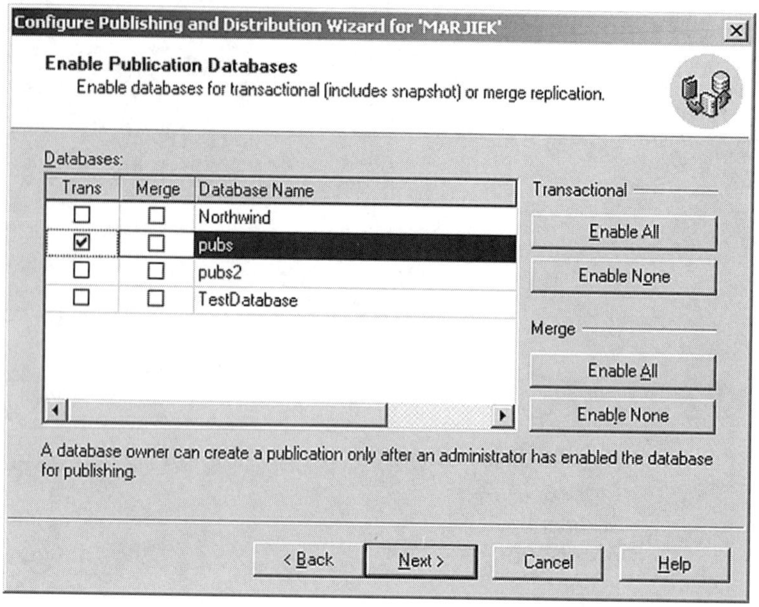

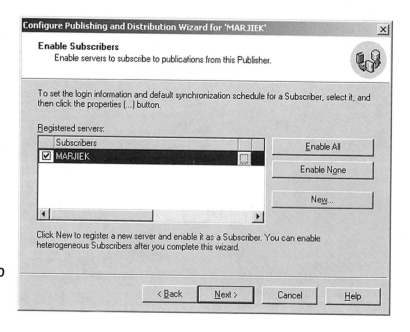

Figure 11.9
Setting up the
databases

Figure 11.10
Setting the
Subscriber

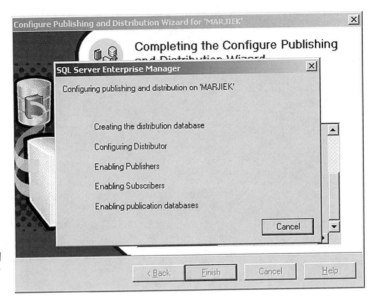

Figure 11.11
Finishing the
wizard

the system will use to get at the published data. That panel also sets the timing for the replication. Leave the defaults and select Next to show the screen in Figure 11.11.

You're presented with a final screen and press Finish to show the progress display you see here. Along the way, you're presented with success messages, like the one shown in Figure 11.12.

You're also given a message that replication monitoring has been added to Enterprise Manager, as shown in Figure 11.13. If you implement replication at your site, you'll find that keeping it going is a bit more complex than just running a wizard. It's not bad; it's just that if something goes awry, you have to resynchronize everything.

I'm not going to spend any time on this monitoring, but you need to if you plan to implement replication. As always, Books Online will help after you've completed this chapter, to give you a complete picture of the monitoring steps you need to take.

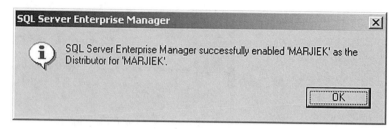

Figure 11.12
Success
message

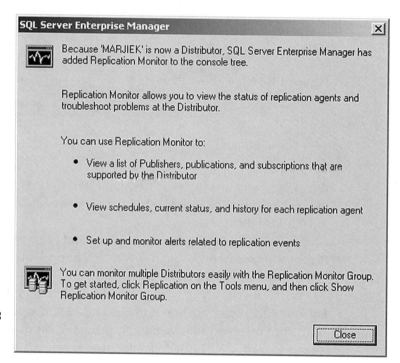

Figure 11.13
Setting the
Distributor

Now that you've set up your Distributor, Publisher, and Subscriber, you need to set up the Publications, Articles, and Subscriptions. Begin by right-clicking the *Publications* object under *Replication* and selecting the *New Publication* menu item that appears, as shown in Figure 11.14. After you make the menu selection, you're shown the opening of the wizard in Figure 11.15.

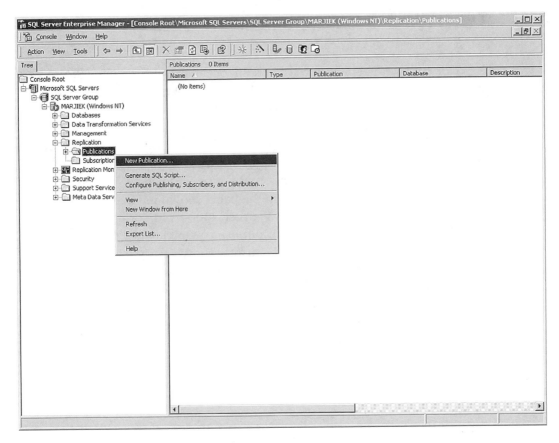

Figure 11.14 Setting up a Publication

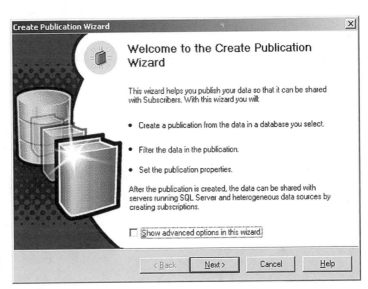

Figure 11.15
Beginning the
wizard

This isn't your typical wizard screen, because there's a checkbox to set advanced options to display during this wizard. We're not going to do that here, but you can use it to partition your data so that only some of it is replicated. Select Next to continue to the screen in Figure 11.16.

Pick the pubs database, just as you did when you set up the Publisher earlier. Select Next to bring up the display shown in Figure 11.17. Here you're allowed to set the type of replication; the type you want is snapshot. Select that and then select Next to bring up the panel shown in Figure 11.18.

Set the Subscriber type as SQL Server 2000—did you notice the other choices? That's right, you can even publish to Oracle and Microsoft Access databases. Select Next to bring up the display shown in Figure 11.19. Here you choose the Articles that you want to publish. Choose just one table, but you can publish other objects or their results as well.

You can also set further defaults for these objects on this panel, but leave the defaults as they are to make this demo as simple as possible. Select Next to bring up the display shown in Figure 11.20.

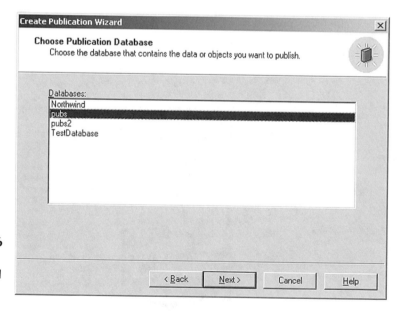

Figure 11.16
Choosing the published databases

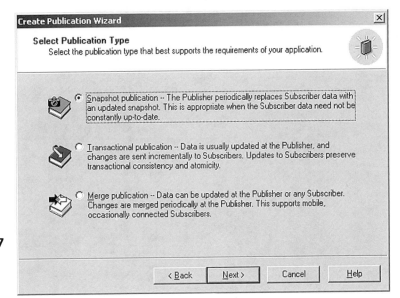

Figure 11.17
Selecting the
replication
type

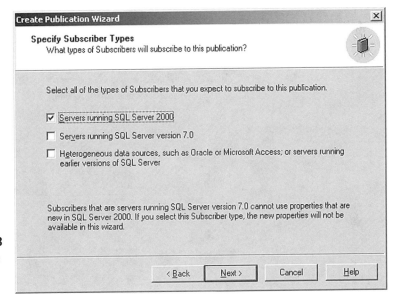

Figure 11.18
Choosing the
subscriber
type

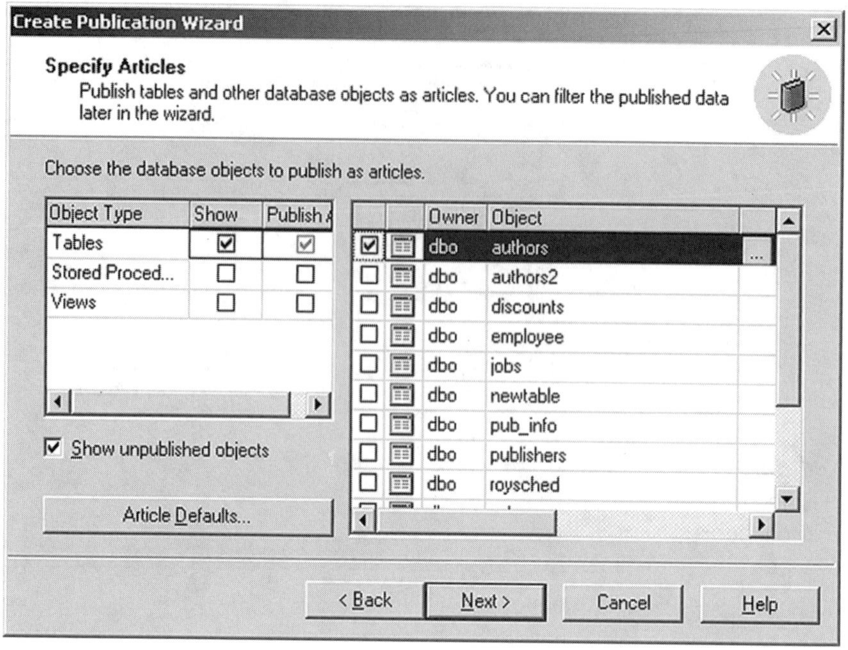

Figure 11.19 Choosing Articles

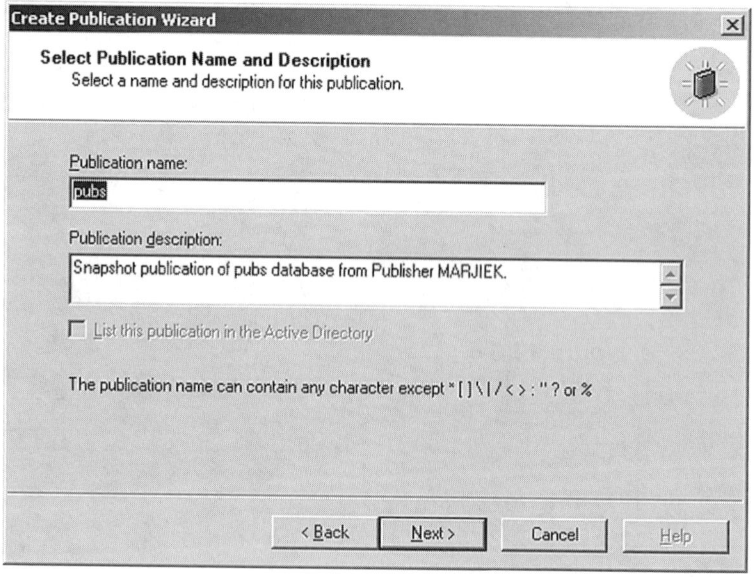

Figure 11.20
Naming the
Publication

Remember that you subscribe to a Publication, not to Articles. Leave the name pubs for this Publication, and select Next to continue to the panel shown in Figure 11.21. Here you can set further options for the Publication, such as filters or allowing anonymous accounts to access the Publication. Granting anonymous access to the Publication allows anyone to subscribe, which is useful for catalogs and the like. Select Next to continue to Figure 11.22.

This is the end panel of the publication wizard, but notice that it tells us that you can monitor the success or failure of the Publication with the newly created Replication Monitor. You'll do that in a moment. For now select Finish, and you're shown the display in Figure 11.23.

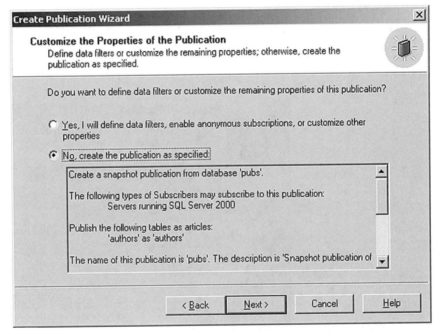

Figure 11.21 Customizing the Publication

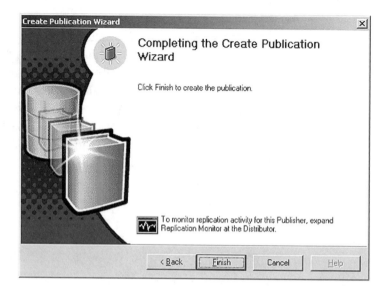

Figure 11.22
Finalizing the
Publication

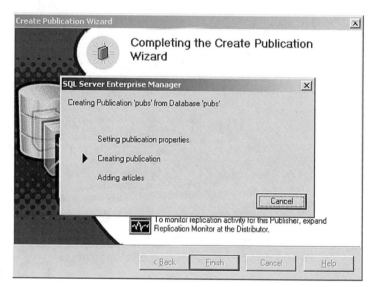

Figure 11.23
Publication
wizard progress

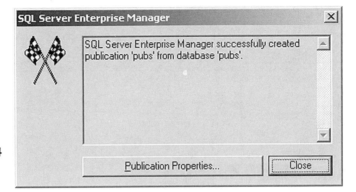

Figure 11.24
Wizard
completion

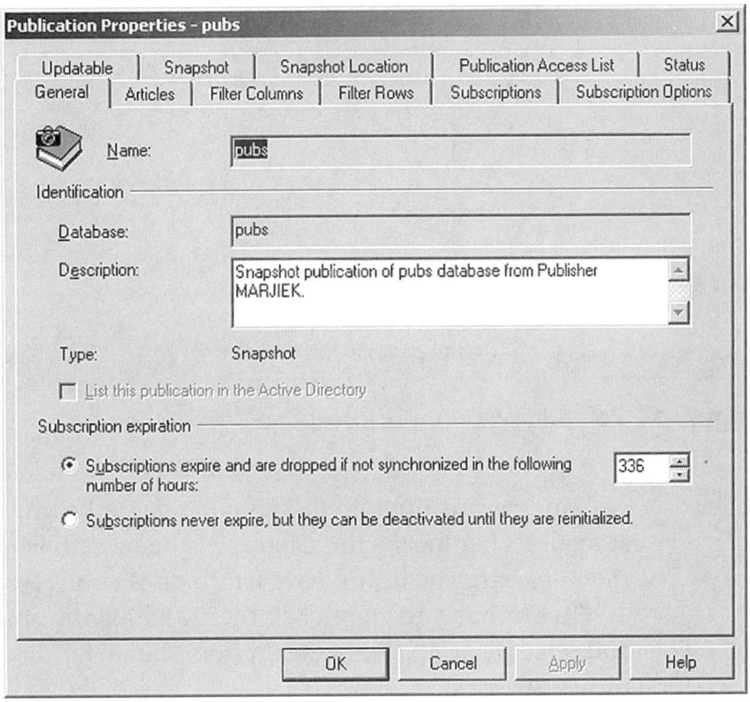

Figure 11.25
Publication
properties

You'll see the progress of the wizard as it moves along, and in time you see the panel shown in Figure 11.24. Close the panel, and the object is displayed in *Enterprise Manager.* Select that object and open its properties, and you're able to edit the previous panels, as shown in Figure 11.25.

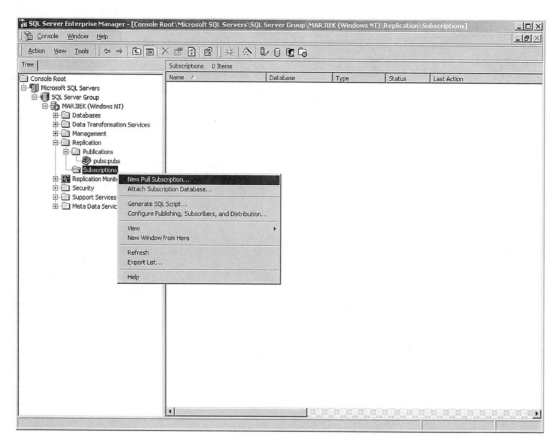

Figure 11.26   Setting up the Subscription

You may also notice there's a hand graphic on the database in Enterprise Manager. That means the database is being published. You're getting close to the home stretch; all you have left to do is configure the Subscription.

To do that, you right-click the Subscriptions object in Enterprise Manager and select New Pull Subscription from the menu that appears, as shown in Figure 11.26.

You're picking this option because in this case you want the Subscriber to show up on its own schedule to get the data. The other option is to set the Publisher to push out the data on schedule. This push function is normally reserved for constant-connected systems, and you're simulating a laptop experience.

Once you make your choice, you're presented with the opening panel shown in Figure 11.27. Again you get the checkbox for advanced options, and again you'll leave the defaults. Select Next to bring up the screen in Figure 11.28.

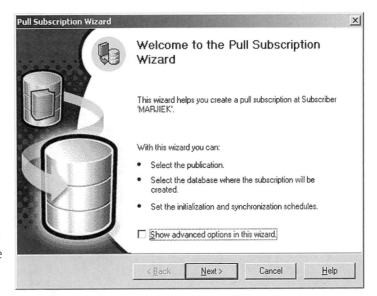

Figure 11.27
Beginning the
subscription
wizard

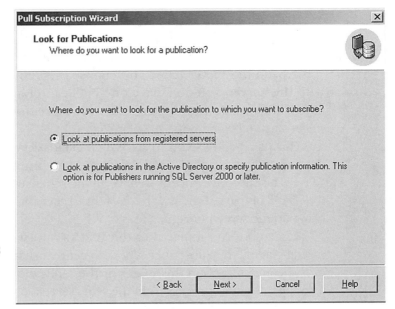

Figure 11.28
Choosing the
Publisher
location

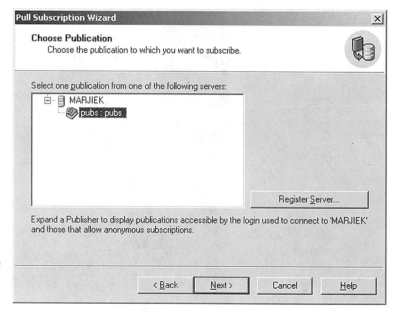

Figure 11.29
Choosing the
Publication

Here you set the location of Publisher the wizard will look for. SQL Server 2000 can make heavy use of Active Directory during this process. For now, leave the first setting and select Next to move to the screen in Figure 11.29.

Expand the server name and choose the Publication that is connected with this server. You only have one Publication in this case, but if you had more, they would show up here. After you make that expansion and selection, select Next to bring up the panel in Figure 11.30.

This panel allows you to set which database will get the data, so choose your test database as shown. Select Next to bring up the screen in Figure 11.31. The Subscriber needs to have all the schema objects installed to receive the data. This part of the wizard does that. Leave the defaults and select Next to bring up the screen in Figure 11.32.

Remember the folder that the first wizard warned you about? In this screen you tell the Subscriber where to get that snapshot data. The Subscriber must be able to access this folder or the replication won't work. You're performing this entire process from the same server, so you shouldn't have a problem by leaving the folder where it is.

Select Next to bring up the screen in Figure 11.33. Here you set the schedule for the replication to occur. You can set the replication to happen all the

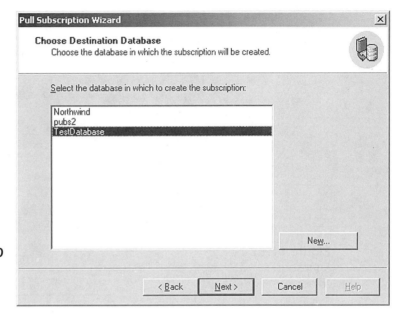

Figure 11.30
Setting the
Subscription
database

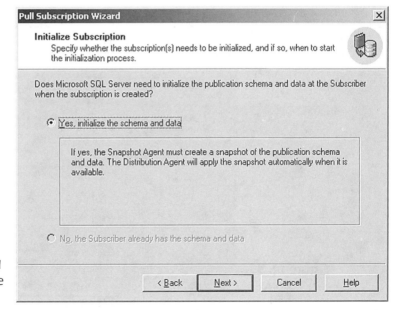

Figure 11.31
Initializing the
schema

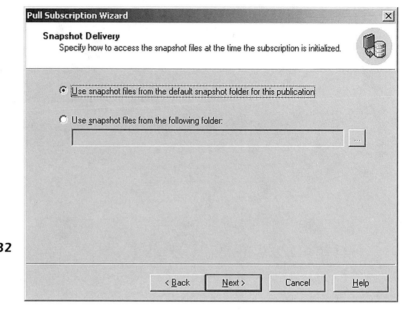

Figure 11.32
Snapshot
folder
selection

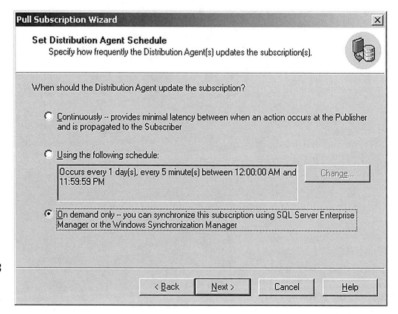

Figure 11.33
Synchroniza-
tion schedule

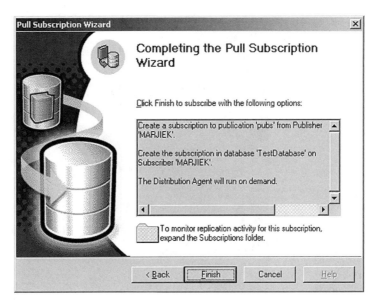

Figure 11.34   Finishing the wizard

time, on a schedule, or on demand. Pick On demand for your Subscription since the test simulates a laptop, and then select Next to bring up the screen in Figure 11.34.

Press Finish here to complete your Subscription with the choices you've made along the way. Once again, you're presented with the progress of the wizard, as shown in Figure 11.35. When the wizard completes, you're given the success message shown in Figure 11.36.

Before you begin the replication, you verify that the data doesn't exist in your destination database. Switch to the pubs object in the Replication Monitor, and start the Snapshot Agent, as shown in Figure 11.37.

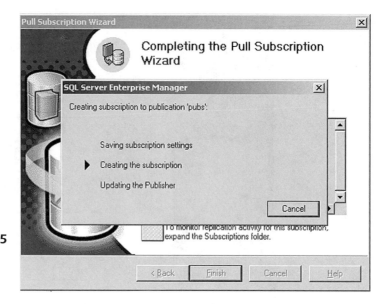

Figure 11.35
Subscription
wizard
progress

Figure 11.36
Subscription
wizard success

Next, select the Subscription you just created and right-click it to bring up the menu. Select *Start Synchronizing* from the menu, as shown in Figure 11.38. You could also start the synchronization from the *Replication Monitor*.

After you apply synchronization, you jump back to the *Replication Monitor*. Remember that an MMC-based tool doesn't refresh the display by itself. Fortu-

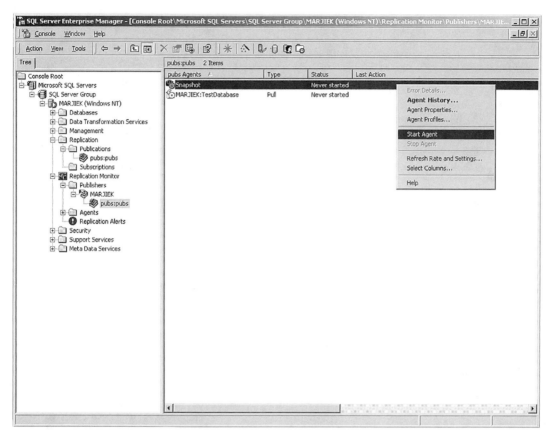

Figure 11.37 *Starting the agent*

nately, the developers of this tool knew this, so they prompt you with a selection to automatically refresh the view. Do that, and the display shown in Figure 11.39 appears. And the table is replicated. Don't be deceived—this is a complex thing to do, and other issues can crop up. The wizard certainly simplifies the replication creation process, though.

Let's move on to the command line.

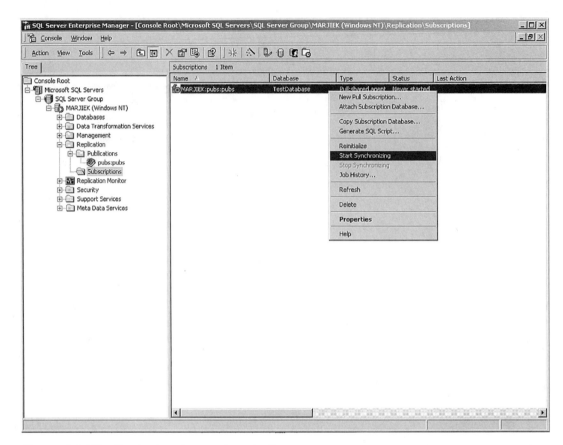

Figure 11.38 Beginning the synchronization

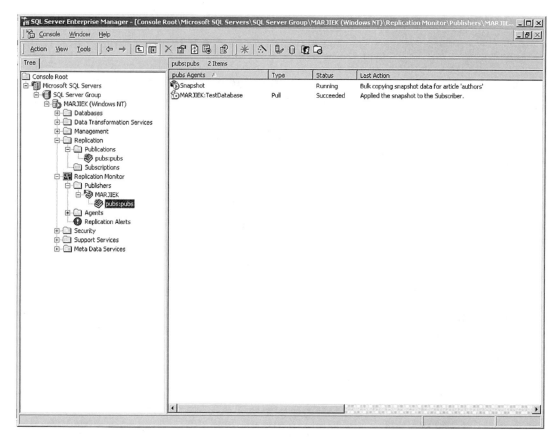

Figure 11.39   *Replication Monitor*

Command Line

By far the easiest way to set up replication is to use the replication wizard through the graphical methods. The wizard protects you from many of the underpinnings of replication, which I expose in this section. Keep in mind, although you can accomplish much of the replication settings from the command line, some parts are best performed by the graphical tools.

Books Online tells this story in much greater detail. However, you might find the following discussion a bit more helpful.

In the Command Line section of past chapters, I've gone through each command step by step, but I think doing that here might be a bit long. Instead, I present the commands in a series of steps, and then in the Examples section, we'll put it into practice.

Replication Stored Procedures

Setting up replication through the command line involves using various stored procedures. You use `sp_addDistributor` to set the server that will be the Distributor, and then create a distribution database using `sp_adddistributiondb`.

The Publication will use Articles on that server. I'll detail that process in a moment, because you need to run certain commands that depend on what type of replication you set up. Next, using `sp_adddistPublisher`, you'll set the server that will act as the Publisher to use that Distributor for the data transfer. To finish off the server side, you then set up the Publication databases by using `sp_replicationdboption` for each database that you want to be able to replicate.

The next commands you issue depend on the type of replication you want to perform. If you want merge replication, run `sp_addmergepublication` to define the Publication. Once you have that Publication, use `sp_addmergeArticle` for each item, like tables and views, that you want to add to the Publication. Next, run `sp_addpublication_snapshot` to create an Agent to put everything in the right place so that the Subscriber will pick it up.

If you're setting up transactional or snapshot replication, run `sp_addpublication` with a special qualifier for the `repl_freq` option called `snapshot` to set the initial creation of the data set. Add the Articles for these two types of replication with the command `sp_addArticle`. There are many ways to filter the Articles, all detailed in *Books Online*.

You must have at least one snapshot of all the data at the beginning so that the replication has a "baseline" to start from. The next command to run is `sp_addpublication_snapshot`, which creates the proper Agent to do the transfers.

Examples

The wizard you went through in the Graphical section already served as a bit of an example, and I described the commands for a replication setup in the Command Line section. In this section, you'll use those commands to perform a replication. The replication you'll set up is a simple snapshot of one table, but you can extrapolate that into more complex examples. I'll be referencing each step that I spoke about earlier to run through this example.

Important note: If you try the code lines in the examples, they might not work! The commands I show depend on many things—language defaults, security mode, drive letters, operating system, whether the SQL Server 2000 system had multiple instances, and many others. Unless your system is set up exactly like mine, the examples might not be successful.

Also, unless your system is a test server, I don't recommend your running these commands. They could change the operation of your server.

Setting the Distributor

As mentioned earlier, you first need to set your Distributor. Specify the name of the server that will serve as the Distributor by using the commands shown in Listing 11.1

Listing 11.1   Setting the Distributor

```
USE master
GO
EXEC sp_addDistributor 'MyServer'
GO
-------------------------------------------------
New login created.
'Distributor_admin' added to role 'sysadmin'.
```

Notice that you had to perform the command from within the *master* database. The first two lines in the command handle that. After that, the command added a login to perform the distribution tasks, along with a lot of other internal activity.

Setting the Publisher

Next, you need to set up your Publication database. This is an intense process that creates the database and then adds lots of tables, stored procedures, and other objects in the database. The process is complex, but the command isn't. Listing 11.2 shows the stored procedure's syntax.

Listing 11.2   Setting the Publication database

```
EXEC sp_adddistributiondb 'DistributionDB'
```

Books Online describes the many parameters this command can take, including the folder on the hard drive that you'd like to set for the data file. Even though you didn't set that option, you need to make sure there is a share on your server pointing to the right places. This is normally a directory called *REPLDATA* within your SQL installation, but you can put it anywhere you want, as long as you specify it in the previous command and make sure everyone can point to it. You may have to share out the directory.

Next, you set the Publisher to use the database you just set. You do that with the commands shown in Listing 11.3. Here you have to do a bit more work. Let's break it down a bit.

Listing 11.3   Publisher-to-distribution database link

```
EXEC sp_adddistPublisher 'MyServer'
, 'DistributionDB'
, 0
, 'sa'
, 'letmein'
, '\\MyServer\REPLDATA'
```

The first parameter is the name of the server, the second is the name of the database you made, and the third indicates the login type for the replication. I've set mine to 0, which means to use SQL Server authentication, and that requires the next two parameters, name and password. Finally, you specify that share I mentioned earlier and then run the command.

Setting the Database

The next part involves setting the database to replicate. You have to tell the entire database that it is a candidate for having Articles replicated from it. You do that with the command shown in Listing 11.4.

Listing 11.4   Setting the database for replication

```
sp_replicationdboption 'pubs2','publish','true'
```

Here you supply the parameters database, option, and value. The database you'll publish from is pubs2; the action you want to perform is publish, because you are setting up a snapshot replication. To set up merge replication, you set this option to merge publish.

The final parameter sets the action to true; if you had specified false, you would have turned the replication option off for this database.

Setting the Publication

Next you need to set a Publication to hold the Articles you wish to publish. Do that with the commands shown in Listing 11.5.

Listing 11.5   Adding the Publication

```
EXEC sp_addpublication 'authors_table'
, @repl_freq='snapshot'
GO
```

Give your Publication a name and include a reference to a type of replication. You're setting up a snapshot, so that's what you'll reference.

Setting the Articles

Now you can add those Articles. We'll keep it simple, setting the *authors* table to be published in its entirety. You do that with the commands shown in Listing 11.6.

Listing 11.6   Setting an Article

```
EXEC sp_addArticle 'authors_table'
, 'authors_table_Article'
, 'authors'
GO
```

Here you've set your Publication to have an Article called *authors_table_Article* and to publish the entire *authors* table. Many parameters are associated with this command, most of them optional. Run this command for each Article you want to add to the Publication.

Setting the Agent

You need to create an Agent to do the work. Use the commands in Listing 11.7 to do that. The only parameter you're specifying here is the name of the Publication you set up earlier.

Listing 11.7   Creating the snapshot agent

```
EXEC sp_addpublication_snapshot 'authors_table'
GO
```

Activating the Replication

Finally you're reading data for your snapshot. This final action queries the data, pulls the files together, and sets the Agent and the rest. The commands to do that are shown in Listing 11.8.

Listing 11.8   Activating the snapshot

```
EXEC sp_changepublication 'authors_table'
, 'status'
, 'active'
GO
```

You created the snapshot earlier, but by default it's placed in a "hold" mode until you're ready. Now you've set the status, and the Publication is ready for

Subscribers to show up and schedule themselves against it. The Subscriptions are best created using the method in the Graphical section, and it's there that you set your schedule. If you're still interested in pursuing the command-line route, read on.

Setting the Subscriber

You need to add a pull subscription for your snapshot, so you run the command shown in Listing 11.9 on the Publisher. This gets all Articles defined for that authors_table Publication. Notice that you set the destination database to TestDB.

Listing 11.9 Setting the full Subscription on the publisher

```
EXEC sp_addsubscription @publication = 'authors_table'
, @Subscriber = 'MyOtherServer'
, @destination_db = 'TestDB'
, @status = 'Active'
GO
```

Now you need to set the schedule, using the commands shown in Listing 11.10. The 2 in this example sets the frequency to be "on demand."

Listing 11.10 Setting the schedule

```
EXEC sp_addSubscriber_schedule @Subscriber = 'MyOtherServer'
, @frequency_type = 2
GO
```

Did you see the @ signs all over the place in the last two listings? Those are references for the parameters. There are many parameters you could specify but don't have to. To specify the one you want for a given setting, you preface the parameter with an @ sign before its identifier. These are detailed further in Books Online.

Next, you move to the Subscriber and run the commands shown in Listing 11.11. You have to make sure you're running these commands from the destination database, or you need to place the USE databasename GO commands before each of the stored procedures.

Listing 11.11 Setting the pull subscription on the Subscriber

```
EXEC sp_addpullsubscription @Publisher = 'MyServer'
, @Publisher_db = 'DistributionDB'
, @publication = 'authors_table'
, @subscription_type = 'pull'
GO
```

Next, you need to add an Agent to do the work, just as the wizard did in the Graphical section. You do that with the commands shown in Listing 11.12.

Listing 11.12   Setting the pull Subscription agent on the Subscriber

```
EXEC sp_addpullsubscription_agent @Publisher = 'MyServer'
, @Publisher_db = 'DistributionDB'
, @publication = 'authors_table'
GO
```

To activate the Agent on the Subscriber, you execute the command shown in Listing 11.13 at the operating system command line. Note that you've placed a return between the dashes for readability, but you won't do that on your server.

Listing 11.13   Starting the pull Subscription agent on the Subscriber

```
snapshot
-Publisher server_name
-PublisherDB Publisher_database
-Publication publication_name
```

Once the command is initiated, the replication is complete.

Resources

Using SQL replication through proxy server:
   http://www.microsoft.com/technet/sql/intrepl.asp
Distributed transactions versus replication:
   http://www.dell.com/us/en/gen/topics/power_ps3q00-martin.htm
Replication server tuning:
   http://www.sql-server-performance.com/replication_tuning.asp
Great SQL Server replication publication:
   http://www.windowsitlibrary.com/Content/77/11/toc.html

Chapter 12

Analysis Services Using OLAP

Chapter at a Glance

Read this chapter to gain a basic understanding of Microsoft's Analysis Services. You'll see a start-to-finish example of how Online Analytical Processing (OLAP) cubes work and how to use Microsoft Excel as an OLAP client.

The Resources section contains references for:

- More OLAP sites
- An excellent tutorial for basic understanding of OLAP
- A reference on estimating the cost of a data warehouse project

Read Chapters 2, 3, and 5 before you read this one.

Overview

Data isn't information. Data is just data. For data to become information, it has to be put together in a meaningful way. Databases store data, and people derive information from that data.

In this chapter, I explore the ways you can use SQL Server 2000's Analysis Services to change data into information. I cover a bit more theory than normal, but rest assured that I'll tie it all together by the end of the chapter.

Analysis Services is a separate installation from SQL Server 2000 and can be installed independently of SQL Server. Analysis Services provides an engine to create OLAP cubes, which are multidimensional data sets. It goes further than OLAP in providing the ability to mine the cubes for patterns of data.

Cubes are formed of various tables of data. These tables are normally denormalized, meaning that they are in a form more suited to reporting than to data input. The tables within a cube source store dimensions, facts, and measures. The dimensions are the categories of the data. Facts are the events, and measures are the numbers within the fact table.

Cube tables are related in structures that form shapes, such as stars or snowflakes. These shapes are determined by the relationship of the data. Star shapes are formed when each dimension table joins to the fact table. Snowflakes are formed when the dimension tables join to each other, and then one or more of them join to the fact table.

Cubes are typically stored using one of three methods:

- ROLAP
- MOLAP
- HOLAP

Relational OLAP (ROLAP) involves pulling the data directly from relational databases, storing only portions of the cube in a separate database. Multidimensional OLAP (MOLAP) involves moving much or all of the data into a separate database. Hybrid OLAP (HOLAP) is a combination of the two storage methods.

Cubes can be accessed from applications by using a language called Multidimensional Expressions (MDX). This language requires knowledge of the data structure before developing the statements.

Microsoft includes several tutorials for Analysis Services, which I use throughout this chapter.

Detail

To help you understand Analysis Services, let's examine the history of the products that became the product Microsoft currently offers.

Analysis Services Evolution

In the past, to change data into information, high-level data analysts would cull all the data that they could get their minds around and try to derive trends or patterns from the items their databases stored. As time went on, software was developed to aid the analysts in their search for meaning. This type of software was called a *decision support system*. The concept was that the data could provide experienced analysts with the information needed to make an intelligent guess, hence the *support system* moniker.

Later, new software was developed that could push a great deal of the number crunching down to the computer, giving less experienced managers the ability to work with this type of analysis as well. This type of software was known as *Online Analytical Processing*, or simply OLAP. This type of software was more accessible, but it wasn't always easy to use, and it carried a heavy expenditure in software and training. With SQL Server 7, Microsoft offered OLAP as part of the basic package.

Data analysis is a field that is changing rapidly, even for the IT industry. Microsoft has improved on an already impressive OLAP package with the product it calls Analysis Services. It isn't simply a marketing rename—this product does more than provide basic decision support or OLAP services. This system also includes a feature called *data mining*. Data mining involves looking *through* the cells of a cube to see patterns that can emerge.

I'm being a bit vague here on purpose. This is a vast discipline, one that many people spend their entire careers in. If you're interested in this field, be sure to check the Resources section. There are a lot more terms, concepts, and practices than I can show you in just one chapter.

Let's look at some of the larger concepts of Analysis Services.

Uses

I've found that the best way to explain this subject is to examine the way the software can be used. You probably store a lot of data in your databases, and you can use that data to answer questions like these:

- How profitable are we? Why?
- Was that ad campaign worth it? Does it do better at a certain time? With a certain media?
- How well is each region or store doing in comparison with the others?
- What products or services have been selling well? When?
- Who are our customers? What are they like? Where are they from?
- How much of each thing should we keep on hand?

Can you find out all this with Analysis Services? Absolutely. It all depends on how much and what type of data you already store and whether you're interested in finding the answers to these questions.

Analysis Services Concepts

So how does it work? I spend the rest of the chapter answering that, but basically it involves getting the data into a format you can use. This usually means moving the data out of the production (OLTP) framework and reworking it into another schema, called a *cube*.

You can think of a cube as an intense spreadsheet. In a standard spreadsheet, there are rows and columns. The rows might be things like the number of shoes sold, and the columns might be the months they were sold in. In the data analysis world, the rows in this example are called *measures* and the columns are called *dimensions*, or the definitions of the measures.

In the spreadsheet example, I've stored a two-dimensional representation of data, the sales and the times they were sold. I might, however, want to know what *type* of shoes sold, say, men's or women's. Adding this "type" dimension to my spreadsheet, which I can't easily do with a spreadsheet, gets me another axis on the data, or a cube of information. Now the "type" column is just one added dimension.

I might also want to know which region sold the men's shoes, adding a *location* dimension. I might further want to add a dimension that involves the customers who bought the shoes, allowing me to answer the question "Who bought the most shoes in the Tampa store in January last year?" That kind of information is extremely valuable to a marketing department as well as other concerns in a company.

Most OLAP services work with cubes. Normally the data is migrated from the production (OLTP) databases and is spread into larger, less optimized tables on another system that is used for cube processing.

Impacts

All this power isn't free. Storage for all this data can be huge—a small 30MB database that I once converted to an OLAP system grew to almost a gigabyte, with just a few dimensions. If you have a few hundred stores reporting four or five dimensions of data each day for a year, you can easily reach into billions of rows. Analysis Services also places a large demand on your processor and memory. You can run Analysis Services only on NT server or 2000 server platforms. Make sure you check *Books Online* for the requirements for this type of server. If you're going to put Analysis Services into place, make sure you read the entire section dealing with the subject in *Books Online* after you read this chapter.

Client Access

Once you've gotten Analysis Services installed, configured, running, and tuned, you access it with one of three tools. You can use Microsoft Excel's Pivot Table Services as a client. This tool provides one of the most powerful views into cubes and the one your managers are probably already familiar with. You can also design your own software using multiple programming environments, including Rapid Application Development (RAD) Integrated Development Environments (IDEs) well suited to data access, such as .NET or Delphi. Finally, you can use these programs with the command-line language MDX to present the answers to cube queries to clients like Web pages.

Analysis Services is a huge improvement over the OLAP services available in Microsoft SQL Server 7. It's also much bigger and more intricate.

Preparing for Analysis Services

Microsoft has included several wizards and tutorials, and I'm going to stick with those for this chapter. Before I start, I need to install the software, a process I detail in the Graphical section. Once the software is installed, I'll proceed to the tutorials. I'll work through more of the concepts there than here, because it's easier to discuss this type of application when you're watching it run in three dimensions, so to speak.

Cubes

The primary concept when using Analysis Services is the idea of cubes, which I introduced in the Overview section earlier. A cube is just a database of tables arranged in a certain way. Keep in mind that the storage of cubes takes place at two levels: the logical design and the physical storage.

The logical design is often represented as a star, with a table in the middle as the collection of all the measures, called a fact table, and the tables that store the things the data is about around the fact table, called dimension tables.

The star isn't the only way to arrange data. The data can be in hierarchical arrangements that feed each other. This is a bit more complex, but the Graphical section shows this arrangement.

There are two main ways to physically store cubes. The first is to obtain much or all of the data directly from the database it is stored in. This type of OLAP is called ROLAP. The other type of storage pulls the data out of the relational database into a separate database, optimized more for queries rather than for data entry. This type is called MOLAP.

Dimensions are the parts of the data that describe the measures. For instance, in a typical cube, you might see a table that contains months, another one for shoes, and one for regions. These dimension tables are normally quite small, because they contain only the discreet measurement areas. They all have identifiers in them that connect them to the fact table. The fact table contains all the measures of those dimensions. This table is usually quite large, because it contains all the data that represents the values in each dimension. This might be a good place for a simple example.

Let's define a dimension table called months, shown in Table 12.1. Next, I'd have another dimension table that contained the discreet values for the kinds of shoes I sell. If I had numbers in the thousands representing men's shoes and numbers in the two thousands representing women's shoes, it might look like Table 12.2.

I would then have a fact table that contained the values of the number of times the months occurred by shoe in my base data, like Table 12.3.

Notice I haven't carried out all the months to their extremes in the fact table. Notice also that all the boxes are filled, meaning I have perfect data for all the periods represented. This is something you don't always have in your production environment.

I can do a little digging with the very small amount of data that I have here. From the previous data, see if you can answer these questions:

- How many shoes did I sell in January?
- What model was my best seller in February?
- Which shoes sell better, men's or women's?

Table 12.1 The months Dimension Table

Key	Month
1	January
2	February
3	March
4	April

Table 12.2 The shoes Dimension Table

Key	Shoe
1	Model 1001
2	Model 1002
3	Model 2001
4	Model 2002

Table 12.3 The fact Table

Month	Shoe	Value
1	1	200
1	2	100
1	3	300
1	4	200
2	1	100
2	2	300
2	3	250
2	4	300

As you can see, even with only two dimensions and a few measures, I can provide marketing with that much-sought-after information they're looking for.

Throw in a region dimension and several thousand rows of measures, and you're just about ready to tackle a real three-dimensional cube.

Graphical

Before you can launch into Analysis Services, you need to install it.

Installation

I'll display some of the installation here, but I won't show you every screen. There are many options during the install that you should be familiar with, and you can read about them further in *Books Online*. Note that Analysis Services is not installed during the initial install.

If you follow this example using your test system, you'll be able to do the same tutorial I use in this chapter.

Pop your SQL Server 2000 CD into the drive. A graphic like the one shown in Figure 12.1 displays. Pick the SQL Server 2000 Components option, and the display shown in Figure 12.2 pops up.

You do what I'm sure you're familiar with as a "Next–Next–Finish" install. Take all the defaults, allowing the software to put itself wherever it wants and

Figure 12.1
Auto-Play
the SQL 2000
Server CD

Figure 12.2
Selecting
Analysis
Services

including things like the tutorial you're going to use for the chapter. Obviously, this is only suitable for a test system. I do advise that you experiment with a test system before you go live on a real installation.

My installation has completed, and if you're following along, you'll notice that there is an extra menu item tacked on to the Microsoft SQL Server menu item in the Start bar.

Running the Tutorial

Now that you've finished the installation, access that menu item to see three new items, Analysis Manager, Books Online, and the MDX Sample Application. You'll use Analysis Manager for everything, most notably the tutorial, which we'll go to right now.

As shown in Figure 12.3, open the Analysis Manager, and you'll notice that the first item in the right-hand pane is the tutorial. Click on the tutorial to start the process, and the first screen you're brought to is a Web page with several tutorial choices, as shown in Figure 12.4.

There are several lessons here, and you should visit them all if you want more than a passing look at Analysis Services. Don't assume, however, that these tutorials by themselves can educate you completely about this huge

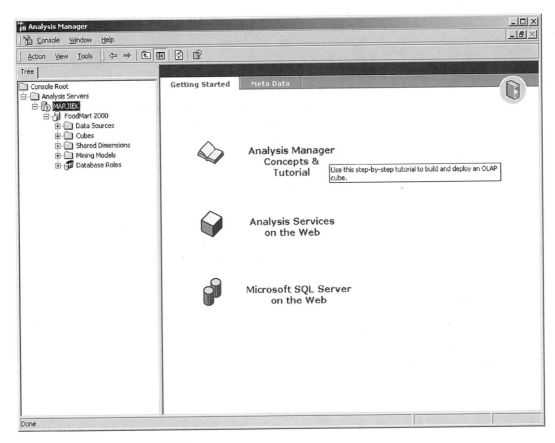

Figure 12.3 The Analysis Manager

product. They are meant more to lightly demonstrate the process you use to build a cube and look at the data from within *Analysis Manager*, as you will do in this chapter.

Although I commend Microsoft highly for including tutorials, you should have this chapter handy to complement the screens you'll go through in the next hour or so.

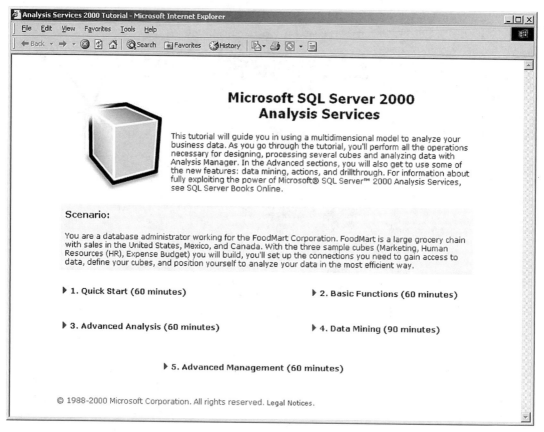

Figure 12.4 The tutorial opening screen

Select the first tutorial, and the screen in Figure 12.5 appears. We'll switch back and forth between the Web page tutorials and the test that you'll do on your test system. Watch the menu bar closely, because Microsoft includes screenshots as well as the ones I show.

The first step in creating a cube of data to work with is to define the source of the data. You don't have to define it here, unless you're using a source that uses ODBC, as this one does. The sample tutorial uses Microsoft

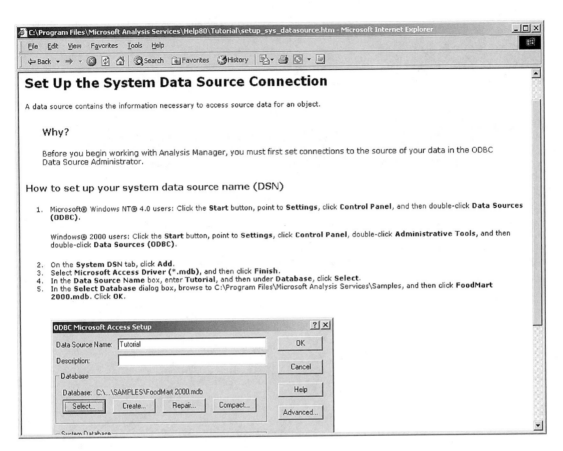

Figure 12.5   Selecting a data source

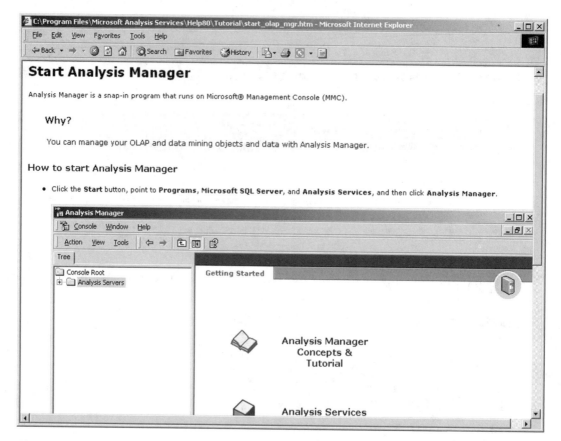

Figure 12.6 *Start Analysis Manager*

Access as the source database. Once you've set up the source ODBC connection, move on to the next part of the tutorial, shown in Figure 12.6.

Since you started the tutorial from inside *Analysis Manager*, we'll consider this step complete. Continue with the tutorial, and you'll see the display shown in Figure 12.7.

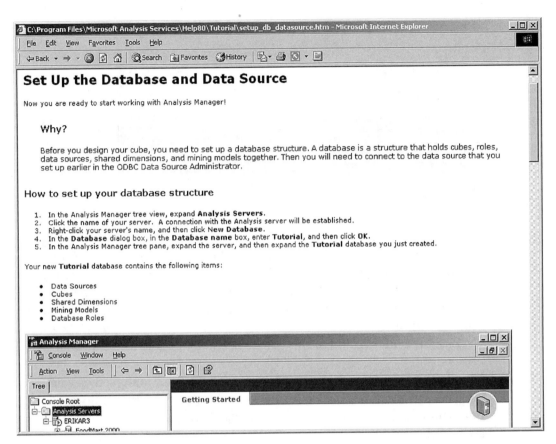

Figure 12.7   Setting up the cube database

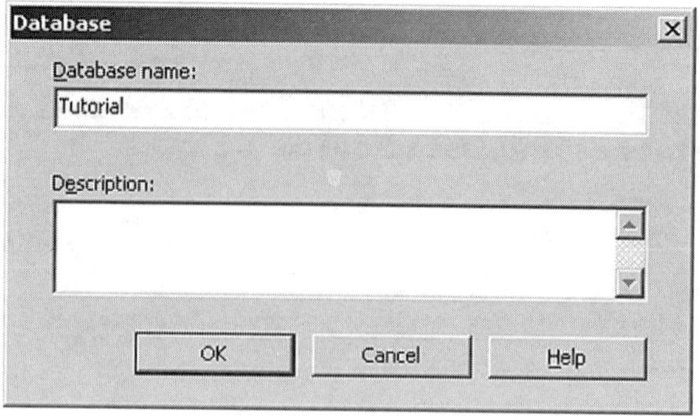

Figure 12.8
Naming the
database

The first thing you need to do is carve out some space on your server to set up the objects you'll work with for the rest of the tutorial. Following the instructions, create a new database by right-clicking the server name and then selecting New Database from the menu that opens. The panel shown in Figure 12.8 appears.

Using the information in this panel, the system is able to create all the tree objects.

Next you need to tie the ODBC-connected database to the cubes you'll create. This database will be a source for the cubes, and you can set up more than one database as a source. Set up your database by right-clicking the Data Sources object and selecting New Data Source, as shown in Figure 12.9.

Once you do that, you'll see the types of sources you can use for your cubes. Select the ODBC driver, as shown in Figure 12.10. Select Next to move to the next tab, and you're shown the display in Figure 12.11.

Pick the name you set up earlier, but notice that there are lots of other settings here that become more pertinent based on the source type. Test the connection, and then close the panel by clicking OK. Now you have your source. We'll move on to the next screen of the tutorial, as shown in Figure 12.12 (see page 418).

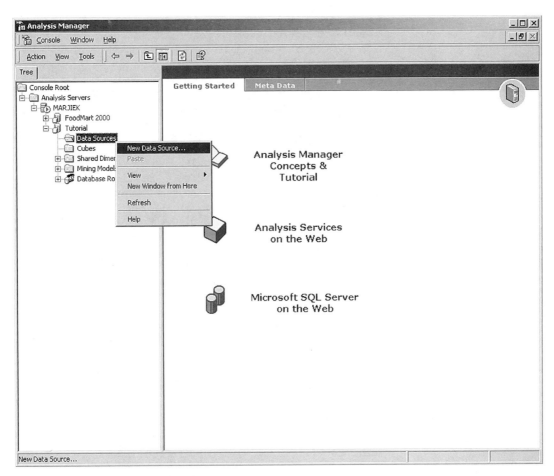

Figure 12.9 Setting up the data source

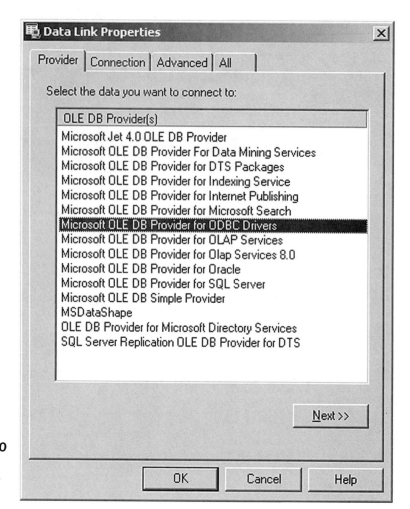

Figure 12.10
Selecting
ODBC as the
data source

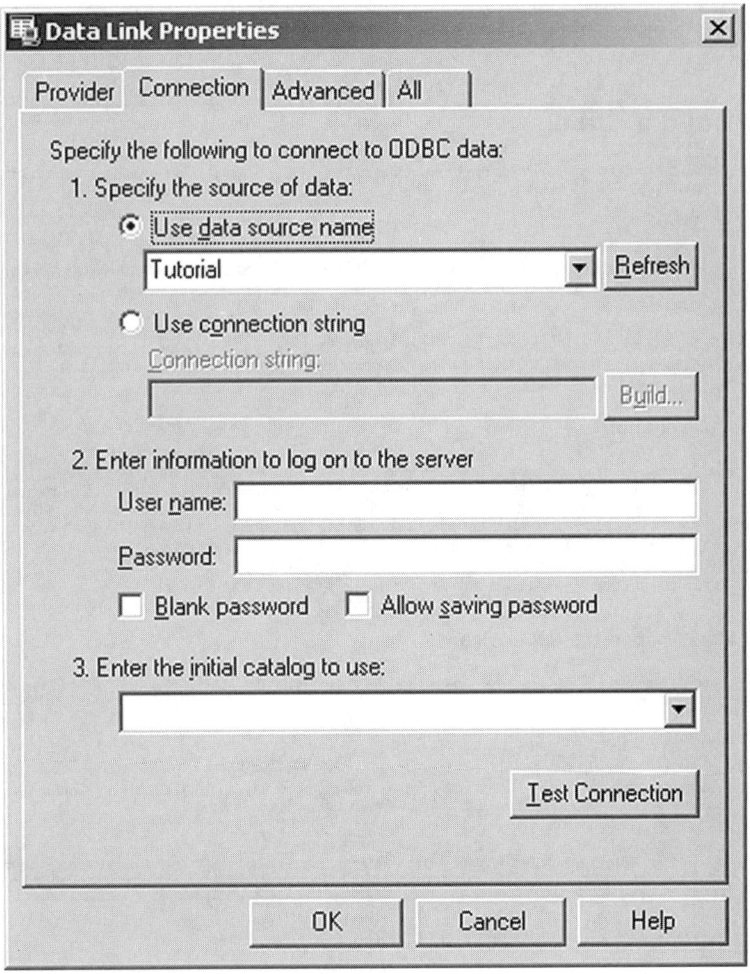

Figure 12.11 Selecting the ODBC DSN name

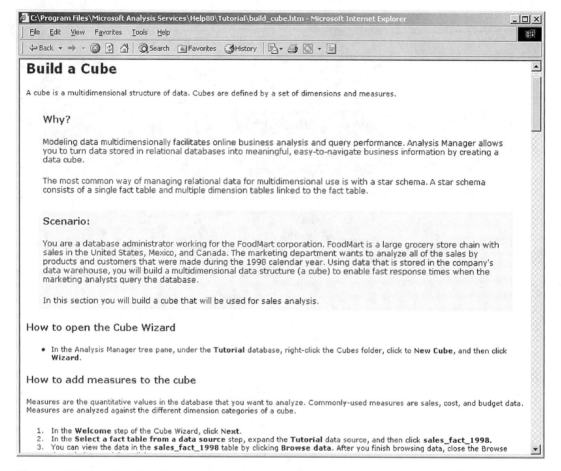

Figure 12.12 Building the cube

Next you're going to start the more involved parts. You're told by the tutorial that you want to analyze data from a large grocery chain. To do this, you need to set up a cube, and you'll do that by creating the fact table containing the measures I spoke about earlier. You'll then create the dimensions you use to analyze the measures.

First, right-click the Cubes object, and select New Cube and then Wizard from the menu that opens. The result is shown in Figure 12.13. Here you see the opening screen, so you'll move on by clicking Next. You see the screen shown in Figure 12.14.

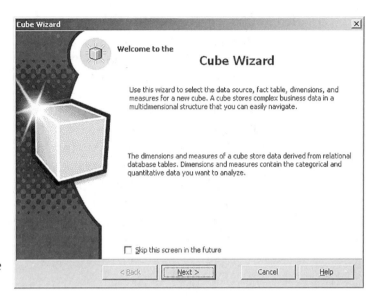

Figure 12.13
The new cube
wizard

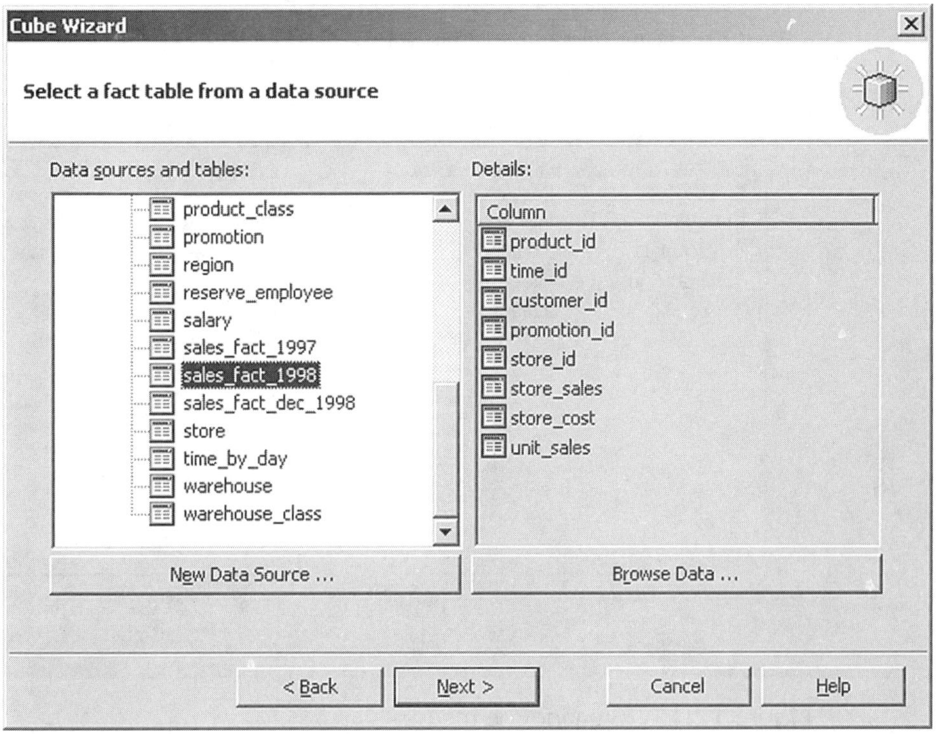

Figure 12.14   The fact table selection

Here you're going to pick the fact table that has the measures you want for your cube. This is cheating a bit, because this database is all prepped and ready for use as a cube. In the wild, this isn't how it works. You'll spend most of your time just getting the database into a format suitable for OLAP.

Getting the data into the format needed for a cube is where DTS comes in; you can use the skills you picked up in Chapter 5 to get the data from your production OLTP format into one better suited to OLAP.

What you're working with is a table that has references (keys) to all the dimensions you'll be including and the values based on those dimensions. This is a great deal like the primitive tables I described earlier.

Press Next to bring up the panel shown in Figure 12.15.

Here you're setting the number columns to act as the measures. If you look closely, you'll see I've included all the columns that are measures and left

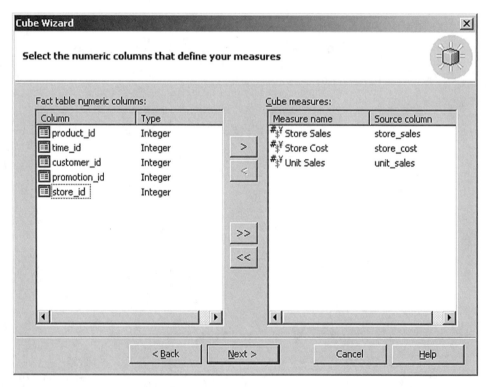

Figure 12.15 Creating the measures

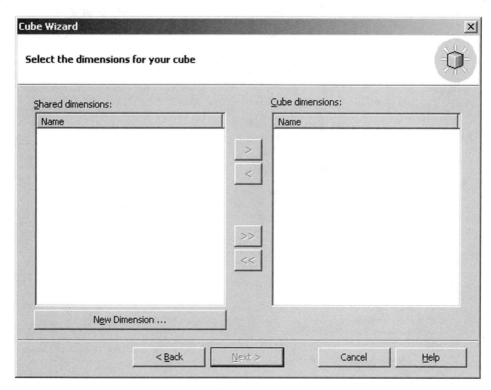

Figure 12.16 *The dimensions panel*

the reference or key columns on the left. Press Next to show the display in Figure 12.16.

You need to tie those dimensions to the fact table. Before you do that, you need to set what the dimension tables are. Press the New Dimension button, which starts a wizard within a wizard, as shown in Figure 12.17. This is just a welcome screen again, so select Next to continue. The screen in Figure 12.18 appears.

You're setting up the structure of how the dimension data will interact with the fact table and with other dimension data. In the most common use, it will form a star shape, hence the name. That's the selection to make; then pick Next to see the display shown in Figure 12.19.

Now select the table that has your first dimension. Pick the time_by_day table, and again you see that this database is already prepped for use as a cube.

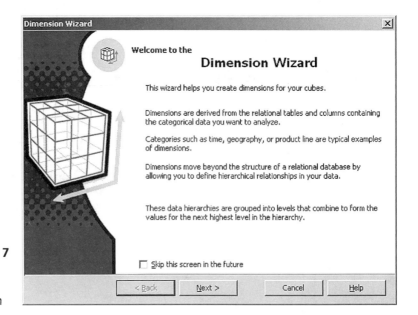

Figure 12.17
Dimension
wizard wel-
come screen

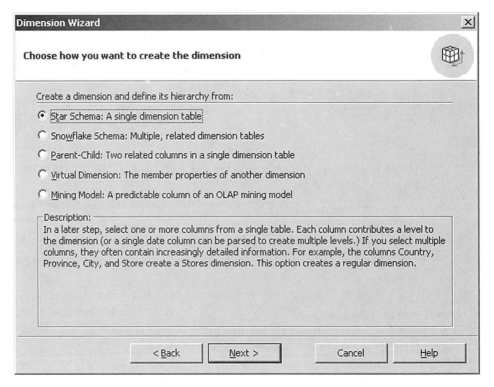

Figure 12.18   Dimension type

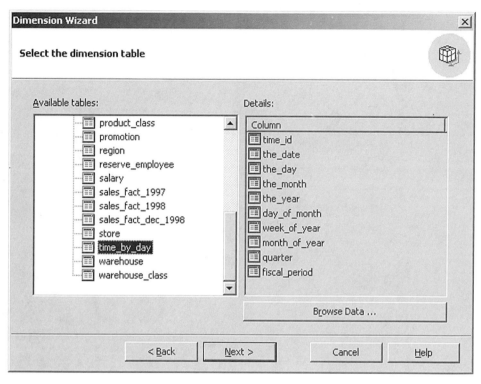

Figure 12.19   First dimension table

This table contains the breakdowns of time periods that might answer questions like "When did the customers buy the most items?" Select Next to bring up the display shown in Figure 12.20.

This is a pivotal point (pardon the pun). Whenever a dimension is based on time, you need to specify that. Time is a tricky thing, because calculating hours, minutes, months, days, and so forth requires specific mathematical functions for each. If the dimension table has data that equates to the datetime type, this is the proper setting.

Sometimes, however, date-based information is stored as a regular old number, such as the quarter or accounting period. In that case, you would *not* pick

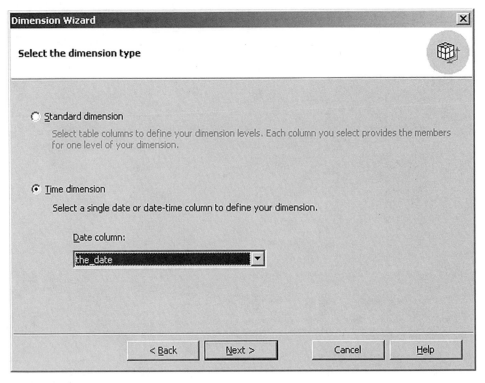

Figure 12.20 Setting the dimension type

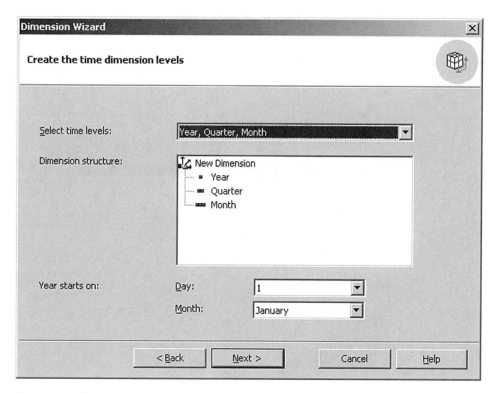

Figure 12.21   *Setting the dimension levels*

this as a time dimension. Pick Next here to bring up the display shown in Figure 12.21.

The concept of *levels* is new here. Levels are ways to further break down a dimension—in this case, you choose the Year, Quarter, Month breakdown because that's how you want to look at the data. You need to select the levels logically based on the breakdowns you have within the dimension table. Select Next to bring up the screen in Figure 12.22.

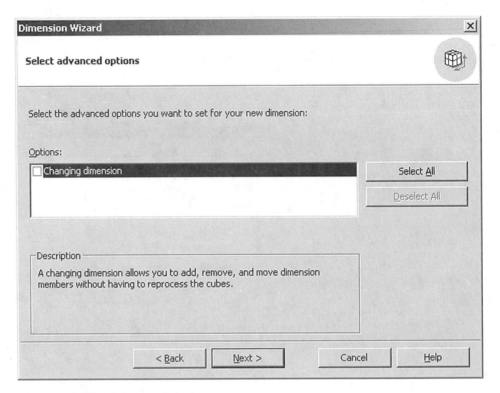

Figure 12.22 Advanced options

By using this panel, you could change more options for your dimensions, but you don't need to now. Select Next here to bring up the screen in Figure 12.23. Next you need to name your dimension, which you do with the name Time. This name represents the grouping; notice that it's singular in number. This is a common way of dimensional naming.

Once you've named the dimension, you can change whether the dimension is visible to other cubes. That can come in very handy, so leave that option checked.

You may have noticed along the way that you have many opportunities to browse the data. This is often useful because you're acting as a developer, and this is one method to make sure you're going to see the proper data in the cube.

Select Finish, and the wizard creates the dimension for you. You now have a completed time dimension. That isn't enough to give you meaningful information though, so continue, and make another dimension. In Figure 12.24, you're shown the completed Time dimension.

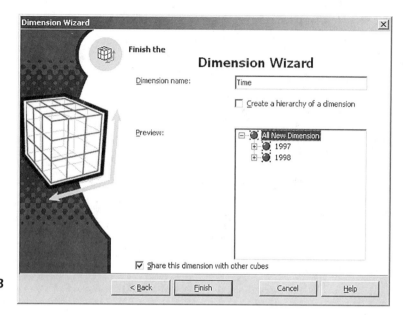

Figure 12.23
Final options

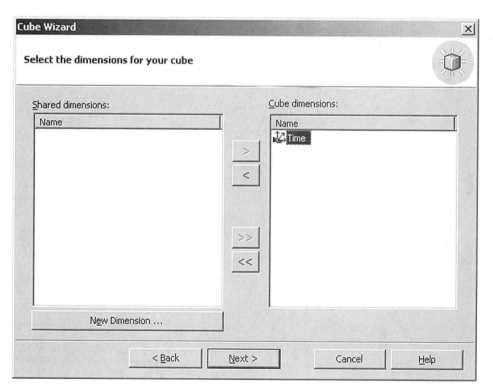

Figure 12.24 The completed dimension

Select the New Dimension . . . button to begin the process all over again. I'll not bore you with the introductory screen again, so skip it and move on to the next screen, as shown in Figure 12.25.

You're asked to pick the table layout, just as you did earlier. This time, however, you're going to use a different type of dimension layout, the Snowflake schema. This type consists of more than one table, which are joined with others to create the dimension with its levels.

Select Next to bring up the screen in Figure 12.26. Select two tables, the product and product_class tables, to allow you to examine the products that are sold and the classes those products have been defined for. For instance, a product that a supermarket sells is oatmeal. Oatmeal belongs to a classification of Cereal. This allows you to ask the questions "What kinds of foods sell well?" and "What Cereal sells the best?"

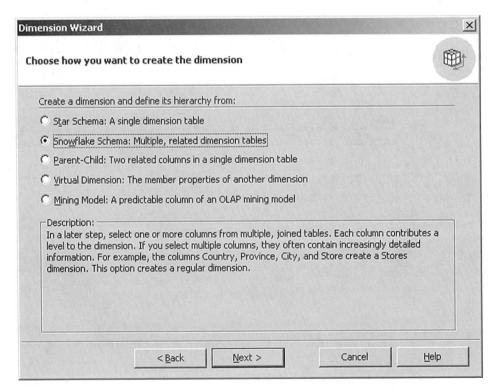

Figure 12.25 Choosing the dimension layout

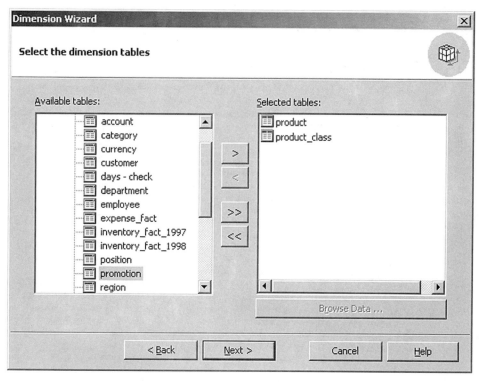

Figure 12.26 Selecting the tables

Next you need to tie the tables together to provide the link that the system will need to say that oatmeal belongs in cereals. This is called a *join*. Click Next to move to that step, as shown in Figure 12.27.

Notice that the tables were automatically joined. SQL Server 2000 determines the most obvious joins based on the column names or "keys" that are already in the table. When this database was created, the tables were made with corresponding key columns. That's what you're going to use here.

If you need to create a join that isn't obvious to SQL Server, or if you want to edit the join, simply click and hold on the column name and drag it on top

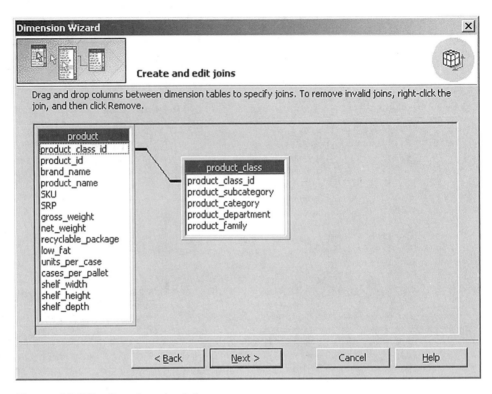

Figure 12.27   Creating the joins

of the column name in the other table. You're finished with this join, so click Next to continue, and you see the screen in Figure 12.28.

Select Product Category, Product Subcategory, and Brand Name as the levels you want to see. Select Next to continue building your cube and bring up the screen shown in Figure 12.29.

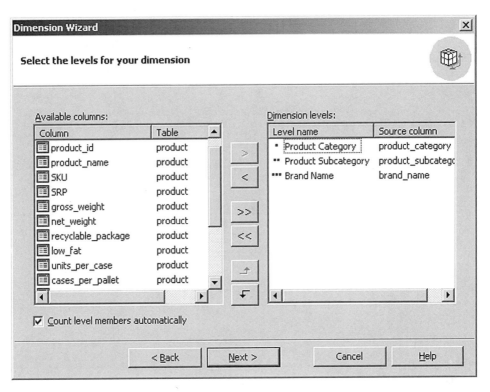

Figure 12.28   Selecting the levels

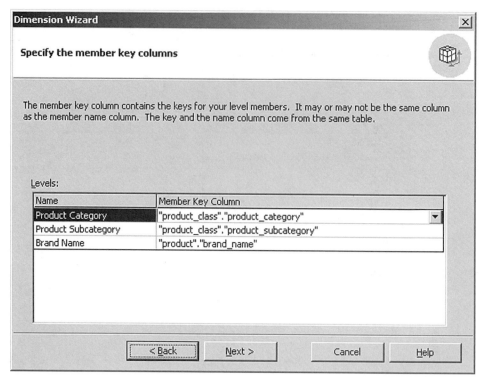

Figure 12.29 *Changing the key columns*

In this screen, you set columns other than the levels to act as the keys for that table. You won't change this, but select one of them so that you can see the pull-down icon. Select Next to bring up the screen in Figure 12.30.

Just as before, you're presented with more options that you can change for the type of schema you'll use. Leave these and press Next to move on to the next screen, shown in Figure 12.31.

Name your new dimension Product, and leave the option selected for sharing the dimension with other cubes. Select Finish, and you see the display shown in Figure 12.32.

As a recap, you've begun your cube; set up a dimension of time where you can break things down by year, quarter, and month; and set dimensions to see products by brand, class, and subclass.

You've already seen the process for creating a dimension with the standard Star schema, so rather than displaying all those screens again, I'll describe what you'll do for the rest of the dimensions you need.

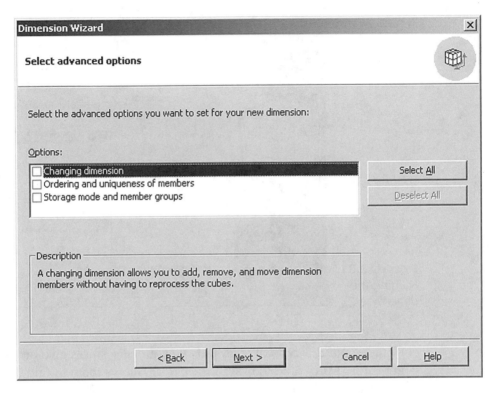

Figure 12.30   Advanced options

If you're following along on your computer, just perform the steps shown here. You can also check the tutorial for the steps, but they're identical to these.

First, you need to create the Customer dimension. Click the New Dimension button, as before. Skip the Welcome screen by clicking Next. In the Choose how you want to create the dimension step, select Star Schema: A single dimension table. Then click Next.

In the Select the dimension table step, pick the customer information by clicking Customer and then Next to continue. You need to set the type of schema to use, so in the Select the dimension type step, leave the Star schema selected and click Next.

Now you have to get the levels that you want to see for the customer data. Under Available columns, double-click the Country, State_Province, City, and lname columns, in that order. This gives you a lot of information about the

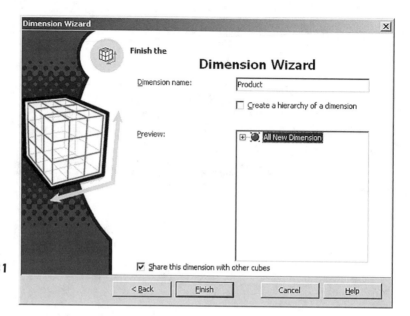

Figure 12.31
Naming the
dimension

customers, and this type of analysis is why grocery stores give out those "discount cards." Every time they scan the card, it allows them to find out just this type of data. Now click Next.

You don't need to change any other options, so in the Specify the member key columns step, click Next. No special options are needed for this table, so in the Select advanced options step, just click Next.

Finally, in the last step of the wizard, name the dimension Customer in the Dimension name box, and leave the Share this dimension with other cubes box selected. To finish, click Finish. Back in the cube wizard, you see the Customer dimension in the Cube dimensions list.

You need to set the data from the individual stores in the field. This helps you answer questions "Which state sells the most? Which city? Which store?" You do that by selecting the New Dimension button and skipping the welcome screen. At the Choose how you want to create the dimension step, select Star Schema: A single dimension table, and then click Next. You're not going to change the type of dimension; just stick with the Star schema.

In the Select the dimension table step, you'll pick your Store table, and then click Next. You won't need to change your dimension type, so just click Next to move on. Now the interesting part starts.

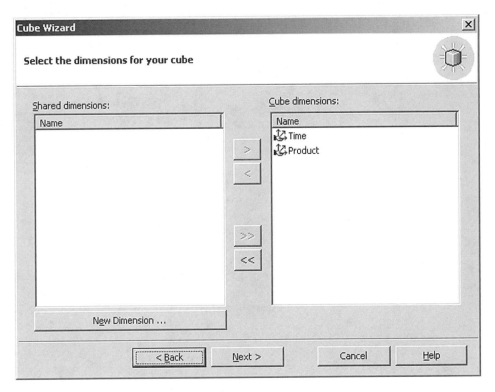

Figure 12.32 The current dimensions

You need to define the levels, so in the *Available columns* screen, double-click the store_country, store_state, store_city, and store_name columns, in that order. Now click Next.

As before, you don't need to change any advanced options, so in the *Specify the member key columns* step, click Next, and in the *Select advanced options* step, click Next.

In the last step of the wizard, name the dimension Store in the *Dimension name* box, and as usual leave the *Share this dimension with other cubes* box selected. Finally, click Finish. In Figure 12.33 on the next page you can see the result of all your labor.

You have all the dimensions, and you have the fact table. SQL Server 2000 will finish the job for you, so press the Next button to bring up the display shown in Figure 12.34. Now you get a warning that it might take a while to

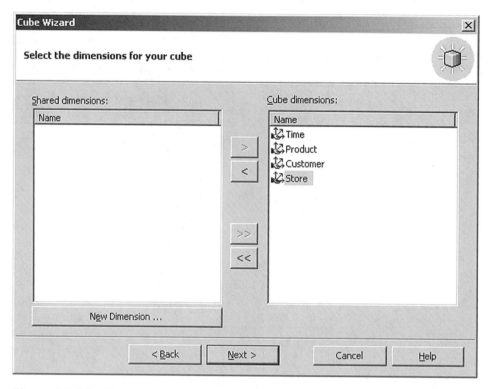

Figure 12.33 The completed dimensions

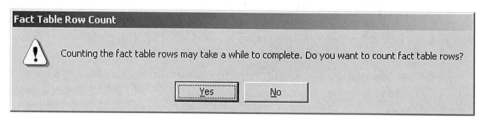

Figure 12.34 Counting the fact table rows

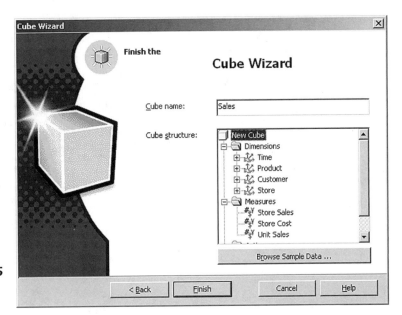

Figure 12.35
Naming the
cube

count all these rows you've asked for. Don't worry—in this instance it won't, but in a real-world database, they aren't kidding. Press Yes, and the screen shown in Figure 12.35 appears.

Name the cube Sales, and press Finish. This lets the cube wizard do all the work to finalize the cube. The wizard closes, and then the cube editor appears, as shown in Figure 12.36.

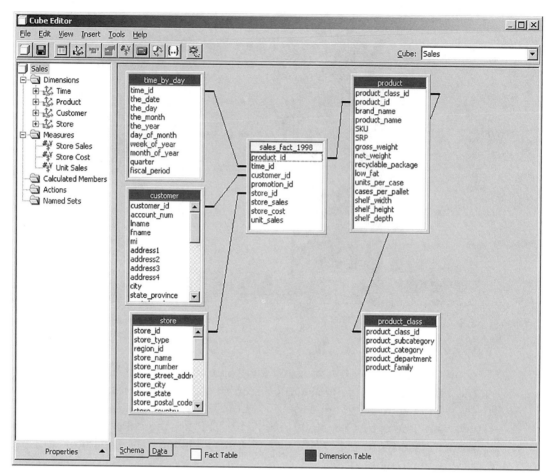

Figure 12.36 The Cube Editor

I've arranged this screen to place the fact table in the center and to group the product information together. You're not done here yet; Microsoft wants you to hang around in the cube editor so that you can see how to make a change to a cube once it's been created. I think that this is a handy thing to do.

Now move on to the next section of the tutorial, as shown in Figure 12.37. What you're told in the tutorial is that you forgot something—what will more

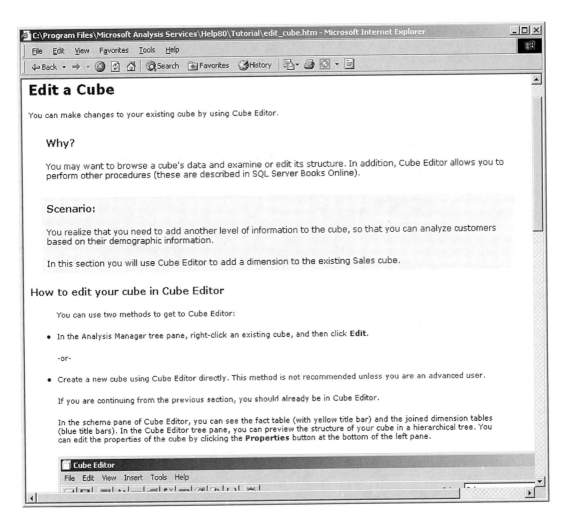

Figure 12.37 *Editing the cube tutorial*

likely happen in the field is that once the information is presented, you or someone else will want to add another factor for examination.

You're going to add a level involving the customers. To do that, click Insert and then Tables in the cube editor's menu bar. Figure 12.38 shows this process.

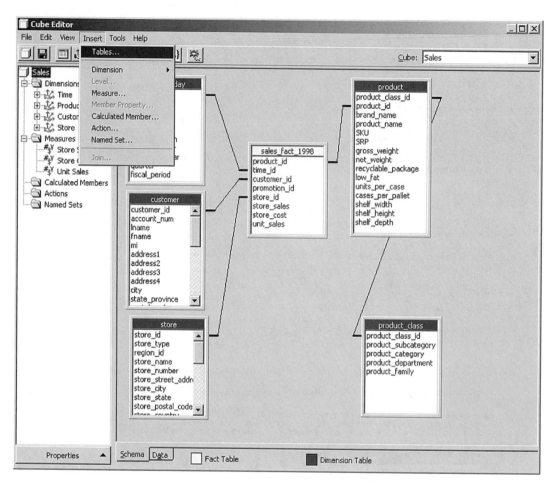

Figure 12.38 Editing the cube

Once you do that, you'll see the screen in Figure 12.39. Select the promotion table. Once you click Add and then Close, you see the display shown in Figure 12.40.

You haven't done nearly the work you did to tie out the other tables, so you'll do that now by double-clicking the promotion_name column. Figure 12.41 appears. Press OK, and then rename the dimension by clicking it in

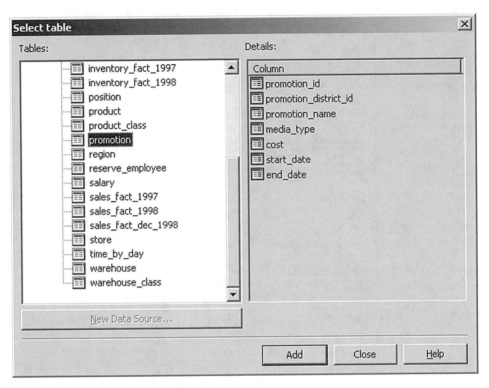

Figure 12.39 Adding the table

the left-hand pane of the editor and typing Promotion, as shown in Figure 12.42. This is done for consistency.

You now have a completed cube. Save the cube by clicking the icon that looks like a disk; the system will ask you if you want to design the storage of the cube. For now, you should say No because this decision warrants its own discussion.

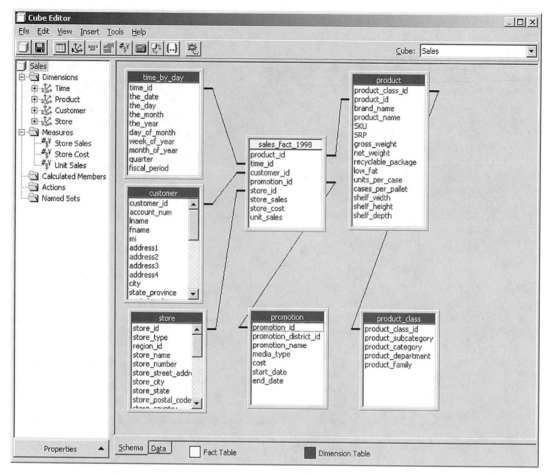

Figure 12.40 The added promotion table

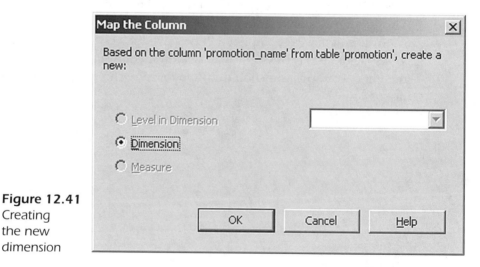

Figure 12.41
Creating
the new
dimension

442

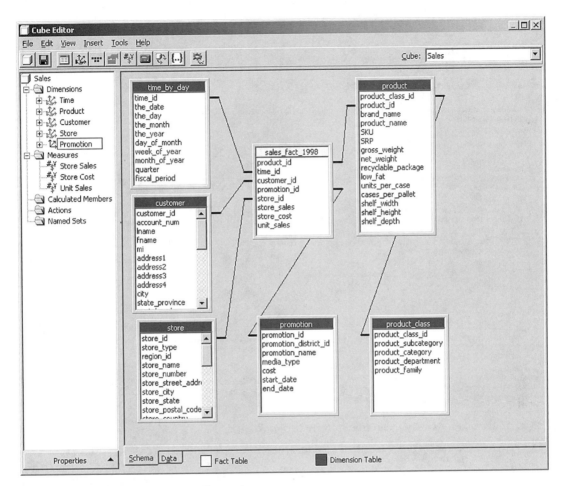

Figure 12.42 Renaming the dimension

You've finished this section of the tutorial, and you can now move on to the next section, as shown in Figure 12.43. Now you set up the way the system physically stores the data cube. There are three choices:

- MOLAP
- ROLAP
- HOLAP

I'm going to oversimplify a bit here again. MOLAP is a storage system completely divorced from the source of the data. ROLAP stores some of the cube

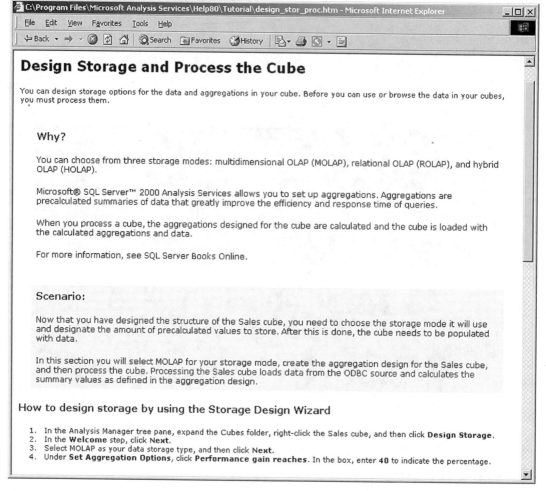

Figure 12.43 The designing storage tutorial

data right in the source, and HOLAP is supposed to be a happy medium between the two. Stick with MOLAP for your storage in this example.

Another part of the storage that you'll determine is how much data to pre-aggregate. *Preaggregate* means that the computer calculates much of the data ahead of time, making it faster to answer a question when it's asked.

The difficulty of this choice is that it will take longer *now* to do that and has the side effect of increasing the amount of storage space needed. Again,

Microsoft includes a handy wizard to do the comparisons, and it offers some trade-offs, so you'll use that to do the work.

First, right-click the *Sales* cube you just made and select *Design Storage* from the menu that appears, as shown in Figure 12.44. After you do that, you'll see the screen shown in Figure 12.45. Nothing to see here, so press Next to bring up the screen in Figure 12.46.

As described earlier, set the data storage to one of three types. There are entire schools of thought about which type is better in which circumstance.

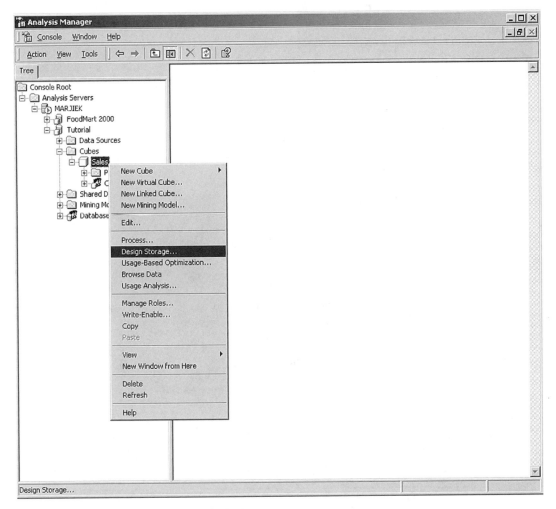

Figure 12.44 *Beginning storage design*

Figure 12.45
Storage welcome screen

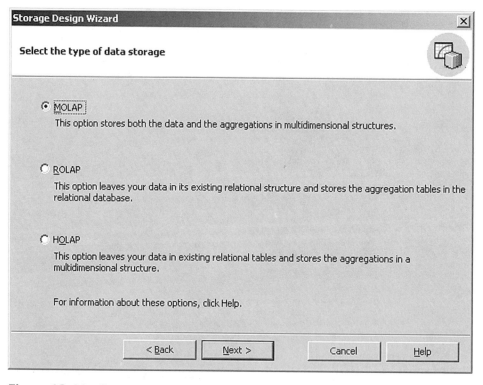

Figure 12.46 Storage type

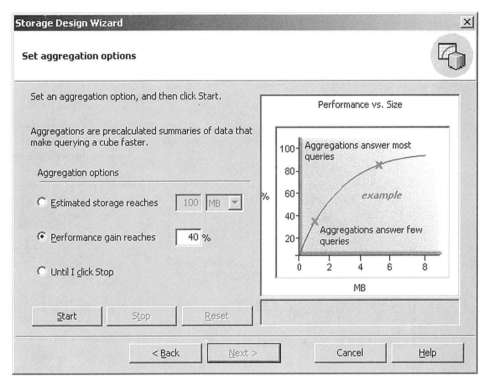

Figure 12.47 *Aggregation options*

Research the Resources section to visit a few sites that contain these discussions. Select MOLAP and press Next to bring up the display shown in Figure 12.47.

Now you set aggregation options. You can choose one of three methods. The first is that the server can only use a certain amount of room to create the aggregations. The second sets what percentage of speed gain the user will get regardless of the space it takes to do that. Finally, you could choose to let the computer work until you say stop.

Choose the middle option and click Start. When the system is done, you see the output shown in Figure 12.48.

The wizard tells you that it will take about 0.3MB to get a 40% gain in performance. If that isn't acceptable, change the option and tell the wizard to start again. That output should be OK, so select Next to tell the system to use these options. The display shown in Figure 12.49 appears.

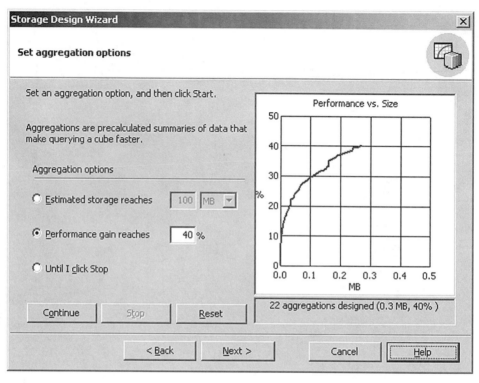

Figure 12.48 Space for performance

Figure 12.49
Saving the
settings

In this screen, you can either save the settings for the storage to be processed later or start the process. Start the process by clicking *Finish*. This process takes a little while, and when the process completes, you see the display shown in Figure 12.50. And with that, you're done. Your cube is complete, data at the ready. Now you can view some amazing things about the raw numbers your database has. You've finished this part of the tutorial, so move to the next section, as shown in Figure 12.51.

Now you're ready to look at the data you configured. To do that, right-click the cube and select *Browse Data* from the menu that appears. You can see that

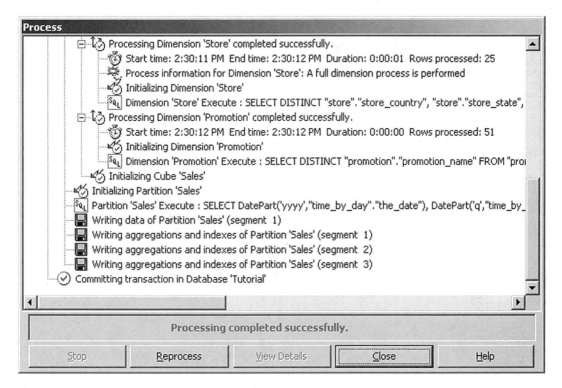

Figure 12.50   *The completed storage wizard*

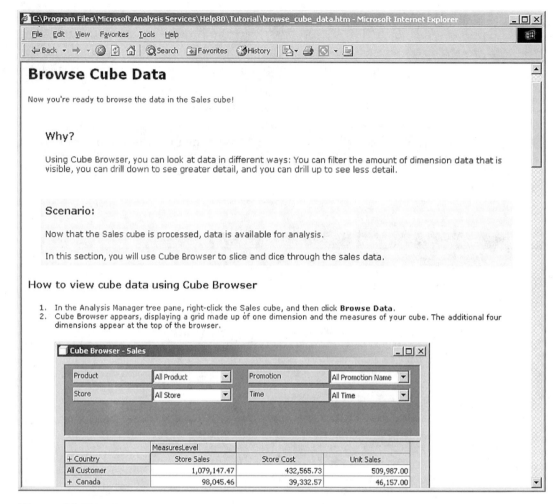

Figure 12.51 Browse-the-cube tutorial

process in Figure 12.52. Once you do that, you see the display that is shown in Figure 12.53. You'll see that the USA has the most customers, followed by Mexico and then Canada.

Expand the USA row by double-clicking it, and you see the display in Figure 12.54.

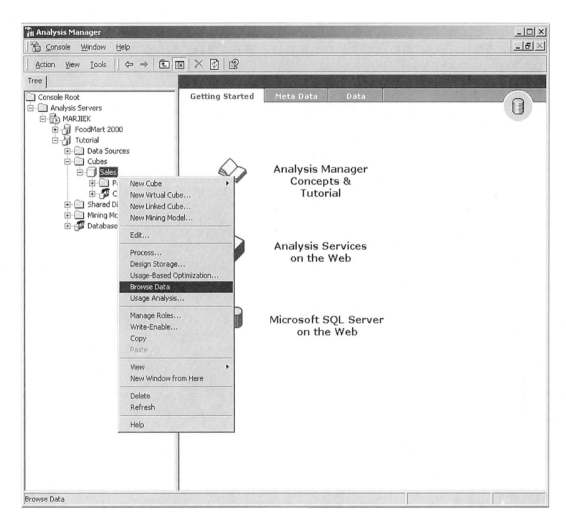

Figure 12.52   Opening the data

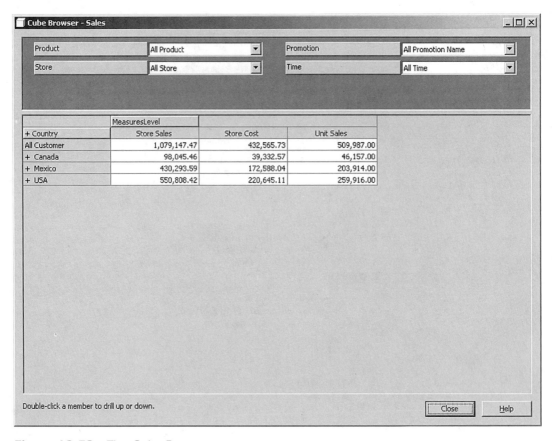

Figure 12.53 The Cube Browser

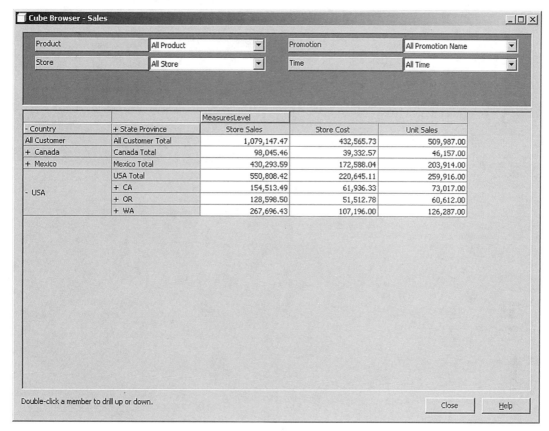

Figure 12.54 Expanding the country level

You can see that Washington has the most customers. Now you can see why you set levels within your dimension and the reason that the order of the level matters. If you use the drop-down menus at the top, you can limit the type of that data that is displayed.

Let's take this to another level (pardon the pun again) and look at products instead of sales. Click the Product dimension button in the top panel and drag that on top of the MeasuresLevel heading. You can see the output of this in Figure 12.55.

You also need to expand the Product dimension so that you can see the subcategories and brands of products. You can also replace the columns spreadsheet view and drag the heading onto the row headings as well. In this fashion, you compare products with customers, customers with stores, promotions with sales, and so forth.

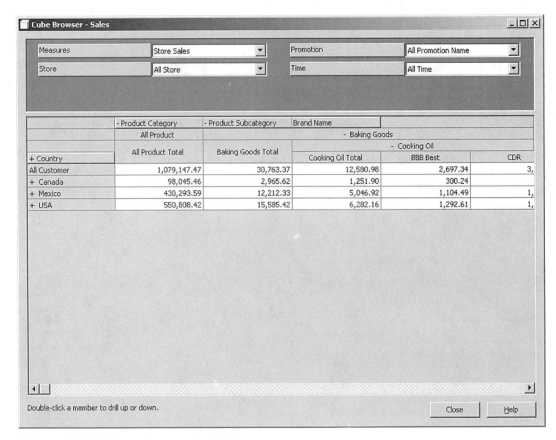

Figure 12.55 Browsing product data

Command Line

In the previous chapters, I've shown that almost anything you can do with graphical tools you can also do with commands. This isn't the case for Analysis Services, because you don't normally build cubes or dimensions by using MDX; you select data from them with MDX commands.

MDX Sample Application

The important thing to keep in mind is that you don't do your work using Query Analyzer or osql. You need a special tool to access the data from a cube—either a program written by a developer or a Web page. Microsoft has included an example of the first kind, called the *MDX Sample Application*. It's in the *Analysis Manager* section of the *SQL Server* menu item in your Start menu.

As shown in shown Figure 12.56, start that on your system. Even though this is called a sample application, you can connect to other servers and even analyze other cubes with the tool. Microsoft doesn't intend for you to supply your users with this tool, however; they fully expect you to use another graphical tool to look at the information. There are many of these, and the Web sites I've referenced at the end of the chapter list the vendors that supply these tools.

We'll stick with this tool for the Command Line section and use Microsoft Excel as your users would in the Examples section. Once you accept the connection parameters, you're dropped into the FoodMart sample database on your server. This isn't the one you made; it's another one that Microsoft includes with the product.

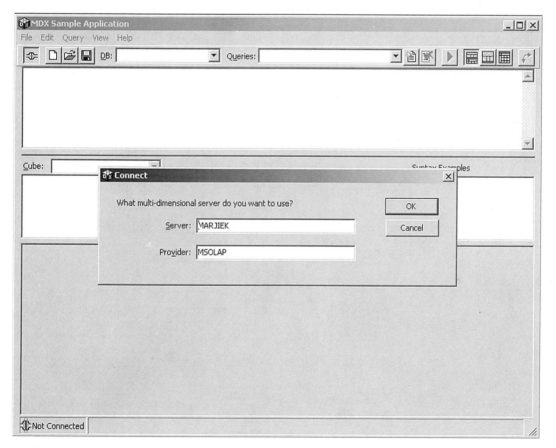

Figure 12.56   *MDX Sample Application*

Notice that you have many panels on this one screen, as shown in Figure 12.57. We're not going to spend too much time on this application, but let's take a quick look at the major parts.

The first icon bar you see allows you to specify the database you want to work with and some predefined queries. One is already displayed in the next window, the query panel. When you select a query, it displays in this panel, and when you press the green arrow icon, the query executes and displays in the bottom panel, called the results panel. You can see an example of this output in Figure 12.58.

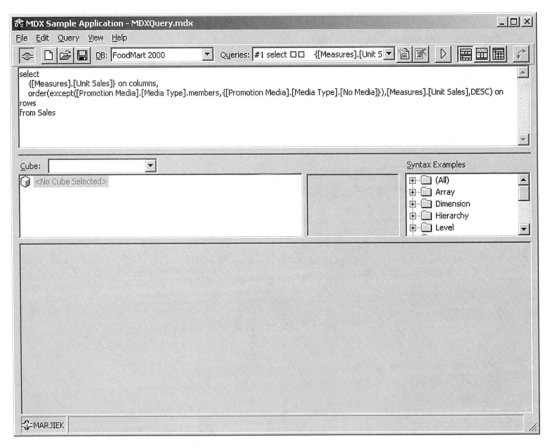

Figure 12.57 Panels in the MDX Sample Application

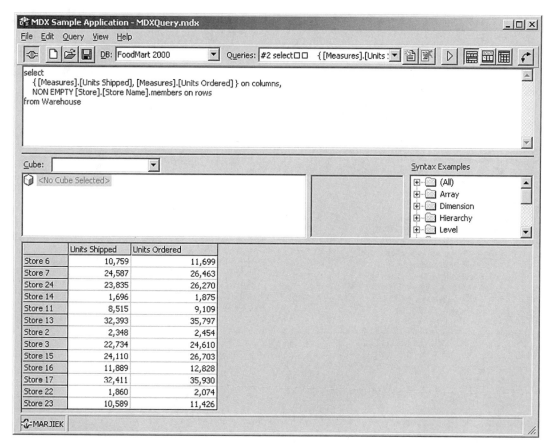

Figure 12.58   Completed query

The next interesting feature of this tool is that it will help design the query. Look at the changes made in Figure 12.59. I've cleared the query panel and typed in the word SELECT. Then in the *Cubes* pull-down selection box, I've chosen the *Sales* cube. Next, I've drilled down to the *Store Type* dimension and then on to the *Deluxe Supermarket* type. When I double-click that entry, it places it after the word SELECT, and I've built my query.

When I started this book, I said that I wouldn't be discussing a lot of SQL syntax. I'm going to continue that tradition here, because I feel that this type of thing is best left to the developer's texts.

There's an excellent explanation of the syntax for MDX in the help documentation for the *MDX Sample Application* as well as in *Books Online*. I urge you

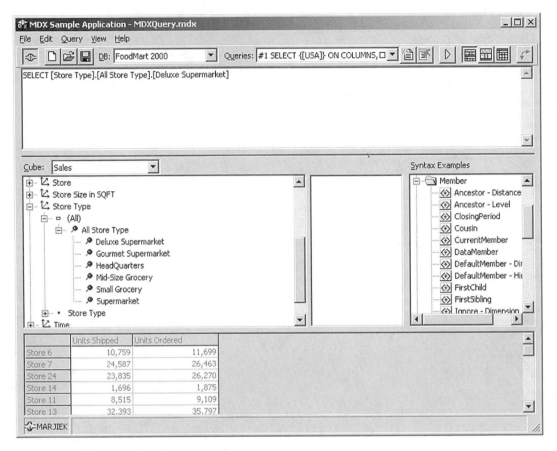

Figure 12.59 Building the query

to pull down the sample queries while you review these references. I've found this is the fastest way to understand these complex queries.

Although I'll not spend a lot of time on MDX queries, I do think it's important for you to see the overall structure of one if you're going to be required to work with them.

I'll assume you know a little about the Structured Query Language (SQL) syntax. When you want to do something in SQL, the command normally has this form:

```
Command - Qualifier - Source - Modifier
```

An example of this is shown in Listing 12.1.

Listing 12.1   Sample SQL query

```
SELECT column_name
FROM table_name
WHERE column_name = 'some value'
```

There is a similar structure when using MDX. The difference is that a standard SELECT statement in SQL is based on a two-dimensional structure. You'll have to use a new way of thinking when you use MDX, because there may be several dimensions in the cube. The new concepts you should incorporate into your SQL way of thinking involve *axes* and *slicers*.

Let's look at the structure in Listing 12.2, direct from Books Online:

Listing 12.2   MDX query structure

```
SELECT [<axis_specification> [, <axis_specification>...]]
FROM [<cube_specification>]
[WHERE [<slicer_specification>]]
```

Axes are the way you specify the dimension you want. The cube specification part is the cube within the database you want to look at, and the slicers specify the "limit" of the data that is returned. It's often a bit difficult to imagine all this, but think of a cube in your mind. I'll keep it simple and only use a few dimensions in this example.

Imagine that the dimensions you're interested in are Store and Time. Recall that within each dimension, you have levels, so you need a way to zoom in on the cells that have the sales figures for the year 2001 and the Boston store. An MDX query for the cells in this fictional cube might have the format shown in Listing 12.3.

Listing 12.3   Sample MDX query

```
SELECT
{ [Measures].[Sales]}
ON COLUMNS, { [Time].[2001]} ON ROWS
FROM Sales
WHERE ( [Store].[USA].[BO] )
```

This is the general layout for an MDX query. Although it gets complex from here, the general principles remain the same. You're just layering on more and more axes and/or slicers. The important concept with MDX is that you need to be familiar with the layout of your cubes before you start.

Although MDX is an important concept for developers, let's look more closely at the way your users will *really* access this information.

Examples

If you're like 90% of the world, you have Microsoft Office installed on your PC. If you do, you already have a client for SQL Server 2000 OLAP cubes.

Microsoft Excel has a built-in Pivot Table feature, and you can use it to monitor the cubes you've created.

Viewing Cube Data with Microsoft Excel

I've got Microsoft Excel version 2000, so that's what you'll see in the following screenshots. The concepts hold true for Office 97 as well. Office XP improves on these concepts even further.

We'll use Excel to create a cube viewer. Remember that your users need to select the Pivot Table option when they install Microsoft Excel, as well as the Microsoft Query product that Excel uses to get at data. To begin, start Microsoft Excel, as shown in Figure 12.60.

Next, open the Data menu item and drill down to the PivotTable and PivotChart selection, as shown in Figure 12.61. Once you've selected that item, you're given another wizard. You can see the screen you're presented with in Figure 12.62.

You can see that you can use data from various locations. You can use data stored in the spreadsheet or pull the data in from another source. The beauty of this option is that the Analysis Services server is busy getting and tracking all the data the users need in their pivot table. Once the cubes are created, the users need only this tool to access the cube.

Select External data source and then Pivot Table to start. Select Next to continue, and you're shown the panel in Figure 12.63.

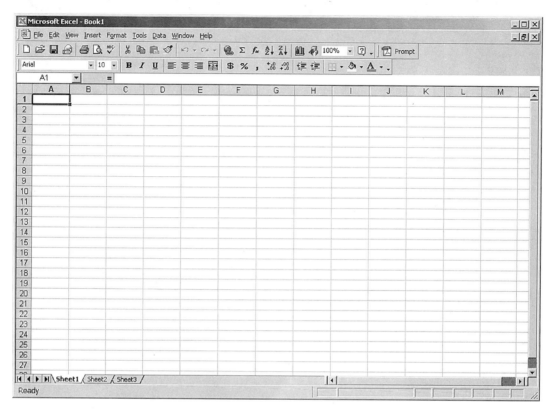

Figure 12.60 Microsoft Excel 2000

Again you see a wizard within a wizard. Click the Get Data button, and you're shown the screen in Figure 12.64. Change to the OLAP Cubes tab to continue your selections. You can see that the FoodMart database is already selected. Select <New Data Source> and then OK to start yet another part of the wizard. The result is shown in Figure 12.65.

Name the source Tutorial and select the higher OLAP source. The older one is for SQL Server 7. Once you select Connect, you see the screen shown in Figure 12.66 on page 464.

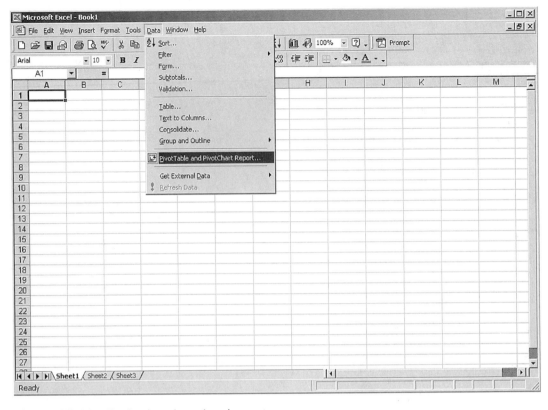

Figure 12.61   Beginning the wizard

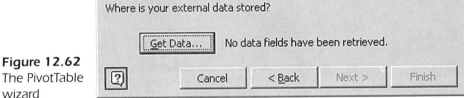

Figure 12.62
The PivotTable
wizard

Figure 12.63
Data source
wizard

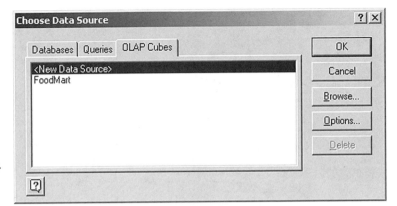

Figure 12.64
Selecting
OLAP cubes

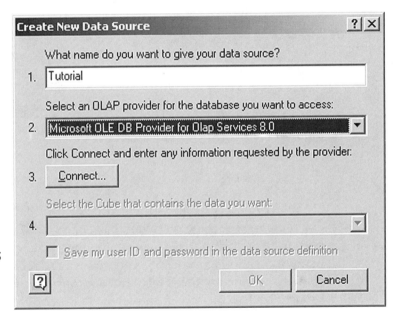

Figure 12.65
Picking the
tutorial cube
database

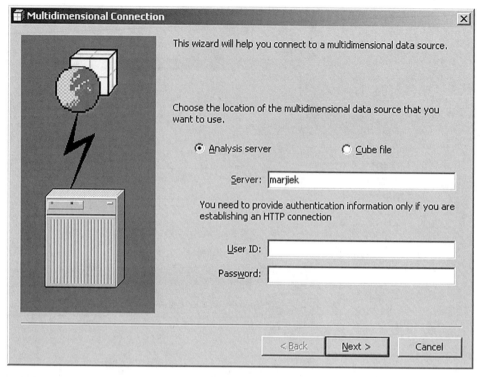

Figure 12.66   Specifying the source

Select *Analysis server* as the source of your data, and then select Next to continue. You see the screen shown in Figure 12.67. Select the database you've been using in the tutorial. Once you've done that, select *Finish*, and you see the panel shown in Figure 12.68. And now you're returned to the selection you started, showing the fields filled out appropriately. Once you select OK, you're brought back to the screen shown in Figure 12.69.

Once you have selected OK, you are brought all the way back to step 2— remember that you were in a wizard within a wizard. You now see the output shown in Figure 12.70.

Click Next, and, as shown in Figure 12.71, you're brought to the final screen. You could import all of this data into a completely new spreadsheet, but leave that option alone and allow the system to put the cells right where they are.

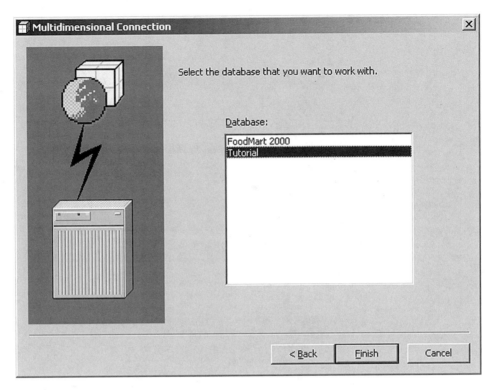

Figure 12.67 Selecting the tutorial database

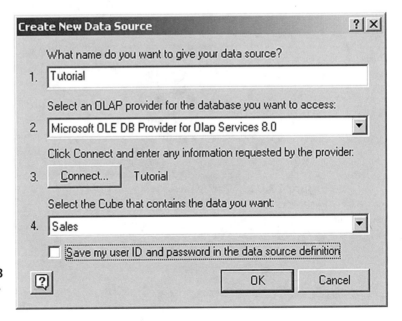

Figure 12.68
Finalizing the
connection

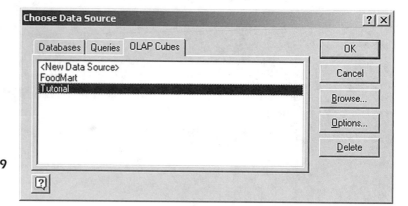

Figure 12.69
The tutorial
source

Figure 12.70
Step 2—
Again

Figure 12.71
Final screen

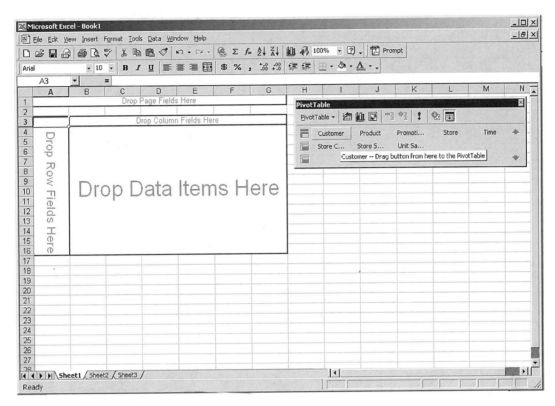

Figure 12.72 Building the cube

In Figure 12.72, you can see your data ready for inclusion into your viewer. I'll drag some fields around and drop them on the places designated on the screen, and, as shown in Figure 12.73, you can see the results. If you've dragged the Customer and Product dimensions onto the left and top panels, and then dragged the Unit Sales measure into the middle pane, your screen will look like this one.

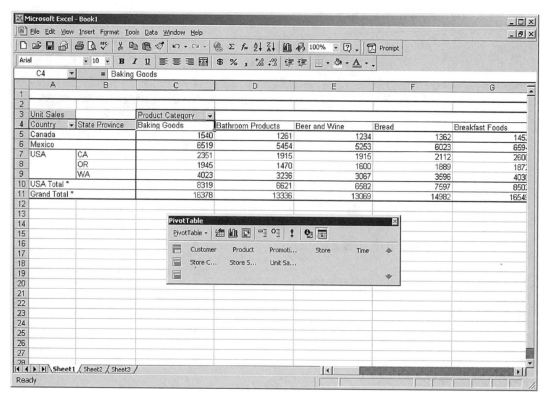

Figure 12.73 Browsing the cube

This is a fairly trivial example; but if you turn your users loose on this kind of exercise, you'll soon see some meaningful information rising from all that data.

Resources

A great collection of OLAP sites:
http://www.altaplana.com/olap/olap.collections.html
An excellent tutorial for basic OLAP:
http://perso.wanadoo.fr/bernard.lupin/english/example.htm
Estimating the cost of data warehousing:
http://www.dmreview.com/portal.cfm?NavID=91&EdID=937&PortalID=25&Topic=55

Chapter **13**

Extensible Markup Language

Chapter at a Glance

Read this chapter for an overview of the Extensible Markup Language (XML) technology in SQL Server 2000.

The Resources section contains references for:

- XML resources
- An XML explanation
- An XML description
- An XML tutorial
- The XML document map
- Another way to access XML data using Visual Basic (VB)
- An XSL Transformations (XSLT) tutorial

Read Chapters 3 and 4 before you read this one.

Overview

The greatest innovations are often the simplest. As computer technology concepts go, XML isn't that complex. In essence it's just a markup language like HTML, but while HTML marks up pages, XML marks up data. The benefit is that XML can be used to transfer data between heterogeneous systems.

SQL Server 2000 includes native support for this new technology, and it's one you should leverage as quickly as possible. The feature provides a way to get the data from your database into an XML document and to read an XML document into your database.

In this chapter, I describe the XML implementation in SQL Server 2000. This chapter won't cover the basics of XML other than the theory; so if XML and SQL Server 2000 are new to you, I highly encourage you to research the Resources section because I only discuss SQL Server, not the intricacies of XML.

The interesting thing about XML isn't just the technology; it's what you can do with it. You can present data you send to the XML document in an HTML browser or use that data with another program. You can read the data from another XML-producing program like Oracle. The beauty of XML is having a single point of entry for all your company's data.

SQL Server 2000's implementation of XML works using Microsoft Internet Information Server. You can run that software on the SQL Server 2000 machine or somewhere else, but either way you need to configure the feature to create the XML/SQL Web site. I do that later in the Graphical section.

Once you have configured the feature, you push data out to these XML documents with a series of commands. Your users can create a query from the URL address bar, or you can create another XML document that already has the query in it. Another extension to this process is to add a style sheet to the XML output and format the data for display in a Web browser.

You can also read XML data into your database. It's a bit limited and not very easy, but the basic premise is that you read the document into memory with a stored procedure and then select data out of a recordset like a table. When you're done, you release the document from memory.

Although I've not seen many people do so, you can also store XML data directly in the database, using the dt:type attribute.

Detail

There's a lot of buzz about XML, and I think it's justified. In concept, it's quite simple, and in practice, it's not hard to produce XML data from SQL Server 2000. The more difficult task lies in *using* that data effectively, so I've included a lot of references at the end of this chapter to help guide you.

I don't spend a great deal of time in this chapter on the query structures or the consuming of the data. Although your situation will dictate the method you should use to both produce and consume the XML documents, I cover the more widely used methods here.

XML is a very new and emerging field, and there are a lot of decisions you'll need to make about when and how to use this technology. I highly advise that you look through each of the references I've provided, especially if you're a developer and plan to use XML. Even as I write this chapter, Microsoft is releasing improvements to the XML implementation in SQL Server 2000.

Structured Documents

The idea behind XML is that of structured documents. It may surprise you to know that this idea isn't new at all. Structured documents were driven by government needs, as many things often are. Documents created by one program should be accessible to other government organizations using different programs. To do this, a document would be stored as plain ASCII text and formatted using a set of agreed-on *tags*, which explained to the reading program (sometimes called a consumer) how to display the document. Because most computers read ASCII, this worked pretty well.

A formatted sentence with a bold font using a program like Microsoft Word looks like this:

This is **bold**.

In a markup language, it looks like this:

```
This is <B>bold</B>.
```

As you probably already know, the tag <B> starts the bolding action, and the slash in front of that B tag ends it. The software you read the document with understands your computer's operating system, video card, fonts, and so forth. It reads the tags and applies the formatting. This is just the sort of thing you're used to working with in an HTML browser.

Tags

XML goes these formatting tags one better. Instead of having agreed-on tags for presentation of text, the tags are used for data. You might precede the words Buck Woody with <name> and end with </name>.

The two types of tags are well-formed and free-form. Well-formed tags are either agreed on by the XML standards body, with titles like XPointer and XLink, or defined in yet another document, called an Extensible Stylesheet Language (XSL) document. I stick with free-form tags in this document, using standards only in the headers of the documents I show. The Resources section has an excellent resource for the well-formed tags.

Table 13.1 Database Record

Authors	
au_id:	172-32-1176
au_lname:	Dull
au_fname:	Ann

The trick is to provide a consumer that knows how to deal with your tags. Microsoft SQL Server 2000 has this tag awareness built into a Dynamic Link Library (DLL) installed on the server. This DLL interprets the tags in predefined ways that SQL Server 2000 understands. It then applies or reads these tags as required.

To become more familiar with this approach, take a glance at the single database record shown in Table 13.1.

The first column shows the columns in a record, and each item can be easily identified by its column name.

XML Documents

Now let's take an example of a simple XML document that contains the same database record. Look at Listing 13.1.

Listing 13.1 Simple XML document

```
<?xml version ='1.0' encoding = 'UTF-8'?>
<authors>
        <author>
        <au_id = '172-32-1176'>
                <au_lname>Dull</au_lname>
                <au_fname>Ann</au_fname>
        </author>
</authors>
```

The first line encodes the document, and the rest are the tags that define data in a hierarchical fashion. That means that until a tag is closed (with the /) the items that follow are part of it. These items are called elements, and the records are referred to as data.

Although you can make up your own tags, there is a defined model for creating an accurate XML document, called a *well-formed* XML document. For a full breakdown of this document model, see the reference in the Resources section for an active map. You should keep this map handy for future reference as you go through this chapter.

Now that you have the concept of what XML output from a SQL database looks like, let's talk a bit more about how you produce it.

Creating XML

The first method involves accessing a configured Web site using a browser or some other program, which then makes requests to the SQL Server 2000 engine. The engine outputs the information as a well-formed XML document. These documents can be parsed by a style sheet if desired and presented to an HTML browser, or they can be accessed directly by another XML consumer program.

To begin the process, you need to configure the SQL Server 2000 XML product extensions for IIS. As I mentioned before, IIS can be installed on the same computer that SQL Server 2000 lives on, but if you're concerned about performance or security, it can be installed on another machine.

Once that's done, you create three directories. The first acts as the *root* or main Web site for the database. Underneath that is a directory for the *templates* that SQL Server 2000 uses in IIS for XML. Templates are the XML documents I mentioned in the Overview section that store queries. Finally, you create a directory that houses the *schema*. Schemas are references for data that XML documents need.

After you create those directories, you create *virtual* directories inside IIS, which are names that point to the physical locations on the hard drive. Along the way, you set the types and locations for these virtual directories so that SQL Server 2000 can use them. Once these extensions are configured, your users can enter queries in the address bar of their Web browser and retrieve XML documents for display. Rather than force your users to enter queries in the URL address bar, you can also produce an XML document that already contains the query. Microsoft calls this a *template* file.

There is a bit of a learning curve for designing good XML queries, which I'll leave to other references. As always, Books Online is the best source of this information, and I've also found the Microsoft SQL Server 2000 Reference Library to be very helpful with this topic.

The queries that I have been discussing so far involve standard Transact SQL (T-SQL) statements, which look like the SELECT * FROM authors variety

Table 13.2   FOR XML Modes

Mode	Description
RAW	Presents each row in the query as an XML element with a generic identifier row.
AUTO	Returns results in a nested XML tree. AUTO sets the tables in the FROM clause as an XML element.
EXPLICIT	Allows you to specify the shape of the XML tree.

that I've used throughout this book. XML queries are a bit different, and you can see this query format in Listing 13.2.

Listing 13.2   FOR XML query layout

```
SELECT somecolumn
FROM sometable
WHERE somecolumn = 'somevalue'
FOR XML AUTO
```

As you can see, the key feature I've added to the standard T-SQL command format is the FOR XML qualifier. This tells SQL Server 2000 that I want the data formatted as XML. I've also added to that qualifier the *mode* of XML command to set the format of the XML data that SQL Server 2000 returns. In this chapter, I use the AUTO mode most of the time, but there are others. Table 13.2 shows a quick rundown of how these modes affect the query.

What I've just described isn't the only way to get XML data from SQL Server 2000, however. A syntax called XPath is another standard way of accessing XML data.

The limitations placed by Microsoft on these types of queries are quite strict, so I'll leave the discussion of XPath to *Books Online* and the Web sites I've referenced at the end of this chapter.

Graphical

You don't need to install anything for XML support in SQL Server 2000, but you do have to run a wizard to configure the Web sites that present and access the XML.

Setting Up for XML

You need to create the three directories I discussed earlier in the Detail section, so let's do that first. After that, you'll set up the IIS extensions, configure the Web site, and type a simple query at the browser. Finally, you'll set up that same query in a template file and examine the results.

Configuring Internet Information Server

Let's begin by creating the directories you need for XML processing. Since you probably installed IIS with the defaults when you installed Windows 2000, the root directory for IIS lives at C:\InetPub\wwwroot, so you'll create the directories you need under that. They could be anywhere, but this location ensures that you keep your Web sites consistent for backup and so forth.

Creating the Directories   You need three directories: one for the root level, another for the schema, and another for templates. You create them by typing the three commands shown in Listing 13.3 at an NT/2000 command prompt.

Listing 13.2   Creating the directories

```
MD C:\InetPub\WWWRoot\pubs
MD C:\InetPub\WWWRoot\pubs\schema
MD C:\InetPub\WWWRoot\pubs\template
```

Configuring IIS   Next you continue the process by selecting Start, Programs, Microsoft SQL Server, Configure SQL XML Support in IIS from the main screen of Windows 2000, as shown in Figure 13.1. Once that utility starts, you'll see the display shown in Figure 13.2.

As shown here, you should drill down to the name of your computer and select the Default Web Site object. Right-click that, and select New and then Virtual Directory from the menu that appears. This brings up the screen shown in Figure 13.3.

A virtual directory is a pointer to the physical path on the hard drive that IIS "adopts" into its logical structure, treating it as a Web site. On this panel you set the name that IIS will use and the physical location on the drive where the root of our database access will begin. This then becomes the name the users enter into their URL address bar in their browsers. If you're familiar with IIS, you've done this before.

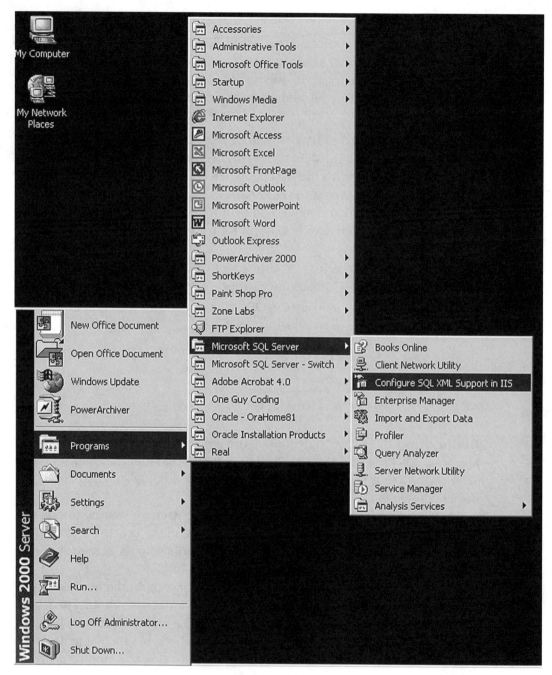

Figure 13.1 Starting the XML configuration

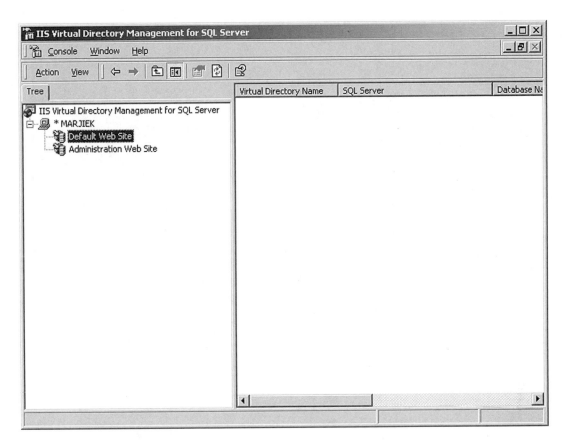

Figure 13.2 The IIS XML manager

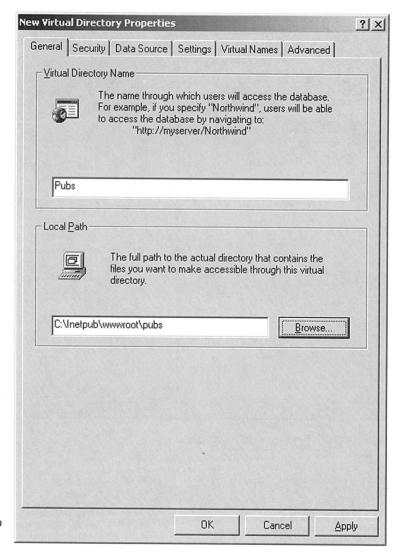

Figure 13.3
Configuring the root Web site

Set your Web site name to Pubs, and set the location to the directory you created earlier. Next, select the Security tab, as shown in Figure 13.4.

This is an important decision point for the Web site. This panel, which isn't normally seen in IIS management, sets the SQL Server 2000 logon for the queries that the users will access. The choices are to always log on as a certain account, use Windows authentication, or set a clear-text logon.

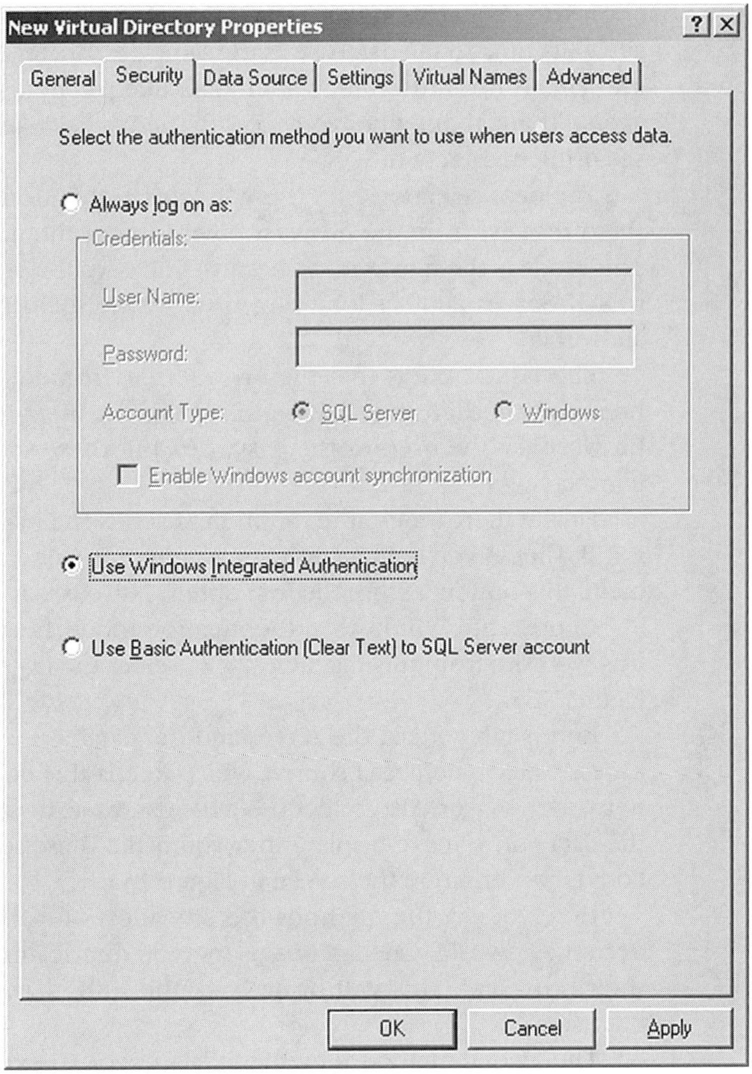

Figure 13.4 The Security tab

If you choose to log on as a certain account, all users who access the Web site will come to the database as the same person, regardless of who they really are. This is often useful for open data like phone lists and so forth, but you should think about who has access to the Web site and what they'll be able to see using this account.

The next selection is to use Windows authentication. This mode prompts IIS to request from the browser environment the name of the current user. This mode is the most secure, because it passes the Windows security through to SQL Server 2000 as long as you've set the security in SQL Server 2000 to allow that.

The issue here is that the browser environment might be at the user's home or another site. There are settings in Internet Explorer to have the browser ask the user for the password, but these settings are best suited for intranets.

Finally, there's a clear-text option; it sends the password along in plain old ASCII. Unless you're in a UNIX environment behind a firewall, I don't recommend this option; I'd use the first option I discussed.

Choose the Windows authentication mode, because you'll be accessing this Web site from this machine. Next, select the *Data Source* tab, as shown in Figure 13.5.

In this tab you set the server and the database you want this Web site to access. Select the *(local)* source, which keeps this connection away from the networking layer. Also select the *pubs* database, because that's the source of the data you want to display. After you make these selections, choose the *Settings* tab to bring up the screen in Figure 13.6.

Here you set the methods this site allows for database access. The first option, *Allow URL Queries*, lets users type queries in the URL address bar of their browsers. This will bring back the XML data directly into the users' browsers.

The second method allows template queries. I explained templates earlier; they are XML documents that contain queries. You normally want to allow that, so select this box as well.

The third option enables XPath queries. As I mentioned earlier, XPath in SQL Server 2000 isn't as easy to use as Transact SQL, but it's useful to have available.

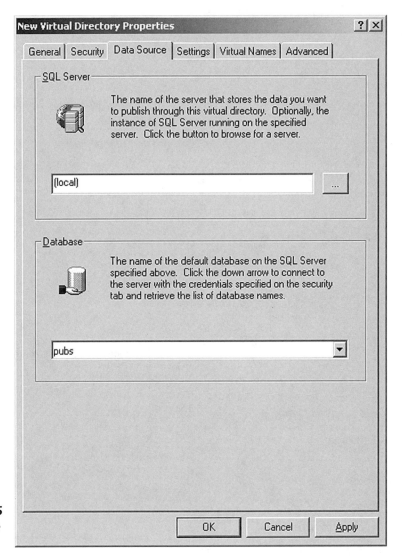

Figure 13.5
Data Source
tab

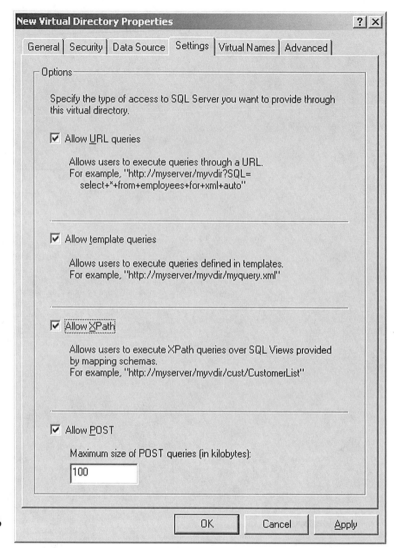

Figure 13.6
Settings tab

The final option, Allow POST, lets the browser communicate back to the Web site. This allows users to pass variables back to the query template file, making templates very extensible. After you've enabled everything, select the Virtual Names tab, as shown in Figure 13.7.

Next you need to define the two directories that house the schema and templates. Select the New button, and the panel that is shown in Figure 13.8 on page 484 appears.

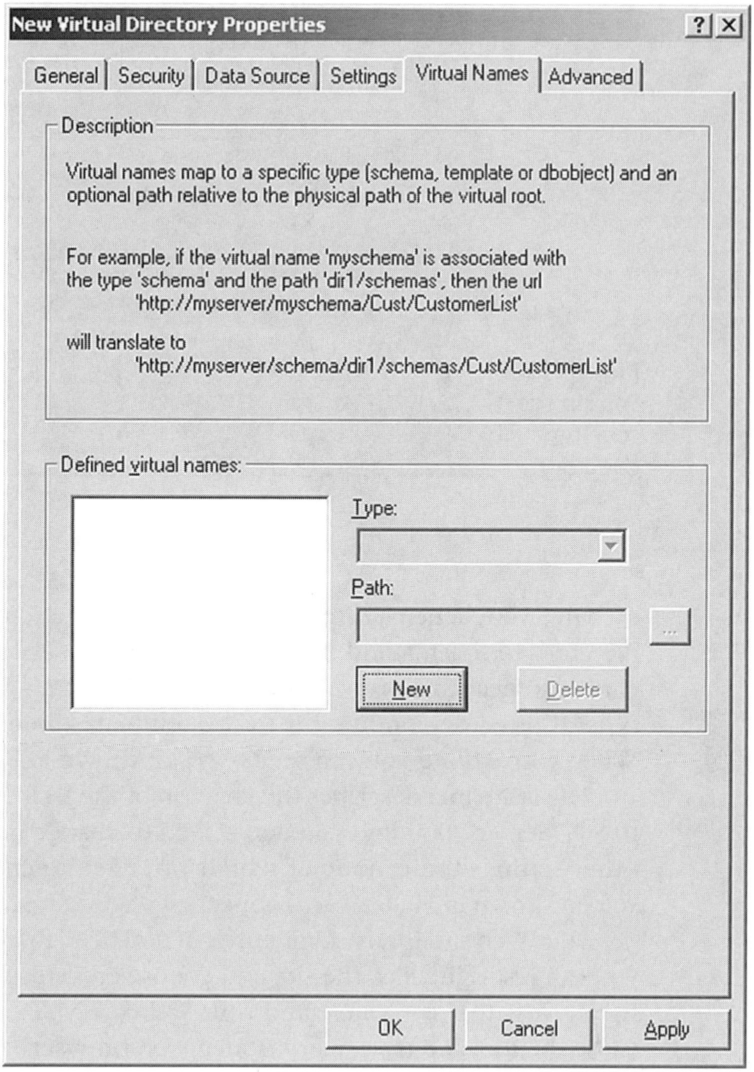

Figure 13.7 Virtual Names tab

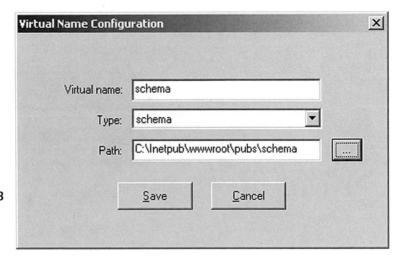

Figure 13.8
Setting the
schema
directory

Give your schema directory the virtual name *schema*. Also set the type of directory to *schema*, and then point that to the schema directory you created earlier. Repeat this process, substituting *template* for both the name and the type of directory, pointing it to the template directory you created earlier. When you're done, you can see the result shown in Figure 13.9.

The last panel describes the location of the DLL that controls how IIS talks to SQL Server 2000, and you don't need to change that. There are a couple of other settings there, none of which you need to change. Select OK, and the screen shown in Figure 13.10 appears.

Your Web site is now configured. If you need to change any of the settings, you can just right-click the site and choose Properties. All the tabs are available there. Now that you've created your Web site, you can begin to work with it. Close the tool and try a query from a Web browser.

Accessing SQL Server 2000 from a Browser URL

The query that you type into a browser URL address bar is similar to those you might type in any command-line tool. The difference is that browsers don't normally tolerate spaces and other "special" characters. For that reason, you place plus signs where spaces would normally be and use other prefacing

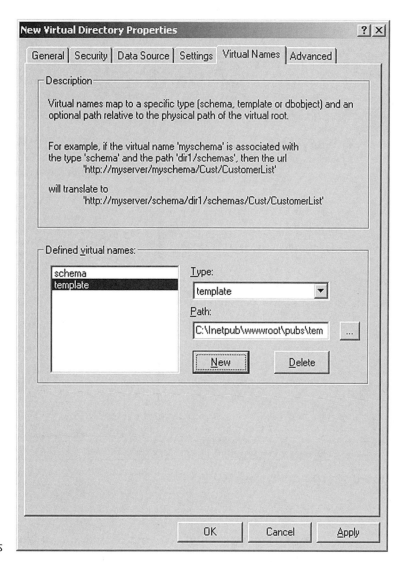

Figure 13.9
Completed
virtual names

characters for percent signs and so forth. These constraints can be found in *Books Online* in the XML section.

For all but the simplest queries, directly typing the query in the URL line isn't always the best choice. There are issues of length and security, but for simple, quick queries, this method can be useful.

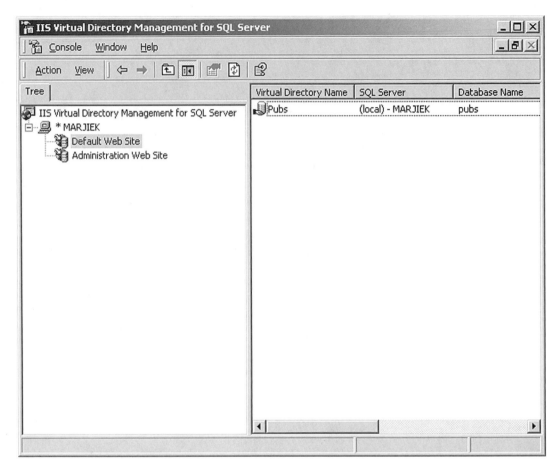

Figure 13.10 Configured Web site

After you've configured your Web site, you can enter the query in your browser as I have in mine. The query is shown in Listing 13.3.

Listing 13.3 URL query

```
http://marjiek/Pubs?sql=SELECT+*+FROM+authors+FOR+XML+AUTO&root=ROOT
```

To break this down a bit, `http://marjiek` sets the server name, `/Pubs` sets the name of the virtual Web you configured earlier, and `?sql=` tells IIS that a SQL query follows. After that is a standard T-SQL query, with those plus signs I mentioned. Finally, at the end, are the words `&root=ROOT`.

I haven't discussed the document model for XML in this chapter, because that goes a little beyond the scope of this book, but it's integral to what is returned to the XML consumer and how it behaves. If you're going much further with XML, you definitely should review the XML document model Web site listed in the Resources section. One of the behaviors the document model requires is a starting point, known as a *Root*. You need to tell SQL Server where to "mount" the data, and you use the words &root=ROOT to do that.

In Figure 13.11 you can see the result returned to the browser. No, it isn't pretty, but it isn't supposed to be. XML marks up *data*, not pages. Keep in mind that this method is often used for retrieving data, not changing or adding it. The process for editing data is a bit more involved and isn't well suited to the URL method. To give your users access to more complex queries, you should use a template.

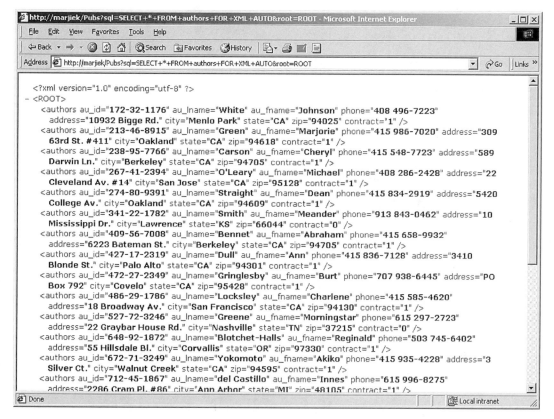

Figure 13.11 Completed Web query

Accessing SQL Server 2000 from a Template Document

You might think that a template is a style mechanism to present data, but that isn't the case. A template is just a specially formatted XML document that stores a query. XML templates are documents that contain a T-SQL query.

To create an XML template document, simply create a text document in the templates virtual directory you define. Reference that XML document in the browser, and the data will be returned to the browser that called it.

A simple XML template is shown in Listing 13.4. I've added numbers to each of the lines for reference, but you need to remove these numbers if you're typing this information yourself.

Listing 13.4 Simple XML template

```
1. <ROOT xmlns:sql="urn:schemas-microsoft-com:xml-sql">
2. <sql:query>
3. SELECT *
4. FROM authors
5. WHERE au_lname LIKE 'B%'
6. FOR XML AUTO
7. </sql:query>
8. </ROOT>
```

The first line in this template tells SQL Server 2000 how to handle the root of the query. Line 2 tells SQL Server that you're beginning a query, which is terminated in line 7. After those tags go the query and the XML mode, and finally in line 8 you terminate the ROOT tag.

You access the output of this template by typing the reference of the XML template file, as shown in Listing 13.5. You can see that you must include the full path of the XML file in the URL.

Listing 13.5 Referencing the XML template

```
http://marjiek/Pubs/template/auquery.xml
```

Using templates can be much more useful than a URL query because your users don't have to know any SQL or the structure of your database. As a matter of fact, much like an ASP page or CGI script, the users can't see the source code. This makes the access much more secure and has the side benefit of fixing the length problem.

You can do a lot more with templates, but for now it's enough to know that this is a great way to access data, and if you need to use this technology, you should pore further into *Books Online*. Let's move on to a discussion of getting that data into more presentable forms.

Formatting XML Data with a Style Sheet

There are a couple of ways to format SQL Server 2000 XML data for use with a browser. The most common way is to use an XML style sheet or XSLT. There's a great tutorial referenced at the end of the chapter for the amazing things you can do with XSLT.

Consider the XML document in Listing 13.6.

Listing 13.6   XML sample document

```
<?xml version="1.0" ?>
<?xml-stylesheet type="text/xsl" href="stores.xsl"?>
  <shoes>
  <sales>
<heading>Amazing Shoes</heading>
</sales>
<data>
<store>
<name>Tampa</name>
<quarter number="1" shoes_sold="100" />
<quarter number="2" shoes_sold="125" />
<quarter number="3" shoes_sold="110" />
</store>
<store>
<name>Melbourne</name>
<quarter number="1" shoes_sold="110" />
<quarter number="2" shoes_sold="115" />
<quarter number="3" shoes_sold="200" />
</store>
</data>
</shoes>
```

Notice the second line in the document. This tells XML to apply a style sheet that we'll make in a moment. This document shows three elements: shoes, sales, and stores. Within these are the data elements quarters and shoes sold. We've only got two stores, but that's enough for this demo.

To transform this data into usable HTML, create an XSL style sheet as shown in Listing 13.7. I've prefaced each line with a number, but you won't do that in a real XSL document.

Listing 13.7   XSL transform

```
1. <?xml version="1.0"?>
2. <xsl:stylesheet xmlns:xsl="http://www.w3.org/1999/XSL/Transform"
3. version="1.0">
4. <xsl:output method="html"/>
5. <xsl:template match="/">
6. <HTML>
7. <HEAD>
```

```
8.  <TITLE><xsl:value-of select="//sales/heading"/></TITLE>
9.  </HEAD>
10. <BODY>
11. <h1><xsl:value-of select="//sales/heading"/></h1>
12. <table>
13. <tr>
14. <th>Store\Quarter</th>
15. <xsl:for-each select="//data/store[1]/quarter">
16. <th>Qtr<xsl:value-of select="@number"/></th>
17. </xsl:for-each>
18. <th>Total</th>
19. </tr>
20. <xsl:for-each select="//data/store">
21. <tr>
22. <th style="text-align:left"><xsl:value-of select="name"/></th>
23. <xsl:for-each select="quarter">
24. <td style="text-align:right">
25. <xsl:value-of select="@shoes_sold"/>
26. </td>
27. </xsl:for-each>
28. <td style="text-align:right;font-weight:bold;">
29. </td>
30. </tr>
31. </xsl:for-each>
32. </table>
33. </BODY>
34. </HTML>
35. </xsl:template>
36. </xsl:stylesheet>
```

This gets a bit more intense, but it isn't as bad as it might seem at first. To move further, I need to assume that you have two pieces of knowledge: the understanding of basic HTML (including tables) and the idea that each beginning tag must have a terminating tag. I won't mention those two ideas again; I'll just explain some of the more interesting XSL bits that go further than that. For a much deeper understanding, see the tutorial I reference at the end of the chapter.

Referring to the line numbers, I'll break down a couple of important parts. In lines 8 and 11, I set the title and heading 1 (H1) to the value inside the heading tag from the XML document. I do this by traversing the XML document's hierarchical structure, moving down the line to the sales element and then on to the heading element.

That's the key to all of this—traversing a hierarchical document. As DBAs, we're used to working with a relational structure, and XML isn't that. It's based on this treelike layout of data.

In line 15 I begin a loop. This sets the beginning for the style sheet to start repeating data. Next, in line 16, I plug in the data. This process continues throughout the document, with the name of the store and the values of the quarters and sales figures.

To reference this style sheet, assuming the XML document is called `stores.xml` and the style sheet is called `stores.xsl`, you type `http://servername/dirname.stores.xml` in your browser. The document displays with the formatted data. I've presented only a simple conceptual model here; a real-world example would be a lot more involved.

You can extend XSL by using Microsoft's version (XSLT) to sort data, do conditional reporting, turn negative values a certain color, and so forth. I've also seen Java graphs, bar charts, and so forth using XML. The only limits on the ways to present XML data are the amount of time you're willing to spend to create them and your design skills.

As I mentioned earlier, XML is a huge technology—and one that's still developing. As you've seen by now, the real beauty of XML doesn't really live in its presentation; it's more a data thing, so keep that in mind as you plan uses for XML in your environment.

Command Line

For the command-line tools, we'll examine the process for creating an XML document within *Query Analyzer*. We'll use this tool to produce an XML document and then examine the process from the other side—accessing XML documents to be used in SQL Server 2000.

Creating an XML Document with Query Analyzer

Open *Query Analyzer* and set the database pull-down list to *pubs*.

If you were to run your XML query right away, you'd have a problem. *Query Analyzer* is set by default to handle the output of a query as wide as 256 characters—more than enough, usually. But because SQL Server 2000 returns the results of your XML query as a single string, the data will exceed the width that the display can handle. You need to set a wider display to receive your data.

From the *menu bar* select *Tools* and then *Options*, and move to the *Results* tab. There you set *Maximum characters per column* to 8096, wide enough for what you need here. You can see the results of that in Figure 13.12. With that setting made, see Listing 13.8 for the command you use to create the XML data.

Listing 13.8   Query Analyzer for XML

```
SELECT * FROM authors FOR XML Auto
```

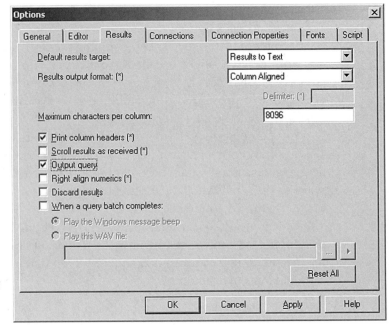

Figure 13.12
Setting the
results length

Now press F5 to see the results. Once you're happy with that, select Query from the menu bar and the Results to File item. This creates the XML base document. Press F5 to run the query again, giving the file the name C:\temp\ test.xml when prompted.

It's easy to create XML data with a simple command, but keep in mind that it's only data, not a full XML document yet. It's missing several elements and has a few extra lines you don't need. We'll clean it up a bit and get it ready for use.

First, remove the header lines at the top and the counts from the bottom of the document. You'll notice several blank lines and dashes at the top of the document—get rid of those. Next include the <ROOT> tag (and a return) at the beginning, and a return and the </ROOT> tag at the end of the document. That gives the document a place to "mount" in the browser's XML interpreter. Finally, make sure each line starts with <authors and that there are no line breaks between those.

After you clean up your document to these specifications and have saved it, double-click the filename to see a simple XML document, ready for use.

You can use just about any query you'd like for producing the XML data. Now that you have the XML document, let's read it back in.

Opening an XML Document as Data

There are a couple of ways to get data into the database from an XML document. Other than direct programming methods, you can use a few basic commands and functions to use XML documents as regular tables, much like a view or temporary table. This is the method we'll use here to read XML documents into SQL Server 2000.

The problem with using XML data in an RDBMS like SQL Server 2000 is that relational databases are just that—relational. XML is hierarchical.

SQL Server 2000 has included two stored procedures to convert that hierarchical XML document into something relational that SQL Server understands. The first stored procedure (sp_xml_preparedocument) loads the XML data into memory, and the second (sp_xml_removedocument) releases that memory area once the operation is complete. In between those stored procedures, you use a function called OPENXML on the FROM predicate to complete the process.

To make this process clear, I'll demonstrate with a bit of T-SQL code in Query Analyzer and then break it down. I've prefaced each line in this example with a number, which you need to remove if you try this yourself. You can see the complete code in Listing 13.9. Note that you've set the database that you're running this command from to pubs. If you don't do that, this won't work.

Listing 13.9   Using an XML document as data

```
1. DECLARE @hdoc int
2. DECLARE @xmldoc varchar(2000)
3. set @xmldoc =
4. '<root>
5. <authors
6. au_id="172-32-1176"
7. au_lname="White"
8. au_fname="Johnson"
9. phone="408 496-7223"
10. address="10932 Bigge Rd."
11. city="Menlo Park"
12. state="CA"
13. zip="94025"
14. contract="1" />
15. </root>'
16. EXEC sp_xml_preparedocument @hdoc OUTPUT, @xmldoc
17. SELECT *
18. FROM OPENXML(@hdoc,'/root/authors')
19. WITH authors
20. EXEC sp_xml_removedocument @hdoc
```

In line 1 you declare a variable to hold something called a *handle*—which is just a pointer in memory where SQL Server 2000 stores the document, and it's required. In line 2 you declare a variable to hold the textual contents of the XML document. In lines 3 through 15, you include the XML document you created earlier.

You only want to include some of it, because you don't want to read through the entire document. Remember to close the document with the </root> tag, because you cut a certain amount of data from the document.

In line 16 you put all these variables to work. The command requires the handle of the document as an input as well as the variable that holds the text. The OUTPUT qualifier is required.

Now that the document has been opened and formatted in memory, you can access the data. In line 18 you use the OPENXML function I mentioned earlier. Shown here, it is simple, but the command structure for this function can become *quite* extensive. The basic format shown requires at least the handle of the document in memory and the row path indicator. You can think of this conceptually as the "mount point" for the document you wish to traverse, but the more technical explanation involves those XPath queries mentioned at the beginning of the chapter. The XPath specification is far too complex to go into here, but the resources available to explore that topic are included at the end of this chapter and in Books Online.

In line 19 you're required to explain to the function how to format the document. You can specify a custom schema or simply use an existing database table to display the column names and so forth. Since you have an authors table in the pubs database with the same schema as this XML document, point to that. If that's not the case with your document, map the columns to the tags as described in Books Online for the OPENXML function.

We've done a simple SELECT here, but you could have just as easily updated data in the pubs database based on the XML document with an UPDATE command, or inserted data with the INSERT command. This is the best way I've seen so far to update XML data into a SQL Server database, but that can also be accomplished programmatically.

Finally, in line 20 you release the memory that you allocated, and the only parameter this stored procedure needs is the handle of the document. This is an important step. I've included the entire XML document in this example, but this isn't how you would normally work with XML. What you can do is to create a stored procedure that accepts the document as a parameter. You might then pass the document as a variable to that stored procedure, which would in turn use the XML document.

A great example of this type of thing can be seen in *Books Online*. Search for *Sample HTML Form to Update Records Using OPENXML*, and read the document for a complete explanation.

Because this is a very advanced topic, I've only scratched the surface of this emerging technology. There are many more ways than I've demonstrated to get data to and from SQL Server 2000 using XML, but these are the quickest methods I've found to put some practical use to this new feature. One of the late-breaking tools I've used recently is the XML Bulk Import feature, available with the second XML patch to SQL Server 2000 on Microsoft's Web site.

In the next section, I demonstrate another simple method to create XML documents from SQL Server 2000.

Examples

One of the best uses I've seen so far for SQL Server 2000's XML features is to create XML documents quickly and easily. Many people have access to Visual Basic, and if you do, you can type in the code in the following listing to create XML documents quickly and easily. If you don't use Visual Basic, C++ and other languages can also produce the documents.

A Simple Visual Basic Program to Create XML Documents from SQL Server 2000

You should not construe the following example as anything other than a learning exercise. I've tried to comment the code as much as possible, but if you're not a developer, you need to take some of the commands on faith. Better still, look them up in MSDN by accessing *msdn.microsoft.com* on the Web and typing the command you're interested in in the "Find" box you see there.

This project demonstrates a simple VB program to create an XML page on your system from a properly configured SQL Server. You can then double-click the filename of the XML document, and if you're using an XML-aware browser, you'll see the output. Read through the exercise to understand one way to do this.

Create a new project, and make sure you move to the Project menu item and select the *References* object. Next locate the *Microsoft ActiveX ADO 2.6* item and select it. Now add a command button called *Command1*, and type the code shown in Listing 13.10.

Listing 13.10 Creating XML from Visual Basic using SQL Server 2000

```
Option Explicit
Private Sub Command1_Click()
  ' This section creates all the connection objects. You'll need to
  ' select Project and then select References. Select the
  ' Microsoft ActiveX ADO Objects 2.6 once you're there.
  Dim dbConn As New ADODB.Connection 'Set up ac onnection to the server
  Dim dbCmd As New ADODB.Command 'Set up a command to the database
  Dim streamIn As New ADODB.Stream 'For reading the data.
  Dim streamOut As New ADODB.Stream 'For writing the data.
  ' Next you set the connection string for your server and database
  ' replace marjiek with your server name.
  Const strConn = "Provider=SQLOLEDB;Data Source=marjiek; _
Initial Catalog=pubs;User ID=sa;Password=letmein"

  ' And open that connection
  dbConn.Open strConn
    ' This sets the active connection to the one we just made
  Set dbCmd.ActiveConnection = dbConn
    ' You'll need to set the XML Dialect - this is a standard for MS
  dbCmd.Dialect = "{5d531cb2-e6ed-11d2-b252-00c04f681b71}"
    ' Create input stream. You'll need to prepend some
  ' data to set the proper XML format.
  streamIn.Open
  streamIn.WriteText "<root xmlns:sql='urn:schemas-microsoft-com:xml-sql'>"
  streamIn.WriteText " <sql:query>select * from authors for xml _ auto</sql:query>"
  streamIn.WriteText "</root>"
  streamIn.Position = 0
  Set dbCmd.CommandStream = streamIn
    ' Create the output stream
  streamOut.Open
  dbCmd.Properties("Output Stream").Value = streamOut
  dbCmd.Properties("Output Encoding") = "UTF-8"
  dbCmd.Execute , , adExecuteStream 'Does the work.
    ' Write the stream to a file.
  Open App.Path + "\authors.xml" For Binary As #1
  streamOut.Position = 0
  Do While Not streamOut.EOS
    Put #1, , streamOut.ReadText(1024) 'writes the file.
  Loop
    ' Close the files and drop all the objects.
  Close #1
  streamOut.Close
  Set streamOut = Nothing
  streamIn.Close
  Set streamIn = Nothing
  dbConn.Close
  Set dbConn = Nothing
End Sub
```

Although this program functions well enough, I've violated more than a few standard programming constructs for the sake of simplicity. For one thing, this program is *closed*, meaning that once the program is compiled into a standalone .exe, you can't change the query, server, user, or password information and the like. For the program to be a bit more extensible, you should add a text box for each of these areas so that you could hit any SQL Server 2000 server and run any query.

There are also better ways to access the server and more efficient ways to write this code, but, again, this is a useful exercise for creating an XML document. I'll leave it to your creative skills to take this example a bit further.

Because this subject is developing (pardon the pun) so rapidly, make sure you visit the references I've included in the Resources section to find the latest service packs, updates, and technology descriptions for XML.

Resources

XML resources:
http://www.xml.com/
An XML explanation:
http://www.15seconds.com/Issue/001102.htm
XML described:
http://www.xml.com/pub/a/98/10/guide0.html
XML tutorial:
http://msdn.microsoft.com/library/psdk/xmlsdk/xmlt5apf.htm
XML document map:
http://msdn.microsoft.com/library/psdk/xmlsdk/xmlp4awg.htm
Another way to access XML data using Visual Basic:
http://msdn.microsoft.com/xml/articles/VBsax2jumpstart.asp
XSLT tutorial:
http://msdn.microsoft.com/library/psdk/xmlsdk/xslp0hpo.htm

Chapter 14

English Query

Chapter at a Glance

Read this chapter to learn about asking plain-English questions from SQL Server 2000 databases.

The Resources section contains references for:

- An English Query overview
- A sample Visual Basic application for English Query
- The interaction between OLAP and English Query
- A discourse on database normalization

Read Chapter 12 before you read this one.

Overview

English Query brings the dream of intelligent user interfaces a lot closer to reality. I'm sure you're familiar with the idea of English communication with a computer ("Open the pod bay doors, Hal") but you may not be aware that this sort of thing already exists. You can try a sample of this technology by going to *www.ask.com* and typing a question. You can also create this technology for yourself by using your own databases, with SQL Server 2000's English Query.

In this chapter, I explain how you can set up your database to answer English questions. The process for the users is simple—they type English sentences, and the server interprets them as SQL commands and returns the data to the users from tables or cubes. The work you have to do to make all this happen isn't difficult, but your application will require a good bit of preplanning.

Up to now I've shied away from asking you to be a data DBA. I've maintained that you can keep a system running without mastering Transact SQL (T-SQL) statements or being able to develop multiuser applications against your database. With English Query, this simply isn't the case. You, or someone who works with you, must understand the structure, layout, and content of your database for an English Query project to be successful. You must also understand the way the intended audience wants to access the data.

In most development efforts, the developers code the application based on restrictions of business rules. With an English Query application, your users have a lot more leeway in the way they access data, so the onus is on you to anticipate the users' decisions and provide the data in that way.

That being said, let's look at the main concepts you should keep in mind when embarking on this development effort. I cover these concepts at a high level in this section, and I develop them more fully in the Detail section that follows.

The first concept you need to keep in mind is that you need to understand your data, and it should be in a highly normalized form. If you're unsure what I mean by normalized, you might want to invest in a good SQL theory book or cover the concept in *Books Online* before you play with this tool. This is known as the *logical* model in English Query, which is unlike the logical model that a design DBA would understand. You should understand the content of the data as well as its physical layout in tables and columns before you continue.

The next important concept is that you need to resist the urge to begin developing with the tools provided before you completely understand that data.

Remember, you'll be working with plain English, which is less than exact for a lot of situations. For instance, consider the word "ship." You understand that word based on the context, such as "ship the order" as opposed to "it came by ship." You will need to understand which way that word is used in your application, because the computer is ignorant of these dual meanings. To do this properly, we come to what I consider the most important concept when designing an English Query application: You should start the entire process by formatting the questions first.

Ask the questions the users might ask, and then ask the users the type of questions they might ask. There's an art to including users as part of the development effort, and in many applications, it's ignored completely or done in name only. If you ignore them here, you're wasting your valuable time. After you understand the data and have formatted the questions your users will ask, you can begin the development cycle.

SQL Server 2000 uses Visual Studio to create English Query projects. A *project* is the precompiled application environment for your English Query application. Within this project are objects that you use to create your application.

Next you define your physical database, and tie out the tables and columns that you'll use. Then, you begin the process of defining your *semantic* model. In this section, you set up the objects in your application and how they work together. This is the English part of English Query.

The first of these objects are *entities*. Think of entities as nouns, such as a person, place, or thing. These entities map to tables and columns in your database.

Sometimes the users call the nouns you have in your database something else. You might store the customer's name in your database in a column called "customers," but your users might call them "buyers" or "clients." You can extend the usefulness of your model by creating a synonym. Be liberal with synonyms; they will help your users get at the data they are looking for.

The next part of the semantic model identifies the relationships between your data's entities (nouns). In this phase, you define what entities have to do with each other. Microsoft calls these relationships *phrasings*, and there are several types. I'll be honest with you—when I first dealt with this topic at work, I dug out my college English textbooks to fully understand these terms, so don't feel bad if you need to do the same.

The first phrasing type is the *name* or *ID*, which defines the column containing the name of the noun. For instance, in the pubs database, au_fnames and au_lnames are the names of authors.

The next phrasing type is the *trait*, which is the attribute the noun has. An example of this in the pubs database is that *authors have addresses*.

The most flexible type of phrasing is the *preposition*. My college textbook tells me "a preposition links a noun with another part of the sentence and shows relationships." Examples of propositions are *under, on, with, in,* and *like*. A question using a preposition might be "Which state does author X live in?"

Another phrasing type is the *subset*, which limits a set of entities, such as "*Some* authors are male." Running a close second for most flexible phrasing type is the *adjective*, as any author will tell you. An adjective describes a noun, such as "a *female* author" or "an *expensive* book." You might have these adjectives in your data (a column for *M* or *F*), but you can also specify SQL conditions for things like "expensive," such as "where cost > 100.00."

Another type of adjective is *measurement*. "How *many* things" or date ranges are measurements that are commonly called for in questions from users, so you should define those as well.

Switching gears a bit, we come to *verb* phrasings. A verb signifies action, so "An author *writes* books" or "Publishers *sell* books." Something to keep in mind here is that you should always use active voice when developing your project. Verbs to avoid are listed in *Books Online*. Verbs are like the key words in an application language.

A final type of phrasing, called the *command*, is quite powerful. Commands can be active in your application and allow users to cause things to happen in the database. You might create a command that allows users to buy a book, such as "I'd like to purchase that book" which would update a table with a sell order.

The concepts I've just described are a great deal like chess, in that they are quite simple to understand but exceedingly complex to master. To see what I mean, combine a few prepositions and diagram the phrase on paper, such as "Which authors have sold the most books to the most publishers?" and you'll see what I mean.

After you've done your planning and drawn everything on paper, you can build your project. If you've never done so, you need to install the English Query engine; then start Visual Studio.

Happily, Microsoft has included wizards that do much of the work for you. If your database is highly normalized and contains the proper key relationships, SQL Server 2000 will derive many entities and relationships for you. If not, you'll end up with a bit more work. As you move through the project, you can make liberal use of a suggestion wizard that watches the questions you ask and suggests entity and relationship definitions.

When you're through with your project, you compile that and it becomes a model that the English Query engine understands. You test the model and then develop the client in Visual Basic, Visual C++, or .NET, or even use another wizard to deploy a set of ASP pages to Internet Information Server (IIS) with just one click.

You're not finished, however. You should save a regression file, which is a list of the current environment, so that, when you make changes, you can make sure you don't break something that did work. And you should plan to make those changes, because your model will need to adapt to be truly effective for your users.

In the next section, we take a closer look at the concepts I've introduced.

Detail

English Query is not part of the initial installation of SQL Server 2000. You need to install that separately, a process I describe in the Graphical section later. You can use English Query against other database sources, such as Oracle.

English Query Uses

After you install the English Query engine, it interprets English questions submitted from your users and creates SQL commands from your data source. This data source is normally a database, but wizards also allow you to access information stored in cubes. This can be a powerful combination for your users.

Not only can they access data in your database, but users can also modify that information or run other commands. If you combine all these features with voice processing software and voice recognition technology, you could phone-enable your entire database!

Understanding the Data Structure

When a painter paints or a chef cooks, an important factor of their success is the variety of palettes that they can choose from. When it comes to English Query, the need to understand your data cannot be overstated. You must know the physical structure of your database. True, you can develop a simple application without an intimate knowledge of your data, but it won't be a very useful one. You should follow a few basic rules to ensure a successful project using English Query.

Your database should be in a normalized form. Normalization involves things like making sure that data is not repeated in a table and that the table contains information for only one item. For instance, if a table contains the title of a book and its type, each book should belong to only one type, or the name will appear twice in the table. There are several formal levels of normalization, and a good explanation is in *Books Online* under the topic Normalization.

Your tables should be related to each other properly. This involves the use of foreign keys, which are fields in one table designed to point to other fields in another table. For instance, the titles table might have a title_id field, which is a value unique to each book. Another table can include a field called title_id as well and point this to the titles table.

Physically defining these relationships allows the wizards in English Query to automatically derive relationships between these tables and do a great deal of the work for you.

Design DBAs are very familiar with these concepts; it's their stock and trade. If you're uncomfortable in this area, you should consult the *Creating and Maintaining Databases* topic in *Books Online*.

Understanding the Data Content

Once you have this physical layout of your database in your pocket, you'll also need to understand the content of the data.

To adequately develop an English Query application, you need to know what answers to expect as you test your questions. This is a simple enough task when the database is something like the *pubs* database I've been demonstrating, but it can become quite daunting when the data involves a multiuser transaction processing database.

Don't let that complexity stop you, and don't try to work the whole project alone. Get help from the developers around you, and involve the whole DBA team.

Developing the Questions

Now that you have the physical layout and content of your database in hand, you can begin the next phase of the design, the questions. I've found that the most successful method is to start formatting the questions your application will answer. Although you can begin by performing the installation, opening the tool, and defining objects and relationships, this approach is doomed from the start. If you don't know where you're going or how to drive, the trip will be long and treacherous.

Start formatting the questions by categorizing them. For instance, you might take a sheet of paper and write as the title "Questions of Measure." On this sheet you might write, "How many books were sold last year?" and "How often does author X write a new book?"

Another sheet might be titled "Questions of Ownership," and the questions on this sheet might be "Who wrote book X?" or "Who publishes book X?" Don't skimp here; the more questions you leave out, the less useful your application will be. True, you can add things to your model later, but this might incur changes that would break other parts of your model.

Remember to include your users in this process. If your users are on the Internet, do a survey to solicit questions. Do not skip this step. If you feel that you can skip it, ask a professional developer how important user input is to application acceptance.

The Semantic Model

You've written all your questions, you have the physical and logical structure, and you're ready to dive into the tools. Even before you open the first tool, you should understand how these physical objects in the database map to those semantic objects I mentioned earlier.

Let's look at the terms you'll use in an English Query project.

Entities

We begin by examining entities, which are the English equivalent of nouns. Nouns are people, places, or things, and you define each one in your project to an entity. These entities should be as fleshed out as possible, and they tie back to tables and columns in your database. In the pubs database, the entities include authors, titles, publishers, and stores.

You don't have to define them all, but the more entities you define, the more things can be questioned in the application.

Synonyms

Sometimes the words you've used in your database (like the au_fname and au_lname columns I mentioned earlier) don't lend themselves to easy understanding by the users. You solve this by relating the entity name to a "friendly" name (more about this process in a moment), and then you apply synonyms, which are words that mean the same thing as other words. I'll create our first entity later in the Graphical section by giving "authors" a synonym of "writers."

You'll appreciate the questions your potential users submitted, because they will help you define what they call a thing. Be as liberal as you can, because your users will quickly become frustrated if they can't figure out what you've called something.

Repeat the definition of your entities until you feel that you've covered all nouns in your database. Submit this to the users to see if you've missed anything, and then move on to the next step.

Relationships

After you have defined your entities, you set up relationships between them. This is where the real work starts.

Your relationships are defined using what Microsoft calls *phrasings*. These phrasings relate the objects in certain ways and use certain types to imply the relationships in English. Let's describe those phrasing types.

Name/ID　The primary phrasing type is the name/ID. This relationship declares which column contains the name of the entity—for instance, "Author names are the names of Authors." This is also the section where you can define the friendly names I spoke about earlier.

Later you'll test your application before deploying it, and you might get the response "I don't understand the word 'author' in the phrase 'author names.'" If this happens, you've left out a name/ID phrasing type. You then need to go back into your project and define the names. You perform this back-and-forth dance quite a bit before you deploy your application.

Trait   Next, there's the trait phrasing type. This is a useful phrasing that sets the attributes the entity has, and this type is one of the easiest to think of.

Here you define things like "Authors have addresses" or "Stores have titles." Ownership is the main part of a trait, and you can put entities together by working from your planning documents and placing the word "have" or "has" after each entity.

Prepositions   Next in line are the prepositions, which link nouns with other parts of a sentence. Prepositions also show relationships. Some common propositions (according to my college textbooks) are shown in Table 14.1.

This can be a difficult type of phrasing to conceptualize, so it's often helpful to write a few questions that contain prepositions. Here's one: "Which books were written *after* book X?" Properly combining entities and prepositions allows you to ask questions like "Who are the authors from Florida?"

Subset   The subset type of phrasing is useful for limiting the results of a question. We do this all the time in spoken English: "Some authors are male." For this to work, you must define this type of relationship by using an existing column in your database, such as an "M" or "F" field in the table that relates to authors.

As I stated earlier, it pays to know the content of your data as well as its physical structure for this very reason. Don't underestimate the usefulness of this type of phrasing, because it mimics the way your users normally ask questions.

Adjectives   One of the most important types of phrasing is the adjective. Just as in English, an English Query adjective describes or modifies a noun. An

Table 14.1 *Common Prepositions*

about	at	down	into	out	toward	within
above	before	during	near	over	under	without
across	behind	except	next	past	until	
after	below	from	of	since	up	
among	beside	in	off	through	upon	
around	by	inside	on	to	with	

"old" dog or a "rich" developer is an example of an adjective in use. English Query breaks adjectives down a little further into three subtypes.

The first is the single adjective phrasing, which allows you to select the conditions that meet the adjective. You might define an "expensive" book as one that costs over $50, and this would answer the question "Can you show me the expensive books?" This adjective type can be also be defined simply by just applying an adjective to the whole entity, by adding the word "good" to books. This would display the entire list of books when asked "Which books are good?" but this is less than useful, unless you're in marketing.

The next subtype of adjective is "entity contains adjectives." This type is used if your database stores adjectives such as an "age" column or the "M" or "F" values for gender. Once again, you need to be very familiar with your database structure to make this choice.

Finally there's the measurement adjective. You'll use this type quite often, because it allows things to be quantified. If you're not storing values that can identify quantities in the database, you can derive certain values by calculating counts or date ranges.

A nifty way to use this subtype is to leave the value blank—this has the effect of prompting the user for the value. For instance, you might define a measurement called "old" but then leave the value blank. When the users ask for the "old" books, they'll be asked what they consider old. Many users have various ideas about a measurement, and using this procedure extends your application.

Now that you've defined your adjectives, you can move on to the verb and command phrasings.

Verbs   Verbs are simple to see—they define action: "Publishers sell books" and so forth. You should define all the verbs you can think of because verbs are used heavily in most spoken English. Remember to use active voice, because English Query can often derive the passive from that but not the other way around.

There are certain verbs that you'll need to avoid defining. English Query in *Books Online* defines these for you; search for *Verbs to Avoid in Command Relationships*.

Commands   Finally, there's the command phrasing type. Until you understand your database thoroughly, you should exercise great caution with this type. Commands allow the users to update, insert, or delete items in the database. They require a strict set of rules so that the command is complete, meaning that it has all the information it needs before execution.

Installing the Product

After you've completed your planning, you can install the engine on the server and begin designing your project. In the Graphical section, I show the first couple of panels for the installation. You have the option of installing just the engine or installing everything. If you pick the "everything" option, you get *Books Online*, samples, Visual Studio, and more.

Visual Studio

Once that's done, you can build a project, putting all your planning to work.

If you've used Visual Studio before, you'll be familiar with this environment. If not, don't worry; it's filled with wizards that can do much of the work for you, such as the *SQL Project Wizard* from the main panel that shows up when you start the program from the *Start* menu.

Using the Project Wizard

Once the wizard starts, follow the prompts to add your database objects, such as tables and columns, and the wizard will derive as much semantic information as it can from your database's physical layout. If your database is normalized, it will do most of the work; if not, you may have to define more of the entities and relationships manually. In either case, you define the database sources and database objects.

Next, you work with the entities and relationships to set the entities and phrasings. Microsoft calls this the semantic model. Then you begin refining the model's semantic model. Using the terms described earlier, review and create any entities and relationships. Constantly refer to your list of questions to put everything into place.

The Model Test Tool

English Query includes a tool to test your questions, called the *Model Test* tool. If you get stuck on a question, you can use the suggestion wizard in the *Model Test* window's toolbar. Type the question you're trying to tie out, and the wizard will respond with "<word> refers to an <entity list>." Use this suggestion to create your entities and semantic relationships.

Building the Project

When you're comfortable that you're getting the answers you want from your project, compile it by selecting the *Build* menu item in the small window in

Visual Studio called the Project Explorer, and your project becomes a model that the English Query engine understands. This model won't work in anything else; it requires the English Query engine to process the English from your application.

Clients

You should test the model before springing it on your users, but you need to decide how you're going to implement it from the client side. You have several options for your client choice. You can always code a Visual Basic application, or you can use Visual C++ or even Active Server Pages (ASP).

If you took the Full option during the English Query installation, you already have sample applications right on your server's hard drive. If you took the defaults, they are located in the `\Program Files\Microsoft English Query\ Samples\Models` directory. Navigate there to see the various subdirectories that have the samples.

Many people decide to use the ASP method because the Visual Studio interface has a Deploy to Web menu item, but you need to have Visual InterDev installed. I deploy our simple model to the Web in the Examples section.

Regression Testing

Another important step that is often left out of many development efforts is regression testing. This involves making sure when you edit a project to include new functionality that it doesn't break the functionality you already have. To be fair, some applications aren't changed to add new functionality that often, or perhaps it may be expected that the things it did before won't work after an upgrade. English Query applications are normally edited as time goes on, because you can give your users so much leeway in the client interface.

Regression testing is a feature built right into the application development environment for English Query. It creates XML documents that can be stored for later use. The XML file stores the questions and answers that you get when you run the tool. Later, after any changes are made, you run the regression test editor again and "play back" the questions. If the answers are the same, the XML file is "promoted" to be the latest successful test. If it fails to get the same answers, a difference file is created for your review.

Now that I've shown you the planning, terms, and process flow for the English Query product, I'll move on to creating one. To do that, I'll show you the first couple of screens for an installation of the product, and then I'll demonstrate a simple model to show some of the tools.

Graphical

In this section, we create a simple English Query application. We'll deploy that application later in the Examples section.

Two tutorials are available from the Start menu item for English Query, one of which is more advanced than what you'll see here and another that is more advanced than the first. You should take time to work through each of the examples after you read this chapter.

Another great source of information is the Books Online additions that are placed in the Start menu. I've always mentioned that Books Online has done a great job with the SQL Server 2000 documentation, and the pages included for English Query are equally good.

We'll begin by displaying the first couple of screens of the product installation. The only real decisions here are the locations and some options, so I'll ask you to take the defaults. I display these screens to alert you to the fact that this is a separate installation.

Installing English Query

After you place the SQL Server 2000 CD in the drive, the display shown in Figure 14.1 appears. Select the SQL Server 2000 Components item, and the panel shown in Figure 14.2 appears.

Just select the item Install English Query and then take the defaults. Selecting the full installation gets all the documentation, the engine, and the samples,

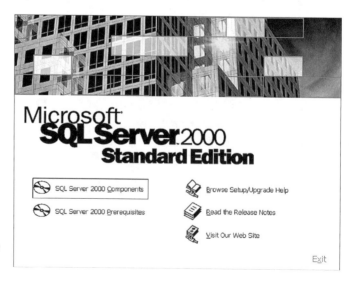

Figure 14.1
Beginning the installation

Figure 14.2
Installing
English
Query

and these are worth the extra drive space they take. Allow the installation to complete. Now you can begin to develop the application.

Creating the Project

The following project isn't intended as a full application, but simply as a guide to help you enter into the development process for an English Query application. I'll show a minimal amount of entities and relationships to be able to concentrate on the process and the tool. Even though it's a limited application, if you're going to do this right, you need to follow the instructions I laid out earlier and plan the application.

Develop the Questions

Each application should start with a need, and your fictional users have come to you with a request: They'd like to be able to ask English questions in a Web browser about the authors in your database. After a bit of questioning, you find they want to know which and how many books each author wrote, and the names and addresses of the authors.

Begin the process by writing the sample questions from the users and having each one review them. You might come up with the following list:

1. Can you show me the names of the authors?
2. What is the phone number of author X?

3. How many authors live in state X?

4. What is author X's address?

5. How many books were written by author X?

6. Does author X have a contract?

7. Which author wrote the most books?

8. Who wrote book X?

These are just a few of the possible questions from the pubs database, but they provide a good starting point. Keep in mind that these questions in their current state provide two benefits: the general areas that the users are interested in and the basis for determining entities and relationships.

You need to do some refining before you use these questions in your project, because a couple of them violate the rules that I defined earlier. For instance, question 5 might be rephrased as "How many books has author X written?" to place it in active voice. Refine your questions as much as you can—this step can't be overemphasized.

Next, you categorize those questions to see which objects you need.

Categorize the Questions

Group the questions from the previous list into general types such as the following:

- Questions of measurement: 3, 5, 7
- Questions of general information: 1, 2, 6
- Questions of verbs: 4, 8

This list will help you in the semantic model later.

Define the Physical Model

Now that you have a few representative questions, you need to define whether your database has the necessary information to answer these questions. If it doesn't, you have a couple of choices to make. You can modify your database to store the information that's missing, or you can strike the questions from the project.

I mentioned earlier that it's important to be familiar with the database structure. To help you display some of that structure, use the sp_help authors

Table 14.2 authors Table Schema

Column	Type	Content
au_id	id	Unique identifier for each author
au_lname	varchar	Author's last name
au_fname	varchar	Author's first name
phone	char	Author's phone number
address	varchar	Author's street address
city	varchar	Author's city
state	char	Author's state
zip	char	Author's ZIP
contract	bit	Contract yes-or-no indicator

command in Query Analyzer against the pubs database. This command was used to produce the chart shown in Table 14.2. Such a chart can help define the data you're working with.

If you look a bit further, you'll find that the other parts of the information you need are stored in the titles table. Using the same sp_help command you used earlier but substituting the name titles for the table name, you can produce the chart shown in Table 14.3.

Table 14.3 titles Table Schema

Column	Type	Content
title_id	tid	Unique indicator for a book
title	varchar	Name of book
type	char	Type of book
pub_id	char	Identifier of the publisher
price	money	Sales price of the book
advance	money	Advance paid to author
royalty	int	Royalty percentage
ytd_sales	int	Cumulative sales of book
notes	varchar	Text notes about the book
pubdate	datetime	Date published

The `sp_help` command doesn't create the last column in the chart; you have to understand the original purpose of the table to do that.

If you examine the tables, you'll notice that there's no way to tie the title of the book to the author who wrote it. That type of relationship brings out yet another understanding you need to properly create an English Query application. You need to understand the relationships your tables have with each other. Microsoft includes the Database Diagram tool in SQL Server 2000 (see Chapter 3), which you can use to display the relationships. You can see a diagram created with the tool in Figure 14.3.

Notice from the diagram that the relationship between authors and titles is enforced through the use of a third table, called titleauthor. This is a common practice in database design that handles the fact that an author might write more than one book, and more than one author might write a single book, called a many-to-many relationship.

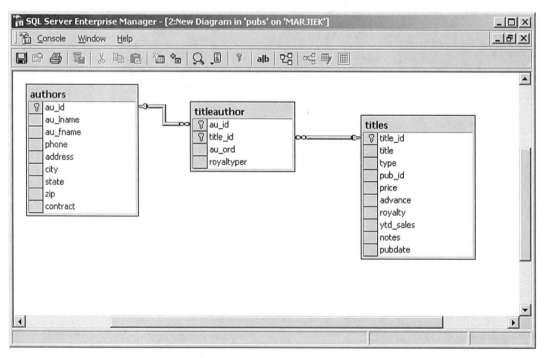

Figure 14.3 Authors and titles relationship

Table 14.4   titleauthor Table Schema

Column	Type	Content
au_id	id	Pointer to author
title_id	tid	Pointer to book
au_ord	tinyint	Order for multiauthor book
royaltyper	int	Royalty breakout for multiauthor book

Now that you're aware of this relationship, use the sp_help command again to define the chart shown in Table 14.4.

Define the physical layout before starting the semantic model because it helps you to know if you have the information to answer the questions. You also need to have the physical model well in hand to define the entities and relationships. You might discover (and probably will) that the database is in less than English Query–friendly format. If so, you may need to edit the structure or add views to get the data into better shape.

The next step is to create the semantic model. Do that on paper before you ever start the software.

Create the Semantic Model

Detail the project on paper by taking all the information in the listings and tables you created earlier and then creating the entities and the relationships.

Mapping Entities to Physical Objects   In the list of questions you developed, you see that you have two main entities: author and title. Obviously, in a real-world example you'd have many more, but this will serve our purposes for the moment.

You'll see in your database that you have objects that will map properly to the entities you've selected, namely the authors and titles tables. Within these tables, you map the entity author to the au_lname and au_fname columns in the authors table, and the entity title to the title column in the titles table.

Most people don't refer to what you're holding in your hand as a title, they call it a book. Many people call authors writers. You need to create *synonyms* for those entities so that the users of the application can get the answers they're looking for. We'll come to that in a moment.

Having documented the first of the entities you need, you next develop the relationships.

Creating Relationships   The relationships are the heart of an English Query application, and it's taken a great deal of time to get to the point where you can properly do that. Working backward, you need entities to create relationships, and you need a physical map to create the entities. You have all that, so it's time to tie out the relationships.

You begin by writing down any trait relationships within the *author* entity, such as the following:

- Authors have names.
- Authors have addresses.
- Authors have phone numbers.

There could be more, but these will do for the questions you've defined. Next, you need to create the *Titles* trait relationships, such as titles have names. In a real-world example, you'd have more trait relationships to define.

Creating Measurements   Earlier you categorized certain questions as measurements. You need to define the counts of the *title* column in your project for these answers.

Creating Verbs   You also categorized certain questions as needing verb relationships. Define those as follows:

- Authors live in states.
- Authors write titles.

As you develop these relationships, keep in mind that entities are related to other entities.

If you look back over your lists, you will be able to see that there are a few relationships that you haven't created entities for. *Address* is one entity, *State* is another. If the tables have been created properly, the wizards will create many of these entities automatically, but remember that it may be necessary to create some entities manually.

Using this example, you've documented enough information to be able to open the tool.

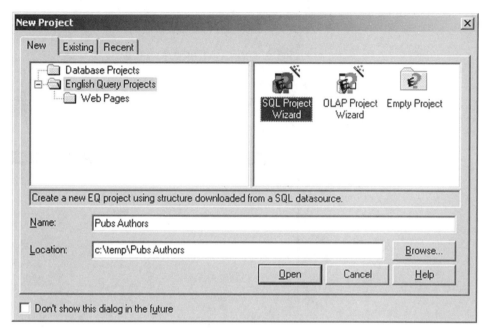

Figure 14.4   *Beginning the English Query design*

Using Visual Studio to Create the Project

Begin by selecting the Start button, then Programs, Microsoft SQL Server, English Query, and Microsoft English Query. The opening screen shown in Figure 14.4 appears.

Set the name of your project and its location. At this point you can choose the SQL Project Wizard, use an OLAP wizard to work with a cube, or just create a blank project. Choose the SQL Project Wizard object and then the Open button. You're shown the screen in Figure 14.5.

This panel sets the source of the tables you'll use in this English Query project. Set the choice to use the Microsoft OLE-DB Provider for SQL Server, and then select the Next button. The screen shown in Figure 14.6 appears.

In this panel type the name of your server, and tell the wizard to use Windows authentication for security. This is an important choice, because this security will be used throughout the application. As I explained in Chapter 12, you should think about what the users are allowed to see and what authentication choices there are. It may be useful to create a user with specific rights and use that authentication for the application.

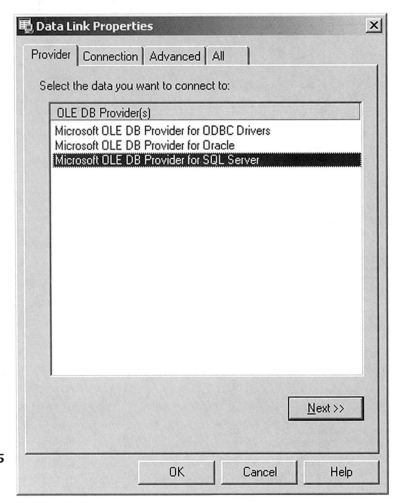

Figure 14.5
Setting the
provider

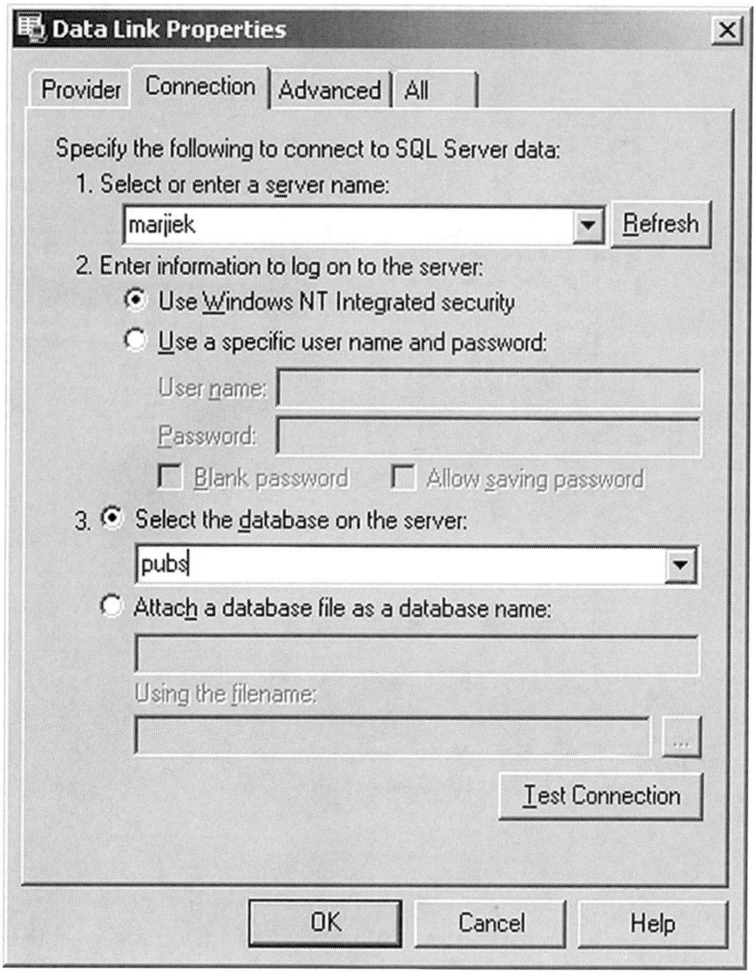

Figure 14.6
Setting the server and database

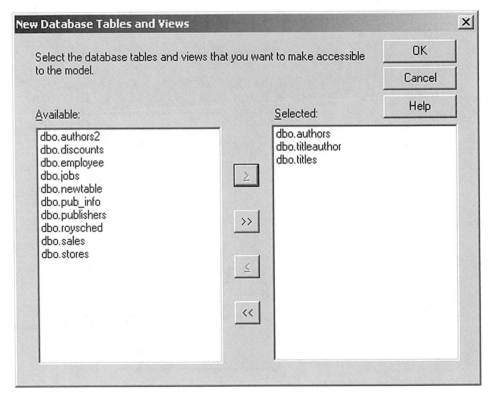

Figure 14.7   *Selecting database objects*

Choose the pubs database and then OK, and the next step of the wizard appears, as shown in Figure 14.7.

At this point in the wizard, select the tables or views you want to work with. These are the physical objects. Based on the documentation you created earlier, you know which tables you need to select. Once you've added the three tables that contain the data, select OK and you're shown the screen in Figure 14.8.

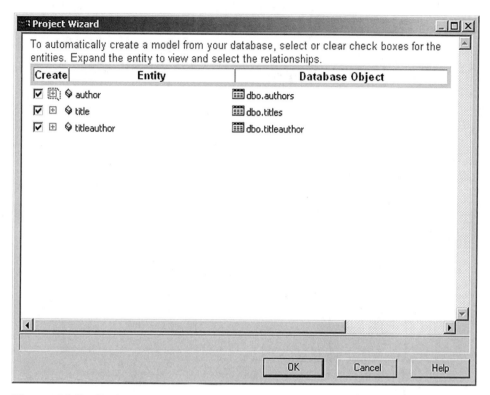

Figure 14.8   Entity creation

The wizard is handling the first part of the semantic model for you. It's made some pretty good guesses for the entities you need, primarily because the design of the table meets the rules of normalization.

In a few places, the wizard made guesses that were inaccurate. I'm not complaining here; I think the wizard is an amazing tool—just don't rely on it blindly. Expand the *author* entity, for instance, as shown in Figure 14.9.

Make a few changes as shown to the trait phrasings that the wizard selected. Not many, mind you, but in Figure 14.9 you can see that you should change relationships such as "Authors *have* author states" to read, "Authors are *in* author states." Continue to review the entities and trait relationships in all the tables. You find that the only changes you need to make are the ones shown in Figure 14.9. After you make your edits, select OK, and you'll see the screen in Figure 14.10.

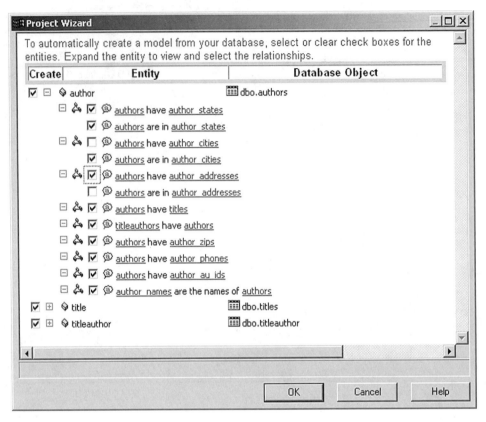

Figure 14.9 Modifying the author entity

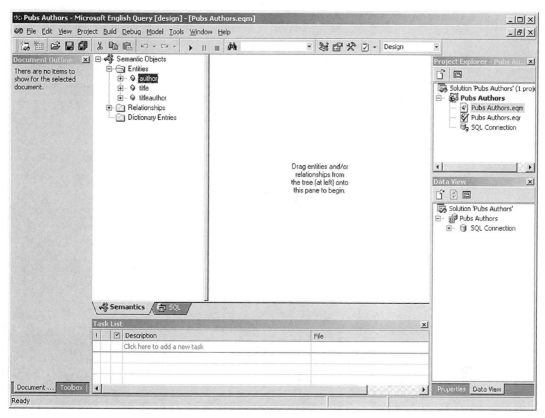

Figure 14.10   The semantic model

If you browse through the objects on the left pane of Visual Studio, you can see that the wizard has already created most of the entities and trait relationships, mostly because of the original good design of the table.

Begin by examining the relationships the wizard created, just in case they need to be modified. You do that by right-clicking the *author* entity and selecting *Show relationships* from the menu that appears. You'll see the panel shown in Figure 14.11.

The panel shows the proper relationships, although the question "What is author X's address?" will only yield the street address, with the entities defined the way they are. That's OK, but you need to consider things like this in your production environment.

After careful examination, you still need to create the verbs and any synonyms for your model, and you'll do that next. Begin with the synonyms for an

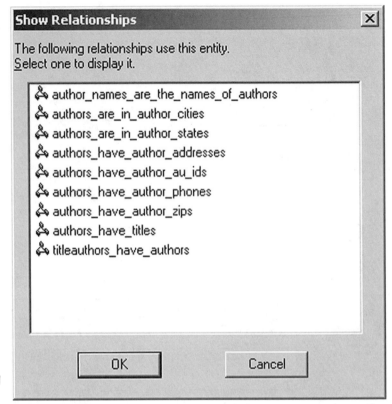

Figure 14.11
Wizard-created
relationships

author. You might recall that I mentioned that sometimes people don't call a writer an author. Try to think of other terms used for this person.

There are a couple of effective methods for defining a synonym. I'll show you the method I use and then explain another way to effectively do the same thing. Right-click the *author* entity in the object browser and then select Edit from the menu that appears. You're shown the screen in Figure 14.12.

On this panel you can see the properties of an entity. Here you might change the columns that tie to an entity and even edit the relationships. For now, you're only interested in the highlighted box at the top left. These are the words that are used to reference this entity.

You'll notice that the dictionary (more on that in a bit) will add many synonyms automatically, and there are two ways to add more. The first is to click the words that are highlighted. That's shown in Figure 14.13.

Here you should add "writer" in the blank box. Notice also that the wizard picked a couple of other words automatically. You probably understand "biog-

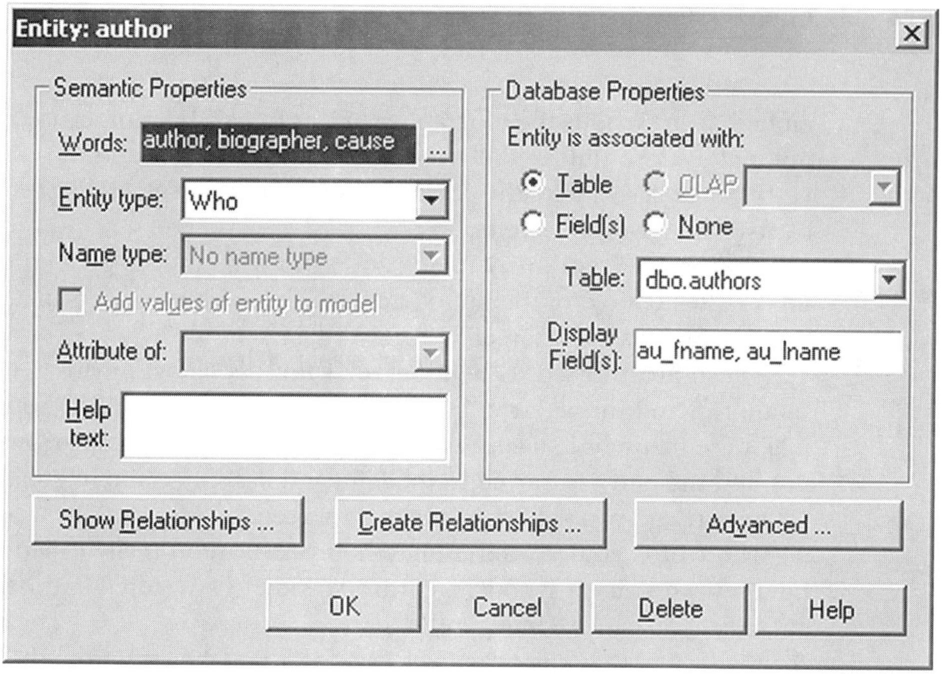

Figure 14.12   author entity edit

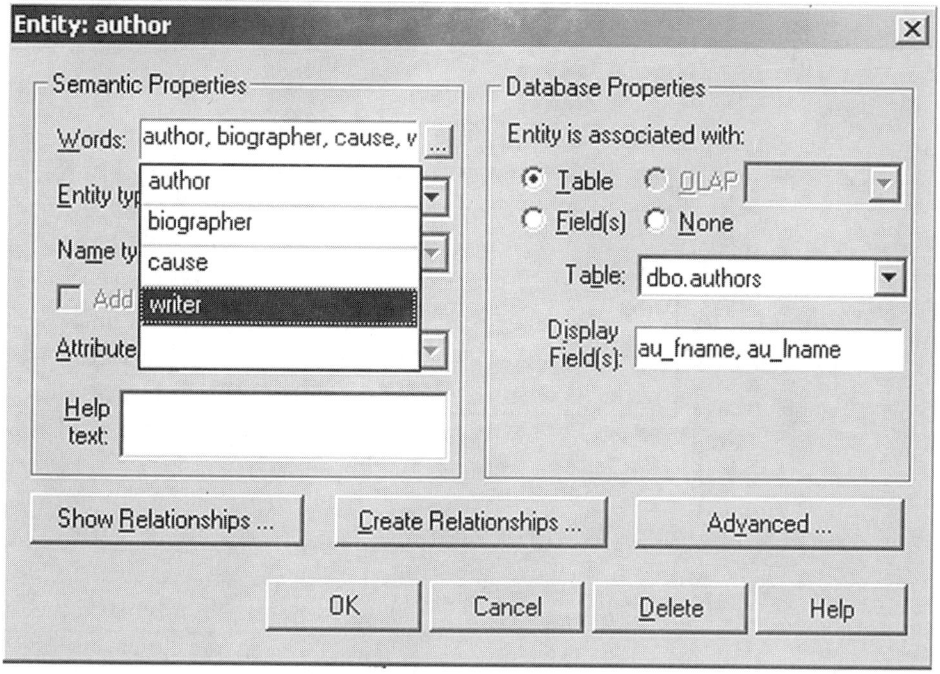

Figure 14.13   Adding a synonym

rapher" as in "Who is the biographer of this book?" but not "cause." This might not make sense unless you remember that the word "author" can also be a verb. Since it isn't in this case, remove that by selecting the entry and backspacing over the letters.

There's one more way to add the synonyms in this panel. Refer to Figure 14.12 and look for the button near the top with three dots in it. Click that, and you're shown the screen in Figure 14.14.

These are the words SQL Server suggests as synonyms for the word "author." Scroll through the list and locate the word "novelist." Your audience might use that word, so click it once (the cursor looks like an arrow when you do), and the entry is moved to the left-hand list. Once you're done, select the OK button, and you're back to the main screen.

The words you created using this process aren't really called synonyms, but they work like a synonym. Formal synonyms are stored in the *dictionary*, an object you can see in Figure 14.10.

Right-click that object and select Add Dictionary Entry from the menu that appears. You're taken to the panel in Figure 14.15. The first type of entry is

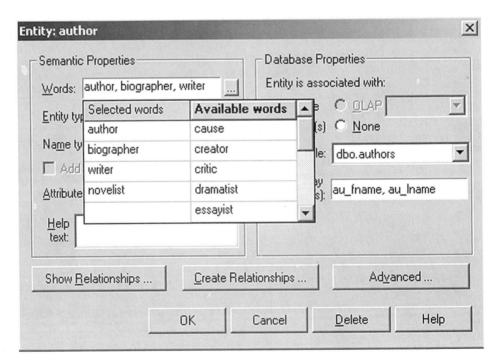

Figure 14.14 Adding predefined synonyms

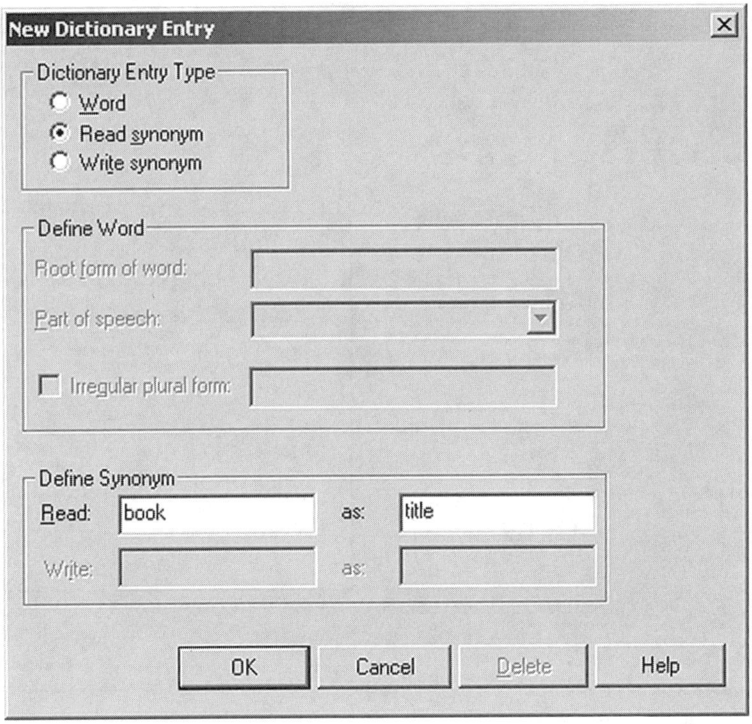

Figure 14.15
Adding a dictionary entry

used to set up words the computer might not understand—irregular words like "you, we, them." These words don't follow the normal way of making a word plural, such as "some, many," or using the past tense, such as "have" and "had." This is pretty deep stuff, and you'll need your college textbook for a few of these.

Select the Read entry type *synonym* and fill in the boxes as shown, which means that when someone types "book," the computer will read "title" as the meaning.

You can also define the words that the computer will read *back* to the user. You could, for instance, tell the computer to say "valued guest" when it would normally write "visitor" as an answer.

When you're done with your changes, select the OK button and you'll see the entry displayed as it is in Figure 14.16. This is a nice view because you can see at a glance the synonyms you've created.

Adding dictionary entries is preferable to entering synonyms at the entity level since the dictionary entries are used for all entities.

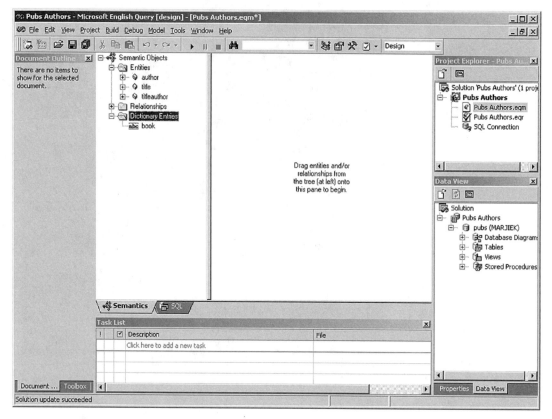

Figure 14.16   The added synonym

You've added two synonyms, one with each method, and reviewed the relationships that the wizard created. Review each of the types that you need, such as traits and adjectives, and you'll find that the wizard has done a great job with most of them. What you're lacking now are the verb relationships.

Begin by reviewing the question categories list, and you'll find that you have two verb relationships to create. Make sure that the statements are made in a *subject–verb–object* mode, such as *authors write books*. If you use that model, the verb relationships are simple to create.

Click on the author entity and drag it to the right-hand panel in Visual Studio; when you let go of the mouse, you'll see the result that is shown in Figure 14.17.

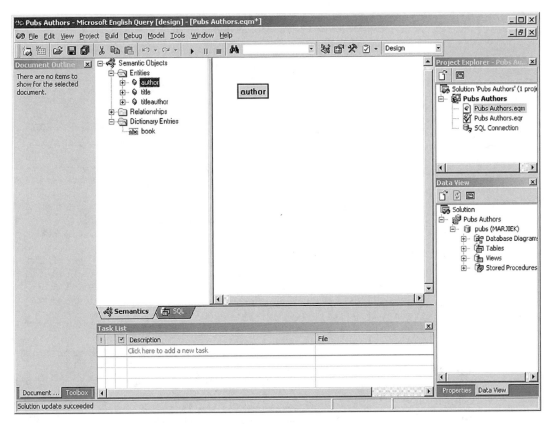

Figure 14.17 The added author entity

Next, right-click the author entity and select Add Relationship from the menu that appears; the result is shown in Figure 14.18. You need to add the other entity that you're trying to relate. To do that, click the top Add button. The results are shown in Figure 14.19.

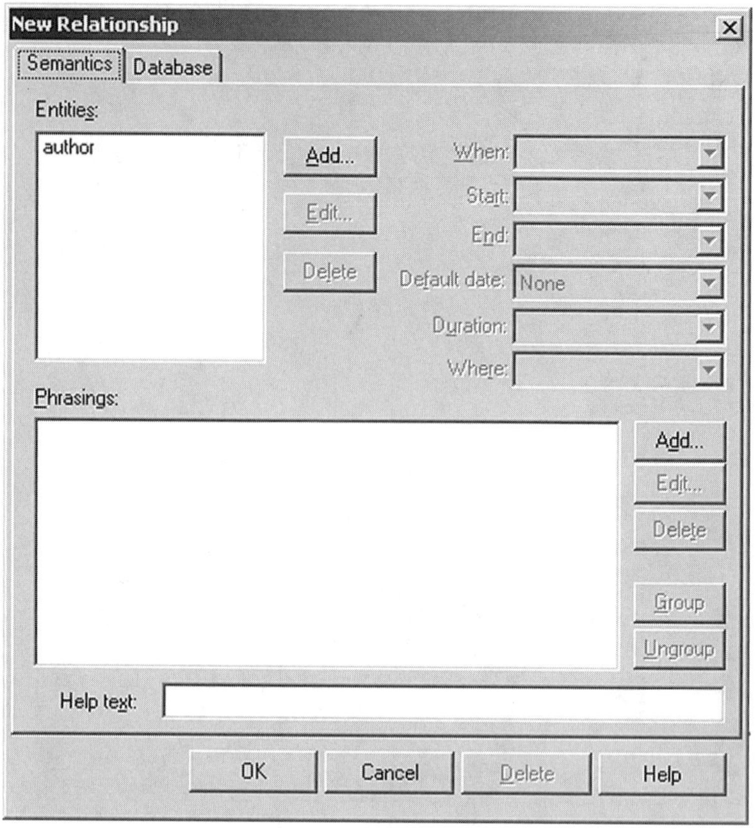

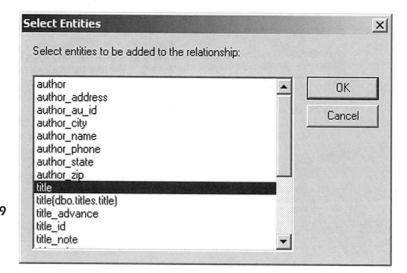

Figure 14.18
Relationship
editor for the
author entity

Figure 14.19
Adding an
entity to the
relationship

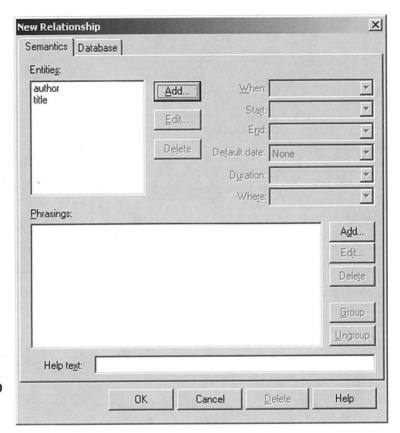

Figure 14.20
Author and
title entities

Notice that I've selected the title entity. If there were other complex re-lationships, such as "authors sell titles to publishers," you'd need to add them here.

Select OK to bring up the screen in Figure 14.20. Next you need to specify how these entities are related. To do that, select the next Add button you see in the Phrasings section, and you're shown the results in Figure 14.21.

This is where all those phrasing types I've mentioned are set. Since you're after a verb, select that, and then select the OK button, which brings up the screen in Figure 14.22.

This is a small panel, but it's the crux of this whole operation. Notice in this panel that you should set the type of the verb phrasing to be subject-verb-object and then select the subject and the object. Next type the verb "write."

You could add a few prepositional phrases here to make the application even more usable. Don't bother with that in this simple example, but you

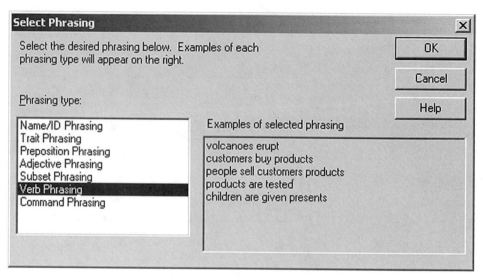

Figure 14.21 Setting the phrasing type

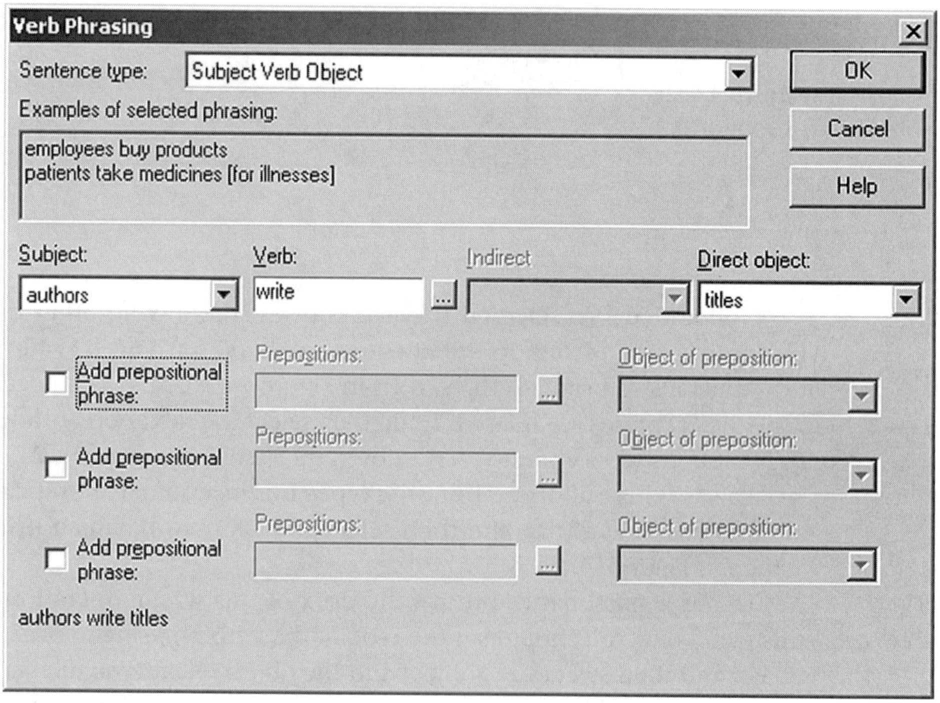

Figure 14.22 Setting the verb phrasing format

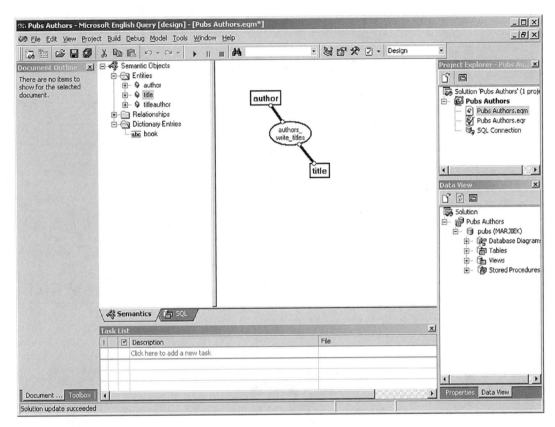

Figure 14.23 The first verb relationship

should take the time to think through all these kinds of decisions. Select OK and then OK again, and the results are shown in Figure 14.23.

At this point you should test the application. Microsoft includes a model-testing tool with the Visual Studio product, so after you save your project, start it by clicking the blue triangle-shaped arrow in the icon bar. You'll see the screen shown in Figure 14.24.

Test what you've done so far by trying out a few questions. To use the most basic question, enter "Can you show me a list of writers?" in the Query box. Press the Enter key, and you see the results in Figure 14.25. Notice that the tool generated two panels. The first shows another way to phrase the question. The next demonstrates the text that would be used in the answer, and the final shows the Transact SQL that the engine generated.

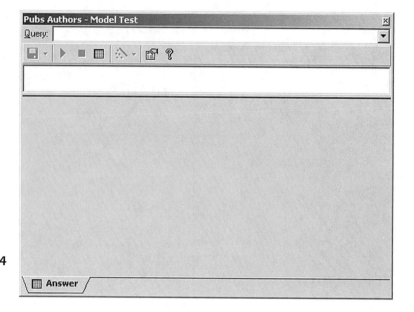

Figure 14.24
The Model
Test tool

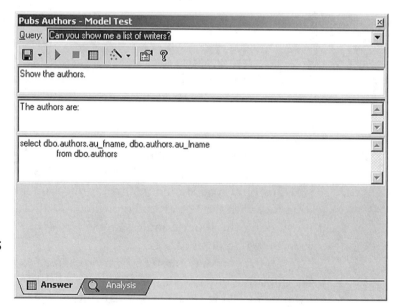

Figure 14.25
An inter-
preted
question

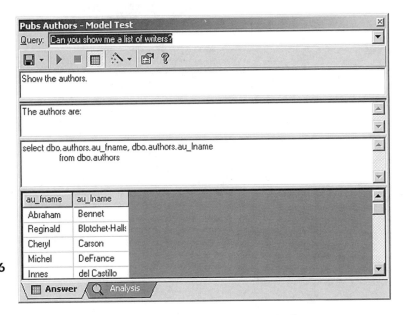

Figure 14.26
Query with
results

You'd normally like to have the question answered, so press the icon that looks like a spreadsheet, and you see the query with the answers that are shown in Figure 14.26.

There are a couple of other interesting bits to this tool. The first is the Analysis tab, shown in Figure 14.27. OK, this pane isn't very interesting *right now*, but as the relationships get more complex, it's quite useful for diagnosing the areas you might need to work on if the question can't be answered.

Another useful tool is the suggestion wizard. Access that by selecting the "magic wand" icon. The panel shown in Figure 14.28 appears. We'll not go through all the panels of the wizard here, but the basic premise is that you enter information about the entities and relationships that are involved with this question, and the wizard assists you with the modifications to your model to get that answer. This part of the tool is useful when you're designing your first application.

Ask the Model Test tool a few more questions, the ones defined in the list you made earlier. For instance, in Figure 14.29 the question is "How many authors are there?" and the computer responds with the correct amount. It does this by counting the number of author entities.

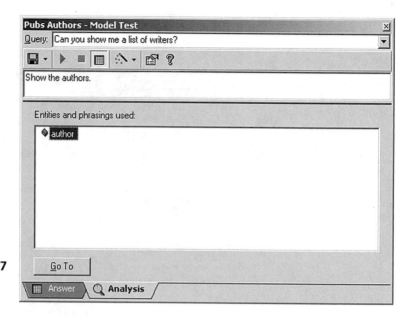

Figure 14.27 The Analysis tab

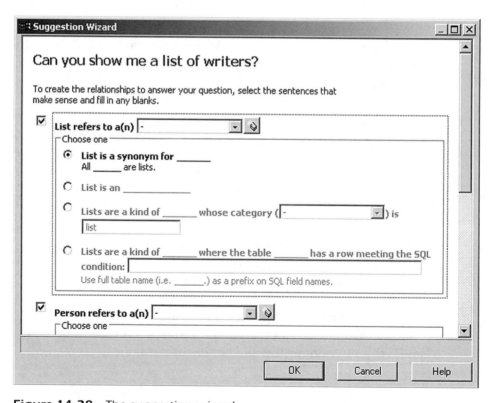

Figure 14.28 The suggestion wizard

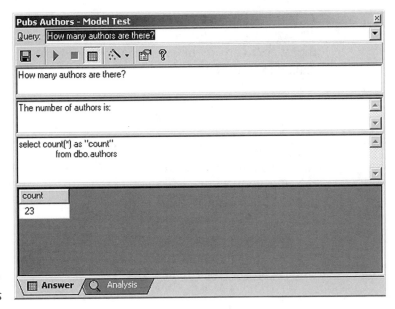

Figure 14.29
Author counts

Work through your entire question list, each time checking to make sure you're receiving the correct answer. If you *don't* get the right answer, you need to edit the entities or relationships until you do. Use the suggestion wizard to assist you with this task.

What happens if a user asks a question the computer can't answer? To find out, ask the tool "Who is Bob?" and press Enter. The system responds by asking for clarification. Your users might be presented with this message as well, and if the clarification they provide helps, the computer will answer the question.

The other response the user might get is the dreaded "I don't understand . . ." type. This means one of two things: Either the user asked a question outside the intended use of the application, or the design needs work. To fix the problem, you can educate your users about phrasing questions properly or start at the beginning of your design process and work through the model again.

That's it! You just have to set up a regression test, as we'll see in the Command Line section.

This has been a simple example of the uses of English Query, and I heartily advise you to work through the other tutorials from Microsoft. They show you other ways to create the same application I have demonstrated as well as more detailed examples.

Command Line

There aren't any command-line tools that access an English Query application. True, all the questions you type are from the command line, but none of the ones that are used within the tools we've defined before, such as Query Analyzer or osql.

I included a regression test in this section because a regression test produces an XML file, and you can edit that with command-line tools or even read it as a recordset (see Chapter 13).

Creating a Regression Test

Regression tests make sure that the questions you typed before will work after you change a model to add functionality. The process is straightforward. You create a regression test file, ask the Model Test tool questions, and save those questions to the regression file. You then run the regression test and it "plays back" the file through the tool, looking for the same answers that it got the first time.

Each project comes with a blank regression test, but I will show you how to create a new one. Stay within the Visual Studio tool and select Project and then select Add Regression Test from the menu, as shown in Figure 14.30.

Once you do that, you see the panel shown in Figure 14.31. Here you set the location of the file that will store the test. Once you select OK, the regression file is added to the Project Explorer pane, which appears in the right-hand side of the Visual Studio environment. Double-click that to bring up the screen shown in Figure 14.32.

Notice that the file is stored as a blank XML file. The next step is to run a few questions and save them to the file. For now run just one, the first one you ran when you started the project.

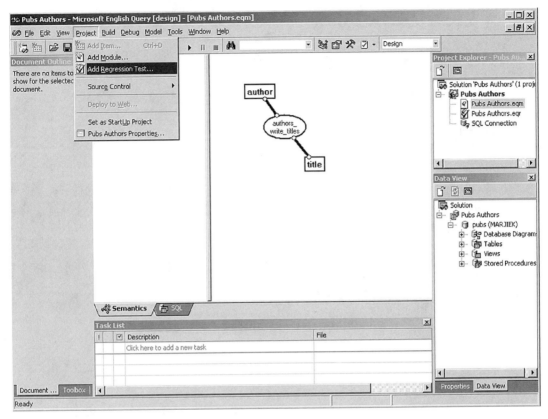

Figure 14.30   Adding a regression test

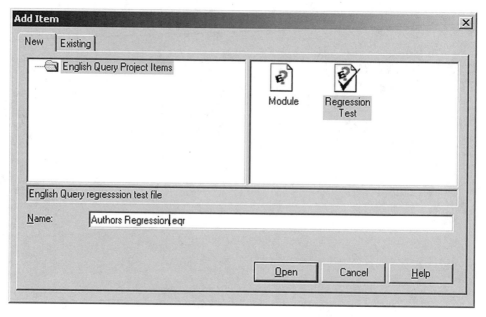

Figure 14.31 Starting the test

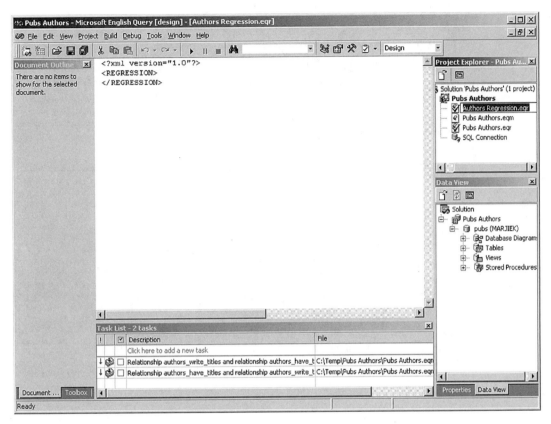

Figure 14.32   The regression test XML panel

Switch to the semantic model by double-clicking the Pubs Authors.eqm object in the Project Explorer in Visual Studio. Press F5 to start the Model Test tool again, and then use the drop-down menu to retrieve your first question. Run that again.

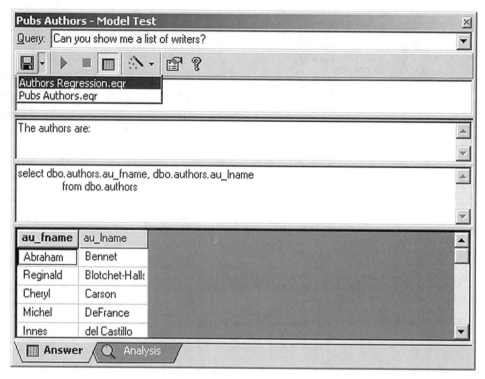

Figure 14.33 Saving the query

Now that you've done all that, select the disk icon, as shown in Figure 14.33. This icon sets where the query is saved. Pick the regression test file you created, and the XML file is automatically created, as shown in Figure 14.34. Let's just save that one query, but normally you should run through as many questions as you can.

Next make any edits to your model that you feel are necessary. At this point, you should run the test to make sure your older questions still work. To run the regression test, right click the regression object and select *Run* from the menu that appears.

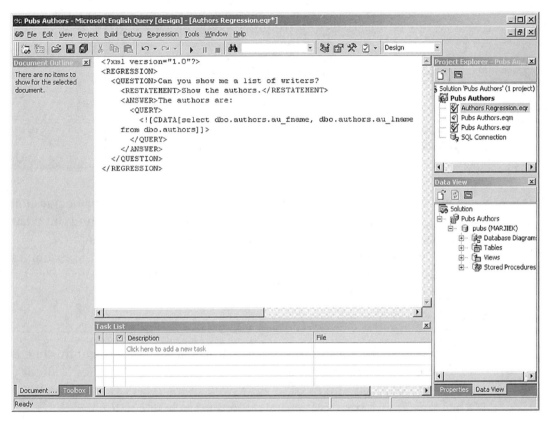

Figure 14.34 The completed XML file

At first, nothing appears to happen. Right-click the object again and select View Output from the menu. This action shows the XML file that was generated using the current (changed) model. Visually, this might not be very helpful. A more helpful command is to right-click the object again and select View Differences. This action displays one of two screens: the one shown in Figure 14.35, indicating success, or a screen that displays a list of the questions that didn't make it.

This panel shows that your model was successful, but you need to take one final step. Because the regression tool creates new XML files each time it's run, you need to make sure that the latest one generated against this model is the one you keep. Do that by right-clicking the object one more time and selecting the Promote item. This sets the latest XML file to be the authority for the test.

Figure 14.35
Regression
differences

What should you do if there are differences? Run the problematic question again in the *Model Test* tool and use the suggestion wizard to find out what broke the model. Then redesign your model to work with the question.

We've gone as far as we need to with this model. Next, in the Examples section, we'll deploy it to the Web so that the users can access it.

Examples

All the previous sections of this chapter flow together as one, and this one is no exception. You may be content to work within the *Model Test* tool for a while, but eventually you need to allow your users to access the application. When you do that, you have several options for a client environment.

The first is a Visual Basic program. I won't spend time in this chapter explaining that, but if you took the *Full* option when you installed English Query, you got several examples, and you can see a Visual Basic application example (if you took the default locations) in C:\Program Files\Microsoft English Query\SAMPLES\Applications\VB.

Your next option is to use Visual C++. The same type of example as for Visual Basic is available (again, if you took the default locations) at C:\Program Files\Microsoft English Query\SAMPLES\Applications\VC.

Finally, you can use ASP technology for Internet Information Server in order to deploy your application. Again, the examples for this type are located at C:\Program Files\Microsoft English Query\SAMPLES\Applications\ASP if you took the default location.

We'll choose the ASP page method for two reasons. The first is that almost everyone has a browser, so there's nothing for the user to install to use your application. Second, the Visual Studio environment provides a wizard right from the menu bar to complete the entire process.

Deploy the Completed Model to the Web

Although there is a wizard that can deploy the model to the Web, there are a couple of restrictions. You need to be an operator on the server that houses Internet Information Server. That's no problem for this example, because you're running all the software on the same box and you're the administrator on that box. You should realize this restriction, however.

The next restriction is that you need to have Visual InterDev installed on the computer where you deploy the application. The wizard is just a hand-off to that environment. It's a good idea to have that installed before you install the English Query software.

Begin back in the Visual Studio project that you created in the beginning of the Graphical section, and open the project, as shown in Figure 14.36. Next, select Project from the main menu and then Deploy To Web, and the screen

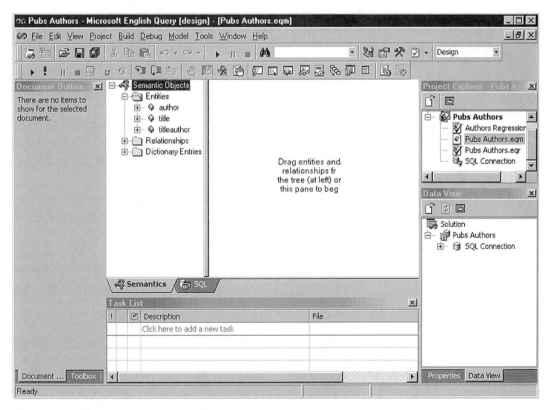

Figure 14.36   *The completed Visual Studio model*

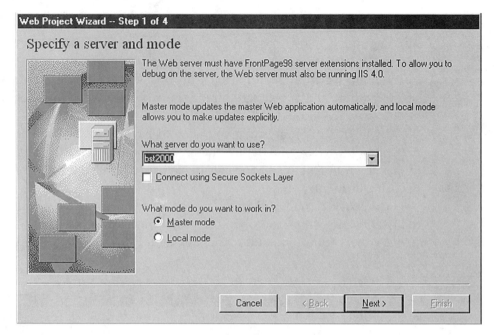

Figure 14.37   Beginning the deployment

shown in Figure 14.37 appears. In this panel you're asked to name the server you're going to use for the Web site. In my case, I select another server in my site, named bst2000. Pick one that works for you, usually the same server you're on.

You're also asked whether you'll be working in *master* or *local* mode. Master mode lets the server do all the work automatically, so that's what you should pick. You also have the choice of using secure sockets, a common practice for many Web sites that allow this type of remote access.

Once you've filled in everything, click the Next button, and your credentials are checked against the requested server. After your credentials are validated, you're shown the screen in Figure 14.38.

Although a treatise on virtual Web sites is a bit beyond the scope of this book, you usually allow the wizard to create the site for you. It's not hard to create a virtual site ahead of time, but unless your Web site has a specific structure, it's not usually necessary either. Leave the selection at the defaults and select Next to bring up the screen in Figure 14.39.

This part of the wizard allows you to choose the layout you want for your new site. This choice sets up the graphical navigation of the application but

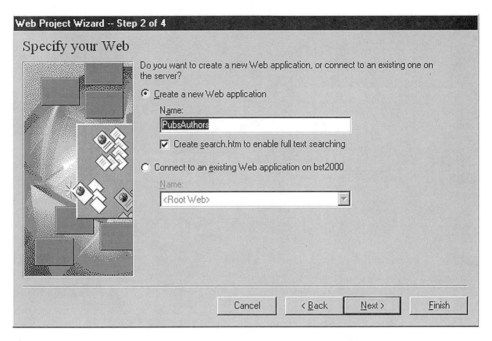

Figure 14.38   Creating the site

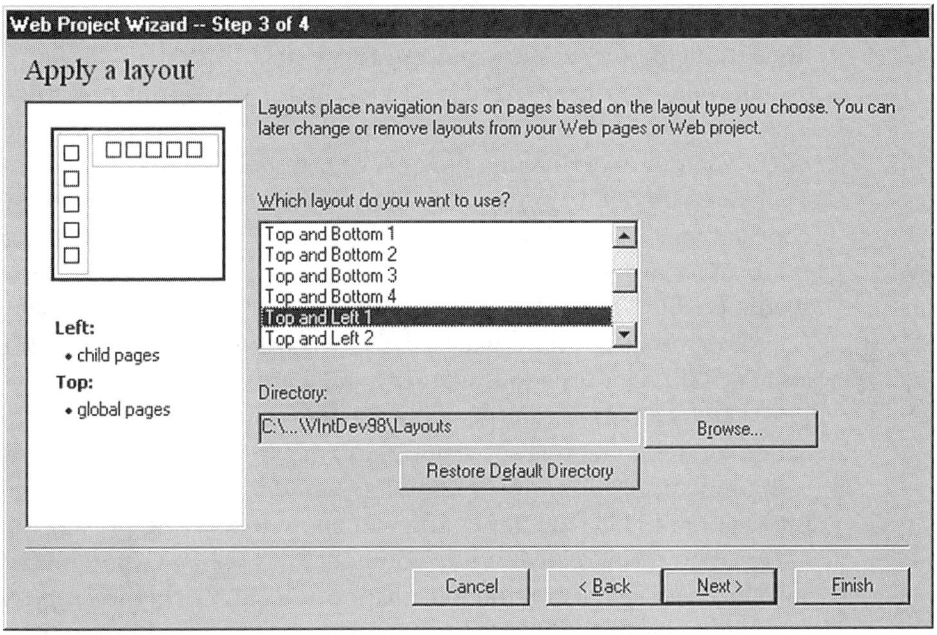

Figure 14.39   Layout choices

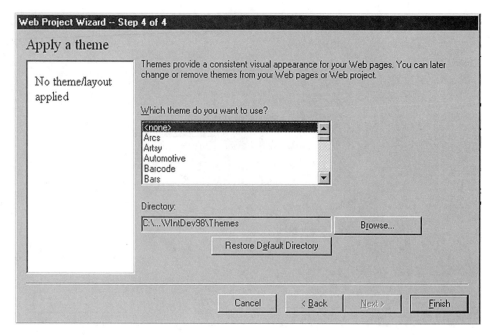

Figure 14.40 Theme choices

not the overall theme. Choose a navigation layout here and select Next to continue to the theme, as shown in Figure 14.40.

Although it's nice to have lots of templates, you normally want a consistent look for your entire site. For that reason, leave off the screen "pretties," but you might want to experiment a little on your test site later.

Once you click Finish, the wizard creates a great deal of HTML and ASP code automatically thanks to Visual InterDev. If you're following along, you see quite a few messages explaining the files that are being transferred to your Web server.

After the files are transferred, the wizard prompts you for the database authentication information, as shown in Figure 14.41.

There is an important distinction here. The first section sets the authentication for designing this application, and the second sets the authentication for using the application. I've mentioned security aspects before, and the same information holds true here. You can allow the wrong person to access the information if you're not careful about your choices on this panel.

Once you've filled in the information, select OK, and the process continues to build more files. When the wizard is complete, you'll see quite a few more

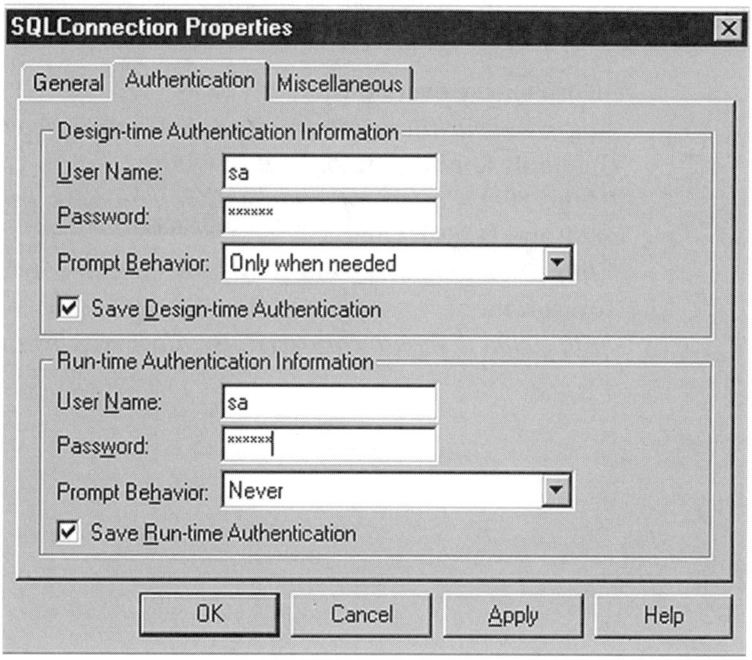

Figure 14.41
Authentication
information

objects in your Project Explorer view of Visual Studio. The deployment wizard generated these items along the way. There isn't a great deal of feedback in Visual Studio, but no news is sometimes good news, especially in this case.

To test the application, open your browser and navigate to the site *http:// WebServername/PubsAuthors/default.asp*. Replace the WebServername part with the IIS server name you published to.

If you ask the application one of the same questions you asked in the Model Test tool, such as "How many writers are there?," you should get the same answer that you did when you used the connected client. Notice that the wizard also built a question-builder application into the page. This gives your users a more structured way of asking questions.

I've found English Query to be one of the "coolest" features inside SQL Server 2000. Although the feature isn't new, the implementation wizards make using the product easy. Open the pod bay doors, Hal.

Resources

English Query overview:

http://www.microsoft.com//sql/evaluation/features/english.asp

VB sample application for English Query:

http://www.microsoft.com/SQL/downloads/vbsample.asp

OLAP and English Query:

http://www.sqlmag.com/Articles/Index.cfm?ArticleID=8035

Normalization:

http://www.swynk.com/friends/putnam/normarticle.asp

Chapter **15**

Working with Instances

Chapter at a Glance

Read this chapter to understand what named instances are and how to set them up and connect to them.

The Resources section contains references for:

- An overview of instances
- A "working with instances" briefing from Microsoft
- A TCP/IP port reference
- An answer for why SQL Server Version 7 tools disappear when instances are installed
- A way of using previous versions of MDAC installations to connect to instances
- Frequently asked questions about instances

Read Chapters 1, 2, and 3 before you read this one.

Overview

Microsoft SQL Server 2000 provides the new feature named instances, which are simply the ability to host more than one installation of SQL Server 2000 on one server. In this chapter, I explain the process for setting up, managing, and accessing named instances.

Although not every SQL Server 2000 installation requires multiple instances, having them can provide the advantage of having different environment settings for each application. Another benefit to having multiple instances is the consolidation it provides, allowing one cost investment of hardware for many applications. Multiple instances also allow separate security accounts to manage several SQL Server 2000 environments on one server.

Having more than one instance on the same server means that there are more services and file locations than if you had one instance. These aren't the only impacts; keep in mind that all this additional load is placed on the same resources the single server has, so increasing RAM or CPUs might be in order.

The devil is in the details, they say, and that's true here as well. Although it isn't that difficult to set up a new instance, connecting to it can sometimes be a challenge. The complexity lies in the protocols.

There are limitations on the protocols you can use, and these protocols might have to be configured a bit to allow successful connections. The only protocols supported for named instances are Named Pipes and TCP/IP. If TCP/IP is used, a separate port must be used for each instance.

Installing a new instance involves starting the SQL Server 2000 installation program again and selecting a new-instance install when prompted. You can connect to a named instance using osql, ODBC, or OLE-DB methods.

Let's take a closer look.

Detail

Instances are not a new concept to other RDBMS systems, such as Oracle, but they are new to SQL Server.

What Are Instances?

Having multiple instances on your server means that you have separate database environments running on the same server. Although previously you could have many databases hosted on one server, they all ran within the common environment of server settings for memory, security, and so forth. If you wanted another environment, you bought another server.

Instances free you from that. Installing multiple instances allows the separation of these environments on the same server. It's a simple concept, but it's powerful when you use it for the right reasons. Books Online has more information about instances under the topic Instances of SQL Server, Overview.

The process for installing a new instance is simple as well, and we do that on the test system in the Graphical section. Accessing the various instances on your server involves qualifying that instance from the client. I cover the exact process in this chapter's Graphical and Command Line sections.

Before you decide to proceed with installing more instances, make sure to read the Impacts section. Even though instances are a great concept, you should implement the feature only when you need to.

Reasons to Implement

Before you implement any new feature, ask yourself "What's the point?" If you don't get a good answer, don't do it. That's especially true here because of those impacts I'll describe later.

There are often good reasons to implement multiple instances on your SQL Server. Let's examine a few of them.

Environmental

Several environmental settings affect the entire SQL Server 2000 installation. Server memory, CPU utilization, Active Directory inclusion, and so forth are just a few of the settings that you can change for each instance. I show a few of these in the Graphical section.

Consolidation

Often you'll want to manage a single, large-scale server for many applications. Your applications might require differing server settings, and having multiple instances allows that feature.

Separation

Although you may want to host several applications on one server, you might want various administrators to manage them. Having completely separate instances gives you the flexibility of keeping one server but managing it as if there were many servers.

Another nice thing about having multiple instances involves service packs. You can install the latest service pack on a single instance without affecting any other instance.

I have an instance at work on a server with a duplicate, although smaller, version of my production database. I'm able to apply service packs to that separate instance and test them against my applications. Previously, I had to maintain a separate "test" server to check these service packs, which meant I was involved in the infamous "server creep" in my company.

Security

Having multiple instances on your server allows one of the most important advantages I've found for the technology: separate security.

There are times that a group of people act as administrators on various applications. Many applications assume that their administrator can make serverwide changes. This isn't a situation that you'll always allow on your server, so having an instance installed that has a system administrator for that instance only is the way to go.

Properties

Having multiple instances installed on one server has its own challenges from an architectural standpoint. In Chapter 2 I explained that when I installed SQL Server 2000 on my server, several services were also installed. These services control the database engine startup and the agent that controls the automation features on my server.

This architecture is repeated with multiple instances, and each has its own set of services. The only difference you'll notice is that the instance services are named with a $ in between the instance name and the service. For example, the naming for the MSSQLServer service becomes MSSQL$InstanceName, and the name for the SQLServerAgent service becomes SQLAgent$InstanceName.

A couple of other services I discussed earlier involve other features for SQL Server 2000, namely the MSTDTC and Microsoft Search services. These stay the same, because they are instance-aware.

The services names are not the only things that are separated by installing multiple instances. Each instance also has its own set of operating system path locations for some of the binaries and the data files. You can look this up on Books Online by searching for File Locations for Multiple Instances of SQL Server. You can also find these locations stored in your server's registry at: HKLM\ Software\Microsoft\Microsoft SQL Server\InstanceName\Setup\SQLPath

Although the file locations for the operation of the server and databases are separated, the tools are common to the server, not to the instances. Tools such as Enterprise Manager and Query Analyzer stay the same regardless of the number of instances you have installed.

Speaking of the number of instances, this isn't something you undertake lightly. There are always trade-offs, and installing multiple instances is no exception.

Impacts

Even though you can install multiple instances on your server, most of the time you should keep only one instance running on your server. Although the idea of having multiple instances can be alluring, remember that there are impacts. Every benefit always has a cost somewhere.

When multiple instances of SQL Server are running on the same computer, each instance uses the standard dynamic memory management algorithm. What that means is that if you've left the default memory settings for each instance, they all grab memory dynamically as they want it. That's fine, but there will be an impact if one application grabs a lot of memory and slows the other.

There are also hard limits to installing multiple instances. You can't install more than 16 instances on one server or cluster. Speaking of clusters, you need to make sure that the instance names are unique across the cluster.

Once you've decided that the benefits outweigh the costs, install the next instance, configure it as you like, and then upgrade your client access to take advantage of it.

Connecting to Multiple Instances

The first installation you create on your SQL Server is called the *default* instance, and you refer to that in the way I've previously described using ODBC or ADO. To access a named instance other than the default, you refer to it in the format Network Name\Instance Name.

The caveat here is the version of MDAC installed on the client. The version is critical. Make sure you have the latest version (2.6 at this writing) on the client, and everything will work seamlessly.

You can use an earlier version of MDAC, but this involves using an *alias*. The process to do that is described in the Resources section, but I advise that you upgrade to the latest MDAC version on each client as soon as possible.

Protocols

SQL Server 2000 doesn't support multiprotocol, Banyan VINES, or AppleTalk network libraries for instances other than the default instance. You can use Named Pipes and TCP/IP. There are some impacts on using even these protocols.

Named Pipes   When you use the Named Pipes protocol, each instance defaults to a network address of \\Computername\Pipe\MSSQL$instancename\ Sql\Query. If you're using this protocol, you're probably in an all-Microsoft network environment, and this is the easiest to set up, albeit a bit slower than TCP/IP.

TCP/IP   TCP/IP is the fastest, most widely used protocol around. Each TCP/IP device has a unique number assigned to it, and each TCP/IP number has several ports assigned to it. Several of these ports are predefined to certain software applications, such as port 80, which is used for HTTP traffic. This way the same IP address can be used for many applications at the same time.

Port 1433 was reserved for Microsoft and, in particular, Microsoft SQL Server. This was assigned in the days when SQL Server could have only one instance. Now that you can have more, you need to choose the others manually or have SQL Server 2000 pick the port automatically. Here's how you do that.

Open the Server Network Utility and set the TCP/IP port to the port you want. Many of the ports are predefined for other programs, so setting this number may cause either the other program to fail or SQL Server 2000 not to answer. Check the Resources section to determine which ports aren't normally used.

Another choice is to set the port to 0 and let SQL Server 2000 choose the next available port. Stop and start SQL Server 2000, then open the utility again, and drill into the TCP/IP properties; you'll see the port SQL Server 2000 used.

On the client side, you can enter the port number, or if MDAC 2.6 or higher is installed, you can check the box marked Dynamically Determine Port in the ODBC DSN setup. I demonstrate this in the Examples section. The effect of this is that SQL Server 2000 sets up a listener on port 1434, which divvies up the port information when it's queried.

As you can see, the most configuration you'll do involves connectivity. Setting up a new instance is much the same as performing a single installation of SQL Server, with all the decisions that go along with it.

Graphical

In this section, you'll perform a second-instance installation of SQL Server 2000. Subsequent instances (up to 16) would work the same way.

Installing a New Instance

The process for installing a new instance is simple, but we'll go through the process here so you can see one before you tackle it on your own server. If you're interested in even more installation information, look up the topic Instances of SQL Server, Named, in Books Online.

To begin, place the SQL Server 2000 CD in the drive. The installation screen auto-plays, as displayed in Figure 15.1. Select the SQL Server 2000 Components menu item, and the next panel, shown in Figure 15.2, appears.

The key to the whole process is just to follow a standard installation path, as I described in Chapter 2. Select Install Database Server, and you're shown the screen in Figure 15.3. This panel is just a description of what's about to happen, so just click Next here, and you see the screen in Figure 15.4.

Figure 15.1
Initial install
screen

Figure 15.2
Beginning the
installation

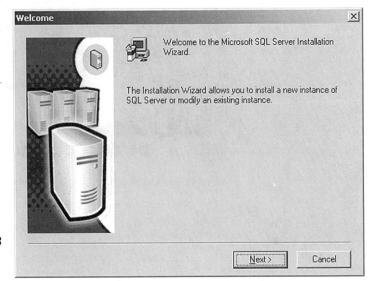

Figure 15.3
Information
screen

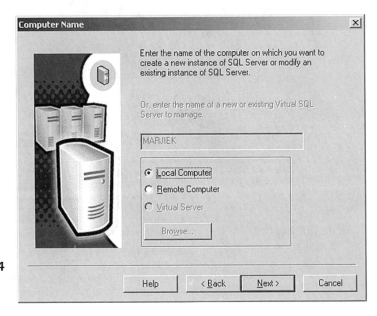

Figure 15.4
Local or
remote

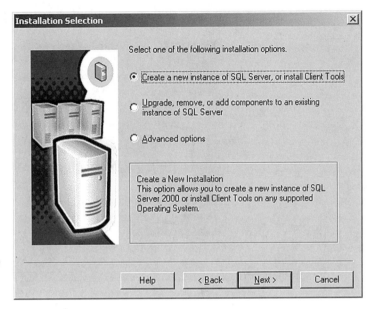

Figure 15.5
Selecting the installation type

You're installing this software on your local server, so pick Local. If you wanted to, you could install this second instance from a workstation, if you had the NT permissions to do so. Kind of a nice feature, but I've never used it. I suppose this might be handy if your server was far away and you had a high-speed link to transfer the files to it.

Once you select Next, the screen in Figure 15.5 appears.

This step is the key. Pick the first option here, Create a New Instance of SQL Server, to tell the install wizard that you want a new instance. Select Next to continue, and you're shown the screen in Figure 15.6.

Remember that even though you're installing this software on the same server, it's an independent installation of SQL Server 2000. Each instance can be installed with differing owner and company information if necessary. If you don't need to change that, just click Next to bring up the screen in Figure 15.7.

This is the standard licensing agreement for SQL Server 2000, so read it and answer Yes to bring up the screen in Figure 15.8. Even though the selection here includes the client tools option, as I mentioned earlier they won't be installed again. After you make your selection, click Next to bring up the screen in Figure 15.9.

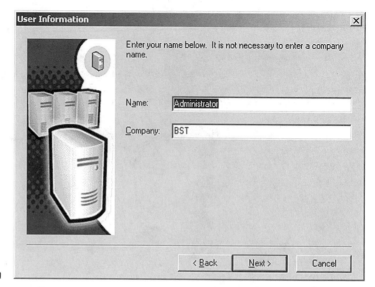

Figure 15.6
Setting the
installation
personalization

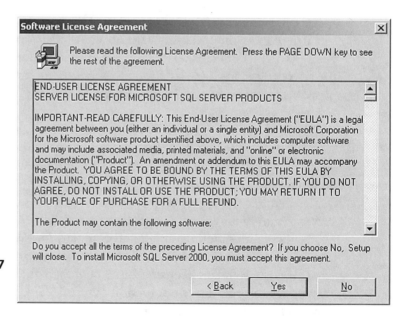

Figure 15.7
Licensing
agreement

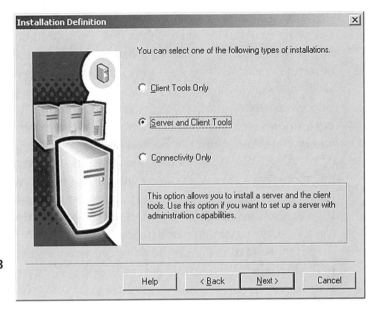

Figure 15.8
Installation
definition

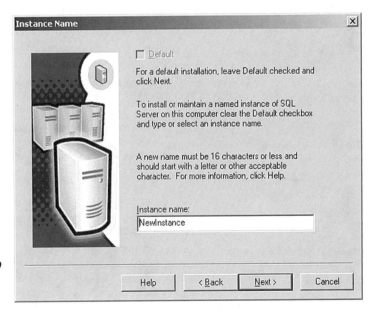

Figure 15.9
Instance
name

Now you get to name the instance. I'll call mine NewInstance so that the following illustrations make sense, but you should choose a short, meaningful name. Why short? If you've ever had to develop an application that had huge object names, you'd vow (as I have) that you'll keep things as short as you can while being as clear as you can.

Select Next to bring up the screen in Figure 15.10. Here select the type of installation you want (see Chapter 2 for more information) and the locations where you want things stored. You should consider the file paths.

Although the binaries' location may not be critical, the data files' location might deserve a review. If you are installing this second instance so that two different administrators can manage their respective databases, make sure that each has the appropriate NTFS access to the proper locations so that the administrators can perform backups or database file manipulations when they need to.

Select Next to bring up the panel shown in Figure 15.11. Just as when you performed the initial installation in Chapter 2, let your administrator account start this instance. When you perform your instance install, you need to consider this choice as well. There are extended stored procedures, for instance, that allow the SQL Server to run an operating system command. If you set this service to start as an administrator, the SQL admin account can do things you might not expect it to be able to do. Fill in the appropriate information and then select Next to bring up the screen in Figure 15.12.

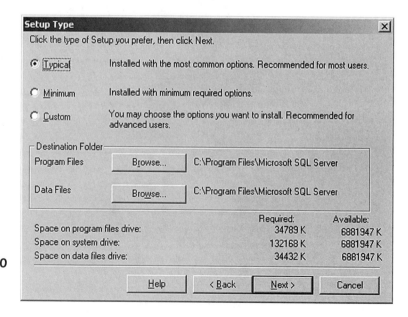

Figure 15.10
Installation
type

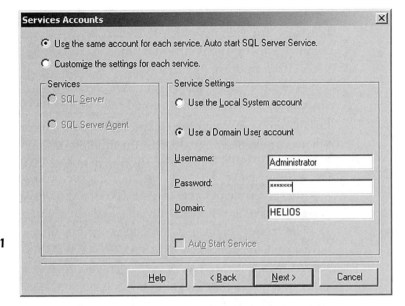

Figure 15.11
Setting the
startup
account

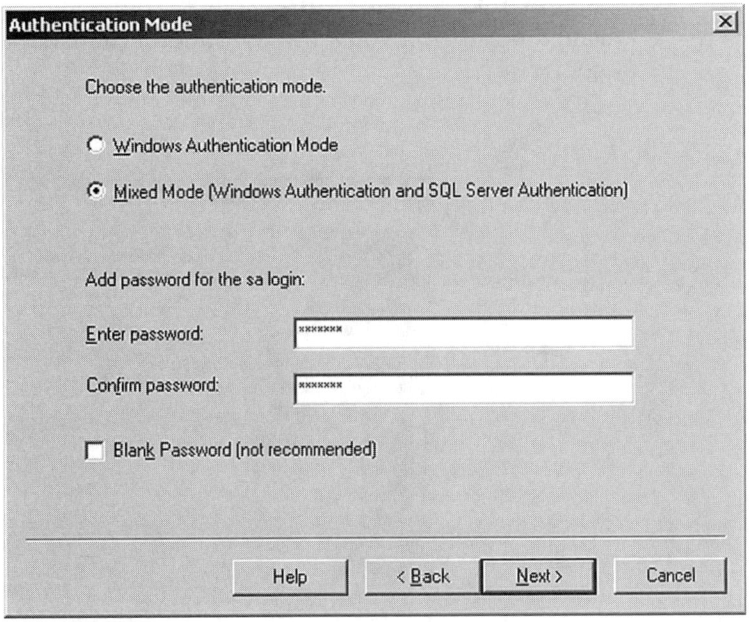

Figure 15.12
Authentica-
tion mode
selection

Here you can select a different authentication mode for this instance. This is how one instance might allow UNIX clients (Mixed Mode) and the other only Windows accounts (Windows Authentication Mode). Select Mixed, fill in the *sa* account's password, and then select Next to bring up the screen in Figure 15.13.

This panel just gives you another chance to press the Back button to make any changes. You don't need to do that, so press Next to bring up the screen in Figure 15.14. You can select the licensing mode here. This is another difference you can set for the instances on the server, but following different licensing modes on one server can be a bit trying. Leave the selection at Processor License and select Next to bring up the screen in Figure 15.15.

After a couple of panels, you're asked to shut down some components so that you don't have to reboot. Go ahead and do that, and then select Next to continue.

The rest of the installation copies various files, and when it completes, you have a new instance on your server. To see what this instance looks like on the server, open *Enterprise Manager*. Once you do, register the new instance just as described in Chapter 2, typing SQLServerName\NewInstance in the name panel when prompted. Replace the SQLServerName part with the name of your SQL Server. The results are shown in Figure 15.16—a new instance as another server. It can be connected to, managed, and controlled as an independent installation.

Now that you have this instance, you need to connect to it. In the Command Line section you'll use *osql*, and in the Examples section you'll connect with ODBC.

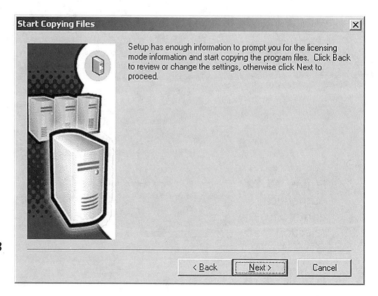

Figure 15.13
Finishing the
selections

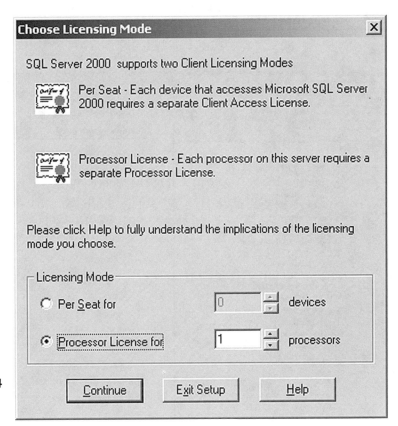

Figure 15.14
Licensing
mode

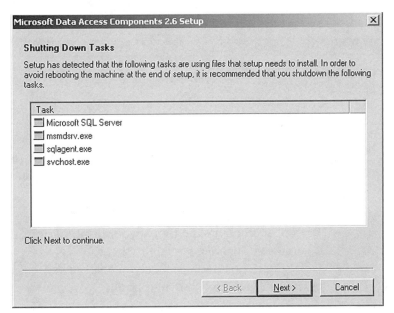

Figure 15.15
Shutting
down
components

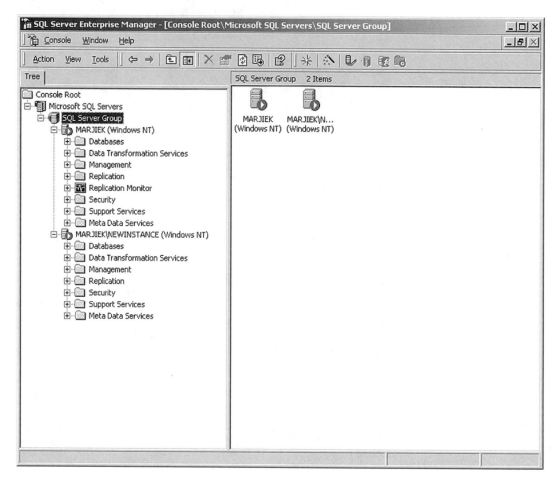

Figure 15.16 Enterprise Manager

Command Line

It isn't difficult to use the new instance in various tools. In Query Analyzer, you just type in the name in the format servername\instancename.

Connecting to the Instance Using osql

The only command-line tool at your disposal (for queries, anyway) is osql. The isql tool can't handle named instances.

Using the named instance you just created, connect to the pubs database, using the command shown in Listing 15.1.

Table 15.1 osql Command Format

osql	Starts the client command
-E	Trusted connection
-S	Server name, including the instance name
-d	Database name
-Q	Query and quit

Listing 15.1 Connecting to an instance with osql

```
osql -E -SSQLServerName\newinstance -dpubs -Q"Select * from authors"
```

Just as you saw in Chapter 4, the osql command breaks down, as shown in Table 15.1. That's all there is to connecting to the instance from osql. Just tacking on the \instancename to the server name does the trick.

Next I demonstrate the ODBC vagaries that I mentioned earlier.

Examples

Connecting with ADO or RDO to a named instance is much the same as using the osql command. Just add the \instancename to the server name connection properties in your application, and the named instance can be used just as the default instance is in your application. If you're checking for illegal characters in the server name in your application, make sure you allow the backslash.

If you're using ODBC, you have a couple of other choices.

Connecting to a Named Instance Using ODBC

Setting up an ODBC connection to a named instance is not that different from setting up one to a default instance. The only trouble you'll experience is with the protocols.

Begin by opening the Control Panel and locating the ODBC applet. Remember that this is in a slightly different place if the OS is Windows 2000, XP, or Windows.NET. You can see the results in Figure 15.17. Move to the *System DSN* tab, and select the *Add* button to start the process, as shown in Figure 15.18. Here select the SQL Server driver, and then select *Finish* to bring up the screen in Figure 15.19.

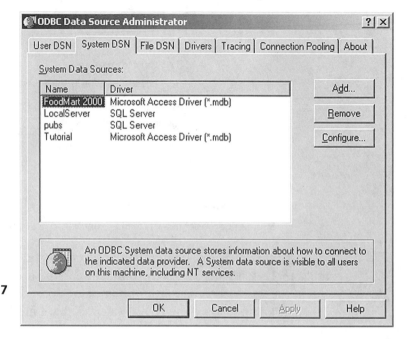

Figure 15.17
The ODBC
applet

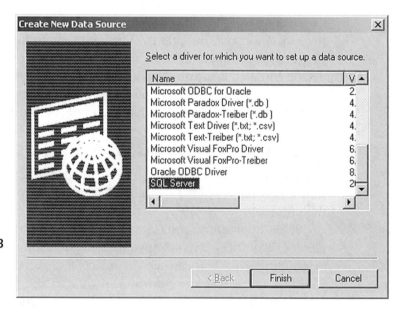

Figure 15.18
Selecting the
connection
type

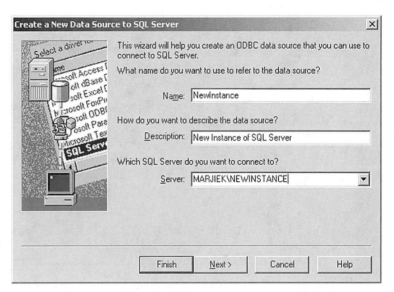

Figure 15.19
Naming the
connection

Fill out three pieces of information here. First, enter a name for the connection. Second, fill in a description for the connection. Finally, enter the server name in the format I've mentioned earlier, *servername\instancename*. Select Next to bring up the screen in Figure 15.20.

Here you choose the authentication type; add a few more clicks and you're normally done. If there is a problem with the protocol, however, this is the

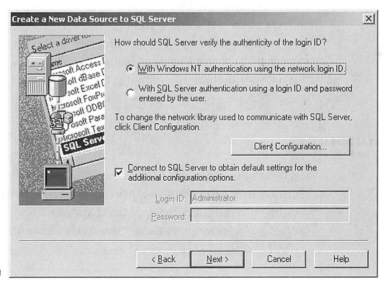

Figure 15.20
ODBC
authentication

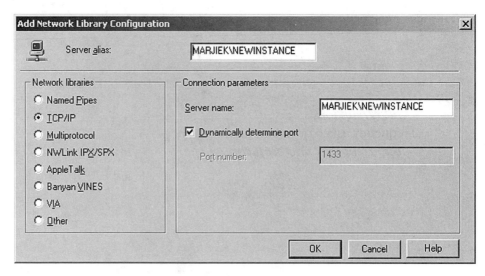

Figure 15.21 TCP/IP properties

place to make the change. Click Client Configuration on this panel to see the protocol choices in Figure 15.21.

This is the panel to use to change the TCP/IP port that the instance is listening on.

Check the Dynamically determine port box to probe the server to see which port listens to the instance name. This works most of the time, but I've had (twice) to check the setting on the server using the Server Network Utility and manually set that port here. Select OK and then Next, Next, Test Connection to verify that the instance is available on the server.

That's all there is to changing the connections for the TCP/IP or Named Pipes protocols.

Resources

Overview of instances:
  http://msdn.microsoft.com/library/psdk/sql/in_runsetup_2xmb.htm
Working-with-instances briefing from Microsoft:
  http://support.microsoft.com/servicedesks/webcasts/wc032201/
    wcblurb032201.asp

TCP/IP port reference:

http://doug.dimick.net/docs/tcpip.php3

SQL Server Version 7 tools disappear when instances are installed:

http://www.storageadmin.com/Articles/Index.cfm?ArticleID=8316

Using previous versions of MDAC installations to connect to instances:

http://support.microsoft.com/support/kb/articles/Q265/8/08.ASP

Frequently asked questions about instances:

http://support.microsoft.com/support/kb/articles/Q260/4/14.ASP

Appendix A

A Sample Server Sizing Exercise

The following exercise should be used for demonstration only. The numbers are suitable only for the test system used throughout this book. For more information on the installation that uses these numbers, see Chapter 2.

RAM

I'll refer to Books Online for the numbers for the memory requirements. There's a lot of room during this phase for imprecision, so make sure you err on the side of having more memory than you think you need.

First, factor the base memory required for running the software. The Microsoft official documentation states that you only need 64MB of RAM to run the software, but I suggest nothing less than 128MB. Because those numbers exclude the operating system requirements, I'll up that to at least 256MB to start.

Next, start adding the various memory requirements for proper server operation. To begin with, Books Online tells me that I need around 6K per open database, which I estimate on my server to be an average of less than 1MB. After that, I add the average number of users at a given time—I'll guess 50 for this example—and multiply that by 1.7MB, giving me 85MB. Then I need to add the numbers for locks and other objects, and I guesstimate around 10MB for those factors. See Books Online for more information.

After adding all these base factors together, I come up with 352MB. These calculations provide me with a good start. I'll actually purchase 512MB of RAM for my server. Don't be surprised if your software vendor tells you to configure SQL Server 2000 with significantly more than this—remember, I'm just setting up an example system.

Storage

Books Online describes the calculations used to estimate this number in the section called *Size of a Table*. I use a very abbreviated version of it here.

First, I estimate how many tables are in my database. Normally, you or someone else has worked up a design, so you have at least an idea of how many tables you will have. I'll say 100 tables will be in my application, simply for demonstration.

Next, I need to estimate the number of rows in each table. To do this completely accurately, you'd estimate the rows in each table separately. I'll fudge a little here for the sake of example and say that each table will have 200 rows.

The next step involves deciding how "wide" the rows are and calculating how much space will be used by a row. To do this, I take the columns individually, add the bytes that I estimate will be stored in each one, and get a total. I'll set this figure at 5K per row, and I'm setting them all the same for the simplicity of this example.

You don't just multiply the rows of data times the number of rows, times the number of tables. Data is stored in SQL Server in units called pages, which are 8K long. Rows have to fit within that page size, so the simplified, modified calculation for a table in my example is:

```
Number of rows / Rows per page = Number of pages
```

Now I take that number and plug it in here:

```
Number of pages * 8,192 = Table size
```

That gives me the table size, and then I multiply that figure times the number of tables:

```
Number of Tables * Table Size = Database Size
```

So now, using the actual figures, I have:

```
200/1 = 200
```

Then I multiply them by the pages:

```
200 * 8,192 = 1,638,400 bytes
```

That works out to roughly 1.6MB for this fictitious database. Now the tables—100 of them—times the 1.6MB figure gives me:

```
100 * 1.6MB = 160MB
```

Obviously, I'll be fine with just about any size drive I can purchase on the market today, but this was just a simple example to illustrate the process.

I'd never use software RAID, because that requires the operating system to calculate each bit that is stored on the hard drive. The following discussion involves only hardware RAID.

I end up with a server that has two RAID controllers, although most new servers have two channels on one controller, which has the same effect. I set one controller, or one channel on that controller, to RAID level 5 with three drives of 4GB each, leaving me 8GB usable. I place the databases on this drive, because of their random access patterns. The other controller I set to RAID level 1 using two drives of 4GB each, giving me 4GB usable. On this drive set I place the log files, because of their sequential nature. Now I've set up my drive system, with the following configuration:

- Drive set 1—RAID 5, 3 drives, 4GB each, leaving 8GB usable
- Drive set 2—RAID 1, 2 drives, 4GB each, leaving 4GB usable

Because I'm using Windows 2000, I can have large bootable drives. So the drive arrangement on my system looks like this:

- Drive C:—Drive set 1, 8GB; operating system, database program, databases
- Drive D:—Drive set 2, 4GB; log files

If I were using Windows NT 4, I would be limited to the amount of drive space that can be used on the bootable drive. My system would look more like this:

- Drive C:—Drive set 1, 2GB; operating system, database program
- Drive D:—Drive set 1, 6GB; databases
- Drive E:—Drive set 2, 4GB; log files

This provides the hardware basis for my test system. Going through an exercise like this is useful, and I offer one last piece of advice: Take any number you come up with in this exercise and double it. You'll need to double that again if you're storing the backups on disk rather than on tape.

Appendix B

Hardware for SQL Server

Chapter 2 details an installation for SQL Server 2000. You may already have your hardware, but if you're waiting to purchase it, this information can be used as a guide.

If we assume you have a SQL Server 2000 installation on a server running the Windows 2000 Server operating system, the primary potential hardware bottlenecks are the following:

- RAM
- CPU
- Storage devices (hard drives)
- NIC

Other factors can affect a server's performance, but those listed here are the heavy hitters as far as hardware is concerned. Let's consider some of the impacts these bottlenecks can have on your implementation.

RAM

Memory is one of the fastest components in your system. SQL Server 2000 is similar to most server packages—it loves memory. SQL Server is auto-configuring when it comes to RAM and automatically uses as much memory as you install on the server. It also moves out of the way when another program wants memory. Both of these behaviors can be overridden.

The more memory you can afford, the better. Here's just one of the ways that SQL Server 2000 uses memory: When data is requested, SQL Server watches the pattern of data access. SQL Server 2000 then develops a *query plan* that is stored in memory, so that the server can have that pattern of data access ready for even faster reference the next time it is requested.

Memory is also taken by many types of caching and by each connection that talks to the server. Memory is taken as well when a user reserves the right to look at a particular set of data, a process called taking a lock.

These are just a few of the ways SQL Server 2000 uses memory, and you can see that the server wants a lot of it.

Most administrators use the "budget method" to determine server hardware. They buy as much server as the budget allows. Although that's a practical method under some circumstances, I like to be a bit more scientific.

In Appendix A I describe an overly simplistic way of taking an educated guess on sizing a server. Take it with a grain of salt and then double the values you come up with.

Most of the time, the vendor determines the type of RAM you can install. If you do have choice, you want ECC EDO RAM on the fastest bus your vendor makes.

CPU

The processor in a server is another fast component of the architecture. The two main types used in servers, as of this writing, are AMD and Intel. Although many server vendors use Intel processors, be sure to consider the processor line from AMD. The AMD processors have some distinct technical enhancements. Processor vendor dominance flip-flops almost monthly as to who has the upper hand in speed, density, and instruction handling, so be sure to talk with your vendor at length about this choice.

Check the Web sites mentioned at the end of Chapter 2 if you're interested in getting the biggest bang for the buck. Most vendors strike a deal with a specific chip manufacturer, however, so you may not have a choice.

Obviously, I'll buy the fastest processor I can find for my example system, but one thing is certain: I'll insist on at least 1MB of L2 cache. I won't go overboard on the technical details, but you can easily gain orders of magnitude of increases in speed by using this increased level of cache so close to your processor and its faster bus. If you're up for a little late-night reading, look up the specifications sometime on how instructions are processed by your CPU, and then compare the differences in throughput on a system having 512K of cache and one that has 1MB.

For my server, I choose a pair of AMD processors, and I'll buy the fastest I can get with 1MB of L2 cache on each.

Storage Devices (Hard Drives)

If you're really looking to increase speed, look no further than your hard drives. They are one of the slowest parts of your computer because they are electromechanical. SQL Server 2000 stores data in two places—new data is written to a file called a log. Users normally don't write directly into the database but write to this log first. Once the server gets the data there, the log writes the data to the database. Once that data is recorded successfully in the database, the log makes a mark on that data, called a checkpoint, signifying that it got there. This is a sequential process. Users read data directly from the database, though, and this reading is done in a random fashion.

The hardware choice you face here is whether to use the Enhanced Integrated Disk Electronics (EIDE) format or the Small Computer System Interface (SCSI) format. The differences between these technologies affect the speed at which the drives spin, the time it takes to locate data, and the transfer rates. Again, if you're looking for the technical specifications, check the Web sites listed at the end of Chapter 2 for the differences between SCSI drives and EIDE.

Even though EIDE drives are becoming faster, it's the transfer of data that matters, the I/O throughput. Here, SCSI is clearly the winner, with (theoretical) transfer rates of up to 80MBps to EIDE's 33MBps. SCSI also allows more devices to be connected to the same bus, which is important for SQL Server 2000 as well.

Another factor to consider is recoverability. You need to be able to recover quickly from a disaster such as a drive failure, preferably with no downtime. To accomplish this, you have two real choices in a mid-level server such as in my example: Redundant Array of Independent Disks (RAID) level 1 and RAID level 5.

NOTE: Microsoft provides software RAID for some of its operating systems. Because the operating system manipulates every bit when software RAID is used, the performance hit on a database server is unbelievable. Never use software RAID on any database server.

RAID level 1 stores the data twice—once on the primary drive and again on another. If the primary drive is lost, the other takes over. You lose 50% of the drive space to this "insurance." This type of RAID is best for sequential data.

RAID level 5 writes the data across three or more drives, currently up to 32, and stores a parity section of data so that if one drive is lost, the others can still function.

To understand this parity function, think of a math problem that looks like this: $3 + x = 5$. You can derive the value of x because you still have the other two numbers. That's RAID level 5. That's a bit oversimplified, but that's roughly the way it works. RAID 5 is best suited for randomly accessed data.

I'll configure my server to have two sets of SCSI drives. The first set will be RAID level 5. I place the databases here because of the low cost of the insurance—roughly 32% or so of the space that I lose to the parity calculations. I also use this RAID level because data is accessed randomly from the database.

The second set of drives I'll use will be RAID level 1—I'll put the database logs here. Remember, RAID level 1 handles sequential writes well. Because RAID level 1 stores the data twice, I lose 50% of the drive space for insurance. However, because logs are normally smaller than databases, the cost of the insurance is lessened.

Now that I've decided on a disk technology and arrangement, I need to choose the size of the drives. Your software vendor using SQL Server as a back end may specify this size for you, but if they don't, read on.

I'll avoid the budget method and try to derive the size of the databases I'll use. You can read about the process I used to derive my numbers in Appendix A.

On all drives, regardless of operating system, I'll use the NTFS file format. I use this file system for several reasons, including its journaling capabilities, speed, and security.

Years ago Microsoft used to recommend a 500MB bootable partition that used the FAT format for recovery. Tools that allow you to boot a diskette to the NTFS format and recover your files have largely outdated this recommendation. The security and performance requirements also outweigh any decisions to use FAT on your server.

There is still one more potential bottleneck in the server to consider—the Network Interface Card (NIC).

NIC

The next slowest part of the server is the Network Interface Card. The fast ones work at roughly 100bps (that's bits, not bytes), so even these cards qualify as very slow devices. Most of the workstations on a network today, as well as the cabling behind the wall, are limited to less than 10bps.

For the server, you should purchase a faster card. Most servers come with a built-in NIC, as does my example server. The important thing is to make sure that your NIC has settings allowing full duplex, which means being able to transmit and receive at the same time, and 32-bit bus-mastering Direct Memory

Access (DMA), especially if you're using Windows 2000 as the operating system. These cards allow more of the processing for the network to be offloaded from your CPU, freeing it to do other work.

My example server comes with a built-in 10/100 full-duplex bus-mastering card.

Remember that this is a test system; you should query your vendor extensively on their experiences with other database servers. Everyone has to work within the constraints of a budget, but many SQL Servers are used for mission-critical systems. You should push to have as much choice as possible in the server selection, and you should use facts like the ones from this book to support your arguments.

Index

Also from Addison-Wesley

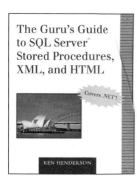

The Guru's Guide to SQL Server™ Stored Procedures, XML, and HTML

By Ken Henderson

0-201-70046-8
Paperback
800 pages with CD-ROM
© 2002

More than just a catalog of coding tricks and syntax subtleties, *The Guru's Guide to SQL Server™ Stored Procedures, XML, and HTML* explores the philosophy of Transact-SQL programming and teaches readers how to apply this philosophy in order to develop their own coding techniques and discover their own solutions to real-world programming problems.

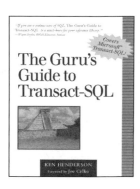

The Guru's Guide to Transact-SQL

By Ken Henderson

0-201-61576-2
Paperback
592 pages with CD-ROM
© 2000

Comprehensive, written in understandable terms, and full of practical information and examples, *The Guru's Guide to Transact-SQL* is an indispensable reference for anyone working with this database development language.

SQL Queries for Mere Mortals

A Hands-On Guide to Data Manipulation in SQL
By Michael J. Hernandez and John L. Viescas

0-201-43336-2
Paperback
528 pages
© 2000

SQL Queries for Mere Mortals will help new users learn the foundations of SQL queries, and will prove an essential reference guide for intermediate and advanced users.

The Practical SQL Handbook, Fourth Edition
Using SQL Variants

By Judith S. Bowman, Sandra L. Emerson,
and Marcy Darnovsky

0-201-70309-2
Paperback
512 pages with CD-ROM
© 2001

This latest edition of the best-selling implementation guide
to the Structured Query Language teaches SQL fundamentals
while providing practical solutions for critical business
applications.

Practical SQL
The Sequel

By Judith S. Bowman

0-201-61638-6
Paperback
352 pages with CD-ROM
© 2001

For those who are working with SQL systems—or preparing
to do so—this book offers information organized by use
rather than by feature. Readers can turn to specific business
problems and learn how to solve them with the appropriate
SQL features.

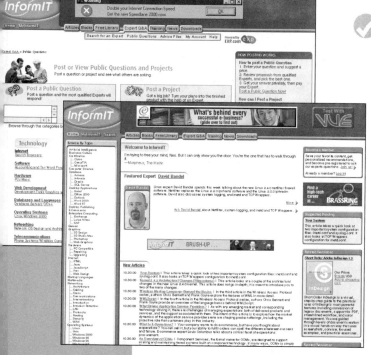